Christopher Columbus: His Story and His Journals

A double historic reprint including

The Life of Christopher Columbus from His Own Letters and Journals

and

Original Narratives of the Voyages of Columbus

ISBN: 978-1-7377062-1-2

Knowledge Keepers Bookstore, 2021

Cover Art:

The First Landing of Christopher Columbus in America, 1862

by Dioscoro Teofilo Puebla Tolin (1832-1901)

BOOK I

The Life of Christopher Columbus From His Own Letters and Journals

AND
OTHER DOCUMENTS OF HIS TIME

by EDWARD EVERETT HALE

CONTENTS

Preparations for a Fourth Expedition

CHAPTER XII: FOURTH VOYAGE 160

The Instructions Given for the Voyage—He is to go to the Mainland of the Indies

A Short Passage

Ovando Forbids the Entrance of Columbus into Harbor
Bobadilla's Squadron and Its Fate

Columbus Sails Westward

Discovers Honduras, and Coasts Along Its Shores
The Search for Gold

Colony Attempted and Abandoned
The Vessels Become Unseaworthy

Refuge at Jamaica

Mutiny Led by the Brothers Porras

Messages to San Domingo

The Eclipse

Arrival of Relief

Columbus Returns to San Domingo, and to Spain

CHAPTER XIII: TWO SAD YEARS 182

Two Sad Years

Isabella's Death

Columbus at Seville

His Illness

Letters to the King

Journeys to Segovia

Salamanca and Valladolid

His Suit There

Philip and Juana

Columbus Executes His Will

Dies

His Burial and the Removal of His Body

His Portraits

His Character

PREFACE

This book contains a life of Columbus, written with the hope of interesting all classes of readers.

His life has often been written, and it has sometimes been well written. The great book of our countryman, Washington Irving, is a noble model of diligent work given to a very difficult subject. And I think every person who has dealt with the life of Columbus since Irving's time, has expressed his gratitude and respect for the author.

According to the custom of biographers, in that time and since, he includes in those volumes the whole history of the West India islands, for the period after Columbus discovered them till his death. He also thinks it his duty to include much of the history of Spain and of the Spanish court. I do not myself believe that it is wise to attempt, in a book of biography, so considerable a study of the history of the time. Whether it be wise or not, I have not attempted it in this book. I have rather attempted to follow closely the personal fortunes of Christopher Columbus, and, to the history around him, I have given only such space as seemed absolutely necessary for the illustration of those fortunes.

1

I have followed on the lines of his own personal narrative wherever we have it. And where this is lost I have used the absolutely contemporary authorities. I have also consulted the later writers, those of the next generation and the generation which followed it. But the more one studies the life of Columbus the more one feels sure that, after the greatness of his discovery was really known, the accounts of the time were overlaid by what modern criticism calls myths, which had grown up in the enthusiasm of those who honored him, and which form no part of real history. If then the reader fails to find some stories with which he is quite familiar in the history, he must not suppose that they are omitted by accident, but must give to the author of the book the credit of having used some discretion in the choice of his authorities.

When I visited Spain in 1882, I was favored by the officers of the Spanish government with every facility for carrying my inquiry as far as a short visit would permit. Since that time Mr. Harrisse[1] has published his invaluable volumes on the life of Columbus. It certainly seems as if every document now existing, which bears upon the history, had been collated by him. The reader will see that I have made full use of this treasure-house.

The Congress of Americanistas, which meets every year, brings forward many curious studies on the history of the continent, but it can scarcely be said to have done much to advance our knowledge of the personal life of Columbus.

The determination of the people of the United States to celebrate fitly the great discovery which has

---

[1] *Notes on Columbus*, by Henry Herrisse, 1866

advanced civilization and changed the face of the world, makes it certain that a new interest has arisen in the life of the great man to whom, in the providence of God, that discovery was due. The author and publishers of this book offer it as their contribution in the great celebration, with the hope that it may be of use, especially in the direction of the studies of the young.

EDWARD E. HALE.
ROXBURY, MASS., June 1st, 1891.

About Edward Everett Hale

Edward was born in Boston, MA in 1822 to a family with famous heritage. His great-uncle was Nathan Hale, the American Revolutionary spy, and Edward Everett, president of Harvard College. He first attended school at the age of two. When he was nine, he was admitted to the Boston Latin School where he studied for the next four years. When Hale was thirteen he attended Harvard College.

Edward held many titles in his life. He was a lifelong minister in the Unitarian church, a journalist, author, and humanitarian. Among his many works include the popular tale, *Man Without A Country*.

According to the Dictionary of Unitarian & Universalist Biography, he married Emily Baldwin Perkins in 1852, granddaughter of the Calvinist preacher Lyman Beecher and niece of Harriet Beecher Stowe, author of *Uncle Tom's Cabin*. They had nine children.

Hale died in 1909.

Introduction to the Knowledge Keepers edition

Christopher Columbus has been of interest to me since I was a teenager and was first introduced to his own writings in the 1980s. As I became an adult, and began to hear of Indigenous People's Day and other outrages against Columbus, I just wanted to say to the world, "You don't know the whole story!" In fact, I dedicated several blog posts over the years to Columbus and his story.

When I began the Knowledge Keepers Home Library series of reprinted history books, Columbus was on my mind for months. I strive, with this series, to provide easy-to-find and affordable old copies of American history to modern readers with the intent to set some records straight. This is definitely needed in the case of Columbus.

I am continually surprised at the number of Americans who assume that Columbus was a greedy, thieving rapist, intent on slaughtering Indians for gold and gain. That is so far from the truth that I know these people have not taken even a few minutes to verify what they've heard.

But where did this idea come from?

One of the main culprits is Howard Zinn. In his book, *A People's History of the United States*, he begins Chapter 1 with a description of peaceful, innocent Indians just minding their own business only days before the evil Columbus arrived on their shores to kill, steal, and destroy. But very few fans of Zinn bothered to check his story. *A People's History* was published in 1980, and in the past forty years, his story somehow became *the* story.

I could write for days on the atrocious state of American education, and especially history education. But if you have picked up this book, you are probably already aware. *A People's History* has become standard reading in too many high schools and colleges. It is a cult favorite. And it's a pack of lies.

Zinn is not the only culprit. There are others. But my point in this book is not to give you the history of false narratives. However, I would like to point you to two books for this purpose:

1. *Debunking Howard Zinn* by Mary Grabar is a fantastic taking-down of Zinn and his erroneous stories. Fun Fact: he was a member of the Communist Party U.S.A. Whether you've read Zinn's *People's History of the United States* or not, you should read this book.
2. *Columbus the Hero* by Rafael is a similar book to *Debunking Zinn*. The author introduces some of the most misunderstood stories of Columbus and his explorations, and with the

help of multiple historical narratives, breaks down each and every falsehood.

Both of these books would make excellent companions to the one you hold in your hand.

Setting historic narratives straight is very important, not to make Columbus out to be a saint (because I don't believe he was), but because Americans need to be intimately acquainted with the true history of their nation. If Columbus can be completely written off for his faults, so can Washington, Jefferson, Bradford, and many others.

Without their history, what do we have left? We have a nation on the brink of something that resembles the fall of Rome and the rise of Soviet Russia.

I spent some time trying to find the best Columbus narrative that I could publish. Having read the journals of Columbus (and some of his fellow explorers), I knew that his actual words were very important. But his own journals don't tell the complete story; there are multiple other narratives written by his brother, son, and friends.

Thanks to the tip of a kind lady at a homeschool convention, I was able to find the Edward Everett Hale book. It is exactly the kind of narrative perfect for readers: facts, straight from Columbus' own writings, woven in an easy-to-follow narrative. This book is BOOK ONE of *Christopher Columbus: His story and His Journals.* As a very necessary historic bonus, I've included in BOOK TWO the actual journals of Columbus. The edition I share here is incredibly annotated with over 600 historical footnotes to clarify just about everything you can think of. I was constantly amazed and overjoyed at the new things I learned just from these footnotes!

Included at the end is a short bibliography of some of the most quoted works in this edition, including the journals of some contemporaries of Columbus, as well as later works of research and collections. If you find the study of Columbus intriguing, you might be interested in adding these books to your home library.

When you read these letters of his, it's apparent what an educated and talented man Columbus was. Like Lewis and Clark, he identified new and strange animals, plants, minerals, and people groups. He was well-versed in the scriptures and biblical prophecy. He was a mapmaker (in a time when the entire world had not been discovered!). He was bold and courageous. I couldn't help thinking that the 21st century critics of his who topple statues and feign moral superiority would not be able to know or do even a fraction of what Columbus did. Despite some miscalculations and misidentifications, and despite some errors in judgement, he was an amazing person who was born to accomplish great things.

As with all of my Knowledge Keepers books, the original text is left intact, with antiquated spellings and punctuation.

This is my favorite Knowledge Keepers project to date. I sincerely hope you make good use of the information in this 2-book volume by learning the true history of Columbus and by sharing it with as many people as possible. Read it to or with your children and grandchildren, give copies as gifts, and teach the next generation how to know the truth and not be offended by it.

Nicki Truesdell

Knowledge Keepers Bookstore

Columbus Day, October 12, 2021

Chapter I: Early Life of Columbus

Christopher Columbus was born in the Republic of
Genoa. The honor of his birth-place has been claimed
by many villages in that Republic, and the house in
which he was born cannot be now pointed out with
certainty. But the best authorities agree that the
children and the grown people of the world have
never been mistaken when they have said: "America
was discovered in 1492 by Christopher Columbus, a
native of Genoa."

His name, and that of his family, is always written
Colombo, in the Italian papers which refer to them,
for more than one hundred years before his time. In
Spain it was always written Colon; in France it is
written as Colomb; while in England it has always
kept its Latin form, Columbus. It has frequently been
said that he himself assumed this form, because
Columba is the Latin word for "Dove," with a fanciful
feeling that, in carrying Christian light to the West,
he had taken the mission of the dove. Thus, he had
first found land where men thought there was ocean,
and he was the messenger of the Holy Spirit to those
who sat in darkness. It has also been assumed that
he took the name of Christopher, "the Christ-bearer,"
for similar reasons. But there is no doubt that he was
baptized "Christopher," and that the family name
had long been Columbo. The coincidences of name are

but two more in a calendar in which poetry delights, and of which history is full.

Christopher Columbus was the oldest son of Dominico Colombo and Suzanna Fontanarossa. This name means Red-fountain. He bad two brothers, Bartholomew and Diego, whom we shall meet again. Diego is the Spanish way of writing the name which we call James.

It seems probable that Christopher was born in the year 1436[2], though some writers have said that he was older than this, and some that he was younger. The record of his birth and that of his baptism have not been found.

His father was not a rich man, but he was able to send Christopher, as a boy, to the University of Pavia, and here he studied grammar, geometry, geography and navigation, astronomy and the Latin language. But this was as a boy studies, for in his fourteenth year he left the university and entered, in hard work, on "the larger college of the world." If the date given above, of his birth, is correct, this was in the year 1450, a few years before the Turks took Constantinople, and, in their invasion of Europe, affected the daily life of everyone, young or old, who lived in the Mediterranean countries. From this time, for fifteen years, it is hard to trace along the life of Columbus. It was the life of an intelligent young seaman, going wherever there was a voyage for him. He says himself, "I passed twenty-three years on the

---

[2] It is now believed that he was born between August 26 and October 31, 1451

sea. I have seen all the Levant[3], all the western coasts, and the North. I have seen England; I have often made the voyage from Lisbon to the Guinea coast." This he wrote in a letter to Ferdinand and Isabella. Again he says, "I went to sea from the most tender age and have continued in a sea life to this day. Whoever gives himself up to this art wants to know the secrets of Nature here below. It is more than forty years that I have been thus engaged. Wherever any one has sailed, there I have sailed."

Whoever goes into the detail of the history of that century will come upon the names of two relatives of his—Colon el Mozo (the Boy, or the Younger) and his uncle, Francesco Colon, both celebrated sailors. The latter of the two was a captain in the fleets of Louis XI of France, and imaginative students may represent him as meeting Quentin Durward at court. Christopher Columbus seems to have made several voyages under the command of the younger of these relatives. He commanded the Genoese galleys near Cyprus in a war which the Genoese had with the Venetians. Between the years 1461 and 1463 the Genoese were acting as allies with King John of Calabria, and Columbus had a command as captain in their navy at that time.

"In 1477," he says, in one of his letters, "in the month of February, I sailed more than a hundred leagues beyond Tile." By this he means Thule, or Iceland. "Of this island the southern part is seventy-three degrees from the equator, not sixty-three degrees, as some geographers pretend." But here he

---

[3] the eastern Mediterranean coastal lands of modern-day Turkey, Syria, and Lebanon

was wrong. The Southern part of Iceland is in the latitude of sixty-three and a half degrees. "The English, chiefly those of Bristol, carry their merchandise, to this island, which is as large as England. When I was there the sea was not frozen, but the tides there are so strong that they rise and fall twenty-six cubits."

The order of his life, after his visit to Iceland, is better known. He was no longer an adventurous sailor-boy, glad of any voyage which offered; he was a man thirty years of age or more. He married in the city of Lisbon and settled himself there. His wife was named Philippa. She was the daughter of an Italian gentleman named Bartolomeo Muniz de Perestrello, who was, like Columbus, a sailor, and was alive to all the new interests which geography then presented to all inquiring minds. This was in the year 1477, and the King of Portugal was pressing the expeditions which, before the end of the century, resulted in the discovery of the route to the Indies by the Cape of Good Hope.

The young couple had to live. Neither the bride nor her husband had any fortune, and Columbus occupied himself as a draftsman, illustrating books, making terrestrial globes, which must have been curiously inaccurate, since they had no Cape of Good Hope and no American Continent, drawing charts for sale, and collecting, where he could, the material for such study. Such charts and maps were beginning to assume new importance in those days of geographical discovery. The value attached to them may be judged from the statement that Vespucius paid one hundred and thirty ducats for one map. This sum would be more than five hundred dollars of our time.

Columbus did not give up his maritime enterprises. He made voyages to the coast of Guinea and in other directions.

It is said that he was in command of one of the vessels of his relative Colon el Mozo, when, in the Portuguese seas, this admiral, with his squadron, engaged four Venetian galleys returning from Flanders. A bloody battle followed. The ship which Christopher Columbus commanded was engaged with a Venetian vessel, to which it set fire. There was danger of an explosion, and Columbus himself, seeing this danger, flung himself into the sea, seized a floating oar, and thus gained the shore. He was not far from Lisbon, and from this time made Lisbon his home for many years.

It seems clear that, from the time when he arrived in Lisbon, for more than twenty years, he was at work trying to interest people in his "great design," of western discovery. He says himself, "I was constantly corresponding with learned men, some ecclesiastics and some laymen, some Latin and some Greek, some Jews and some Moors." The astronomer Toscanelli was one of these correspondents.

We must not suppose that the idea of the roundness of the earth was invented by Columbus. Although there were other theories about its shape, many intelligent men well understood that the earth was a globe, and that the Indies, though they were always reached from Europe by going to the East, must be on the west of Europe also. There is a very funny story in the travels of Mandeville, in which a traveler is represented as having gone, mostly on foot, through all the countries of Asia, but finally determines to return to Norway, his home. In his farthest eastern investigation, he hears some people calling their cattle by a peculiar cry, which he had never heard before. After he returned home, it was necessary for him to take a day's journey westward to look after some cattle he had lost. Finding these cattle, he also heard the same cry of people calling cattle, which he had heard in the extreme East, and now learned, for the first time, that he had gone round the world on foot, to turn and come back by the same route, when he was only a day's journey from home. Columbus was acquainted with such stories as this, and also had the astronomical knowledge which almost made him know that the world was round, "and, like a ball, goes spinning in the air." The difficulty was to persuade other people that, because of this roundness, it would be possible to attain Asia by sailing to the West.

Now all the geographers of repute supposed that there was not nearly so large a distance as there proved to be, in truth, between Europe and Asia. Thus, in the geography of Ptolemy, which was the standard book at that time, one hundred and thirty-five degrees, a little more than one-third of the earth's circumference, is given to the space between the extreme eastern part of the Indies and the Canary Islands. In fact, as we now know, the distance is one hundred and eighty degrees, half the world's circumference. Had Columbus believed there was any such immense distance, he would never have undertaken his voyage.

Almost all the detailed knowledge of the Indies which the people of his time had, was given by the explorations of Marco Polo, a Venetian traveler of the thirteenth century, whose book had long been in the possession of European readers. It is a very entertaining book now, and may well be recommended to young people who like stories of adventure. Marco Polo had visited the court of the Great Khan of Tartary at Pekin, the prince who brought the Chinese Empire into very much the condition in which it now[4] is. He had, also, given accounts of Japan (or Cipango), which he had himself never visited. Columbus knew, therefore, that, well east of the Indies, was the island of Cipango, and he aimed at that island, because he supposed that that was the nearest point to Europe, as in fact it is. And when finally he arrived at Cuba, as the reader will see, he thought he was in Japan.

Columbus's father-in-law had himself been the Portuguese governor of the island of Porto Santo, where he had founded a colony. He, therefore, was interested in western explorations, and probably from him Columbus collected some of the statements which are known to have influenced him, with regard to floating matters from the West, which are constantly borne upon that island by the great currents of the sea.

The historians are fond of bringing together all the intimations which are given in the Greek and Latin classics, and in later authors, with regard to a land beyond Asia. Perhaps the most famous of them is that of Seneca, "In the later years there shall come

---

[4] 1892

days in which Ocean shall loose his chains, and a great land shall appear . . . and Thule shall not be the last of the worlds."

In a letter which Toscanelli wrote to Columbus in 1474, he inclosed a copy of a letter which he had already sent to an officer of Alphonso V, the King of Portugal. In writing to Columbus, he says, *"I see that you have a great and noble desire to go into that country (of the East) where the spices come from, and in reply to your letter I send you a copy of that which I addressed some years ago to my attached friend in the service of the most serene King of Portugal. He had an order from his Highness to write me on this subject. . .*

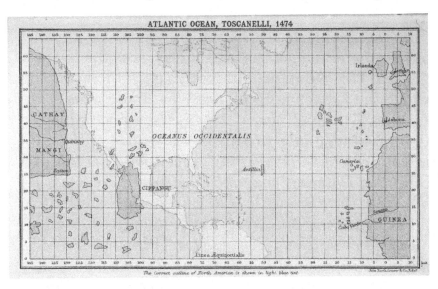

If I had a globe in my hand, I could show you what is needed. But I prefer to mark out the route on a

chart like a marine chart[5], which will be an assistance to your intelligence and enterprise. On this chart I have myself drawn the whole extremity of our western shore from Ireland as far down as the coast of Guinea toward the South, with all the islands which are to be found on this route. Opposite this (that is, the shores of Ireland and Africa) I have placed directly at the West the beginning of the Indies with the islands and places where you will land.[6] You will see for yourself how many miles you must keep from the arctic pole toward the equator, and at what distance you will arrive at these regions so fertile and productive of spices and precious stones."

In Toscanelli's letter, he not only indicates Japan, but, in the middle of the ocean, he places the island of Antilia. This old name afterwards gave the name by which the French still call the West Indies, Les Antilles. Toscanelli gives the exact distance which Columbus will have to sail: *"From Lisbon to the famous city of Quisay (Hang-tcheou-fou, then the capital of China) if you take the direct route toward the West, the distance will be thirty-nine hundred miles. And from Antilia to Japan it will be two hundred and twenty-five leagues."* Toscanelli says again, *"You see that the voyage that you wish to attempt is much legs difficult than would be thought.*

---

[5] Map: A literary & historical atlas of America, by Bartholomew, J. G. (John George), 1860-1920; Brooke, G. C. (George Cyril), 1884-; Rhys, Ernest. Publication date: 1911. Publisher London : J.M. Dent & Sons ; New York : E.P. Dutton & Co.

You would be sure of this if you met as many people as I do who have been in the country of spices."

While there were so many suggestions made that it would be possible to cross the Atlantic, there was one man who determined to do this. This man was Christopher Columbus. But he knew well that he could not do it alone. He must have money enough for an expedition, he must have authority to enlist crews for that expedition, and he must have power to govern those crews when they should arrive in the Indies. In our times such adventures have been conducted by mercantile corporations, but in those times no one thought of doing any such thing without the direct assistance and support of some monarch.

It is easy now to see and to say that Columbus himself was singularly well fitted to take the charge of the expedition of discovery. He was an excellent sailor and at the same time he was a learned geographer and a good mathematician. He was living in Portugal, the kings of which country had, for many years, fostered the exploration of the coast of Africa, and were pushing expeditions farther and farther South.

In doing this, they were, in a fashion, making new discoveries. For Europe was wholly ignorant of the western coast of Africa, beyond the Canaries, when their expeditions began. But all men of learning knew that, five hundred years before the Christian era, Hanno, a Carthaginian, had sailed round Africa under the direction of the senate of Carthage. The efforts of the King of Portugal were to repeat the voyage made by Hanno. In 1441, Gonzales and Tristam sailed as far as Sierra Leone. They brought back some blacks as slaves, and this was the beginning of the slave[7] trade.

In 1446 the Portuguese took possession of the Azores, the most western points of the Old World. Step by step they advanced southward, and became familiar with the African coast. Bold navigators were eager to find the East, and at last success came. Under the king's orders, in August, 1477, three caravels sailed from the Tagus, under Bartolomeo Diaz, for southern discovery. Diaz was himself brave enough to be willing to go on to the Red Sea, after he made the great discovery of the Cape of Good Hope, but his crews mutinied, after he had gone much farther than his predecessors, and compelled him to return. He passed the southern cape of Africa and went forty miles farther. He called it the Cape of Torments, "Cabo Tormentoso," so terrible were the storms he met there. But when King John heard his report he gave it that name of good omen which it has borne ever since, the name of the "Cape of Good Hope."

In the midst of such endeavors to reach the East Indies by the long voyage down the coast of Africa and across an unknown ocean, Columbus was urging all people who cared, to try the route directly west. If the world was round, as the sun and moon were, and as so many men of learning believed, India or the Indies must be to the west of Portugal. The value of direct trade with the Indies would be enormous. Europe had already acquired a taste for the spices of India and had confidence in the drugs of India. The

---

[7] The African slave trade (*noted because slavery has existed on all continents and for all races since ancient times*)

silks and other articles of clothing made in India, and the carpets of India, were well known and prized. Marco Polo and others had given an impression that there was much gold in India; and the pearls and precious stones of India excited the imagination of all who read his travels.

The immense value of such a commerce may be estimated from one fact. When, a generation after this time, one ship only of all the squadron of Magellan returned to Cadiz, after the first voyage round the world, she was loaded with spices from the Moluccas[8]. These spices were sold by the Spanish government for so large a sum of money that the king was remunerated for the whole cost of the expedition, and even made a very large profit from a transaction which had cost a great deal in its outfit.

Columbus was able, therefore, to offer mercantile adventurers the promise of great profit in case of success; and at this time kings were willing to take their share of such profits as might accrue.

The letter of Toscanelli, the Italian geographer, which has been spoken of, was addressed to Alphonso V, the King of Portugal. To him and his successor, John the Second, Columbus explained the probability of success, and each of them, as it would seem, had confidence in it. But King John made the great mistake of intrusting Columbus's plan to another person for experiment. He was selfish enough, and mean enough, to fit out a ship privately and intrust its command to another seaman, bidding him sail west in search of the Indies, while he pretended that

---

[8] The Maluku Islands or the Moluccas are an archipelago in eastern Indonesia

he was on a voyage to the Cape de Verde Islands. He was, in fact, to follow the route indicated by Columbus. The vessel sailed. But, fortunately for the fame of Columbus, she met a terrible storm, and her officers, in terror, turned from the unknown ocean and returned to Lisbon. Columbus himself tells this story. It was in disgust with the bad faith the king showed in this transaction that he left Lisbon to offer his great project to the King and Queen of Spain.

In a similar way, a generation afterward, Magellan, who was in the service of the King of Portugal, was disgusted by insults which he received at his court, and exiled himself to Spain. He offered to the Spanish king his plan for sailing round the world and it was accepted. He sailed in a Spanish fleet, and to his discoveries Spain owes the possession of the Philippine Islands. Twice, therefore, did kings of Portugal lose for themselves, their children and their kingdom, the fame and the recompense which belong to such great discoveries.

The wife of Columbus had died and he was without a home. He left Lisbon with his only son, Diego, in or near the end of the year 1484.

Chapter II: His Plans for Discovery

It has been supposed that when Columbus left Lisbon he was oppressed by debts. At a subsequent period, when King John wanted to recall him, he offered to protect him against any creditors. But on the other hand, it is thought that at this time he visited Genoa, and made some provision for the comfort of his father, who was now an old man. Christopher Columbus, himself, according to the usual opinion regarding his birth, was now almost fifty years old[9].

It is probable that at this time he urged on his countrymen, the Genoese, the importance of his great plan; and tried to interest them to make the great endeavor, for the purpose of reaching the Indies by a western route. As it proved, the discovery of the route by the Cape of Good Hope was, commercially, a great injury to Genoa and the other maritime cities of Italy. Before this time, the eastern trade of Europe came by the ports of the eastern Mediterranean, and the Italian cities. Columbus's offer to Genoa was therefore one which, if her statesmen could have foreseen the future, they would have considered eagerly.

But Genoa was greatly depressed at this period. In her wars with the Turks she had been, on the whole,

---

[9] If he was actually born in 1451, he would have been around 40 years old.

not successful. She had lost Caffa, her station in the Crimea, and her possessions in the Archipelago were threatened. The government did not accept Columbus's proposals, and he was obliged to return with them to Spain. He went first to distinguished noblemen, in the South of Spain, who were of liberal and adventurous disposition. One was the Duke of Medina Celi, and one the Duke of Medina Sidonia. Each of these grandees entertained him at their courts, and heard his proposals.

The Duke of Medina Celi was so much interested in them, that at one time he proposed to give Columbus the direction of four vessels which he had in the harbor of Cadiz. But, of a sudden, he changed his mind. The enterprise was so vast, he said, that it should be under the direction of the crown. And, without losing confidence in it, he gave to Columbus an introduction to the king and queen, in which he cordially recommended him to their patronage.

This king and queen were King Ferdinand of Aragon, and Queen Isabella of Castile. The marriage of these two had united Spain. Their affection for each other made the union real, and the energy, courage and wisdom of both made their reign successful and glorious. Of all its glories the greatest, as it has proved, was connected with the life and discoveries of the sailor who was now to approach them. He had been disloyally treated by Portugal, he had been dismissed by Genoa. He had not succeeded with the great dukes. Now he was to press his adventure upon a king and queen who were engaged in a difficult war with the Moors, who still held a considerable part of the peninsula of Spain.

The king and queen were residing at Cordova, a rich and beautiful city, which they had taken from the Moors. Under their rule Cordova had been the most important seat of learning in Europe. Here Columbus tarried at the house of Alonso de Quintinilla, who became an ardent convert to his theory, and introduced him to important friends. By their agency, arrangements were made, in which Columbus should present his views to the king. The time was not such as he could have wished. All Cordova was alive with the preparation for a great campaign against the enemy. But King Ferdinand made arrangements to hear Columbus; it does not appear that, at the first hearing, Isabella was present at the interview. But Ferdinand, although in the midst of his military cares, was interested in the proposals made by Columbus. He liked the man. He was pleased by the modesty and dignity with which he brought forward his proposals. Columbus spoke, as he tells us, as one specially appointed by God Himself to carry out this discovery. The king did not, however, at once adopt the scheme, but gave out that a council of men of learning should be called together to consider it.

Columbus himself says that he entered the service of the sovereigns January 26, 1486. The council to which he was referred was held in the university city of Salamanca, in that year. It gave to him a full opportunity to explain his theory. It consisted of a fair representation of the learning of the time. But most of the men who met had formed their opinions on the subjects involved, and were too old to change them. A part of them were priests of the church, in the habit of looking to sacred Scripture as their only authority, when the pope had given no instruction in detail. Of these some took literally expressions in the Old Testament, which they supposed to be fatal to the plans of Columbus. Such was the phrase in the 104th Psalm, that God stretches out the heavens like a curtain. The expression in the book of Hebrews, that the heavens are extended as a tent, was also quoted, in the same view.

Quotations from the early Fathers of the church were more fatal to the new plan than those from the Scripture.

On the other hand there were men who cordially supported Columbus's wishes, and there were more when the congress parted than when it met. Its sessions occupied a considerable part of the summer, but it was not for years that it rendered any decision.

The king, queen and court, meanwhile, were occupied in war with the Moors. Columbus was once and again summoned to attend the court, and more than once money was advanced to him to enable him to do so. Once he began new negotiations with King John, and from him he received a letter inviting him to return to Portugal. He received a similar letter from King Henry VII of England inviting him to his court. Nothing was determined on in Spain. To this day, the people of that country are thought to have a habit of postponement to tomorrow of that which perplexes them. In 1489, according to Ortiz de Zuniga, Columbus fought in battle in the king's army.

When, however, in the winter of 1490, it was announced that the army was to take the field again, never to leave its camp till Grenada had fallen, Columbus felt that he must make one last endeavor.

He insisted that he must have an answer regarding his plans of discovery. The confessor of the queen, Fernando da Talavera, was commanded to obtain the definite answer of the men of learning. Alas! it was fatal to Columbus's hopes. They said that it was not right that great princes should undertake such enterprises on grounds as weak as those which he relied upon.

The sovereigns themselves, however, were more favorable; so was a minority of the council of Salamanca. And the confessor was instructed to tell him that their expenses in the war forbade them from sending him out as a discoverer, but that, when that was well over, they had hopes that they might commission him. This was the end of five years of solicitation, in which he had put his trust in princes. Columbus regarded the answer, as well he might, as only a courtly measure of refusal. And he retired in disgust from the court at Seville.

He determined to lay his plans before the King of France. He was traveling with this purpose, with his son, Diego, now a boy of ten or twelve years of age, when he arrived at night at the hospitable convent of Saint Mary of Rabida, which has been made celebrated by that incident. It is about three miles south of what was then the seaport of Palos, one of the active ports of commercial Spain. The convent stands on level ground high above the sea; but a steep road runs down to the shore of the ocean. Some of its windows and corridors look out upon the ocean on the west and south, and the inmates still show the room in which Columbus used to write, and the inkstand which served his purposes while he lived there. It is maintained as a monument of history by the Spanish government.[10]

At the door of this convent he asked for bread and water for his boy. The prior of the convent was named Juan Perez de Marchena. He was attracted by the appearance of Columbus, still more by his conversation, and invited him to remain as their guest.

When he learned that his new friend was about to offer to France the advantages of a discovery so great as that proposed, he begged him to make one effort more at home. He sent for some friends, Fernandos, a physician at Palos, and for the brothers Pinzon, who now appear for the first time in a story where their part is distinguished. Together they all persuaded Columbus to send one messenger more to wait upon their sovereigns. The man sent was Rodriguez, a pilot of Lepe, who found access to the queen because Juan Perez, the prior, had formerly been her confessor. She had confidence in him, as she had, indeed, in Columbus. And in fourteen days the friendly pilot came back from Santa Fe with a kind letter from the queen to her friend, bidding him return at once to court. Perez de Marchena saddled his mule at once and before midnight was on his way to see his royal mistress.

Santa Fe was half camp, half city. It had been built in what is called the Vega, the great fruitful plain which extends for many miles to the westward of

---

[10] Monastery of Santa María de La Rábida and the Columbus Memorial Places in Huelva was nominated as a World Heritage site in 2016; according to UNESCO, it is still tentative in 2021. (https://whc.unesco.org/en/tentativelists/6080/)

Grenada. The court and army were here as they pressed their attack on that city. Perez de Marchena had ready access to Queen Isabella, and pressed his suit well. He was supported by one of her favorites, the Marquesa de Moya. In reply to their solicitations, she asked that Columbus should return to her, and ordered that twenty thousand maravedis should be sent to him for his traveling expenses.

This sum was immediately sent by Perez to his friend. Columbus bought a mule, exchanged his worn clothes for better ones, and started, as he was bidden, for the camp.

He arrived there just after the great victory, by which the king and queen had obtained their wish— had taken the noble city of Grenada and ended Moorish[11] rule in Spain. King, queen, court and army were preparing to enter the Alhambra in triumph. Whoever tries to imagine the scene, in which the great procession entered through the gates, so long sealed, or of the moment when the royal banner of Spain was first flying out upon the Tower of the Vela, must remember that Columbus, elate, at last, with hopes for his own great discovery, saw the triumph and joined in the display.

But his success was not immediate, even now. Fernando de Talavera, who had had the direction of the wise council of Salamanca, was now Archbishop of Grenada, whose see had been conferred on him after the victory. He was not the friend of Columbus. And when, at what seemed the final interview with king and queen, he heard Columbus claim the right to one-tenth of all the profits of the enterprise, he

---

[11] Muslim

protested against such lavish recompense of an adventurer. He was now the confessor of Isabella, as Juan Perez, the friendly prior, had been before. Columbus, however, was proud and firm. He would not yield to the terms prepared by the archbishop. He preferred to break off the negotiation, and again retired from court. He determined, as he had before, to lay his plans before the King of France.

Spain would have lost the honor and the reward of the great discovery, as Portugal and Genoa had lost them, but for Luis de St. Angel, and the queen herself. St. Angel had been the friend of Columbus. He was an important officer, the treasurer of the church revenues of Aragon. He now insisted upon an audience from the queen. It would seem that Ferdinand, though King of Aragon, was not present. St. Angel spoke eloquently. The friendly Marchioness of Moya spoke eagerly and persuasively. Isabella was at last fired with zeal. Columbus should go, and the enterprise should be hers.

It is here that the incident belongs, represented in the statue by Mr. Mead, and that of Miss Hosmer. The sum required for the discovery of a world was only three thousand crowns. Two vessels were all that Columbus asked for, with the pay of their crews. But where were three thousand crowns? The treasury was empty, and the king was now averse to any action. It was at this moment that Isabella said, "The enterprise is mine, for the Crown of Castile. I pledge my jewels for the funds."

The funds were in fact advanced by St. Angel, from the ecclesiastical revenues under his control. They were repaid from the gold brought in the first voyage.

But, always afterward, Isabella regarded the Indies as a Castilian possession. The most important officers in its administration, indeed most of the emigrants, were always from Castile.

Columbus, meanwhile, was on his way back to Palos, on his mule, alone. But at a bridge, still pointed out, a royal courier overtook him, bidding him return. The spot has been made the scene of more than one picture, which represents the crisis, in which the despair of one moment changed to the glad hope which was to lead to certainty.

He returned to Isabella for the last time, before that great return in which he came as a conqueror, to display to her the riches of the New World. The king yielded a slow and doubtful assent. Isabella took the enterprise in her own hands. She and Columbus agreed at once, and articles were drawn up which gave him the place of admiral for life on all lands he might discover; gave him one-tenth of all pearls, precious stones, gold, silver, spices and other merchandise to be obtained in his admiralty, and gave him the right to nominate three candidates from whom the governor of each province should be selected by the crown. He was to be the judge of all disputes arising from such traffic as was proposed; and he was to have one-eighth part of the profit, and bear one-eighth part of the cost of it.

With this glad news he returned at once to Palos. The Pinzons, who had been such loyal friends, were to take part in the enterprise. He carried with him a royal order, commanding the people of Palos to fit out two caravels within ten days, and to place them and their crews at the disposal of Columbus. The third vessel proposed was to be fitted out by him and his friends. The crews were to be paid four months' wages in advance, and Columbus was to have full command, to do what he chose, if he did not interfere with the Portuguese discoveries.

On the 23rd of May, Columbus went to the church of San Giorgio in Palos, with his friend, the prior of St. Mary's convent, and other important people, and the royal order was read with great solemnity.

But it excited at first only indignation or dismay. The expedition was most unpopular. Sailors refused to enlist, and the authorities, who had already offended the crown, so that they had to furnish these vessels, as it were, as a fine, refused to do what they were bidden. Other orders from Court were necessary. But it seems to have been the courage and determination of the Pinzons which carried the preparations through. After weeks had been lost, Martin Alonso Pinzon and his brothers said they would go in person on the expedition. They were well-known merchants and seamen, and were much respected. Sailors were impressed, by the royal authority, and the needful stores were taken in the same way. It seems now strange that so much difficulty should have surrounded an expedition in itself so small. But the plan met then all the superstition, terror and other prejudice of the time.

All that Columbus asked or needed was three small vessels and their stores and crews. The largest ships engaged were little larger than the large yachts, whose races every summer delight the people of America. The *Gallega* and the *Pinta* were the two largest. They were called caravels, a name then given to the smallest three-masted vessels. Columbus once uses it for a vessel of forty tons; but it generally applied in Portuguese or Spanish use to a vessel, ranging one hundred and twenty to one hundred and forty Spanish "toneles." This word represents a capacity about one-tenth larger than that expressed by our English "ton."

The reader should remember that most of the commerce of the time was the coasting commerce of the Mediterranean, and that it was not well that the ships should draw much water. The fleet of Columbus, as it sailed, consisted of the *Gallega* (the Galician), of which he changed the name to the *Santa Maria*, and of the *Pinta* and the *Nina*. Of these the first two were of a tonnage which we should rate as about one hundred and thirty tons. The *Nina* was much smaller, not more than fifty tons. One writer says that they were all without full decks, that is, that such decks as they had did not extend from stem to stern. But the other authorities speak as if the Nina only was an open vessel, and the two larger were decked. Columbus himself took command of the *Santa Maria*, Martin Alonso Pinzon of the *Pinta*, and his brothers, Francis Martin and Vicente Yanez, of the *Nina*. The whole company in all three ships numbered one hundred and twenty men.

Mr. Harrisse shows that the expense to the crown amounted to 1,140,000 maravedis. This, as he counts it, is about sixty-four thousand dollars of our money[12]. To this Columbus was to add one-eighth of the cost. His friends, the Pinzons, seem to have advanced this, and to have been afterwards repaid.

---

[12] 1892; in 2021 this amount is valued at close to $2 million

Las Casas and Herrera both say that the sum thus added was much more than one-eighth of the cost and amounted to half a million maravedis.

Chapter III: The Great Voyage

At last all was ready. That is to say, the fleet was so far ready that Columbus was ready to start. The vessels were small, as we think of vessels, but he was not dissatisfied. He says in the beginning of his journal, "I armed three vessels very fit for such an enterprise." He had left Grenada as late as the twelfth of May. He had crossed Spain to Palos[13], and in less than three months had fitted out the ships and was ready for sea.

The harbor of Palos is now ruined. Mud and gravel, brought down by the River Tinto, have filled up the bay, so that even small boats cannot approach the shore. The traveler finds, however, the island of Saltes, quite outside the bay, much as Columbus left it. It is a small spit of sand, covered with shells and with a few seashore herbs. His own account of the great voyage begins with the words:[14]

"Friday, August 3, 1492. Set sail from the bar of Saltes at 8 o'clock, and proceeded with a strong breeze till sunset sixty miles, or fifteen leagues south, afterward southwest and south by west, which is in the direction of the Canaries."

---

[13] Author's note: Palos is now so insignificant a place that on some important maps of Spain it will not be found. It is on the east side of the Tinto river; and Huelva, on the west side, has taken its place.
[14] See Book II of this edition, page 226 for the full journal of Columbus.

It appears, therefore, that the great voyage, the most important and successful ever made, began on Friday, the day which is said to be so much disliked by sailors. Columbus never alludes to this superstition.

He had always meant to sail first for the Canaries, which were the most western land then known in the latitude of his voyage. From Lisbon to the famous city of "Quisay," or "Quinsay," in Asia, Toscanelli, his learned correspondent, supposed the distance to be less than one thousand leagues westward. From the Canary islands, on that supposition, the distance would be ten degrees less. The distance to Cipango, or Japan, would be much less.

As it proved, the squadron had to make some stay at the Canaries. The rudder of the Pinta was disabled, and she proved leaky. It was suspected that the owners, from whom she had been forcibly taken, had intentionally disabled her, or that possibly the crew had injured her. But Columbus says in his journal that Martin Alonso Pinzon, captain of the Pinta, was a man of capacity and courage, and that this quieted his apprehensions. From the ninth of August to the second of September, nearly four weeks were spent by the Pinta and her crew at the Grand Canary island, and she was repaired.

She proved afterwards a serviceable vessel, the fastest of the fleet. At the Canaries they heard stories of lands seen to the westward, to which Columbus refers in his journal.

On the sixth of September they sailed from Gomera and on the eighth they lost sight of land. Nor did they see land again for thirty-three days. Such was the length of the great voyage. All the time, most naturally, they were wishing for signs, not of land perhaps, but which might show whether this great ocean were really different from other seas. On the whole the voyage was not a dangerous one.

According to the Admiral's reckoning—and in his own journal Columbus always calls himself the Admiral—its length was one thousand and eighty-nine leagues. This was not far from right, the real distance being, in a direct line, three thousand one hundred and forty nautical miles, or three thousand six hundred and twenty statute miles.[15] It would not be considered a very long voyage for small vessels now. In general the course was west. Sometimes, for special reasons, they sailed south of west. If they had sailed precisely west they would have struck the shore of the United States a little north of the spot where St. Augustine now is, about the northern line of Florida.

Had the coast of Asia been, indeed, as near as Toscanelli and Columbus supposed, this latitude of the Canary islands would have been quite near the mouth of the Yang-tse-Kiang river, in China, which was what Columbus was seeking. For nearly a generation afterwards he and his followers supposed that the coast of that region was what they had found.

It was on Saturday, the eighth of September, that they lost sight of Teneriffe.

---

[15] [Author's note] The computations from Santa Cruz, in the Canaries, to San Salvador give this result, as kindly made for us by Lieutenant Mozer, of the United States navy.

On the eleventh they saw a large piece of the mast of a ship afloat.

On the fourteenth they saw a "tropic-bird," which the sailors thought was never seen more than twenty-five leagues from land; but it must be remembered, that, outside of the Mediterranean, few of the sailors had ever been farther themselves.

On the sixteenth they began to meet "large patches of weeds, very green, which appeared to have been recently washed away from land."

This was their first knowledge of the "Sargasso sea," a curious tract in mid-Atlantic which is always green with floating seaweeds. "The continent we shall find farther on," wrote the confident Admiral.

An observation of the sun on the seventeenth proved what had been suspected before, that the needles of the compasses were not pointing precisely to the north. The variation of the needle, since that time, has been a recognized fact. But this observation at so critical a time first disclosed it. The crew were naturally alarmed. Here was evidence that, in the great ocean, common laws were not to be relied upon. But they had great respect for Columbus's knowledge of such subjects. He told them that it was not the north which had changed, nor the needle, which was true to the north, but the polar star revolved, like other stars, and for the time they were satisfied.

The same day they saw weeds which he was sure were land weeds. From them he took a living crab, whose unintentional voyage eastward was a great encouragement to the bolder adventurer westward. Columbus kept the crab, saying that such were never found eighty leagues from land. In fact this poor crab was at least nine hundred and seventy leagues from the Bahamas, as this same journal proves.

On the eighteenth the Pinta ran ahead of the other vessels, Martin Alonso was so sure that he should reach land that night. But it was not to come so soon.

Columbus every day announced to his crew a less distance as the result of the day than they had really sailed. For he was afraid of their distrust, and did not dare let them know how far they were from home. The private journal, therefore, has such entries as this, "Sailed more than fifty-five leagues, wrote down only forty-eight." That is, he wrote on the daily log, which was open to inspection, a distance some leagues less than they had really made.

On the twentieth pelicans are spoken of, on the twenty-first "such abundance of weeds that the ocean seemed covered with them," "the sea smooth as a river, and the finest air in the world. Saw a whale, an indication of land, as they always keep near the coast." To later times, this note, also, shows how ignorant Columbus then was of mid-ocean.

On the twenty-second, to the Admiral's relief, there was a head wind; for the crew began to think that with perpetual east winds they would never return to Spain. They had been in what are known as the trade winds.

On the twenty-third the smoother water gave place to a rough sea, and he writes that this "was favorable to me, as it happened formerly to Moses when he led the Jews from Egypt."

The next day, thanks to the headwinds, their progress was less.

On the twenty-fifth, Pinzon, of the Pinta, felt sure that they were near the outer islands of Asia as they appeared on the Toscanelli map, and at sunset called out with joy that he saw land, claiming a reward for such news. The crews of both vessels sang "Glory to God in the highest," and the crew of the little *Nina* were sure that the bank was land. On this occasion they changed from a western course to the southwest. But alas! the land was a fog-bank and the reward never came to Martin Pinzon.

On the twenty-sixth, again "the sea was like a river." This was Wednesday.

In three days they sailed sixty-nine leagues. Saturday was calm. They saw a bird called "'Rabihorcado,' which never alights at sea, nor goes twenty leagues from land," wrote the confident Columbus; "Nothing is wanting but the singing of the nightingale," he says.

Sunday, the thirtieth, brought "tropic-birds" again, "a very clear sign of land." Monday the journal shows them seven hundred and seven leagues from Ferro. Tuesday a white gull was the only visitor. Wednesday they had pardelas and great quantities of seaweed. Columbus began to be sure that they had passed "the islands" and were nearing the continent of Asia. Thursday they had a flock of pardelas, two pelicans, a rabihorcado and a gull. Friday, the fifth of October, brought pardelas and flying-fishes.

We have copied these simple intimations from the journal to show how constantly Columbus supposed that he was near the coast of Asia. On the sixth of October Pinzon asked that the course might be changed to the southwest. But Columbus held on.

On the seventh the Nina was ahead, and fired a gun and hoisted her flag in token that she saw land. But again they were disappointed. Columbus gave directions to keep close order at sunrise and sunset.

The next day he did change the course to west southwest, following flights of birds from the north which went in that direction.

On the eighth "the sea was like the river at Seville," the weeds were very few and they took land birds on board the ships.

On the ninth they sailed southwest five leagues, and then with a change of wind went west by north. All night they heard the birds of passage passing.

On the tenth of October the men made remonstrance, which has been exaggerated in history into a revolt. It is said, in books of authority, that Columbus begged them to sail west only three days more. But in the private journal of the tenth he says simply: "The seamen complained of the length of the voyage. They did not wish to go any farther. The Admiral did his best to renew their courage, and reminded them of the profits which would come to them. He added, boldly, that no complaints would change his purpose, that he had set out to go to the Indies, and that with the Lord's assistance he should keep on until he came there." This is the only passage in the journal which has any resemblance to the account of the mutiny.

If it happened, as Oviedo says, three days before the discovery, it would have been on the eighth of October. On that day the entry is, "Steered west southwest, and sailed day and night eleven or twelve leagues—at times, during the night, fifteen miles an hour—if the log can be relied upon. Found the sea like the river at Seville, thanks to God. The air was as soft as that of Seville in April, and so fragrant that it was delicious to breathe it. The weeds appeared very fresh. Many land birds, one of which they took, flying towards the southwest, also grajaos, ducks and a pelican were seen."

This is not the account of a mutiny. And the discovery of Columbus's own journal makes that certain, which was probable before, that the romantic account of the despair of the crews was embroidered on the narrative after the event, and by people who wanted to improve the story. It was, perhaps, borrowed from a story of Diaz's voyage. We have followed the daily record to show how constantly they supposed, on the other hand, that they were always nearing land.

With the eleventh of October, came certainty. The eleventh is sometimes spoken of as the day of discovery, and sometimes the twelfth, when they landed on the first island of the new world.

The whole original record of the discovery is this: "Oct. 11, course to west and southwest. Heavier sea than they had known, pardelas and a green branch near the caravel of the Admiral. From the Pinta they see a branch of a tree, a stake and a smaller stake, which they draw in, and which appears to have been cut with iron, and a piece of cane. Besides these, there is a land shrub and a little bit of board. The crew of the Nina saw other signs of land and a branch covered with thorns and flowers. With these tokens every-one breathes again and is delighted. They sail twenty-seven leagues on this course.

"The Admiral orders that they shall resume a westerly course at sunset. They make twelve miles each hour; up till two hours after midnight they made ninety miles.

"The Pinta, the best sailer of the three, was ahead. She makes signals, already agreed upon, that she has discovered land. A sailor named Rodrigo de Triana was the first to see this land. For the Admiral being on the castle of the poop of the ship at ten at night really saw a light, but it was so shut in by darkness that he did not like to say that it was a sign of land. Still he called up Pedro Gutierrez, the king's chamberlain, and said to him that there seemed to be a light, and asked him to look. He did so and saw it. He said the same to Rodrigo Sanchez of Segovia, who had been sent by the king and queen as inspector in the fleet, but he saw nothing, being indeed in a place where he could see nothing.

"After the Admiral spoke of it, the light was seen once or twice. It was like a wax candle, raised and lowered, which would appear to few to be a sign of land. But the Admiral was certain that it was a sign of land. Therefore when they said the 'Salve,' which all the sailors are used to say and sing in their fashion, the Admiral ordered them to look out well from the forecastle, and he would give at once a silk jacket to the man who first saw land, besides the other rewards which the sovereigns had ordered, which were 10,000 maravedis, to be paid as an annuity forever to the man who saw it first.

"At two hours after midnight land appeared, from which they were about two leagues off."

This is the one account of the discovery written at the time. It is worth copying and reading at full in its little details, for it contrasts curiously with the embellished accounts which appear in the next generation. Thus the historian Oviedo says, in a dramatic way:

"One of the ship boys on the largest ship, a native of Lepe, cried 'Fire!' 'Land!' Immediately a servant of Columbus replied, 'The Admiral had said that already.' Soon after, Columbus said, 'I said so some time ago, and that I saw that fire on the land.'" And so indeed it happened that Thursday, at two hours after midnight, the Admiral called a gentleman named Escobedos, officer of the wardrobe of the king, and told him that he saw fire. And at the break of day, at the time Columbus had predicted the day before, they saw from the largest ship the island which the Indians call Guanahani[16] to the north of them.

"And the first man to see the land, when day came, was Rodrigo of Triana, on the eleventh day of October, 1492."

Nothing is more certain than that this was really on the twelfth.

The reward for first seeing land was eventually awarded to Columbus, and it was regularly paid him through his life. It was the annual payment of 10,000 maravedis. A maravedi was then a little less than six cents of our currency[17]. The annuity was, therefore, about six hundred dollars a year.

---

[16] An island in the Bahamas; now San Salvador
[17] 1892

The worth of a maravedi varied, from time to time, so that the calculations of the value of any number of maravedis are very confusing. Before the coin went out of use it was worth only half a cent.

Chapter IV: The Landing on the Twelfth of October

It was on Friday, the twelfth of October, that they saw this island, which was an island of the Lucayos group, called, says Las Casas, "in the tongue of the Indians, Guanahani." Soon they saw people naked, and the Admiral went ashore in the armed boat, with Martin Alonzo Pinzon and, Vicente Yanez, his brother, who was captain of the Nina. The Admiral unfurled the Royal Standard, and the captain's two standards of the Greek Cross, which the Admiral raised on all the ships as a sign, with an F. and a Y.; over each letter a crown; one on one side of the {"iron cross symbol"} and the other on the other. When they were ashore they saw very green trees and much water, and fruits of different kinds.

"The Admiral called the two captains and the others who went ashore, and Rodrigo Descovedo, Notary of the whole fleet, and Rodrigo Sanchez of Segovia, and he said that they must give him their faith and witness how he took possession before all others, as in fact he did take possession of the said island for the king and the queen, his lord and lady. . . . Soon many people of the island assembled. These which follow are the very words of the Admiral, in his book of his first navigation and discovery of these Indies."

October 11-12. "So that they may feel great friendship for us, and because I knew that they were a people who would be better delivered and converted to our Holy Faith by love than by force, I gave to some of them red caps and glass bells which they put round their necks, and many other things of little value, in which they took much pleasure, and they remained so friendly to us that it was wonderful.

"Afterwards they came swimming to the ship's boats where we were. And they brought us parrots and cotton-thread in skeins, and javelins and many other things. And they bartered them with us for other things, which we gave them, such as little glass beads and little bells. In short, they took everything, and gave of what they had with good will. But it seemed to me that they were a people very destitute of everything.

"They all went as naked as their mothers bore them, and the women as well, although I only saw one who was really young. And all the men I saw were young, for I saw none more than thirty years of age; very well made, with very handsome persons, and very good faces; their hair thick like the hairs of horses' tails, and cut short. They bring their hair above their eyebrows, except a little behind, which they wear long, and never cut. Some of them paint themselves blackish (and they are of the color of the inhabitants of the Canaries, neither black nor white), and some paint themselves white, and some red, and some with whatever they can get. And some of them paint their faces, and some all their bodies, and some only the eyes, and some only the nose.

"They do not bear arms nor do they know them, for I showed them swords and they took them by the edge, and they cut themselves through ignorance. They have no iron at all; their javelins are rods without iron, and some of them have a fish's tooth at the end, and some of them other things. They are all of good stature, and good graceful appearance, well made. I saw some who had scars of wounds in their bodies, and I made signs to them (to ask) what that was, and they showed me how people came there from other islands which lay around, and tried to take them captive and they defended themselves. And I believed, and I (still) believe, that they came there from the mainland to take them for captives.

"They would be good servants, and of good disposition, for I see that they repeat very quickly everything which is said to them. And I believe that they could easily be made Christians, for it seems to me that they have no belief. I, if it please our Lord, will take six of them to your Highnesses at the time of my departure, so that they may learn to talk. No wild creature of any sort have I seen, except parrots, in this island."

All these are the words of the Admiral, says Las Casas. The journal of the next day is in these words:

Saturday, October 13. "As soon as the day broke, many of these men came to the beach, all young, as I have said, and all of good stature, a very handsome race. Their hair is not woolly, but straight and coarse, like horse hair, and all with much wider foreheads and heads than any other people I have seen up to this time. And their eyes are very fine and not small, and they are not black at all, but of the color of the Canary Islanders. And nothing else could be expected, since it is on one line of latitude with the Island of Ferro, in the Canaries.

"They came to the ship with almadias[18], which are made of the trunk of a tree, like a long boat, and all of one piece—and made in a very wonderful manner in the

---

[18] Arabic word for raft or float; here it means canoes.

fashion of the country—and large enough for some of them to hold forty or forty-five men. And others are smaller, down to such as hold one man alone. They row with a shovel like a baker's, and it goes wonderfully well. And if it overturns, immediately they all go to swimming and they right it, and bale it with calabashes which they carry.

They brought skeins of spun cotton, and parrots, and javelins, and other little things which it would be wearisome to write down, and they gave everything for whatever was given to them.

"And I strove attentively to learn whether there were gold. And I saw that some of them had a little piece of gold hung in a hole which they have in their noses. And by signs I was able to understand that going to the south, or going round the island to the southward, there was a king there who had great vessels of it, and had very much of it. I tried to persuade them to go there; and afterward I saw that they did not understand about going.[19]

"I determined to wait till the next afternoon, and then to start for the southwest, for many of them told me that there was land to the south and southwest and northwest, and that those from the northwest came often to fight with them,

---

[19] To this first found land, called by the natives Guanahani, Columbus gave the name of San Salvador. There is, however, great doubt whether this is the island known by that name on the maps. Of late years the impression has generally been that the island thus discovered is that now known as Watling's island. In 1860 Admiral Fox, of the United States navy, visited all these islands, and studied the whole question anew, visiting the islands himself and working backwards to the account of Columbus's subsequent voyage, so as to fix the spot from which that voyage began. Admiral Fox decides that the island of discovery was neither San Salvador nor Watling's island, but the Samana island of the same group. The subject is so curious that we copy his results at more length in appendix A, p. 195.

and so to go on to the southwest to seek gold and precious stones.

"This island is very large and very flat and with very green trees, and many waters, and a very large lake in the midst, without any mountain. And all of it is green, so that it is a pleasure to see it. And these people are so gentle, and desirous to have our articles and thinking that nothing can be given them unless they give something and do not keep it back. They take what they can, and at once jump (into the water) and swim (away). But all that they have they give for whatever is given them. For they barter even for pieces of porringus, and of broken glass cups, so that I saw sixteen skeins of cotton given for three Portuguese centis, that is a blanca of Castile, and there was more than twenty-five pounds of spun cotton in them. This I shall forbid, and not let anyone take (it); but I shall have it all taken for your Highnesses, if there is any quantity of it.

"It grows here in this island, but for a short time I could not believe it at all. And there is found here also the gold which they wear hanging to their noses; but so as not to lose time I mean to go to see whether I can reach the island of Cipango.

"Now as it was night they all went ashore with their almadias."

Sunday, October 14. "At daybreak I had the ship's boat and the boats of the caravels made ready, and I sailed along the island, toward the north-northeast, to see the other port, what there was (there), and also to see the towns, and I soon saw two or three, and the people, who all were coming to the shore, calling us and giving thanks to God. Some brought us water, others things to eat. Others, when they saw that I did not care to go ashore, threw themselves into the sea and came swimming, and we understood that they asked us if we had come from heaven. And an old man came into the boat, and others called all (the rest) men and women, with a loud voice: 'Come and see the men who have come from heaven; bring them food and drink.'

"There came many of them and many women, each one with something, giving thanks to God, casting themselves on the ground, and raising their heads toward heaven. And afterwards they called us with shouts to come ashore.

"But I feared (to do so), for I saw a great reef of rocks which encircles all that island. And in it there is bottom and harbor for as many ships as there are in all Christendom, and its entrance very narrow. It is true that there are some shallows inside this ring, but the sea is no rougher than in a well.

"And I was moved to see all this, this morning, so that I might be able to give an account of it all to your Highnesses, and also (to find out) where I might make a fortress. And I saw a piece of land formed like an island, although it is not one, in which there were six houses, which could be cut off in two days so as to become an island; although I do not see that it is necessary, as this people is very ignorant of arms, as your Highnesses will see from seven whom I had taken, to carry them off to learn our speech and to bring them back again. But your Highnesses, when you direct, can take them all to Castile, or keep them captives in this same island, for with fifty men you can keep them all subjected, and make them do whatever you like.

"And close to the said islet are groves of trees, the most beautiful I have seen, and as green and full of leaves as those of Castile in the months of April and May, and much water.

"I looked at all that harbor and then I returned to the ship and set sail, and I saw so many islands that I could not decide to which I should go first. And those men whom I had taken said to me by signs that there were so very many that they were without number, and they repeated by name more than a hundred. At last I set sail for the largest one, and there I determined to go. And so I am doing, and it will be five leagues from the island of San Salvador, and farther from some of the rest, nearer to others. They all are very flat, without mountains and very fertile, and all inhabited. And they make war upon each other although they are very simple, and (they are) very beautifully formed."

Monday, October 15, Columbus, on arriving at the island for which he had set sail, went on to a cape, near which he anchored at about sunset. He gave the island the name of Santa Maria de la Concepcion.[20]

"At about sunset I anchored near the said cape to know if there were gold there, for the men whom I had taken at the Island of San Salvador told me that there they wore very large rings of gold on their legs and arms. I think that all they said was for a trick, in order to make their escape. However, I did not wish to pass by any island without taking possession of it.

"And I anchored, and was there till today, Tuesday, when at the break of day I went ashore with the armed boats, and landed.

"They (the inhabitants), who were many, as naked and in the same condition as those of San Salvador, let us land on the island, and gave us what we asked of them.

"I set out for the ship. And there was a large almadia which had come to board the caravel Nina, and one of the

---

[20] This is supposed to be Caico del Norte.

men from we Island of San Salvador threw himself into the sea, took this boat, and made off; and the night before, at midnight, another jumped out. And the almadia went back so fast that there never was a boat which could come up with her, although we had a considerable advantage. It reached the shore, and they left the almadia, and some of my company landed after them, and they all fled like hens.

"And the almadia, which they had left, we took to the caravel Nina, to which from another headland there was coming another little almadia, with a man who came to barter a skein of cotton. And some of the sailors threw themselves into the sea, because he did not wish to enter the caravel, and took him. And I, who was on the stern of the ship, and saw it all, sent for him and gave him a red cap and some little green glass beads which I put on his arm, and two small bells which I put at his ears, and I had his almadia returned, and sent him ashore.

"And I set sail at once to go to the other large island which I saw at the west, and commanded the other almadia to be set adrift, which the caravel Nina was towing astern. And then I saw on land, when the man landed, to whom I had given the above mentioned things (and I had not consented to take the skein of cotton, though he wished to give it to me), all the others went to him and thought it a great wonder, and it seemed to them that we were good people, and that the other man, who had fled, had done us some harm, and that therefore we were carrying him off. And this was why I treated the other man as I did, commanding him to be released, and gave him the said things, so that they might have this opinion of us, and so that another time, when your Highnesses send here again, they may be well disposed. And all that I gave him was not worth four maravedis."

Columbus had set sail at ten o'clock for a "large island" he mentions, which he called Fernandina, where, from the tales of the Indian captives, he expected to find gold. Half way between this island and Santa Maria, he met with "a man alone in an almadia which was passing" (from one island to the other), "and he was carrying a little of their bread, as big as one's fist, and a calabash of water and a piece of red earth made into dust, and then kneaded, and some dry leaves, which must be a thing much valued among them, since at San Salvador they brought them to me as a present.[21] And he had a little basket of their sort, in which he had a string of little glass bells and two blancas, by which I knew that he came from the Island of San Salvador. He came to the ship; I took him on board, for so he asked, and made him put his almadia in the ship, and keep all he was carrying. And I commanded to give him bread and honey to eat, and something to drink.

"And thus I will take him over to Fernandina, and I will give him all his property so that he may give good accounts of us, so that, if it please our Lord, when your Highnesses send there, those who come may receive honor, and they may give us of all they have."

Columbus continued sailing for the island he named Fernandina, now called Inagua Chica. There was a calm all day and he did not arrive in time to anchor safely before dark. He therefore waited till morning, and anchored near a town. Here the man had gone, who had been picked up the day before, and he had given such good accounts that all night long the ship had been boarded by almadias, bringing supplies. Columbus directed some trifle to be given to each of the islanders, and that they should be given "honey of sugar" to eat. He sent the ship's boat ashore for water and

---

[21] Was this perhaps tobacco?

the inhabitants not only pointed it out but helped to put the water-casks on board.

"This people," he says, "is like those of the aforesaid islands, and has the same speech and the same customs, except that these seem to me a somewhat more domestic race, and more intelligent. And I saw also in this island cotton cloths made like mantles.

"It is a very green island and flat and very fertile, and I have no doubt that all the year through they sow panizo (panic-grass) and harvest it, and so with everything else. And I saw many trees, of very different form from ours, and many of them which had branches of many sorts, and all on one trunk. And one branch is of one sort and one of another, and so different that it is the greatest wonder in the world. One branch has its leaves like canes, and another like the lentisk; and so on one tree five or six of these kinds; and all so different. Nor are they grafted, for it might be said that grafting does it, but they grow on the mountains, nor do these people care for them.

"Here the fishes are so different from ours that it is wonderful. There are some like cocks of the finest colors in the world, blue, yellow, red and of all colors, and others painted in a thousand ways. And the colors are so fine that there is no man who does not wonder at them and take great pleasure in seeing them. Also, there are whales. As for wild creatures on shore, I saw none of any sort, except parrots and lizards; a boy told me that he saw a great snake. Neither sheep nor goats nor any other animal did I see; although I have been here a very short time, that is, half a day, but if there had been any I could not have failed to see some of them."

Wednesday, October 17. He left the town at noon and prepared to sail round the island. He had meant to go by the south and southeast. But as Martin Alonzo Pinzon, captain of the Pinta, had heard, from one of the Indians he had on board, that it would be quicker to start by the northwest, and as the wind was favorable for this course, Columbus took it. He found a fine harbor two leagues further on, where he found some friendly Indians, and sent a party ashore for water. "During this time," he says, "I went (to look at) these trees, which were the most beautiful things to see which have been seen; there was as much verdure in the same degree as in the month of May in Andalusia, and all the trees were as different from ours as the day from the night. And so (were) the fruits, and the herbs, and the stones and everything. The truth is that some trees had a resemblance to others which there are in Castile, but there was a very great difference. And other trees of other sorts were such that there is no one who could liken them to others of Castile.

"The others who went for water told me how they had been in their houses, and that they were very well swept and clean, and their beds and furniture (made) of things which are like nets of cotton.[22] Their houses are all like pavilions, and very high and good chimneys.[23]

"But I did not see, among many towns which I saw, any of more than twelve or fifteen houses. And there they had dogs. And there they found one man who had on his nose a piece of gold which was like half a castellano, on which there were cut letters.[24] I blamed them for not bargaining for it, and giving as much as was asked, to see what it was,

---

[22] They are called Hamacas.

[23] Las Casas says they were not meant for smoke but as a crown, for they have no opening below for the smoke.

[24] A castellano was a piece of gold, money, weighing about one-sixth of an ounce.

and whose coin it was; and they answered me that they did not dare to barter it."

He continued towards the northwest, then turned his course to the east-southeast, east and southeast. The weather being thick and heavy, and "threatening immediate rain. So all these days since I have been in these Indies it has rained little or much."

Friday, October 19. Columbus, who had not landed the day before, now sent two caravels, one to the east and southeast and the other to the south-southeast, while he himself, with the Santa Maria, the SHIP, as he calls it, went to the southeast. He ordered the caravels to keep their courses till noon, and then join him. This they did, at an island to the east, which he named Isabella, the Indians whom he had with him calling it Saomete. It has been supposed to be the island now called Inagua Grande.

"All this coast," says the Admiral, "and the part of the island which I saw, is all nearly flat, and the island the most beautiful thing I ever saw, for if the others are very beautiful this one is more so." He anchored at a cape which was so beautiful that he named it Cabo Fermoso, the Beautiful Cape, "so green and so beautiful," he says, "like all the other things and lands of these islands, that I do not know where to go first, nor can I weary my eyes with seeing such beautiful verdure and so different from ours. And I believe that there are in them many herbs and many trees, which are of great value in Spain for dyes (or tinctures) and for medicines of spicery. But I do not know them, which I greatly regret. And as I came here to this cape there came such a good and sweet odor of flowers or trees from the land that it was the sweetest thing in the world."

He heard that there was a king in the interior who wore clothes and much gold, and though, as he says, the Indians had so little gold that whatever small quantity of it the king wore it would appear large to them, he decided to visit him the next day. He did not do so, however, as he found the water too shallow in his immediate neighborhood, and then had not enough wind to go on, except at night.

Sunday morning, October 21, he anchored, apparently more to the west, and after having dined, landed. He found but one house, from which the inhabitants were absent; he directed that nothing in it should be touched. He speaks again of the great beauty of the island, even greater than that of the others he had seen. "The singing of the birds," he says, "seems as if a man would never seek to leave this place, and the flocks of parrots which darken the sun, and fowls and birds of so many kinds and so different from ours that it is wonderful. And then there are trees of a thousand sorts, and all with fruit of their kinds. And all have such an odor that it is wonderful, so that I am the most afflicted man in the world not to know them."

They killed a serpent in one of the lakes upon this island, which Las Casas says is the Guana, or what we call the Iguana.

In seeking for good water, the Spaniards found a town, from which the inhabitants were going to fly. But some of them rallied, and one of them approached the visitors. Columbus gave him some little bells and glass beads, with which he was much pleased. The Admiral asked him for water, and they brought it gladly to the shore in calabashes.

He still wished to see the king of whom the Indians had spoken, but meant afterward to go to "another very great island, which I believe must be Cipango, which they call Colba." This is probably a mistake in the manuscript for

Cuba, which is what is meant. It continues, "and to that other island which they call Bosio" (probably Bohio) "and the others which are on the way, I will see these in passing. But still, I am determined to go to the mainland and to the city of Quisay and to give your Highnesses' letters to the Grand Khan, and seek a reply and come back with it."

He remained at this island during the twenty-second and twenty-third of October, waiting first for the king, who did not appear, and then for a favorable wind. "To sail round these islands," he says, "one needs many sorts of wind, and it does not blow as men would like." At midnight, between the twenty-third and twenty-fourth, he weighed anchor in order to start for Cuba.

"I have heard these people say that it was very large and of great traffic," he says, "and that there were in it gold and spices, and great ships and merchants. And they showed me that I should go to it by the west-southwest, and I think so. For I think that if I may trust the signs which all the Indians of these islands have made me, and those whom I am carrying in the ships, for by the tongue I do not understand them, it (Cuba) is the Island of Cipango,[25] of which wonderful things are told, and on the globes which I have seen and in the painted maps, it is in this district."

The next day they saw seven or eight islands, which are supposed to be the eastern and southern keys of the Grand Bank of Bahama. He anchored to the south of them on the twenty-sixth of October, and on the next day sailed once more for Cuba.

On Sunday, October 28, he arrived there, in what is now called the Puerto de Nipe; he named it the Puerto de San Salvador. Here, as he went on, he was again charmed by the beautiful country. He found palms "of another sort,"

---

[25] This was the name the old geographers gave to Japan.

says Las Casas, "from those of Guinea, and from ours." He found the island the "most beautiful which eyes have seen, full of very good ports and deep rivers," and that apparently the sea is never rough there, as the grass grows down to the water's edge. This greenness to the sea's edge is still observed there. "Up till that time," says Las Casas, "he had not experienced in all these islands that the sea was rough." He had occasion to learn about it later. He mentions also that the island is mountainous.

Chapter V: The Landing on Cuba

When Columbus landed, at some distance farther along the coast, he found the best houses he had yet seen, very large, like pavilions, and very neat within; not in streets but set about here and there. They were all built of palm branches. Here were dogs which never barked (supposed to be the *almiqui*), wild birds tamed in the houses and "wonderful arrangements of nets,[26] and fish-hooks and fishing apparatus. There were also carved masks and other images. Not a thing was touched." The inhabitants had fled.

He went on to the northwest, and saw a cape which he named Cabo de Palmas. The Indians on board the Pinta said that beyond this cape was a river and that at four days' journey from this was what they called "Cuba." Now they had been coasting along the Island of Cuba for two or three days. But Martin Pinzon, the captain of the Pinta, understood this Cuba to be a city, and that this land was the mainland, running far to the north. Columbus until he died believed that it was the mainland.

Martin Pinzon also understood that the king of that land was at war with the Grand Khan, whom they called Cami. The Admiral determined to go to the river the Indians mentioned, and to send to the king the letter of the sovereigns. He meant to send with it a sailor who had been

---

[26] These were probably hammocks.

to Guinea, and some of the Guanahani Indians. He was encouraged, probably, by the name of Carni, in thinking that he was really near the Grand Khan.

He did not, however, send off these messengers at once, as the wind and the nature of the coast proved unfit for his going up the river the Indians had spoken of. He went back to the town where he had been two days before.

Once more he found that the people had fled, but "after a good while a man appeared," and the Admiral sent ashore one of the Indians he had with him. This man shouted to the Indians on shore that they must not be afraid, as these were good people, and did harm to no man, nor did they belong to the Grand Khan, but they gave, of what they had, in many islands where they had been. He now jumped into the sea and swam ashore, and two of the inhabitants took him in their arms and brought him to a house where they asked him questions. When he had reassured them, they began to come out to the ships in their canoes, with "spun cotton and others of their little things." But the Admiral commanded that nothing should be taken from them, so that they might know that he was seeking nothing but gold, or, as they called it, *nucay*.

He saw no gold here, but one of them had a piece of wrought silver hanging to his nose. They made signs, that before three days many merchants would come from the inland country to trade with the Spaniards, and that they would bring news from the king, who, according to their signs, was four days' journey away. "And it is certain" says the Admiral, "that this is the mainland, and that I am before Zayto and Quinsay, a hundred leagues more or less from both of them, and this is clearly shown by the tide, which comes in a different manner from that in which it has done up to this time; and yesterday when I went to the northwest I found that it was cold."

Always supposing that he was near Japan, which they called Cipango, Columbus continued to sail along the northern coast of Cuba and explored about half that shore. He then returned to the east, governed by the assurances of the natives that on an island named Babegue he would find men who used hammers with which to beat gold into ingots. This gold, as he understood them, was collected on the shore at night, while the people lighted up the darkness with candles.

At the point where he turned back, he had hauled his ships up on the shore to repair them. From this point, on the second of November, he sent two officers inland, one of whom was a Jew, who knew Chaldee, Hebrew and a little Arabic, in the hope that they should find some one who could speak these languages. With them went one of the Guanahani Indians, and one from the neighborhood.

They returned on the night between the fifth and sixth of November. Twelve leagues off they had found a village of about fifty large houses, made in the form of tents. This village had about a thousand inhabitants, according to the explorers. They had received the ambassadors with cordial kindness, believing that they had descended from heaven.

They even took them in their arms and thus carried them to the finest house of all. They gave them seats, and then sat round them on the ground in a circle. They kissed their feet and hands, and touched them, to make sure whether they were really men of flesh and bone.

It was on this expedition that the first observation was made of that gift of America to the world, which has worked its way so deep and far into general use. They met men and women who "carried live coals, so as to draw into their mouths the smoke of burning herbs." This was the account of the first observers. But Las Casas says that the dry herbs were wrapped in another leaf as dry. He says that "they lighted one end of the little stick thus formed, and sucked in or absorbed the smoke by the other, with which," he says, "they put their flesh to sleep, and it nearly intoxicates them, and thus they say that they feel no fatigue. These *mosquetes*, as we should call them, they call *tobacos*. I knew Spaniards on this Island of Hispaniola who were accustomed to take them, who, on being reproved for it as a vice, replied that it was not in their power (in their hand) to leave off taking them. I do not know what savour or profit they found in them." This is clearly a cigar.

The third or fourth of November, then, 1892, with the addition of nine days to change the style from old to new, may be taken by lovers of tobacco as the fourth centennial of the day when Europeans first learned the use of the cigar.

On the eleventh of November the repairs were completed.

He says that the Sunday before, November 11 it had seemed to him that it would be good to take some persons, from those of that river, to carry to the sovereigns, so that "they might learn our tongue, so as to know what there is in the country, and so that when they come back they may be tongues to the Christians, and receive our customs and the things of the faith. Because I saw and know," says the Admiral, "that this people has no religion (*secta*) nor are they idolaters, but very mild and without knowing what evil is, nor how to kill others, nor how to take them, and without arms, and so timorous that from one of our men ten of them fly, although they do sport with them, and ready to believe and knowing that there is a God in heaven, and sure that we have come from heaven; and very ready at any prayer which we tell them to repeat, and they make the sign of the cross.

"So your Highnesses should determine to make them Christians, for I believe that if they begin, in a short time they will have accomplished converting to our holy faith a multitude of towns." "Without doubt there are in these lands the greatest quantities of gold, for not without cause do these Indians whom I am bringing say that there are places in these isles where they dig out gold and wear it on their necks, in their ears and on their arms and legs, and the bracelets are very thick.

"And also there are stones and precious pearls, and unnumbered spices. And in this Rio de Mares, from which I departed last night, without doubt there is the greatest quantity of mastic, and there might be more if more were desired. For the trees, if planted, take root, and there are many of them and very great and they have the leaf like a lentisk, and their fruit, except that the trees and the fruit are larger, is such as Pliny describes, and I have seen in the Island of Chios in the Archipelago.

"And I had many of these trees tapped to see if they would send out resin, so as to draw it out. And as it rained all the time I was at the said river, I could not get any of it, except a very little which I am bringing to your Highnesses. And besides, it may be that it is not the time to tap them, for I believe that this should be done at the time when the trees begin to leave out from the winter and seek to send out their flowers, and now they have the fruit nearly ripe.

"And also here there might be had a great store of cotton, and I believe that it might be sold very well here without taking it to Spain, in the great cities of the Great Khan, which will doubtless be discovered, and many others of other lords, who will then have to serve your Highnesses. And here will be given them other things from Spain, from the lands of the East, since these are ours in the West.

"And here there is also aloes everywhere, although this is not a thing to make great account of, but the mastic should be well considered, because it is not found except in the said island of Chios, and I believe that they get from it quite 50,000 ducats if I remember aright. And this is the best harbor which I have seen thus far—deep and easy of access, so that this would be a good place for a large town."

The notes in Columbus's journals are of the more interest and value, because they show his impressions at the moment when he wrote. However mistaken those impressions, he never corrects them afterwards. Although, while he was in Cuba, he never found the Grand Khan, he never recalls the hopes which he has expressed.

He had discovered the island on its northern side by sailing southwest from the Lucayos or Bahamas. From the eleventh of November until the sixth of December he was occupied in coasting along the northern shore, eventually returning eastward, when he crossed the channel which parts Cuba from Hayti.

The first course was east, a quarter southeast, and on the sixteenth, they entered Port-au-Prince, and took possession, raising a cross there. At Port-au-Prince, to his surprise, he found on a point of rock two large logs, mortised into each other in the shape of a cross, so "that you would have said a carpenter could not have proportioned them better."

On the nineteenth the course was north-northeast; on the twenty-first they took a course south, a quarter southwest, seeking in these changes the island of "Babeque," which the Indians had spoken of as rich with gold. On the day last named Pinzon left the Admiral in the Pinta, and they did not meet again for more than a month.

Columbus touched at various points on Cuba and the neighboring islands. He sought, without success, for pearls, and always pressed his inquiries for gold. He was determined to find the island of Bohio, greatly to the terror of the poor Indians, whom he had on board: they said that its natives had but one eye, in the middle of their foreheads, and that they were well armed and ate their prisoners.

He landed in the bay of Moa, and then, keeping near the coast, sailed towards the Capo del Pico, now called Cape Vacz. At Puerto Santo he was detained some days by bad weather. On the fourth of December he continued his eastward voyage, and on the next day saw far off the mountains of Hayti, which was the Bohio he sought for.

Chapter VI: Discovery of Hayti or Espanola

On the sixth of December they crossed from the eastern
cape of Cuba to the northwestern point of the island, which
we call Hayti or San Domingo. He says he gave it this
name because "the plains appeared to him almost exactly
like those of Castile, but yet more beautiful."

He coasted eastward along the northern side of the island,
hoping that it might be the continent, and always inquiring
for gold when he landed; but the Indians, as before, referred
him to yet another land, still further south, which they still
called Bohio. It was not surrounded by water, they said.
The word "caniba," which is the origin of our word
"cannibal," and refers to the fierce Caribs, came often into
their talk. The sound of the syllable *can* made Columbus
more sure that he was now approaching the dominions of
the Grand Khan of eastern Asia, of whom Marco Polo had
informed Europe so fully.

On the twelfth of the month, after a landing in which a
cross had been erected, three sailors went inland, pursuing
the Indians. They captured a young woman whom they
brought to the fleet. She wore a large ring of gold in her
nose. She was able to understand the other Indians whom
they had on board. Columbus dressed her, gave her some
imitation pearls, rings and other finery, and then put her on
shore with three Indians and three of his own men.

The men returned the next day without going to the Indian village. Columbus then sent out nine men, with an Indian, who found a town of a thousand huts about four and a half leagues from the ship. They thought the population was three thousand. The village in Cuba is spoken of as having twenty people to a house. Here the houses were smaller or the count of the numbers extravagant. The people approached the explorers carefully, and with tokens of respect. Soon they gained confidence and brought out food for them: fish, and bread made from roots, "which tasted exactly as if it were made of chestnuts."

In the midst of this festival, the woman, who had been sent back from the ship so graciously, appeared borne on the shoulders of men who were led by her husband.

The Spaniards thought these natives of St. Domingo much whiter than those of the other islands. Columbus says that two of the women, if dressed in Castilian costume, would be counted to be Spaniards. He says that the heat of the country is intense, and that if these people lived in a cooler region they would be of lighter color.

On the fourteenth of December he continued his voyage eastward, and on the fifteenth landed on the little island north of Hayti, which he called Tortuga, or Turtle island. At midnight on the sixteenth he sailed, and landed on Hispaniola again. Five hundred Indians met him, accompanied by their king, a fine young man of about twenty years of age. He had around him several counselors, one of whom appeared to be his tutor. To the steady questions where gold could be found, the reply as steady was made that it was in "the Island of Babeque." This island, they said, was only two days off, and they pointed out the route. The interview ended in an offer by the king to the Admiral of all that he had. The explorers never found this mysterious Babeque, unless, as Bishop Las Casas guessed, Babeque and Jamaica be the same.

The king visited Columbus on his ship in the evening, and Columbus entertained him with European food. With so cordial a beginning of intimacy, it was natural that the visitors should spend two or three days with these people. The king would not believe that any sovereigns of Castile could be more powerful than the men he saw. He and those around him all believed that they came direct from heaven.

Columbus was always asking for gold. He gave strict orders that it should always be paid for, when it was taken. To the islanders it was merely a matter of ornament, and they gladly exchanged it for the glass beads, the rings or the bells, which seemed to them more ornamental. One of the caciques or chiefs, evidently a man of distinction and authority, had little bits of gold which he exchanged for pieces of glass. It proved that he had clipped them off from a larger piece, and he went back into his cabin, cut that to pieces, and then exchanged all those in trade for the white man's commodities. Well pleased with his bargain, he then told the Spaniards that he would go and get much more and would come and trade with them again.

On the eighteenth of December, the wind not serving well, they waited the return of the chief whom they had first seen. In the afternoon he appeared, seated in a palanquin, which was carried by four men, and escorted by more than two hundred of his people. He was accompanied by a counselor and preceptor who did not leave him. He came on board the ship when Columbus was at table. He would not permit him to leave his place, and readily took a seat at his side, when it was offered. Columbus offered him European food and drink; he tasted of each, and then gave what was offered to his attendants. The ceremonious

Spaniards found a remarkable dignity in his air and gestures. After the repast, one of his servants brought a handsome belt, elegantly wrought, which he presented to Columbus, with two small pieces of gold, also delicately wrought.

Columbus observed that this cacique looked with interest on the hangings of his ship-bed, and made a present of them to him, in return for his offering, with some amber beads from his own neck, some red shoes and a flask of orange flower water.

On the nineteenth, after these agreeable hospitalities, the squadron sailed again, and on the twentieth arrived at a harbor which Columbus pronounced the finest he had ever seen. The reception he met here and the impressions he formed of Hispaniola determined him to make a colony on that island. It may be said that on this determination the course of his after life turned. This harbor is now known as the Bay of Azul.

The men, whom he sent on shore, found a large village not far from the shore, where they were most cordially received. The natives begged the Europeans to stay with them, and as it proved, Columbus accepted the invitation for a part of his crew. On the first day three different chiefs came to visit him, in a friendly way, with their retinues. The next day more than a hundred and twenty canoes visited the ship, bringing with them such presents as the people thought would be acceptable. Among these were bread from the cassava root, fish, water in earthen jars, and the seeds of spices. These spices they would stir in with water to make a drink which they thought healthful.

On the same day Columbus sent an embassy of six men to a large town in the interior. The chief by giving his hand "to the secretary" pledged himself for their safe return.

The twenty-third was Sunday. It was spent as the day before had been, in mutual civilities. The natives would offer their presents, and say "take, take," in their own language. Five chiefs were among the visitors of the day. From their accounts Columbus was satisfied that there was much gold in the island, as indeed, to the misery and destruction of its inhabitants, there proved to be. He thought it was larger than England. But he was mistaken. In his journal of the next day he mentions Civao, a land to the west, where they told him that there was gold, and again he thought he was approaching Cipango, or Japan.

The next day he left these hospitable people, raising anchor in the morning, and with a light land wind continued towards the west. At eleven in the evening Columbus retired to rest. While he slept, on Christmas Day, there occurred an accident which changed all plans for the expedition so far as any had been formed, and from which there followed the establishment of the ill-fated first colony. The evening was calm when Columbus himself retired to sleep, and the master of the vessel followed his example, entrusting the helm to one of the boys. Every person on the ship, excepting this boy, was asleep, and he seems to have been awake to little purpose.

The young steersman let the ship drift upon a ridge of rock, although, as Columbus says, indignantly, there were breakers abundant to show the danger. So soon as she struck, the boy cried out, and Columbus was the first to wake. He says, by way of apology for himself, that for thirty-six hours he had not slept until now. The master of the ship followed him. But it was too late. The tide, such as there was, was ebbing, and the Santa Maria was hopelessly aground. Columbus ordered the masts cut away, but this did not relieve her.

He sent out his boat with directions to carry aft an anchor and cable, but its crew escaped to the Nina with their tale of disaster. The Nina's people would not receive them, reproached them as traitors, and in their own vessel came to the scene of danger. Columbus was obliged to transfer to her the crew of the Santa Maria.

So soon as it was day, their friendly ally, Guacanagari, came on board. With tears in his eyes, he made the kindest and most judicious offers of assistance. He saw Columbus's dejection, and tried to relieve him by expressions of his sympathy. He set aside on shore two large houses to receive the stores that were on the Santa Maria, and appointed as many large canoes as could be used to remove these stores to the land. He assured Columbus that not a bit of the cargo or stores should be lost, and this loyal promise was fulfilled to the letter.

The weather continued favorable. The sea was so light that everything on board the Santa Maria was removed safely. Then it was that Columbus, tempted by the beauty of the place, by the friendship of the natives, and by the evident wishes of his men, determined to leave a colony, which should be supported by the stores of the Santa Maria, until the rest of the party could go back to Spain and bring or send reinforcements. The king was well pleased with this suggestion, and promised all assistance for the plan. A vault was dug and built, in which the stores could be placed, and on this a house was built for the home of the colonists, so far as they cared to live within doors.

The chief sent a canoe in search of Martin Pinzon and the Pinta, to tell them of the disaster. But the messengers returned without finding them. At the camp, which was to be a city, all was industriously pressed, with the assistance of the friendly natives. Columbus, having no vessel but the little Nina left, determined to return to Europe with the news of his discovery, and to leave nearly forty men ashore.

It would appear that the men, themselves, were eager to stay. The luxury of the climate and the friendly overtures of the people delighted them, They had no need to build substantial houses. So far as houses were needed, those of the natives were sufficient. All the preparations which Columbus thought necessary were made in the week between the twenty-sixth of December and the second of January. On that day he expected to sail eastward, but unfavorable winds prevented.

He landed his men again, and by the exhibition of a pretended battle with European arms, he showed the natives the military force of their new neighbors. He fired a shot from an arquebuse against the wreck of the Santa Maria, so that the Indians might see the power of his artillery. The Indian chief expressed his regret at the approaching departure, and the Spaniards thought that one of his courtiers said that the chief had ordered him to make a statue of pure gold as large as the Admiral.

Columbus explained to the friendly chief that with such arms as the sovereigns of Castile commanded they could readily destroy the dreaded Caribs. And he thought he had made such an impression that the islanders would be the firm friends of the colonists.

"I have bidden them build a solid tower and defense, over a vault. Not that I think this necessary against the natives, for I am satisfied that with a handful of people I could conquer the whole island, were it necessary, although it is, as far as I can judge, larger than Portugal, and twice as thickly peopled." In this cheerful estimate of the people

Columbus was wholly wrong, as the sad events proved before the year had gone by.

He left thirty-nine men to be the garrison of this fort; and the colony which was to discover the mine of gold. In command he placed Diego da Arana, Pedro Gutierres and Rodrigo de Segovia. To us, who have more experience of colonies and colonists than he had had, it does not seem to promise well that Rodrigo was "the king's chamberlain and an officer of the first lord of the household." Of these three, Diego da Arana was to be the governor, and the other two his lieutenants. The rest were all sailors, but among them there were Columbus's secretary, an alguazil, or person commissioned in the civil service at home, an "arquebusier," who was also a good engineer, a tailor, a ship carpenter, a cooper and a physician. So the little colony had its share of artificers and men of practical skill. They all staid willingly, delighted with the prospects of their new home.

On the third of January Columbus sailed for Europe in the little Nina. With her own crew and the addition she received from the Santa Maria, she must have been badly crowded. Fortunately for all parties, on Sunday, the third day of the voyage, while they were still in sight of land, the Pinta came in sight. Martin Pinzon came on board the Nina and offered excuses for his absence. Columbus was not really satisfied with them, but he affected to be, as this was no moment for a quarrel. He believed that Pinzon had left him, that, in the Pinta, he might be alone when he discovered the rich gold-bearing island of Babeque or Baneque. Although the determination was made to return, another week was spent in slow coasting, or in waiting for wind. It brought frequent opportunities for meeting the natives, in one of which they showed a desire to take some of their visitors captive. This would only have been a return for a capture made by Pinzon of several of their number, whom Columbus, on his meeting Pinzon, had freed. In this encounter two of the Indians were wounded, one by a sword, one by an arrow. It would seem that he did not show them the power of firearms.

This was in the Bay of Samana, which Columbus called "The Bay of Arrows," from the skirmish or quarrel which took place there. They then sailed sixty-four miles cast, a quarter northeast, and thought they saw the land of the Caribs, which he was seeking. But here, at length, his authority over his crew failed. The men were eager to go home;—did not, perhaps, like the idea of fight with the man-eating Caribs. There was a good western wind, and on the evening of the sixteenth of January Columbus gave way and they bore away for home.

Columbus had satisfied himself in this week that there were many islands east of him which he had not hit upon, and that to the easternmost of these, from the Canaries, the distance would prove not more than four hundred leagues. In this supposition he was wholly wrong, though a chain of islands does extend to the southeast.

He seems to have observed the singular regularity by which the trade winds bore him steadily westward as he came over. He had no wish to visit the Canary Islands again, and with more wisdom than could have been expected, from his slight knowledge of the Atlantic winds, he bore north. Until the fourteenth of February the voyage was prosperous and uneventful. One day the captive Indians amused the sailors by swimming. There is frequent mention of the green growth of the Sargasso sea. But on the fourteenth all this changed. The simple journal thus describes the terrible tempest which endangered the two vessels, and seemed, at the moment, to cut off the hope of their return to Europe.

"Monday, February 14.—This night the wind increased still more; the waves were terrible. Coming from two opposite directions, they crossed each other, and stopped the progress of the vessel, which could neither proceed nor get out from among them; and as they began continually to break over the ship, the Admiral caused the main-sail to be lowered. She proceeded thus during three hours, and made twenty miles. The sea became heavier and heavier, and the wind more and more violent. Seeing the danger imminent, he allowed himself to drift in whatever direction the wind took him, because he could do nothing else. Then the Pinta, of which Martin Alonzo Pinzon was the commander, began to drift also; but she disappeared very soon, although all through the night the Admiral made signals with lights to her, and she answered as long as she could, till she was prevented, probably by the force of the tempest, and by her deviation from the course which the Admiral followed." Columbus did not see the Pinta again until she arrived at Palos. He was himself driven fifty-four miles towards the northeast.

The journal continues. "After sunrise the strength of the wind increased, and the sea became still more terrible. The Admiral all this time kept his mainsail lowered, so that the vessel might rise from among the waves which washed over it, and which threatened to sink it. The Admiral followed, at first, the direction of east-northeast, and afterwards due northeast. He sailed about six hours in this direction, and thus made seven leagues and a half. He gave orders that every sailor should draw lots as to who should make a pilgrimage to Santa Maria of Guadeloupe, to carry her a five-pound wax candle. And each one took a vow that he to whom the lot fell should make the pilgrimage.

"For this purpose, he gave orders to take as many dry peas as there were persons in the ship, and to cut, with a knife, a cross upon one of them, and to put them all into a cap, and to shake them up well. The first who put his hand in was the Admiral. He drew out the dry pea marked with the cross; so it was upon him that the lot fell, and he regarded himself, after that, as a pilgrim, obliged to carry into effect the vow which he had thus taken. They drew lots a second time, to select a person to go as pilgrim to Our Lady of Lorette, which is within the boundaries of Ancona, making a part of the States of the Church: it is a place where the Holy Virgin has worked and continues to work many and great miracles. The lot having fallen this time upon a sailor of the harbor of Santa Maria, named Pedro de Villa, the Admiral promised to give him all the money necessary for the expenses. He decided that a third pilgrim should be sent to watch one night at Santa Clara of Moguer, and to have a mass said there. For this purpose, they again shook up the dry peas, not forgetting that one which was marked with the cross, and the lot fell once again to the Admiral himself. He then took, as did all his crew, the vow that, on the first shore which they might reach, they would go in their shirts, in a procession, to make a prayer in some church in invocation of Our Lady."

"Besides the general vows, or those taken by all in common, each man made his own special vow, because nobody expected to escape. The storm which they experienced was so terrible, that all regarded themselves as lost; what increased the danger was the circumstance that the vessel lacked ballast, because the consumption of food, water and wine had greatly diminished her load. The hope of the continuance of weather as fine as that which they had experienced in all the islands, was the reason why the Admiral had not provided his vessel with the proper amount of ballast. Moreover, his plan had been to ballast it in the Women's Island, whither he had from the first determined to go. The remedy which the Admiral employed was to fill with sea water, as soon as possible, all the empty barrels which had previously held either wine or fresh water. In this way the difficulty was remedied.

"The Admiral tells here the reasons for fearing that our Saviour would allow him to become the victim of this tempest, and other reasons which made him hope that God would come to his assistance, and cause him to arrive safe and sound, so that intelligence such as that which he was conveying to the king and queen would not perish with him. The strong desire which he had to be the bearer of intelligence so important, and to prove the truth of all which he had said, and that all which he had tried to discover had really been discovered, seemed to contribute precisely to inspire him with the greatest fear that he could not succeed. He confessed, himself, that every mosquito that passed before his eyes was enough to annoy and trouble him. He attributed this to his little faith, and his lack of confidence in Divine Providence. On the other hand, he was re-animated by the favors which God had shown him in granting to him so great a triumph as that which he had achieved, in all his discoveries, in fulfilling all his wishes, and in granting that, after having experienced in Castile so many rebuffs and disappointments, all his hopes should at last be more than surpassed. In one word, as the sovereign master of the universe, had, in the outset, distinguished him in granting all his requests, before he had carried out his expedition for God's greatest glory, and before it had succeeded, he was compelled to believe now that God would preserve him to complete the work which he had begun." Such is Las Casas's abridgment of Columbus's words.

"For which reasons he said he ought to have had no fear of the tempest that was raging. But his weakness and anguish did not leave him a moment's calm. He also said that his greatest grief was the thought of leaving his two boys orphans. They were at Cordova, at their studies. What would become of them in a strange land, without father or mother? for the king and queen, being ignorant of the services he had rendered them in this voyage, and of the good news which he was bringing to them, would not be bound by any consideration to serve as their protectors.

"Full of this thought, he sought, even in the storm, some means of apprising their highnesses of the victory which the Lord had granted him, in permitting him to discover in the Indies all which he had sought in his voyage, and to let them know that these coasts were free from storms, which is proved, he said, by the growth of herbage and trees even to the edge of the sea. With this purpose, that, if he perished in this tempest, the king and queen might have some news of his voyage, he took a parchment and wrote on it all that he could of his discoveries, and urgently begged that whoever found it would carry it to the king and queen. He rolled up this parchment in a piece of waxed linen, closed this parcel tightly, and tied it up securely; he had brought to him a large wooden barrel, within which he placed it, without anybody's knowing what it was. Everybody thought the proceeding was some act of devotion. He then caused it to be thrown into the sea."[27]

---

[27] Within a few months, in the summer of 1890, a well known English publisher has issued an interesting and ingenious edition, of what pretended to be a facsimile of this document. The reader is asked to believe that the lost barrel has just now been found on the western coast of England. But publishers and purchasers know alike that this is only an amusing suggestion of what might have been.

The sudden and heavy showers, and the squalls which followed some time afterwards, changed the wind, which turned to the west. They had the wind thus abaft, and he sailed thus during five hours with the foresail only, having always the troubled sea, and made at once two leagues and a half towards the northeast. He had lowered the main topmast lest a wave might carry it away.

With a heavy wind astern, so that the sea frequently broke over the little Nina, she made eastward rapidly, and at daybreak on the fifteenth they saw land. The Admiral knew that he had made the Azores, he had been steadily directing the course that way; some of the seamen thought they were at Madeira, and some hopeful ones thought they saw the rock of Cintra in Portugal. Columbus did not land till the eighteenth, when he sent some men on shore, upon the island of Santa Maria. His news of discovery was at first received with enthusiasm.

But there followed a period of disagreeable negotiation with Castaneda, the governor of the Azores. Pretending great courtesy and hospitality, but really acting upon the orders of the king of Portugal, he did his best to disable Columbus and even seized some of his crew and kept them prisoners for some days. When Columbus once had them on board again, he gave up his plans for taking ballast and water on these inhospitable islands, and sailed for Europe.

He had again a stormy passage. Again they were in imminent danger. "But God was good enough to save him. He caused the crew to draw lots to send to Notre Dame de la Cintra, at the island of Huelva, a pilgrim who should come there in his shirt. The lot fell upon himself. All the crew, including the Admiral, vowed to fast on bread and water on the first Saturday which should come after the arrival of the vessel. He had proceeded sixty miles before the sails were torn; then they went under masts and shrouds on account of the unusual strength of the wind, and the roughness of the sea, which pressed them almost on all sides. They saw indications of the nearness of the land; they were in fact, very near Lisbon."

At Lisbon, after a reception which was at first cordial, the Portuguese officers showed an inhospitality like that of Castaneda at the Azores. But the king himself showed more dignity and courtesy. He received the storm-tossed Admiral with distinction, and permitted him to refit his shattered vessel with all he needed. Columbus took this occasion to write to his own sovereigns.

On the thirteenth he sailed again, and on the fifteenth entered the bay and harbor of Palos, which he had left six months and a half before. He had sailed on Friday. He had discovered America on Friday. And on Friday he safely returned to his home.

His journal of the voyage ends with these words:

"I see by this voyage that God has wonderfully proved what I say, as anybody may convince himself, by reading this narrative, by the signal wonders which he has worked during the course of my voyage, and in favor of myself, who have been for so long a time at the court of your Highnesses in opposition and contrary to the opinions of so many distinguished personages of your household, who all opposed me, treating my project as a dream, and my undertaking as a chimera. And I hope still, nevertheless, in our Lord, this voyage will bring the greatest honor to Christianity, although it has been performed with so much ease."

Chapter VII: Columbus is Called to Meet the King and Queen

The letter which Columbus sent from Lisbon to the king and queen was everywhere published.[28] It excited the enthusiasm first of Spain and then of the world. This letter found in the earlier editions is now one of the most choice curiosities of libraries. Well it may be, for it is the first public announcement of the greatest event of modern history.

Ferdinand and Isabella directed him to wait upon them at once at court. It happened that they were then residing at Barcelona, on the eastern coast of Spain, so that the journey required to fulfill their wishes carried him quite across the kingdom. It was a journey of triumph. The people came together in throngs to meet this peaceful conqueror who brought with him such amazing illustrations of his discovery.

The letter bearing instructions for him to proceed to Barcelona was addressed "To Don Christopher

---

[28] See Book II of this edition, p. 433.

Columbus, our Admiral of the Ocean Sea, Viceroy and Governor of the islands discovered in the Indies." So far was he now raised above the rank of a poor adventurer, who had for seven years attended the court in its movements, seeking an opportunity to explain his proposals.

As he approached Barcelona he was met by a large company of people, including many persons of rank. A little procession was formed of the party of the Admiral. Six Indians of the islands who had survived the voyage, led the way. They were painted according to their custom in various colors, and ornamented with the fatal gold of their countries, which had given to the discovery such interest in the eyes of those who looked on.

Columbus had brought ten Indians away with him, but one had died on the voyage and he had left three sick at Palos. Those whom he brought to Barcelona, were baptized in presence of the king and queen.

After the Indians, were brought many curious objects which had come from the islands, such as stuffed birds and beasts and living paroquets, which perhaps spoke in the language of their own country, and rare plants, so different from those of Spain. Ornaments of gold were displayed, which would give the people some idea of the wealth of the islands. Last of all came Columbus, elegantly mounted and surrounded by a brilliant cavalcade of young Spaniards. The crowd of wondering people pressed around them. Balconies and windows were crowded with women looking on. Even the roofs were crowded with spectators.

The king and queen awaited Columbus in a large hall, where they were seated on a rich dais covered with gold brocade. It was in the palace known as the "*Casa de la Deputacion*" which the kings of Aragon made their residence when they were in Barcelona. A body of the most distinguished lords and ladies of Spain were in attendance. As Columbus entered the hall the king and queen arose. He fell on his knee that he might kiss their hands but they bade him rise and then sit and give an account of his voyage.

Columbus spoke with dignity and simplicity which commanded respect, while all listened with sympathy. He showed some of the treasures he had brought, and spoke with certainty of the discoveries which had been made, as only precursors of those yet to come. When his short narrative was ended, all the company knelt and united in chanting the "*Te Deum*," "We Praise Thee, O God." Las Casas, describing the joy and hope of that occasion says, "it seems as if they had a foretaste of the joys of paradise."

It would seem as if those whose duty it is to prepare fit celebrations of the periods of the great discovery, could hardly do better than to produce on the twenty-fourth of April, 1893, a reproduction of the solemn pageant in which, in Barcelona, four centuries before, the Spanish court commemorated the great discovery.

From this time, for several weeks, a series of pageants and festivities surrounded him. At no other period of his life were such honors paid to him. It was at one of the banquets, at which he was present, that the incident of the egg, so often told in connection with the great discovery, took place. A flippant courtier—of that large class of people who stay at home when great deeds are done, and afterwards depreciate the doers of them—had the impertinence to ask Columbus, if the adventure so much praised was not, after all, a very simple matter. He probably said "a short voyage of four or five weeks; was it anything more?" Columbus replied by giving him an egg which was on the table, and asking him if he could stand it on one end. He said he could not, and the other guests said that they could not. Columbus tapped it on the table so as to break the end of the shell, and the egg stood erect. "It is easy enough," he said, "when any one has shown you how."

It is well to remember, that if after years showed that the ruler of Spain wearied in his gratitude, Columbus was, at the time, welcomed with the enthusiasm which he deserved. From the very grains of gold brought home in this first triumph, the queen, Isabella, had the golden illumination wrought of a most beautiful missal-book.

Distinguished artists decorated the book, and the portraits of sovereigns then on the throne appear as the representations of King David, King Solomon, the Queen of Sheba and other royal personages. This book she gave afterwards to her grandson, Charles V, of whom it has been said that perhaps no man in modern times has done the world more harm.

This precious book, bearing on its gilded leaves the first fruits of America, is now preserved in the Royal Library at Madrid.

The time was not occupied merely in shows and banquets. There was no difficulty now, about funds for a second expedition. Directions were given that it might be set forward as quickly as possible, and on an imposing scale. For it was feared at court that King John of Portugal, the successful rival of Spain, thus far, in maritime adventure, might anticipate further discovery. The sovereigns at once sent an embassy to the pope, not simply to announce the discovery, but to obtain from him a decree confirming similar discoveries in the same direction. There was at least one precedent for such action. A former pope had granted to Portugal all the lands it might discover in Africa, south of Cape Bojador, and the Spanish crown had assented by treaty to this arrangement. Ferdinand and Isabella could now refer to this precedent, in asking for a grant to them of their discoveries on the western side of the Atlantic. The pope now reigning was Alexander II. He had not long filled the papal chair. He was an ambitious and prudent sovereign—a native of Spain—and, although he would gladly have pleased the king of Portugal, he was quite unwilling to displease the Spanish sovereigns. The Roman court received with respect the request made to them. The pope expressed his joy at the hopes thrown out for the conversion of the heathen, which the Spanish sovereigns had expressed, as Columbus had always done. And so prompt were the Spanish requests, and so ready the pope's answer, that as early as May 3, 1493, a papal bull was issued to meet the wishes of Spain.

This bull determined for Spain and for Portugal, that all discoveries made west of a meridian line one hundred leagues west of the Azores should belong to Spain. All discoveries east of that line should belong to Portugal. No reference was made to other maritime powers, and it does not seem to have been supposed that other states had any rights in such matters. The line thus arranged for the two nations was changed by their own agreement, in 1494, for a north and south line three hundred and fifty leagues west of the Cape de Verde Islands. The difference between the two lines was not supposed to be important.

The decision thus made was long respected. Under a mistaken impression as to the longitude of the Philippine Islands in the East Indies, Spain has held those islands, under this line of division, ever since their discovery by Magellan. She considered herself entitled to all the islands and lands between the meridian thus drawn in the Atlantic and the similar meridian one hundred and eighty degrees away, on exactly the other side of the world.

Under the same line of division, Portugal held, for three centuries and more, Brazil, which projects so far eastward into the Atlantic as to cross this line of division.

Fearful, all the time, that neither the pope's decree, nor any diplomacy would prevent the king of Portugal from attempting to seize lands at the west, the Spanish court pressed with eagerness arrangements for a second expedition. It was to be on a large and generous scale and to take out a thousand men. For this was the first plan, though the number afterwards was increased to fifteen hundred. To give efficiency to all the measures of colonization, what we should call a new department of administration was formed, and at the head of it was placed Juan Rodriguez de Fonseca.

Fonseca held this high and responsible position for thirty years. He early conceived a great dislike of Columbus, who, in some transactions before this expedition sailed, appealed to the sovereigns to set aside a decision of Fonseca's, and succeeded. For all the period while he managed the Indian affairs of Spain, Fonseca kept his own interests in sight more closely than those of Spain or of the colonists; and not Columbus only, but every other official of Spain in the West Indies, had reason to regret the appointment.

The king of Portugal and the sovereigns of Spain began complicated and suspicious negotiations with each other regarding the new discoveries. Eventually, as has been said, they acceded to the pope's proposal and decree. But, at first, distrusting each other, and concealing their real purposes, in the worst style of the diplomacy of that time, they attempted treaties for the adjustment between themselves of the right to lands not yet discovered by either. Of these negotiations, the important result was that which has been named,—the change of the meridian of division from that proposed by the pope. It is curious now to see that the king of Portugal proposed a line of division, which would run east and west, so that Spain should have the new territories north of the latitude of the Grand Canary, and Portugal all to the south.

In the midst of negotiation, the king and queen and Columbus knew that whoever was first on the ground of discovery would have the great advantage. There was a rumor in Spain that Portugal had already sent out vessels to the west. Everything was pressed with alacrity at Cadiz. The expedition was to be under Columbus's absolute command. Seamen of reputation were engaged to serve under him. Seventeen vessels were to take out a colony. Horses as well as cattle and other domestic animals were provided. Seeds and plants of different kinds were sent out, and to this first colonization by Spain, America owes the sugar-cane, and perhaps some other of her tropical productions.

Columbus remained in Barcelona until the twenty-third of May. But before that time, the important orders for the expedition had been given. He then went to Cadiz himself, and gave his personal attention to the preparations. Applications were eagerly pressed, from all quarters, for permission to go. Young men of high family were eager to try the great adventure. It was necessary to enlarge the number from that at first proposed. The increase of expense, ordered as the plans enlarged, did not please Fonseca. To quarrels between him and Columbus at this time have been referred the persecutions which Columbus afterwards suffered. In this case the king sustained Columbus in all his requisitions, and Fonseca was obliged to answer them.

So rapidly were all these preparations made, that, in a little more than a year from the sailing of the first expedition, the second, on a scale so much larger, was ready for sea.

Chapter VIII: The Second Expedition Sails

There is not in history a sharper contrast, or one more dramatic, than that between the first voyage of Columbus and the second. In the first voyage, three little ships left the port of Palos, most of the men of their crews unwilling, after infinite difficulty in preparation, and in the midst of the fears of all who stayed behind.

In the second voyage, a magnificent fleet, equipped with all that the royal service could command, crowded with eager adventurers who are excited by expectations of romance and of success, goes on the very same adventure.

In the first voyage, Columbus has but just turned the corner after the struggles and failures of eight years. He is a penniless adventurer who has staked all his reputation on a scheme in which he has hardly any support. In the second case, Columbus is the governor-general, for aught he knows, of half the world, of all the countries he is to discover; and he knows enough, and all men around him know enough, to see that his domain may be a principality indeed.

Success brings with it its disadvantages. The world has learned since, if it did not know it then, that one hundred and fifty sailors, used to the hard work and deprivations of a seafaring life, would be a much more efficient force for purposes of discovery, than a thousand and more courtiers who have left the presence of the king and queen in the hope of personal advancement or of romantic adventure. Those dainty people, who would have been soldiers if there were no gunpowder, are not men to found states; and the men who have lived in the ante-chambers of courts are not people who co-operate sympathetically with an experienced man of affairs like Columbus.

From this time forward this is to be but a sad history, and the sadness, nay, the cruelty of the story, results largely from the composition of the body of men whom Columbus took with him on this occasion. It is no longer coopers and blacksmiths and boatswains and sailmakers who surround him. These were officers of court, whose titles even cannot be translated into modern language, so artificial were their habits and so conventional the duties to which they had been accustomed. Such men it was, who made poor Columbus endless trouble. Such men it was, who, at the last, dragged him down from his noble position, so that he died unhonored, dispirited and poor. To the same misfortune, probably, do we owe it that, for a history of this voyage, we have no longer authority so charming as the simple, gossipy journal which Columbus kept through the first voyage, of which the greater part has happily been preserved. It may be that he was too much pressed by his varied duties to keep up such a journal. For it is alas! an unfortunate condition of human life, that men are most apt to write journals when they have nothing to tell, and that in the midst of high activity, the record of that activity is not made by the actor. In the present case, a certain Doctor Chanca, a native of Seville, had been taken on board Columbus's ship, perhaps with the wish that he should be the historian of the expedition. It may be that in the fact that his journal was sent home is the reason why the Admiral's, if he kept one, has never been preserved. Doctor Chanca's narrative is our principal contemporary account of the voyage.[29] From later authorities much can be added to it, but all of them put together are not, for the purposes of history, equal to the simple contemporaneous statement which we could have had, had Columbus's own journal been preserved.

The great fleet sailed from Cadiz on the twenty-fifth day of September, in the year 1493, rather more than thirteen months after the sailing of the little fleet from Palos of the year before. They touched at the Grand Canary as before, but at this time their vessels were in good condition and there was no dissatisfaction among the crews. From this time the voyage across the ocean was short. On the third day of November, 11 the Sunday after All Saints Day had dawned, a pilot on the ship cried out to the captain that he saw land. "So great was the joy among the people, that it was marvellous to hear the shouts of pleasure on all hands. And for this there was much reason because the people were so much fatigued by the hard life and by the water which they drank that they all hoped for land with much desire."

The reader will see that this is the ejaculation of a tired landsman; one might say, of a tired scholar, who

[29] *See Book II of this edition, p. 439.*

was glad that even the short voyage was at an end. Some of the pilots supposed that the distance which they had run was eight hundred leagues from Ferro; others thought it was seven hundred and eighty. As the light increased, there were two islands in sight the first was mountainous, being the island of "Dominica," which still retains that name, of the Sunday when it was discovered; the other, the island of Maria Galante, is more level, but like the first, as it is described by Dr. Chanca, it was well wooded. The island received its name from the ship that Columbus commanded. In all, they discovered six islands on this day.

Finding no harbor which satisfied him in Dominica, Columbus landed on the island of Maria Galante, and took possession of it in the name of the king and queen. Dr. Chanca expresses the amazement which everyone had felt on the other voyage, at the immense variety of trees, of fruits and of flowers, which to this hour is the joy of the traveller in the West Indies.

"In this island was such thickness of forest that it was wonderful, and such a variety of trees, unknown to anyone, that it was terrible, some with fruit, some with flowers, so that everything was green. There were wild fruits of different sorts, which some not very wise men tried, and, on merely tasting them, touching them with their tongues, their faces swelled and they had such great burning and pain that they seemed to rage (or to have hydrophobia). They were cured with cold things." This fruit is supposed to have been the manchireel,[30] which is known to produce such effects.

They found no inhabitants on this island and went on to another, now called Guadeloupe. It received this name from its resemblance to a province of the same name in Spain. They drew near a mountain upon it which "seemed to be trying to reach the sky," upon which was a beautiful waterfall, so white with foam that at a distance some of the sailors thought it was not water, but white rocks. The Admiral sent a light caravel to coast along and find harbor. This vessel discovered some houses, and the captain went ashore and found the inhabitants in them. They fled at once, and he entered the houses. There he found that they had taken nothing away. There was much cotton, "spun and to be spun," and other goods of theirs, and he took a little of everything, among other things, two parrots, larger and different from what had been seen before. He also took four or five bones of the legs and arms of men. This last discovery made the Spaniards suppose that these islands were those of Caribs, inhabited by the cannibals of whom they had heard in the first voyage.

They went on along the coast, passing by some little villages, from which the inhabitants fled, "as soon as they saw the sails." The Admiral decided to send ashore to make investigations, and next morning "certain captains" landed. At dinnertime some of them returned, bringing with them a boy of

---

[30]The manchineel (Hippomane mancinella), or death apple tree, is a very poisonous species found around the Caribbean and northern tropics. (https://science.howstuffworks.com/life/botany/manchineel-tree.htm)

fourteen, who said that he was one of the captives of the people of the island. The others divided, and one party "took a little boy and brought him on board." Another party took a number of women, some of them natives of the island, and others captives, who came of their own accord. One captain, Diego Marquez, with his men, went off from the others and lost his way with his party. After four days he came out on the coast, and by following that, he succeeded in coming to the fleet. Their friends supposed them to have been killed and eaten by the Caribs, as, since some of them were pilots and able to set their course by the pole-star, it seemed impossible that they should lose themselves.

During the first day Columbus spent here, many men and women came to the water's edge, "looking at the fleet and wondering at such a new thing; and when any boat came ashore to talk with them, saying, 'tayno, tayno,' which means good. But they were all ready to run when they seemed in danger, so that of the men only two could be taken by force or free-will. There were taken more than twenty women of the captives, and of their free-will came other women, born in other islands, who were stolen away and taken by force. Certain captive boys came to us. In this harbor we were eight days on account of the loss of the said captain."

They found great quantities of human bones on shore, and skulls hanging like pots or cups about the houses. They saw few men. The women said that this was because ten canoes had gone on a robbing or kidnapping expedition to other islands. "This people," says Doctor Chanca, "appeared to us more polite than those who live in the other islands we have seen, though they all have straw houses." But he goes on to say that these houses are better made and provided, and that more of both men's and women's work appeared in them. They had not only plenty of spun and unspun cotton, but many cotton mantles, "so well woven that they yield in nothing (or owe nothing) to those of our country."

When the women, who had been found captives, were asked who the people of the island were, they replied that they were Caribs. "When they heard that we abhorred such people for their evil use of eating men's flesh, they rejoiced much." But even in the captivity which all shared, they showed fear of their old masters.

"The customs of this people, the Caribs," says Dr. Chanca, "are beastly;" and it would be difficult not to agree with him, in spite of the "politeness" and comparative civilization he has spoken of.

They occupied three islands, and lived in harmony with each other, but made war in their canoes on all the other islands in the neighborhood. They used arrows in warfare, but had no iron. Some of them used arrow-heads of tortoise shell, others sharply toothed fish-bones, which could do a good deal of damage among unarmed men. "But for people of our nation, they are not arms to be feared much."

These Caribs carried off both men and women on their robbing expeditions. They slaughtered and ate the men, and kept the women as slaves; they were, in short, incredibly cruel. Three of the captive boys ran away and joined the Spaniards.

They had twice sent out expeditions after the lost captain, Diego Marquez, and another party had returned without news of him, on the very day on which he and his men came in. They brought with them ten captives, boys and women. They were received with great joy. "He and those that were with him, arrived so destroyed by the mountain, that it was pitiful to see them. When they were asked how they had lost themselves, they said that it was the thickness of the trees, so great that they could not see the sky, and that some of them, who were mariners, had climbed up the trees to look at the star (the Polestar) and that they never could see it."

One of the accounts of this voyage[31] relates that the captive women, who had taken refuge with the Spaniards, were persuaded by them to entice some of the Caribs to the beach. "But these men, when they had seen our people, all struck by terror, or the consciousness of their evil deeds, looking at each other, suddenly drew together, and very lightly, like a flight of birds, fled away to the valleys of the woods. Our men then, not having succeeded in taking any cannibals, retired to the ships and broke the Indians' canoes."

They left Guadeloupe on Sunday, the tenth of November. They passed several islands, but stopped at none of them, as they were in haste to arrive at the settlement of La Navidad in Hispaniola, made on the first voyage. They did, however, make some stay at an island which seemed well populated. This was that of San Martin. The Admiral sent a boat ashore

---

[31] That of Peter Martyr; *De Orbe Novo, The Eight Decades of Peter Martyr D'Anghera*

100

to ask what people lived on the island, and to ask his way, although, as he afterwards found, his own calculations were so correct that he did not need any help. The boat's crew took some captives, and as it was going back to the ships, a canoe came up in which were four men, two women and a boy. They were so astonished at seeing the fleet, that they remained, wondering what it could be, "two Lombard-shot from the ship," and did not see the boat till it was close to them. They now tried to get off, but were so pressed by the boat that they could not. "The Caribs, as soon as they saw that flight did not profit them, with much boldness laid hands on their bows, the women as well as the men. And I say with much boldness, because they were no more than four men and two women, and ours more than twenty-five, of whom they wounded two. To one they gave two arrow-shots in the breast, and to the other one in the ribs. And if we had not had shields and tablachutas, and had not come up quickly with the boat and overturned their canoe, they would have shot the most of our men with their arrows. And after their canoe was overturned, they remained in the water swimming, and at times getting foothold, for there were some shallow places there. And our men had much ado to take them, for they still kept on shooting as they could. And with all this, not one of them could be taken, except one badly wounded with a lance-thrust, who died, whom thus wounded they carried to the ships."

Another account of this fight says that the canoe was commanded by one of the women, who seemed to be a queen, who had a son "of cruel look, robust, with a lion's face, who followed her." This account represents the queen's son to have been wounded, as well as the man who died. "The Caribs differed from the other Indians in having long hair; the others wore theirs braided and a hundred thousand differences made in their heads, with crosses and other paintings of different sorts, each one as he desires, which they do with sharp canes." The Indians, both the Caribs and the others, were beardless, unless by a great exception. The Caribs, who had been taken prisoners here, had their eyes and eyebrows blackened, "which, it seems to me, they do as an ornament, and with that they appear more frightful." They heard from these prisoners of much gold at an island called Cayre.

They left San Martin on the same day, and passed the island of Santa Cruz, and the next day (November 15) they saw a great number of islands, which the Admiral named Santa Ursula and the Eleven Thousand Virgins. This seemed "a country fit for metals," but the fleet made no stay there. They did stop for two days at an island called Burenquen. The Admiral named it San Juan Bautista (Saint John Baptist). It is what we now call Porto Rico. He was not able to communicate with any of the inhabitants, as they lived in such fear of the Caribs that they all fled. All these islands were new to the Admiral and all "very beautiful and of very good land, but this one seemed better than all of them."

On Friday, the twenty-second of November, they landed at the island of Hispaniola, or Hayti, which they so much desired. None of the party who had made the first voyage were acquainted with this part of the island; but they conjectured what it was, from what the Indian captive women told them.

The part of the island where they arrived was called Hayti, another part Xamana, and the third Bohio. "It is a very singular country," says Dr. Chanca, "where there are numberless great rivers and great mountain ridges and great level valleys. I think the grass never dries in the whole year. I do not think that there is any winter in this (island) nor in the others, for at Christmas are found many birds' nests, some with birds, and some with eggs." The only four-footed animals found in these islands were what Dr. Chanca calls dogs of various colors, and one animal like a young rabbit, which climbed trees. Many persons ate these last and said they were very good. There were many small snakes, and few lizards, because the Indians were so fond of eating them. "They made as much of a feast of them as we would do of pheasants."

"There are in this island and the others numberless birds, of those of our country, and many others which never were seen there. Of our domestic birds, none have ever been seen here, except that in Zuruquia there were some ducks in the houses, most of them white as snow, and others black."

They coasted along this island for several days, to the place where the Admiral had left his settlement. While passing the region of Xamana, they set ashore one of the Indians whom they had carried off on the first voyage. They "gave him some little things which the Admiral had commanded him to give away." Another account adds that of the ten Indian men who had been carried off on the first voyage, seven had already died on account of the change of air and food. Two of the three whom the Admiral was bringing back, swam ashore at night. "The Admiral cared for this but little, thinking that he should have enough interpreters among those whom he had left in the island, and whom he hoped to find there again." It seems certain that one Indian remained faithful to the Spaniards; he was named Diego Colon, after the Admiral's brother.

On the day that the captive Indian was set ashore, a Biscayan sailor died, who had been wounded by the Caribs in the fight between the boat's crew and the canoe. A boat's crew was sent ashore to bury him, and as they came to land there came out "many Indians, of whom some wore gold at the neck and at the ears. They sought to come with the Christians to the ships, and they did not like to bring them, because they had not had permission from the Admiral." The Indians then sent two of their number in a little canoe to one of the caravels, where they were received kindly, and sent to speak with the Admiral.

"They said, through an interpreter, that a certain king sent them to know what people we were, and to ask that we might be kind enough to land, as they had much gold and would give it to him, and of what they had to eat. The Admiral commanded silken shirts and caps and other little things to be given them, and told them that as he was going where Guacanagari was, he could not stop, that another time he would be able to see him. And with that, they (the Indians) went away."

They stopped two days at a harbor which they called Monte Christi, to see if it were a suitable place for a town, for the Admiral did not feel altogether satisfied with the place where the settlement of La Navidad had been made on the first voyage. This Monte Christi was near "a great river of very good water" (the Santiago). But it is all an inundated region, and very unfit to live in.

"As they were going along, viewing the river and land, some of our men found, in a place close by the river, two dead men, one with: a cord (lazo) around his neck, and the other with one around his foot. This was the first day. On the next day following, they found two other dead men farther on than these others. One of these was in such a position that it could be known that he had a plentiful beard. Some of our men suspected more ill than good, and with reason, as the Indians are all beardless, as I have said."

This port was not far from the port where the Spanish settlement had been made on the first voyage, so that there was great reason for these anxieties. They set sail once more for the settlement, and arrived opposite the harbor of La Navidad on the twenty-seventh of November. As they were approaching the harbor, a canoe came towards them, with five or six Indians on board, but, as the Admiral kept on his course without waiting for them, they went back.

The Spaniards arrived outside the port of La Navidad so late that they did not dare to enter it that night. "The Admiral commanded two Lombards to be fired, to see if the Christians replied, who had been left with the said Guacanagari, (this was the friendly cacique Guacanagari of the first voyage), for they too had Lombards," "They never replied, nor did fires nor signs of houses appear in that place, at which the people were much discouraged, and they had the suspicion that was natural in such a case."

"Being thus all very sad, when four or five hours of the night had passed, there came the same canoe which they had seen the evening before. The Indians in it asked for the Admiral and the captain of one of the caravels of the first voyage. They were taken to the Admiral's ship, but would not come on board until they had spoken with him and seen him." They asked for a light, and as soon as they knew him, they entered the ship. They came from Guacanagari, and one of them was his cousin.

They brought with them golden masks, one for the Admiral and another for one of the captains who had been with him on the first voyage, probably Vicente Yanez Pinzon. Such masks were much valued among the Indians, and are thought to have been meant to put upon idols, so that they were given to the Spaniards as tokens of great respect. The Indian party remained on board for three hours, conversing with the Admiral and apparently very glad to see him again. When they were asked about the colonists of La Navidad, they said that they were all well, but that some of them had died from sickness, and that others had been killed in quarrels among themselves. Their own cacique, Guacanagari, had been attacked by two other chiefs, Caonabo and Mayreni. They had burned his village, and he had been wounded in the leg, so that he could not come to meet the Spaniards that night. As the Indians went away, however, they promised that they would bring him to visit them the next day. So the explorers remained "consoled for that night."

Next day, however, events were less reassuring. None of last night's party came back and nothing was seen of the cacique. The Spaniards, however, thought that the Indians might have been accidentally overturned in their canoe, as it was a small one, and as wine had been given them several times during their visit.

While he was still waiting for them, the Admiral sent some of his men to the place where La Navidad had stood. They found that the strong fort with a palisade was burned down and demolished. They also found some cloaks and other clothes which had been carried off by the Indians, who seemed uneasy, and at first would not come near the party.

"This did not appear well" to the Spaniards, as the Admiral had told them how many canoes had come out to visit him in that very place on the other voyage. They tried to make friends, however, threw out to them some bells, beads and other presents, and finally a relation of the cacique and three others ventured to the boat, and were taken on board ship.

These men frankly admitted that the "Christians" were all dead. The Spaniards had been told so the night before by their Indian interpreter, but they had refused to believe him. They were now told that the King of Canoaboa[32] and the King Mayreni had killed them and burned the village.

---

[32] Canoaboa" was thought to mean "Land of Gold."

They said, as the others had done, that Guacanagari was wounded in the thigh and they, like the others, said they would go and summon him. The Spaniards made them some presents, and they, too, disappeared.

Early the next morning the Admiral himself, with a party, including Dr. Chanca, went ashore.

"And we went where the town used to be, which we saw all burnt, and the clothes of the Christians were found on the grass there. At that time we saw no dead body. There were among us many different opinions, some suspecting that Guacanagari himself was (concerned) in the betrayal or death of the Christians, and to others it did not appear so, as his town was burnt, so that the thing was very doubtful."

The Admiral directed the whole place to be searched for gold, as he had left orders that if any quantity of it were found, it should be buried. While this search was being made, he and a few others went to look for a suitable place for a new settlement. They arrived at a village of seven or eight houses, which the inhabitants deserted at once. Here they found many things belonging to the Christians, such as stockings, pieces of cloth, and "a very pretty mantle which had not been unfolded since it was brought from Castile." These, the Spaniards thought, could not have been obtained by barter. There was also one of the anchors of the ship which had gone ashore on the first voyage.

When they returned to the site of La Navidad they found many Indians, who had become bold enough to come to barter gold. They had shown the place where the bodies of eleven Spaniards lay "covered already by the grass which had grown over them." They all "with one voice" said that Canoaboa and Mayreni had killed them. But as, at the same time, they complained that some of the Christians had taken three Indian wives, and some four, it seemed likely that a just resentment on the part of the islanders had had something to do with their death.

The next day the Admiral sent out a caravel to seek for a suitable place for a town, and he himself went out to look for one in a different direction. He found a secure harbor and a good place for a settlement, But he thought it too far from the place where he expected to find a gold mine. On his return, he found the caravel he had sent out. As it was coasting along the island, a canoe had come out to it, with two Indians on board, one of whom was a brother of Guacanagari. This man begged the party to come and visit the cacique. The "principal men" accordingly went on shore, and found him in bed, apparently suffering from his wounded thigh, which he showed them in bandages. They judged from appearances that he was telling them the truth.

He said to them, "by signs as best he could," that since he was thus wounded, they were to invite the Admiral to come to visit him. As they were going away, he gave each of them a golden jewel, as each "appeared to him to deserve it." "This gold," says Dr. Chanca, "is made in very delicate sheets, like our gold leaf, because they use it for making masks and to plate upon bitumen. They also wear it on the head and for earrings and nose-rings, and therefore they beat it very thin as they only wear it for its beauty and not for its value."

The Admiral decided to go to the cacique on the next day. He was visited early in the day by his brother, who hurried on the visit.

The Admiral went on shore and all the best people (*gente de pro*) with him, "handsomely dressed, as would be suitable in a capital city." They carried presents with them, as they had already received gold from him.

"When we arrived, we found him lying in his bed, according to their custom, hanging in the air, the bed being made of cotton like a net. He did not rise, but from the bed made a semblance of courtesy, as best he knew how. He showed much feeling, with tears in his eyes, at the death of the Christians, and began to talk of it, showing, as best he could, how some died of sickness, and how others had gone to Canoaboa to seek for the gold mine, and that they had been killed there, and how the others had been killed in their town."

He presented to the Admiral some gold and precious stones. One of the accounts says that there were eight hundred beads of a stone called ciba, one hundred of gold, a golden coronet, and three small calabashes filled with gold dust. Columbus, in return, made him a present.

"I and a navy surgeon were there," says Dr. Chanca. "The Admiral now said that we were learned in the infirmities of men, and asked if he would show us the wound. He replied that it pleased him to do so. I said that it would be necessary, if he could, for him to go out of the house, since with the multitudes of people it was dark, and we could not see well. He did it immediately, as I believe, more from timidity than from choice. The surgeon came to him and began to take off the bandage. Then he said to the Admiral that the injury was caused by ciba, that is, by a stone. When it was unbandaged we managed to examine it. It is certain that he was no more injured in that leg than in the other, although he pretended that it was very painful."

The Spaniards did not know what to believe. But it seemed certain that an attack of some enemy upon these Indians had taken place, and the Admiral determined to continue upon good terms with them. Nor did he change this policy toward Guacanagari. How far that chief had tried to prevent the massacre will never be known. The detail of the story was never fully drawn from the natives. The Spaniards had been cruel and licentious in their dealing with the Indians. They had quarrelled among themselves, and the indignant natives, in revenge, had destroyed them all.

Chapter IX: The New Colony

Columbus had hoped, with reason, to send back a part of the vessels which made up his large squadron, with gold collected in the year by the colonists at La Navidad. In truth, when, in 1501, the system of gold-washing-had been developed, the colony yielded twelve hundred pounds of gold in one year. The search for gold, from the beginning, broke up all intelligent plans for geographical discovery or for colonization. In this case, it was almost too clear that there was nothing but bad news to send back to Spain. Columbus went forward, however, as well as he could, with the establishment of a new colony, and with the search for gold.

He sent out expeditions of discovery to open relations with the natives, and to find the best places for washing and mining for gold. Melchior Meldonado commanded three hundred men, in the first of these expeditions. They came to a good harbor at the mouth of a river, where they saw a fine house, which they supposed might be the home of Guacanagari. They met an armed party of one hundred Indians; but these men put away their weapons when signals of peace were made, and brought presents in token of good-will.

The house to which they went was round, with a hemispherical roof or dome. It was thirty-two paces in diameter, divided by wicker work into different rooms. Smaller houses, for persons of rank lower than the chiefs, surrounded it. The natives told the explorers that Guacanagari himself had retired to the hills.

On receiving the report of these explorers Columbus sent out Ojeda with a hundred men, and Corvalan with a similar party in different directions. These officers, in their report, described the operation of gold-washing, much as it is known to explorers in mining regions to-day. The natives made a deep ditch into which the gold bearing sand should settle. For more important work they had flat baskets in which they shook the sand and parted it from the gold. With the left hand they dipped up sand, handled this skilfully or "dextrously" with the right hand, so that in a few minutes they could give grains of gold to the gratified explorers. Ojeda brought home to Columbus one nugget which weighed nine ounces.

They also brought tidings of the King of Canoaboa, of whom they had heard before, and he is called by the name of Caunebo himself. He was afterwards carried, as a prisoner or as a hostage, on the way to Spain; but died on the passage.

Columbus was able to dispatch the returning ships, with the encouraging reports brought in by Meldonado and Ojeda, but with very little gold. But he was obliged to ask for fresh supplies of food for the colony—even in the midst of the plenty which he described; for he had found already what all such leaders find, the difficulty of training men to use food to which they were not accustomed. He sent also his Carib prisoners, begging that they might be trained to a knowledge of the Christian religion and of the Spanish language. He saw, already, how much he should need interpreters. The fleet sailed on the second of February, and its reports were, on the whole, favorably received.

Columbus chose for the new city an elevation, ten leagues east of Monte Christi, and at first gave to his colony the name of Martha. It is the Isabella of the subsequent history.

The colonists were delighted with the fertility of the soil under the tropical climate. Andalusia itself had not prepared them for it. They planted seeds of peas, beans, lettuces, cabbages and other vegetables, and declared that they grew more in eight days than they would have grown in twenty at home. They had fresh vegetables in sixteen days after they planted them; but for melons, pumpkins and other fruits of that sort, they are generous enough to allow thirty days.

They had carried out roots and suckers of the sugar-cane. In fifteen days the shoots were a cubit high. A farmer who had planted wheat in the beginning of February had ripe grain in the beginning of April; so that they were sure of, at least, two crops in a year.

But the fertility of the soil was the only favorable token which the island first exhibited. The climate was enervating and sickly. The labor on the new city was hard and discouraging. Columbus found that his colonists were badly fitted for their duty, or not fitted for it at all. Court gentlemen did not want to work. Priests expected to be put on better diet than any other people. Columbus—though he lost his own popularity—insisted on putting all on equal fare, in sharing the supplies he had brought from Spain. It did not require a long time to prove that the selection of the site of the colony was unfortunate. Columbus himself gave way to the general disease. While he was ill, a mutiny broke out which he had to suppress by strong measures.

Bornal Diaz, who ranked as comptroller of the expedition, and Fermin Cedo, an assayer, made a plot for seizing the remaining ships and sailing for Europe. News of the mutiny was brought to Columbus. He found a document in the writing of Diaz, drawn as a memorial, accusing Columbus himself of grave crimes. He confined Diaz on board a ship to be sent to Spain with the memorial. He punished the mutineers of lower rank. He took the guns and naval munitions from four of the vessels, and entrusted them all to a person in whom he had absolute confidence.

On the report of the exploring parties, four names were given to as many divisions of the island. Junna was the most western, Attibunia the most eastern, Jachen the northern and Naiba the southern. Columbus himself, seeing the fortifications of the city well begun, undertook, in March, an exploration, of the island, with a force of five hundred men.

It was in the course of this exploration that one of the natives brought in a gold-bearing stone which weighed an ounce. He was satisfied with a little bell in exchange. He was surprised at the wonder expressed by the Spaniards, and showing a stone as large as a pomegranate, he said that he had nuggets of gold as large as this at his home. Other Indians brought in gold-bearing stones which weighed more than an ounce. At their homes, also, but not in sight, alas, was a block of gold as large as an infant's head.

Columbus himself thought it best to take as many men as he could into the mountain region. He left the new city under the care of his brother, Diego, and with all the force of healthy men which he could muster, making a little army of nearly five hundred men, he marched away from the sickly seaboard into the interior. The simple natives were astonished by the display of cavalry and other men in armor. After a few days of a delightful march, in the beauty of spring in that country, he entered upon the long sought Cibao. He relinquished his first idea of founding another city here, but did build a fortress called St. Thomas, in joking reference to Cedo and others, who had asserted that these regions produced no gold. While building this fortress, as it was proudly called, he sent a young cavalier named Luxan for further exploration.

Luxan returned with stories even greater than they had heard of before, but with no gold, "because he had no orders to do so." He had found ripe grapes. And at last they had found a region called Cipangi, *cipan* signifying stone. This name recalled the memory of Cipango, or Japan. With tidings as encouraging as this, Columbus returned to his city. He appointed his brother and Pedro Margarita governors of the city, and left with three ships for the further exploration of Cuba, which he had left only partly examined in his first voyage. He believed that it was the mainland of Asia. And as has been said, such was his belief till he died, and that of his countrymen. Cuba was not known to be an island for many years afterwards. He was now again in the career which pleased him, and for which he was fitted. He was always ill at ease in administering a colony, or ruling the men who were engaged in it. He was happy and contented when he was discovering. He had been eager to follow the southern coast of Cuba, as he had followed the north in his first voyage. And now he had his opportunity. Having commissioned his brother Diego and Margarita and appointed also a council of four other gentlemen, he sailed to explore new coasts, on the twenty-fourth of April.

He was soon tempted from his western course that he might examine Jamaica, of which he saw the distant lines on the south. "This island," says the account of the time, "is larger than Sicily. It has only one mountain, which rises from the coast on every side, little by little, until you come to the middle of the island and the ascent is so gradual that, whether you rise or descend, you hardly know whether you are rising or descending." Columbus found the island well peopled, and from what he saw of the natives, thought them more ingenious, and better artificers, than any Indians he had seen before. But when he proposed to land, they generally showed themselves prepared to resist him. He therefore deferred a full examination of the island to his return, and, with the first favorable wind, pressed on toward the southern coast of Cuba. He insisted on calling this the "Golden Chersonesus" of the East. This name had been given by the old geographers to the peninsula now known as Malacca.

Crossing the narrow channel between Jamaica and Cuba, he began coasting that island westward. If the reader will examine the map, he will find many small keys and islands south of Cuba, which, before any survey had been made, seriously retarded his westward course. In every case he was obliged to make a separate examination to be sure where the real coast of the island was, all the time believing it was the continent of Asia. One of the narratives says, with a pardonable exaggeration, that in all this voyage he thus discovered seven hundred islands. His own estimate was that he sailed two hundred and twenty-two leagues westward in the exploration which now engaged him.

The month of May and the beginning of June were occupied with such explorations. The natives proved friendly, as the natives of the northern side of Cuba had proved two years before. They had, in general, heard of the visit of the Spaniards; but their wonder and admiration seem to have been none the less now that they saw the reality.

On one occasion the hopes of all the party, that they should find themselves at the court of the Grand Khan, were greatly quickened. A Spaniard had gone into a forest alone, hunting. Suddenly he saw a man clothed in white, or thought he did, whom he supposed to be a friar of the order of Saint Mary de Mercedes, who was with the expedition. But, almost immediately, ten other friars dressed in the same costume, appeared, and then as many as thirty. The Spaniard was frightened at the multiplication of their number, it hardly appears why, as they were all men of peace, or should have been, whatever their number. He called out to his companions, and bade them escape. But the men in white called out to him, and waved their hands, as if to assure him that there was no danger. He did not trust them, however, but rushed back to the shore and the ship, as fast as he could, to report what he had seen to the Admiral.

Here, at last, was reason for hope that they had found one of the Asiatic missions of the Church. Columbus at once landed a party, instructing them to go forty miles inland, if necessary, to find people. But this party found neither path nor roadway, although the country was rich and fertile. Another party brought back rich bunches of grapes, and other native fruits. But neither party saw any friars of the order of Saint Mary. And it is now supposed that the Spaniard saw a peaceful flock of white cranes. The traveller Humboldt describes one occasion, in which the town of Angostura was put to alarm by the appearance of a flock of cranes known as soldados, or "soldiers," which were, as people supposed, a band of Indians.

In his interviews with the natives at one point and another, upon the coast, Columbus was delighted with their simplicity, their hospitality, and their kindly dealing with each other. On one occasion, when the Mass was celebrated, a large number of them were present, and joined in the service, as well as they could, with respect and devotion. An old man as much as eighty years old, as the Spaniards thought, brought to the Admiral a basket full of fruit, as a present. Then he said, by an interpreter:

"We have heard how you have enveloped, by your power, all these countries, and how much afraid of you the people have been. But I have to exhort you, and to tell you that there are two ways when men leave this body. One is dark and dismal; it is for those who have injured the race of men. The other is delightful and pleasant; it is for those who, while alive, have loved peace and the repose of mankind. If, then, you remember that you are mortal, and what these retributions are, you will do no harm to any one."

Columbus told him in reply that he had known of the two roads after death, and that he was well pleased to find that the natives of these lands knew of them; for he had not expected this. He said that the king and queen of Spain had sent him with the express mission of bringing these tidings to them. In particular, that he was charged with the duty of punishing the Caribs and all other men of impure life, and of rewarding and honoring all pure and innocent men. This statement so delighted the old prophet that he was eager to accompany Columbus on a mission so noble, and it was only by the urgent entreaty of his wife and children that he stayed with them. He found it hard to believe that Columbus was inferior in rank or command to any other sovereign.

The beauty of the island and the hospitality of the natives, however, were not enough to dispose the crews to continue this exploration further. They were all convinced that they were on the coast of Asia. Columbus did not mean that afterwards any one should accuse him of abandoning the discovery of that coast too soon. Calling to their attention the distance they had sailed, he sent round a written declaration for the signature of every person on the ships. Every man and boy put his name to it. It expressed their certainty that they were on the cape which made the end of the eastern Indies, and that any one who chose could proceed thence westward to Spain by land. This extraordinary declaration was attested officially by a notary, and still exists.

It was executed in a bay at the extreme southwestern corner of Cuba. It has been remarked by Munoz, that at that moment, in that place, a ship boy at the masthead could have looked over the group of low islands and seen the open sea, which would have shown that Cuba was an island.

The facts, which were controlling, were these, that the vessels were leaky and the crews sick and discontented. On the thirteenth of June, Columbus stood to the southeast. He discovered the island now known as the Island of Pines. He called it Evangelista. He anchored here and took in water. In an interview, not unlike that described, in which the old Cuban expressed his desire to return with Columbus, it is said that an Evangelistan chief made the same offer, but was withheld by the remonstrances, of his wife and children. A similar incident is reported in the visit to Jamaica, which soon followed. Columbus made a careful examination of that island. Then he crossed to Hispaniola, where, from the Indians, he received such accounts from the new town of Isabella as assured him that all was well there.

With his own indomitable zeal, he determined now to go to the Carib islands and administer to them the vengeance he had ready. But his own frame was not strong enough for his will. He sank exhausted, in a sort of lethargy. The officers of his ship, supposing he was dying, put about the vessels and the little squadron arrived, none too soon as it proved, at Isabella.

He was as resolute as ever in his determination to crush the Caribs, and prevent their incursions upon those innocent islanders to whom he had made so many promises of protection. But he fell ill, and for a short time at least was wholly unconscious. The officers in command took occasion of his illness, and of their right to manage the vessels, to turn back to the city of Isabella. He arrived there "as one half dead," and his explorations and discoveries for this voyage were thus brought to an end. To his great delight he found there his brother Bartholomew, whom he had not seen for eight years. Bartholomew had accompanied Diaz in the famous voyage in which he discovered the Cape of Good Hope. Returning to Europe in 1488 he had gone to England, with a message from Christopher Columbus, asking King Henry the Seventh to interest himself in the great adventure he proposed.

The authorities differ as to the reception which Henry gave to this great proposal. Up to the present time, no notice has been found of his visit in the English archives. The earliest notice of America, in the papers preserved there, is a note of a present of ten pounds "to hym that found the new land," who was Cabot, after his first voyage. Bartholomew Columbus was in England on the tenth of February, 1488; how much later is not known. Returning from England he staid in France, in the service of Madama de Bourbon. This was either Anne of Beaujeu, or the widow of the Admiral Louis de Bourbon. Bartholomew was living in Paris when he heard of his brother's great discovery.

He had now been appointed by the Spanish sovereigns to command a fleet of three vessels, which had been sent out to provision the new colony. He had sailed from Cadiz on the thirtieth of April, 1494, and he arrived at Isabella on St. John's Day of the same year.

Columbus welcomed him with delight, and immediately made him his first-lieutenant in command of the colony. There needed a strong hand for the management of the colony, for the quarrels which had existed before Columbus went on his Cuban voyage had not diminished in his absence. Pedro Margarita and Father Boil are spoken of as those who had made the most trouble. They had come determined to make a fortune rapidly, and they did not propose to give up such a hope to the slow processes of ordinary colonization. Columbus knew very well that those who had returned to Spain had carried with them complaints as to his own course. He would have been glad on some accounts to return, himself, at once; but he did not think that the natives of the islands were sufficiently under the power of the new colony to be left in safety.

First of all he sent back four caravels, which had recently arrived from Europe, with five hundred Indians whom he had taken as slaves. He consigned them to Juan de Fonseca's care. He was eager himself to say that he sent them out that they might be converted, to Christianity, and that they might learn the Spanish language and be of use as interpreters.

But, at the same time, he pointed out how easy it would be to make a source of revenue to the Crown from such involuntary emigration. To Isabella's credit it is to be said, that she protested against the whole thing immediately; and so far as appears, no further shipments were made in exactly the same way. But these poor wretches were not sent back to the islands, as she perhaps thought they were. Fonseca did not hesitate to sell them, or apprentice them, to use our modern phrase, and it is said by Bernaldez that they all died. His bitter phrase is that Fonseca took no more care of them than if they had been wild animals.

Columbus did not recover his health, so as to take a very active part in affairs for five months after his arrival at San Domingo. He was well aware that the Indians were vigorously organized, with the intention of driving his people from the island, or treating the colony as they had treated the colony of Navidad. He called the chief of the Cipangi, named Guarionexius, for consultation. The interpreter Didacus, who had served them so faithfully, married the king's sister, and it was hoped that this would be a bond of amity between the two nations.

Columbus sent Ojeda into the gold mountains with fifty armed men to make an alliance with Canabao. Canabao met this party with a good deal of perplexity. He undoubtedly knew that he had given the Spaniards good reason for doubting him. It is said that he had put to death twenty Spaniards by treasonable means, but it is to be remembered that this is the statement of his enemies. He, however, came to Columbus with a large body of his people, all armed. When he was asked why he brought so large a force with him, he said that so great a king as he, could not go anywhere without a fitting military escort. But Ojeda did not hesitate to take him prisoner and carry him into Isabella, bound. As has been said, he was eventually sent to Spain, but he died on the passage.

Columbus made another fortress, or tower, on the border of King Guarionexius's country, between his kingdom and Cipango. He gave to this post the name of the "Tower of the Conception," and meant it to be a rallying point for the miners and others, in case of any uprising of the natives against them. This proved to be an important centre for mining operations. From this place, what we should call a nugget of gold, which one of the chiefs brought in, was sent to Spain. It weighed twenty ounces. A good deal of interest attached also to the discovery of amber, one mass of which weighed three hundred pounds. Such discoveries renewed the interest and hope which had been excited in Spain by the first accounts of Hispaniola.

Columbus satisfied himself that he left the island really subdued; and in this impression he was not mistaken. Certain that his presence in Spain was needed, if he would maintain his own character against the attacks of the disaffected Spaniards who had gone before him, he set sail on the Nina on the tenth of March, taking with him as a consort a caravel which had been built at Isabella. He did not arrive in Cadiz till the eleventh of June, having been absent from Spain two years and nine months.

His return to Spain at this time gave Isabella another opportunity to show the firmness of her character, and the determination to which alone belongs success.

The excitement and popularity which attended the return from the first voyage had come to an end. Spain was in the period of reaction. The disappointment which naturally follows undue expectations and extravagant prophecies, was, in this instance, confirmed by the return of discontented adventurers. Four hundred years have accustomed the world to this reflex flow of disappointed colonists, unable or unwilling to work, who come back from a new land to say that its resources have been exaggerated. In this case, where everything was measured by the standard of gold, it was certainly true that the supply of gold received from the islands was very small as compared with the expenses of the expedition which had been sent out.

Five hundred Indians, who came to be taught the language, entering Spain as slaves, were but a poor return for the expenses in which the nation, not to say individuals, had been involved. The people of Spain, therefore, so far as they could show their feeling, were prejudiced against Columbus and those who surrounded him. They heard with incredulity the accounts of Cuba which he gave, and were quite indifferent to the geographical theories by which he wanted to prove that it was a part of Asia. He believed that the rich mines, which he had really found in Hispaniola, were the same as those of Ophir. But after five years of waiting, the Spanish public cared but little for such conjectures.

As he arrived in Cadiz, he found three vessels, under Nino, about to sail with supplies. These were much needed, for the relief of the preceding year, sent out in four vessels, had been lost by shipwreck. Columbus was able to add a letter of his own to the governor of Isabella, begging him to conform to the wishes expressed by the king and queen in the dispatches taken by Nino. He recommended diligence in exploring the new mines, and that a seaport should be founded in their neighborhood. At the same time he received a gracious letter from the king and queen, congratulating him on his return, and asking him to court as soon as he should recover from his fatigue.

Columbus was encouraged by the tone of this letter. He had chosen to act as if he were in disgrace, and dressed himself in humble garb, as if he were a Franciscan monk, wearing his beard as the brethren of those orders do. Perhaps this was in fulfillment of one of those vows which, as we know, he frequently made in periods of despondency.

He went to Burgos, where Ferdinand and Isabella were residing, and on the way made such a display of treasure as he had done on the celebrated march to Barcelona. Canabao, the fierce cacique of Hispaniola, had died on the voyage, but his brother and nephew still lived, and he took them to the king and queen, glittering on state occasions with golden ornaments. One chain of gold which the brother wore, is said to have been worth more than three thousand dollars of our time. In the procession Columbus carried various masks and other images, made by the Indians in fantastic shapes, which attracted the curiosity which in all nations surrounds the idols of a foreign creed.

The sovereigns received him cordially. No reference was made to the complaints of the adventurers who had returned. However the sovereigns may have been impressed by these, they were still confident in Columbus and in his merits, and do not seem to have wished to receive the partial accounts of his accusers. On his part, he pressed the importance of a new expedition, in order that they might annex to their dominions the eastern part of Asia. He wanted for this purpose eight ships. He was willing to leave two in the island of Hispaniola, and he hoped that he might have six for a voyage of discovery. The sovereigns assented readily to his proposal, and at the time probably intended to carry out his wishes.

But Spain had something else to do than to annex Asia or to discover America; and the fulfillment of the promises made so cordially in 1496, was destined to await the exigencies of European war and diplomacy. In fact, he did not sail upon the third expedition for nearly two years after his arrival in Cadiz.

In the autumn of 1496, an order was given for a sum amounting to nearly a hundred thousand dollars of our time, for the equipment of the promised squadron. At the same time Columbus was relieved from the necessity by which he was bound in his original contract, to furnish at least one-eighth of the money necessary in any of these expeditions. This burden was becoming too heavy for him to bear. It was agreed, however, that in the event of any profit resulting to the crown, he should be entitled to one-eighth of it for three ensuing years. This concession must be considered as an evidence that he was still in favor. At the end of three years both parties were to fall back upon the original contract.

But these noble promises, which must have been so encouraging to him, could not be fulfilled, as it proved. For the exigencies of war, the particular money which was to be advanced to Columbus was used for the repair of a fortress upon the frontier. Instead of this, Columbus was to receive his money from the gold brought by Nino on his return. Alas, it proved that a report that he had returned with so much gold, meant that he had Indian prisoners, from the sale of whom he expected to realize this money. And poor Columbus was virtually consigned to building and fitting out his ship from the result of a slave-trade, which was condemned by Isabella, and which he knew was wretchedly unprofitable.

A difficulty almost equally great resulted from the unpopularity of the expedition. People did not volunteer eagerly, as they had done, the minds of men being poisoned by the reports of emigrants, who had gone out in high hope, and had returned disappointed. It even became necessary to commute the sentences of criminals who had been sentenced to banishment, so that they might be transported into the new settlements, where they were to work without pay. Even these expedients did not much hasten the progress of the expedition.

Fonseca, the steady enemy of Columbus, was placed in command again at this time. The queen was overwhelmed with affliction by the death of Prince Juan; and it seemed to Columbus and his friends that every petty difficulty was placed in the way of preparation. When at length six vessels were fitted for sea, it was only after the wear and tear of constant opposition from officials in command; and the expedition, as it proved, was not what Columbus had hoped for, for his purposes.

On the thirtieth of May, however, in 1498, he was able to sail. As this was the period when the Catholic church celebrates the mystery of the Trinity, he determined and promised that the first land which he discovered should receive that sacred name. He was well convinced of the existence of a continent farther south than the islands among which he had cruised, and intended to strike that continent, as in fact he did, in the outset of his voyage.

Chapter 10: The Third Voyage

For the narrative of the third voyage, we are fortunate in having once more a contemporary account by Columbus himself.[33] The more important part of his expedition was partly over when he was able to write a careful letter to the king and queen, which is still preserved. It is lighted up by bursts of the religious enthusiasm which governed him from the beginning. All the more does it show the character of the man, and it impresses upon us, what is never to be forgotten, the mixture in his motive of the enthusiasm of a discoverer, the eager religious feeling which might have quickened a crusader, and the prospects of what we should call business adventure, by which he tries to conciliate persons whose views are less exalted than his own.

In addressing the king and queen, who are called "very high and very powerful princes," he reminds them that his undertaking to discover the West Indies began in the inspiration of the Holy Spirit, which appointed him as a messenger for this enterprise. He asks them to remember that he has always addressed them as with that intention.

He reminds them of the seven or eight years in which he was urging his cause and that it was not enough that he should have showed the religious side

---

[33] *See Book II of this edition, p. 476.*

of it, that he was obliged to argue for the temporal view as well. But their decision, for which he praises them indirectly, was made, he says, in the face of the ridicule of all, excepting the two priests, Marcheza and the Archbishop of Segovia. "And everything will pass away excepting the word of God, who spoke so clearly of these lands by the voice of Isaiah in so many places, affirming that His name should be divulged to the nations from Spain." He goes on in a review of the earlier voyages, and after this preface gives his account of the voyage of 1498.

They sailed from Santa Lucca the thirtieth of May, and went down to Madeira to avoid the hostile squadron of the French who were awaiting him at Cape St. Vincent. In the history by Herrara, of another generation, this squadron is said to be Portuguese. From Maderia, they passed to the Canary Islands, from which, with one ship and two caravels, he makes his voyage, sending the other three vessels to Hispaniola. After making the Cape de Verde Islands, he sailed southwest. He had very hot weather for eight days, and in the hope of finding cooler weather changed his course to the westward.

On the thirty-first of July, they made land, which proved to be the cape now known as Galeota, the southeastern cape of the island of Trinidad. The country was as green at this season as the orchards of Valencia in March. Passing five leagues farther on, he lands to refit his vessels and take on board wood and water. The next day a large canoe from the east, with twenty-four men, well armed, appeared.

The Admiral wished to communicate with them, but they refused, although he showed them basins and other things which he thought would attract them. Failing in this effort, he directed some of the boys of the crew to dance and play a tambourine on the poop of the ship. But this conciliatory measure had as little success as the other. The natives strung their bows, took up their shields and began to shoot the dancers. Columbus stopped the entertainment, therefore, and ordered some balls shot at them, upon which they left him. With the other vessel they opened more friendly communication, but when the pilot went to Columbus and asked leave to land with them, they went off, nor were any of them or theirs seen again.

On his arrival at Punta de Icacocos, at the southern point of Trinidad, he observes the very strong currents which are always noticed by voyagers, running with as much fury as the Guadalquiver in time of flood. In the night a terrible wave came from the south, "a hill as high as a ship," so that even in writing of it he feels fear. But no misfortune came from it.

Sailing the next day, he found the water comparatively fresh. He is, in fact, in the current produced by the great river Orinoco, which affects, in a remarkable way, all the tide-flow of those seas. Sailing north, he passes different points of the Island of Trinidad, and makes out the Punta de la Pena and the mainland. He still observes the freshness of the water and the severity of the currents.

As he sails farther westward, he observes fleets, and he sends his people ashore. They find no inhabitants at first, but eventually meet people who tell him the enemy of this country is Paria. Of these he took on board four. The king sent him an invitation to land, and numbers of the people came in canoes, many of whom wore gold and pearls. These pearls came to them from the north. Columbus did not venture to land here because the provisions of his vessels were already failing him.

He describes the people, as of much the same color as those who have been observed before, and were ready for intercourse, and of good appearance. Two prominent persons came to meet them, whom he thought to be father and son. The house to which the Spaniards were led was large, with many seats. An entertainment was brought forward, in which there were many sorts of fruits, and wine of many kinds. It was not made from grapes, however, and he supposed it must be made of different sorts of fruits.

A part of the entertainment was of maize, "which is a sort of corn which grows here, with a spike like a spindle." The Indians and their guests parted with regret that they could not understand each other's conversation. All this passed in the house of the elder Indian. The younger then took them to his house, where a similar collation was served, and they then returned to the ship, Columbus being in haste to press on, both on account of his want of supplies and the failure of his own health. He says he was still suffering from diseases which he had contracted on the last voyage, and with blindness. "That then his eyes did not give him as much pain, nor were they bloodshot as much as they are now."

He describes the people whom they at first visited as of fine stature, easy bearing, with long straight hair, and wearing worked handkerchiefs on their heads. At a little distance it seemed as if these were made of silk, like the gauze veil with which the Spaniards were familiar, from Moorish usage.

"Others," he says, "wore larger handkerchiefs round their waists, like the panete of the Spaniards." By this phrase he means a full garment hanging over the knees, either trousers or petticoats. These people were whiter in color than the Indians he had seen before. They all wore something at the neck and arms, with many pieces of gold at the neck. The canoes were much larger than he had seen, better in build and lighter; they had a cabin in the middle for the princes and their women.

He made many inquiries for gold, but was told he must go farther on, but he was advised not to go there, because his men would be in danger of being eaten. At first, Columbus supposed that this meant that the inhabitants of the gold-bearing countries were cannibals, but he satisfied himself afterwards that the natives meant that they would be eaten by beasts. With regard to pearls, also, he got some information that he should find them when he had gone farther west and farther north.

After these agreeable courtesies, the little fleet raised its anchors and sailed west. Columbus sent one caravel to investigate the river. Finding that he should not succeed in that direction, and that he had no available way either north or south, he leaves by the same entrance by which he had entered. The water is still very fresh, and he is satisfied, correctly as we know, that these currents were caused by the entrance of the great river of water.

On the thirteenth of August he leaves the island by what he calls the northern mouth of the river (Boca Grande), and begins to strike salt water again.

At this part of Columbus's letter there is a very curious discussion of temperature, which shows that this careful observer, even at that time, made out the difference between what are called isothermal curves and the curves of latitude. He observes that he cannot make any estimate of what his temperature will be on the American coast from what he has observed on the coast of Africa.

He begins now to doubt whether the world is spherical, and is disposed to believe that it is shaped like a pear, and he tries to make a theory of the difference of temperature from this suggestion. We hardly need to follow this now. We know he was entirely wrong in his conjecture. "Pliny and others," he says, "thought the world spherical, because on their part of it it was a hemisphere." They were ignorant of the section over which he was sailing, which he considers to be that of a pear cut in the wrong way. His demonstration is, that in similar latitudes to the eastward it is very hot and the people are black, while at Trinidad or on the mainland it is comfortable and the people are a fine race of men, whiter than any others whom he has seen in the Indies. The sun in the constellation of the Virgin is over their heads, and all this comes from their being higher up, nearer the air than they would have been had they been on the African coast.

With this curious speculation he unites some inferences from Scripture, and goes back to the account in the Book of Genesis and concludes that the earthly Paradise was in the distant east. He says, however, that if he could go on, on the equinoctial line, the air would grow more temperate, with greater changes in the stars and in the water. He does not think it possible that anyone can go to the extreme height of the mountain where the earthly Paradise is to be found, for no one is to be permitted to enter there but by the will of God, but he believes that in this voyage he is approaching it.

Any reader who is interested in this curious speculation of Columbus should refer to the "Divina Comedia" of Dante, where Dante himself held a somewhat similar view, and describes his entrance into the terrestrial paradise under the guidance of Beatrice. It is a rather curious fact, which discoverers of the last three centuries have established, that the point, on this world, which is opposite the city of Jerusalem, where all these enthusiasts supposed the terrestrial Paradise would be found, is in truth in the Pacific Ocean not far from Pitcairn's Island, in the very region where so many voyagers have thought that they found the climate and soil which to the terrestrial Paradise belong.

Columbus expresses his dissent from the recent theory, which was that of Dante, supposing that the earthly Paradise was at the top of a sharp mountain. On the other hand, he supposes that this mountain rises gently, but yet that no person can go to the top.

This is his curious "excursion," made, perhaps, because Columbus had the time to write it.

The journal now recurs to more earthly affairs. Passing out from the mouth of the "Dragon," he found the sea running westward and the wind gentle. He notices that the waters are swept westward as the trade winds are. In this way he accounts for there being so many islands in that part of the earth, the mainland having been eaten away by the constant flow of the waves. He thinks their very shape indicates this, they being narrow from north to south and longer from east to west. Although some of the islands differ in this, special reasons maybe given for the difference. He brings in many of the old authorities to show, what we now know to be entirely false, that there is much more land than water on the surface of the globe.

All this curious speculation as to the make-up of the world encourages him to beg their Highnesses to go on with the noble work which they have begun. He explains to them that he plants the cross on every cape and proclaims the sovereignty of their Majesties and of the Christian religion. He prays that this may continue. The only objection to it is the expense, but Columbus begs their Highnesses to remember how much more money is spent for the mere formalities of the elegancies of the court. He begs them to consider the credit attaching to plans of discovery and quickens their ambition by reference to the efforts of the princes of Portugal.

This letter closes by the expression of his determination to go on with his three ships for further discoveries.

This letter was written from San Domingo on the eighth of October. He had already made the great discovery of the mainland of South America, though he did not yet know that he had touched the continent. He had intentionally gone farther south than before, and had therefore struck the island of Trinidad, to which, as he had promised, he gave the name which it still bears. A sailor first saw the summits of three mountains, and gave the cry of land. As the ships approached, it was seen that these three mountains were united at the base. Columbus was delighted by the omen, as he regarded it, which thus connected his discovery with the vow which he had made on Trinity Sunday.

As the reader has seen, he first passed between this great island and the mainland. The open gulf there described is now known as the Gulf of Paria. The observation which he made as to the freshness of the water caused by the flow of the Orinoco, has been made by all navigators since. It may be said that he was then really in the mouth of the Orinoco.

Young readers, at least, will be specially interested to remember that it was in this region that Robinson Crusoe's island was placed by Defoe; and if they will carefully read his life they will find discussions there of the flow of the "great River Orinoco." Crossing this gulf, Columbus had touched upon the coast of Paria, and thus became the first discoverer of South America. It is determined, by careful geographers, that the discovery of the continent of North America, had been made before this time by the Cabots, sailing under the orders of England.

Columbus was greatly encouraged by the discovery of fine pearls among the natives of Paria. Here he found one more proof that he was on the eastern coast of Asia, from which coast pearls had been brought by the caravans on which, till now, Europe had depended for its Asiatic supplies. He gave the name "Gulf of Pearls" to the estuary which makes the mouth of the River Paria.

He would gladly have spent more time in exploring this region; but the sea-stores of his vessel were exhausted, he was suffering from a difficulty with his eyes, caused by overwatching, and was also a cripple from gout. He resisted the temptation, therefore, to make further explorations on the coast of Paria, and passed westward and northwestward. He made many discoveries of islands in the Caribbean Sea as he went northwest, and he arrived at the colony of San Domingo, on the thirtieth of August. He had hoped for rest after his difficult voyage; but he found the island in confusion which seemed hopeless.

His brother Bartholomew, from all the accounts we have, would seem to have administered its affairs with justice and decision; but the problem he had in hand was one which could not be solved so as to satisfy all the critics. Close around him he had a body of adventurers, almost all of whom were nothing but adventurers. With the help of these adventurers, he had to repress Indian hostilities, and to keep in order the natives who had been insulted and injured in every conceivable way by the settlers.

He was expected to send home gold to Spain with every vessel; he knew perfectly well that Spain was clamoring with indignation because he did not succeed in doing so. But on the island itself he had to meet, from day to day, conspiracies of Spaniards and what are called insurrections of natives. These insurrections consisted simply in their assertion of such rights as they had to the beautiful land which the Spaniards were taking away from them.

At the moment when Columbus landed, there was an instant of tranquility. But the natives, whom he remembered only six years ago as so happy and cheerful and hospitable, had fled as far as they could. They showed in every way their distrust of those who were trying to become their masters. On the other hand, soldiers and emigrants were eager to leave the island if they could. They were near starvation, or if they did not starve they were using food to which they were not accustomed. The eagerness with which, in 1493, men had wished to rush to this land of promise, was succeeded by an equal eagerness, in 1498, to go home from it.

As soon as he arrived, Columbus issued a proclamation, approving of the measures of his brother in his absence, and denouncing the rebels with whom Bartholomew had been contending. He found the difficulties which surrounded him were of the most serious character. He had not force enough to take up arms against the rebels of different names. He offered pardon to them in the name of the sovereigns, and that they refused.

Columbus was obliged, in order to maintain any show of authority, to propose to the sovereigns that they should arbitrate between his brother and Roldan, who was the chief of the rebel party. He called to the minds of Ferdinand and Isabella his own eager desire to return to San Domingo sooner, and ascribed the difficulties which had arisen, in large measure, to his long delay. He said he should send home the more worthless men by every ship.

He asked that preachers might be sent out to convert the Indians and to reform the dissolute

Spaniards. He asked for officers of revenue, and for a learned judge. He begged at the same time that, for two years longer, the colony might be permitted to employ the Indians as slaves, but he promised they would only use such as they captured in war and insurrections.

By the same vessel the rebels sent out letters charging Columbus and his brother with the grossest oppression and injustice. All these letters came to court by one messenger. Columbus was then left to manage as best he could, in the months which must pass, before he could receive an answer.

He was not wholly without success. That is to say, no actual battles took place between the parties before the answer returned. But when it returned, it proved to be written by his worst enemy, Fonseca. It was a genuine Spanish answer to a letter which required immediate decision. That is to say, Columbus was simply told that the whole matter must be left in suspense till the sovereigns could make such an investigation as they wished. The hope, therefore, of some help from home was wholly disappointed.

Roldan, the chief of the rebels, was encouraged by this news to take higher ground than even he had ventured on before. He now proposed that he should send fifteen of his company to Spain, also that those who remained should not only be pardoned, but should have lands granted them; third, that a public proclamation should be made that all charges against him had been false; and fourth, that he should hold the office of chief judge, which he had held before the rebellion.

Columbus was obliged to accede to terms as insolent as these, and the rebels even added a stipulation, that if he should fail in fulfilling either of these articles, they might compel him to comply, by force or any other means. Thus was he hampered in the very position where, by the king's orders, and indeed, one would say, by the right of discovery, he was the supreme master.

For himself, he determined to return with Bartholomew to Spain, and he made some preparations to do so. But at this time he learned, from the western part of the island, that four strange ships had arrived there. He could not feel that it was safe to leave the colony in such a condition of latent rebellion as he knew it to be in; he wrote again to the sovereigns, and said directly that his capitulation with the rebels had been extorted by force, and that he did not consider that the sovereigns, or that he himself, were bound by it. He pressed some of the requests which he had made before, and asked that his son Diego, who was no longer a boy, might be sent out to him.

It proved that the ships which had arrived at the west of the island were under the command of Ojeda, who will be remembered as a bold cavalier in the adventures of the second voyage. Acting under a general permission which had been given for private adventurers, Ojeda had brought out this squadron, and, when Columbus communicated with him, was engaged in cutting dye-woods and shipping slaves.

Columbus sent Roldan, who had been the head of the rebels, to inquire on what ground he was there. Ojeda produced a license signed by Fonseca, authorizing him to sail on a voyage of discovery. It proved that Columbus's letters describing the pearls of Paria had awakened curiosity and enthusiasm, and, while the crown had passed them by so coldly, Ojeda and a body of adventurers had obtained a license and had fitted out four ships for adventure. The special interest of this voyage for us, is that it is supposed that Vespucci, a Florentine merchant, made at this time his first expedition to America.

Vespucci was not a professional seaman, but he was interested in geography, and had made many voyages before this time. So soon as it was announced that Ojeda was on the coast, the rebels of San Domingo selected him as a new leader. He announced to Columbus, rather coolly, that he could probably redress the grievances which these men had. He undoubtedly knew that he had the protection of Fonseca at home. Fortunately for Columbus, Roldan did not mean to give up his place as "leader of the opposition;" and it may be said that the difficulty between the two was a certain advantage to Columbus in maintaining his authority.

Meanwhile, all wishes on his part to continue his discoveries were futile, while he was engaged in the almost hopeless duty of reconciling various adventurers and conciliating people who had no interests but their own. In Spain, his enemies were doing everything in their power to undermine his reputation. His statements were read more and more coldly, and at last, on the twenty-first and twenty-sixth of May, 1499, letters were written to him instructing him to deliver into the hands of Bobadilla, a new commandant, all the fortresses any ships, houses and other royal property which he held, and to give faith and obedience to any instructions given by Bobadilla. That is to say, Bobadilla was sent out as a commander who was to take precedence of every one on the spot. He was an officer of the royal household, probably a favorite at court, and was selected for the difficult task of reconciling all difficulties, and bringing the new colony into loyal allegiance to the crown. He sailed for San Domingo in the middle of July, 1500, and arrived on the twenty-third of August.

On his arrival, he found that Columbus and his brother Bartholomew were both absent from the city, being in fact engaged in efforts to set what may be called the provinces in order. The young Diego Columbus was commander in their absence. The morning after he arrived, Bobadilla attended mass, and then, with the people assembled around the door of the church, he directed that his commission should be read. He was to investigate the rebellion, he was to seize the persons of delinquents and punish them with rigor, and he was to command the Admiral to assist him in these duties.

He then bade Diego surrender to him certain prisoners, and ordered that their accusers should appear before him. To this Diego replied that his brother held superior powers to any which Bobadilla could possess; he asked for a copy of the commission, which was declined, until Columbus himself should arrive. Bobadilla then took the oath of office, and produced, for the first time, the order which has been described above, ordering Columbus to deliver up all the royal property. He won the popular favor by reading an order which directed him to pay all arrears of wages due to all persons in the royal service.

But when he came before the fortress, he found that the commander declined to surrender it. He said he held the fortress for the king by the command of the Admiral, and would not deliver it until he should arrive. Bobadilla, however, "assailed the portal;" that is to say, he broke open the gate. No one offered any opposition, and the commander and his first-lieutenant were taken prisoners. He went farther, taking up his residence in Columbus's house, and seizing his papers. So soon as Columbus received account of Bobadilla's arrival, he wrote to him in careful terms, welcoming him to the island. He cautioned him against precipitate measures, told him that he himself was on the point of going to Spain, and that he would soon leave him in command, with everything explained. Bobadilla gave no answer to these letters; and when Columbus received from the sovereigns the letter of the twenty-sixth of May, he made no longer any hesitation, but reported in person at the city of San Domingo.

He traveled without guards or retinue, but Bobadilla had made hostile preparations, as if Columbus meant to come with military force. Columbus preferred to show his own loyalty to the crown and to remove suspicion. But no sooner did he arrive in the city than Bobadilla gave orders that he should be put in irons and confined in the fortress. Up to this moment, Bobadilla had been sustained by the popular favor of those around him; but the indignity of placing chains upon Columbus seems to have made a change in the fickle impressions of the little town.

Columbus, himself, behaved with magnanimity, and made no complaint. Bobadilla asked him to bid his brother return to San Domingo, and he complied. He begged his brother to submit to the authority of the sovereigns, and Bartholomew immediately did so. On his arrival in San Domingo he was also put in irons, as his brother Diego had been, and was confined on board a caravel. As soon as a set of charges could be made up to send to Spain with Columbus, the vessels, with the prisoners, set sail.

The master of the caravel, Martin, was profoundly grieved by the severe treatment to which the great navigator was subjected. He would gladly have taken off his irons, but Columbus would not consent. "I was commanded by the king and queen," he said, "to submit to whatever Bobadilla should order in their name. He has put these chains on me by their authority. I will wear them until the king and queen bid me take them off. I will preserve them afterwards as relics and memorials of the reward of my services." His son, Fernando, who tells this story, says that he did so, that they were always hanging in his cabinet, and that he asked that they might be buried with him when he died.

From this expression of Fernando Columbus, there has arisen, what Mr. Harrisse calls, a "pure legend," that the chains were placed in the coffin of Columbus. Mr. Harrisse shows good reason for thinking that this was not so. "Although disposed to believe that, in a moment of just indignation, Columbus expressed the wish that these tokens of the ingratitude of which he had been the victim should be buried, with him, I do not believe that they were ever placed in his coffin."

It will thus be seen that the third voyage added to the knowledge of the civilized world the information which Columbus had gained regarding Paria and the island of Trinidad. For other purposes of discovery, it was fruitless.

Chapter XI: Spain 1500, 1501

Columbus was right in insisting on wearing his chains. They became rather an ornament than a disgrace. So soon as it was announced in Spain that the great discoverer had been so treated by Bobadilla, a wave of popular indignation swept through the people and reached the court. Ferdinand and Isabella, themselves, had never intended to give such powers to their favorite, that he should disgrace a man so much his superior.

They instantly sent orders to Cadiz that Columbus should be received with all honor. So soon as he arrived he had been able to send, to Dona Juana de la Torre, a lady high in favor at court, a private letter, in which he made a proud defense of himself. This letter is still preserved, and it is of the first interest, as showing his own character, and as showing what were the real hardships which he had undergone.[34]

The Lady Juana read this letter to Isabella. Her own indignation, which probably had been kindled by the general news that Columbus had been chained, rose to the highest. She received him, therefore, when he arrived at court, with all the more cordiality. Ferdinand was either obliged to pretend to join with her in her indignation, or he had really felt distressed by the behavior of his subordinate.

---

[34] *See Book I, Appendix B and Book II, p. 533 of this edition.*

They did not wait for any documents from Bobadilla. As has been said, they wrote cordially to Columbus; they also ordered that two thousand ducats should be paid him for his expenses, and they bade him appear at Grenada at court. He did appear there on the seventeenth of December, attended by an honorable retinue, and in the proper costume of a gentleman in favor with the king and queen.

When the queen met him she was moved to tears, and Columbus, finding himself so kindly received, threw himself upon his knees. For some time he could not express himself except by tears and sobs. His sovereigns raised him from the ground and encouraged him by gracious words.

So soon as he recovered his self-possession he made such an address as he had occasion to make more than once in his life, and showed the eloquence which is possible to a man of affairs. He could well boast of his loyalty to the Spanish crown; and he might well say that, whether he were or were not experienced in government, he had been surrounded by such difficulties in administration as hardly any other man had had to go through. But really, it was hardly necessary that he should vindicate himself.

The stupidity of his enemies had injured their cause more than any carelessness of Columbus could have done. The sovereigns expressed their indignation at Bobadilla's proceedings, and, indeed, declared at once that he should be dismissed from command. They never took any public notice of the charges which he had sent home; on the other hand, they received Columbus with dignity and favor, and assured him that he should be reinstated in all his privileges.

The time at which he arrived was, in a certain sense, favorable for his future plans, so far as he had formed any. On the other hand, the condition of affairs was wholly changed from what it was when he began his great discoveries, and the changes were in some degree unfavorable. Vasco da Gama had succeeded in the great enterprise by which he had doubled the Cape of Good Hope, had arrived at the Indies by the route of the Indian ocean, and his squadron had successfully returned.

This great adventure, with the commercial and other results which would certainly follow it, had quickened the mind of all Europe, as the discovery by Columbus had quickened it eight years before. So far, any plan for the discoveries over which Columbus was always brooding, would be favorably received. But, on the other hand, in eight years since the first voyage, a large body of skillful adventurers had entered upon the career which then no one chose to share with him. The Pinzon brothers were among these; Ojeda, already known to the reader, was another; and Vespucci, as the reader knows, an intelligent and wise student, had engaged himself in such discoveries.

The rumors of the voyages of the Cabots, much farther north than those made by Columbus, had gone through all Europe. In a word, Columbus was now only one of several skilful pilots and voyagers, and his plans were to be considered side by side with those which were coming forward almost every day, for new discoveries, either by the eastern route, of which Vasco da Gama had shown the practicability, or by the western route, which Columbus himself had first essayed.

It is to be remembered, as well, that Columbus was now an old man, and, whatever were his successes as a discoverer, he had not succeeded as a commander. There might have been reasons for his failure; but failure is failure, and men do not accord to an unsuccessful leader the honors which they are ready to give to a successful discoverer. When, therefore, he offered his new plans at court, he should have been well aware that they could not be received, as if he were the only one who could make suggestions. Probably he was aware of this. He was also obliged, whether he would or would not, to give up the idea that he was to be the commander of the regions which he discovered.

It had been easy enough to grant him this command before there was so much as an inch of land known, over which it would make him the master. But now that it was known that large islands, and probably a part of the continent of Asia, were to be submitted to his sway if he had it, there was every reason why the sovereigns should be unwilling to maintain for him the broad rights which they had been willing to give when a scratch of the pen was all that was needful to give them.

Bobadilla was recalled; so far well. But neither Ferdinand nor Isabella chose to place Columbus again in his command. They did choose Don Nicola Ovando, a younger man, to take the place of Bobadilla, to send him home, and to take the charge of the colony.

From the colony itself, the worst accounts were received. If Columbus and his brother had failed, Bobadilla had failed more disgracefully. Indeed, he had begun by the policy of King Log, as an improvement on the policy of King Stork. He had favored all rebels, he had pardoned them, he had even paid them for the time which they had spent in rebellion; and the natural result was utter disorder and license.

It does not appear that he was a bad man; he was a man wholly unused to command; he was an imprudent man, and was weak. He had compromised the crown by the easy terms on which he had rented and sold estates; he had been obliged, in order to maintain the revenue, to work the natives with more severity than ever. He knew very well that the system, under which he was working could not last long. One of his maxims was, "Do the best with your time," and he was constantly sacrificing future advantages for such present results as he could achieve.

The Indians, who had been treated badly enough before, were worse treated now. And during his short administration, if it may be called an administration,—during the time when he was nominally at the head of affairs—he was reducing the island to lower and lower depths. He did succeed in obtaining a large product of gold, but the abuses of his government were not atoned for by such remittances. Worst of all, the wrongs of the natives touched the sensitiveness of Isabella, and she was eager that his successor should be appointed, and should sail, to put an end to these calamities.

The preparations which were made for Ovando's expedition, for the recall of Bobadilla, and for a reform, if it were possible, in the administration of the colony, all set back any preparations for a new expedition of discovery on the part of Columbus. He was not forgotten; his accounts were to be examined and any deficiencies made up to him; he was to receive the arrears of his revenue; he was permitted to have an agent who should see that he received his share in future. To this agency he appointed Alonzo Sanchez de Carvajal, and the sovereigns gave orders that this agent should be treated with respect.

Other preparations were made, so that Ovando might arrive with a strong reinforcement for the colony. He sailed with thirty ships, the size of these vessels ranging from one hundred and fifty Spanish *toneles* to one bark of twenty-five. It will be remembered that the Spanish *tonele* is larger by about ten per cent than our English ton. Twenty-five hundred persons embarked as colonists in the vessels, and, for the first time, men took their families with them.

Everything was done to give dignity to the appointment of Ovando, and it was hoped that by sending out families of respectable character, who were to be distributed in four towns, there might be a better basis given to the settlement. This measure had been insisted upon by Columbus.

This fleet put to sea on the thirteenth of February, 1502. It met, at the very outset, a terrible storm, and one hundred and twenty of the passengers were lost by the foundering of a ship. The impression was at first given in Spain that the whole fleet had been lost;

but this proved to be a mistake. The others assembled at the Canaries, and arrived in San Domingo on the fifteenth of April.

Columbus himself never lost confidence in his own star. He was sure that he was divinely sent, and that his mission was to open the way to the Indies, for the religious advancement of mankind. If Vasco de Gama had discovered a shorter way than men knew before, Christopher Columbus should discover one shorter still, and this discovery should tend to the glory of God. It seemed to him that the simplest way in which he could make men understand this, was to show that the Holy Sepulchre might, now and thus, be recovered from the infidel.

Far from urging geographical curiosity as an object, he proposed rather the recovery of the Holy Sepulchre. That is, there was to be a new and last crusade, and the money for this enterprise was to be furnished from the gold of the farthest East. He was close at the door of this farthest East; and as has been said, he believed that Cuba was the Ophir of Solomon, and he supposed, that a very little farther voyaging would open all the treasures which Marco Polo had described, and would bring the territory, which had made the Great Khan so rich, into the possession of the king of Spain.

He showed to Ferdinand and Isabella that, if they would once more let him go forward, on the adventure which had been checked untimely by the cruelty of Bobadilla, this time they would have wealth which would place them at the head of the Christian sovereigns of the world.

While he was inactive at Seville, and the great squadron was being prepared which Ovando was to command, he wrote what is known as the "Book of Prophecies,"[35] in which he attempted to convince the Catholic kings of the necessity of carrying forward the enterprise which he proposed. He urged haste, because he believed the world was only to last a hundred and fifty-five years longer; and, with so much before them to be done, it was necessary that they should begin.

He remembered an old vow that he had undertaken, that, within seven years of the time of his discovery, he would furnish fifty thousand foot soldiers and five thousand horsemen for the recovery of the Holy Sepulchre. He now arranged in order prophecies from the Holy Scripture, passages from the writings of the Fathers, and whatever else suggested itself, mystical and hopeful, as to the success of an enterprise by which the new world could be used for the conversion of the Gentiles and for the improvement of the Christianity of the old world.

He had the assistance of a Carthusian monk, who seems to have been skilled in literary work, and the two arranged these passages in order, illustrated them with poetry, and collected them into a manuscript volume which was sent to the sovereigns.

Columbus accompanied the Book of Prophecies with one of his own long letters, written with the utmost fervor. In this letter he begins, as Peter the Hermit might do, by urging the sovereigns to set on foot a crusade. If they are tempted to consider his advice extravagant, he asks them how his first

---

[35] *Book of Prophecies* by Christopher Columbus.

scheme of discovery was treated. He shows that, as heaven had chosen him to discover the new world, heaven has also chosen him to discover the Holy Sepulchre. God himself had opened his eyes that he might make the great discovery, which has reflected such honor upon them and theirs.

"If his hopes had been answered," says a Catholic writer, "the modern question of holy places, which is the Gordian knot of the religious politics of the future, would have been solved long ago by the gold of the new world, or would have been cut by the sword of its discoverer. We should not have seen nations which are separated from the Roman communion, both Protestant and Pantheistic governments, coming audaciously into contest for privileges, which, by the rights of old possession, by the rights of martyrdom and chivalry, belong to the Holy Catholic Church, the Apostolic Church, the Roman Church, and after her to France, her oldest daughter."

Columbus now supposed that the share of the western wealth which would belong to him would be sufficient for him to equip and arm a hundred thousand infantry and ten thousand horsemen.

At the moment when the Christian hero made this pious calculation he had not enough of this revenue with which "to buy a cloak," This is the remark of the enthusiastic biographer from whom we have already quoted.

It is not literally true, but it is true that Columbus was living in the most modest way at the time when he was pressing his ambitious schemes upon the court. At the same time, he wrote a poem with which he undertook to press the same great enterprise upon his readers. It was called "The End of Man," *"Memorare novissima tua, et non peccabis in eternum."*[36]

In his letter to the king and queen he says, "Animated as by a heavenly fire, I came to your Highnesses; all who heard of my enterprise mocked it; all the sciences I had acquired profited me as nothing; seven years did I pass in your royal court, disputing the case with persons of great authority and learned in all the arts, and in the end they decided that all was vain. In your Highnesses alone remained faith and constancy. Who will doubt that this light was from the Holy Scriptures, illumining you, as well as myself, with rays of marvellous brightness."

It is probable that the king and queen were, to a certain extent, influenced by his enthusiasm. It is certain that they knew that something was due to their reputation and to his success. By whatever motive led, they encouraged him with hopes that he might be sent forward again, this time, not as commander of a colony, but as a discoverer. Discovery was indeed the business which he understood, and to which alone he should ever have been commissioned.

It is to be remembered that the language of crusaders was not then a matter of antiquity, and was not used as if it alluded to bygone affairs. It was but a few years since the Saracens had been driven out of Spain, and all men regarded them as being the enemies of Christianity and of Europe, who could not be neglected. More than this, Spain was beginning to

---

[36] Ecclesiasticus 7:40, Latin Vulgate

receive very large and important revenues from the islands.

It is said that the annual revenues from Hispaniola already amounted to twelve millions of our dollars.[37] It was not unnatural that the king and queen, willing to throw off the disgrace which they had incurred from Bobadilla's cruelty, should not only send Ovando to replace him, but should, though in an humble fashion, give to Columbus an opportunity to show that his plans were not chimerical.

---

[37] 1892

Chapter XII: Fourth Voyage

It seems a pity now that, after his third voyage, Columbus did not remain in Spain and enjoy, as an old man could, the honors which he had earned and the respect which now waited upon him. Had this been so, the world would have been spared the mortification which attends the thought that the old man to whom it owes so much suffered almost everything in one last effort, failed in that effort, and died with the mortification of failure. But it is to be remembered that Columbus was not a man to cultivate the love of leisure. He had no love of leisure to cultivate. His life had been an active one. He had attempted the solution of a certain problem which he had not solved, and every day of leisure, even every occasion of effort and every word of flattery, must have quickened in him new wishes to take the prize which seemed so near, and to achieve the possibility which had thus far eluded him.

From time to time, therefore, he had addressed new memorials to the sovereigns proposing a new expedition; and at last, by an instruction which is dated on the fourteenth of March, in the year 1502, a fourth voyage was set on foot at the charge of the king and queen,—an instruction not to stop at Hispaniola, but, for the saving of time, to pass by that island. This is a graceful way of intimating to him that he is not to mix himself up with the rights and wrongs of the new settlement.

The letter goes on to say, that the sovereigns have communicated with the King of Portugal, and that they have explained to him that Columbus is pressing his discoveries at the west and will not interfere with those of the Portuguese in the east. He is instructed to regard the Portuguese explorers as his friends, and to make no quarrel with them. He is instructed to take with him his sons, Fernando and Diego. This is probably at his request.

The prime object of the instruction is still to strike the mainland of the Indies. All the instructions are, "You will make a direct voyage, if the weather does not prevent you, for discovering the islands and the mainland of the Indies in that part which belongs to us." He is to take possession of these islands and of this mainland, and to inform the sovereigns in regard to his discoveries, and the experience of former voyages has taught them that great care must be taken to avoid private speculation in "gold, silver, pearls, precious stones, spices and other things of different quality." For this purpose special instructions are given.

Of this voyage we have Columbus's own official account.[38]

There were four vessels, three of which were rated as caravels. The fourth was very small. The chief vessel was commanded by Diego Tristan; the second, the *Santiago,* by Francisco de Porras; the third, the *Viscaina* (Biscayan), by Bartholomew de Fiesco; and

---

[38] *See Book II of this edition, p. 551.*

the little *Gallician* by Pedro de Torreros. None of these vessels, as the reader will see, was ever to return to Spain. From de Porras and his brother, Columbus and the expedition were to receive disastrous blows.

It must be observed that he is once more in his proper position of a discoverer. He has no government or other charge of colonies entrusted to him. His brother Bartholomew and his youngest son Fernando, sail with him.

The little squadron sailed from the bay of Cadiz on the eleventh of May, 1502. They touched at Sicilla,— a little port on the coast of Morocco,—to relieve its people, a Portuguese garrison, who had been besieged by the Moors. But finding them out of danger, Columbus went at once to the Grand Canary island, and had a favorable passage.

From the Grand Canary to the island which he calls "the first island of the Indies," and which he named Martinino, his voyage was only seventeen days long. This island was either the St. Lucia or the Martinique of today. Hence he passed to Dominica, and thence crossed to San Domingo, to make repairs, as he said. For, as has been said, he had been especially ordered not to interfere in the affairs of the settlement.

He did not disobey his orders. He says distinctly that he intended to pass along the southern shore of San Domingo, and thence take a departure for the continent. But he says, that his principal vessel sailed very ill—could not carry much canvas, and delayed the rest of the squadron. This weakness must have increased after the voyage across the ocean. For this reason he hoped to exchange it for another ship at San Domingo.

But he did not enter the harbor. He sent a letter to Ovando, now the governor, and asked his permission. He added, to the request he made, a statement that a tempest was at hand which he did not like to meet in the offing. Ovando, however, refused any permission to enter. He was, in fact, just dispatching a fleet to Spain, with Bobadilla, Columbus's old enemy, whom Ovando had replaced in his turn.

Columbus, in an eager wish to be of use, by a returning messenger begged Ovando to delay this fleet till the gale had passed. But the seamen ridiculed him and his gale, and begged Ovando to send the fleet home.

He did so. Bobadilla and his fleet put to sea. In ten days a West India hurricane struck them. The ship on which Columbus's enemies, Bobadilla and Roldan, sailed, was sunk with them and the gold accumulated for years. Of the whole fleet, only one vessel, called the weakest of all, reached Spain. This ship carried four thousand pieces of gold, which were the property of the Admiral. Columbus's own little squadron, meanwhile—thanks probably to the seamanship of himself and his brother—weathered the storm, and he found refuge in the harbor which he had himself named "the beautiful," El Hermoso, in the western part of San Domingo.

Another storm delayed him at a port which he called Port Brasil. The word Brasil was the name which the Spaniards gave to the red log-wood, so valuable in dyeing, and various places received that name, where this wood was found. The name is derived from "Brasas,"—coals,—in allusion, probably, to the bright red color of the dye.

Sailing from this place, on Saturday, the sixteenth of June, they made sight of the island of Jamaica, but he pressed on without making any examination of the country, for four days sailing west and south-west. He then changed his course, and sailed for two days to the northwest and again two days to the north.

On Sunday, the twenty fourth of July, they saw land. This was the key now known as Cuyago, and they were at last close upon the mainland. After exploring this island they sailed again on Wednesday, the twenty-seventh, southwest and quarter southwest about ninety miles, and again they saw land, which is supposed to be the island of Guanaja or Bonacca, near the coast of Honduras.

The Indians on this island had some gold and some pearls. They had seen whites before. Columbus calls them men of good stature. Sailing from this island, he struck the mainland near Truxillo, about ten leagues from the island of Guanaja. He soon found the harbor, which we still know as the harbor of Truxillo, and from this point Columbus began a careful investigation of the coast.

He observed, what all navigators have since observed, the lack of harbors. He passed along as far as the river now known as the Tinto, where he took possession in the name of the sovereigns, calling this river the River of Possession. He found the natives savage, and the country of little account for his purposes. Still passing southward, he passed what we call the Mosquito Coast, to which he found the natives gave the name of Cariay.

These people were well disposed and willing to treat with them. They had some cotton, they had some gold. They wore very little clothing, and they painted their bodies, as most of the natives of the islands had done. He saw what he thought to be pigs and large mountain cats.

Still passing southward, running into such bays or other harbors as they found, he entered the "Admiral's Bay," in a country which had the name of Cerabaro, or Zerabora. Here an Indian brought a plate of gold and some other pieces of gold, and Columbus was encouraged in his hopes of finding more.

The natives told him that if he would keep on he would find another bay which they called Arburarno, which is supposed to be the Laguna Chiriqui. They said the people, of that country, lived in the mountains. Here Columbus noticed the fact,—one which has given to philologists one of their central difficulties for four hundred years since,—that as he passed from one point to another of the American shores, the Indians did not understand each other's language. "Every ten or twenty leagues they did not understand each other." In entering the river Veragua, the Indians appeared armed with lances and arrows, some of them having gold also. Here, also, the people did not live upon the shore, but two or three leagues back in the interior, and they only came to the sea by their canoes upon the rivers.

The next province was then called Cobraba, but Columbus made no landing for want of a proper harbor. All his courses since he struck the continent had been in a southeasterly direction. That an expedition for westward discovery should be sailing eastward, seemed in itself a contradiction. What irritated the crews still more was, that the wind seemed always against them.

From the second to the ninth of November, 1502, the little fleet lay at anchor in the spacious harbor, which he called Puerto Bello, "the beautiful harbor." It is still known by that name. A considerable Spanish city grew up there, which became well known to the world in the last century by the attack upon it by the English in the years 1739 and 1742.

The formation of the coast compelled them to pass eastward as they went on. But the currents of the Gulf flow in the opposite direction. Here there were steady winds from the east and the northeast. The ships were pierced by the *teredo*,[39] which eats through thick timbers, and is so destructive that the seamen of later times have learned to sheath the hulls of their vessels with copper.

The seamen thought that they were under the malign influence of some adverse spell. And after a month Columbus gave way to their remonstrances, and abandoned his search for a channel to India. He was the more ready to do this because he was satisfied that the land by which he lay was connected with the coast which other Spaniards had already discovered. He therefore sailed westward again, retracing his course to explore the gold mines of Veragua.

But the winds could change as quickly as his purposes, and now for nearly a fortnight they had to

---

[39] A ship-worm.

fight a tropical tempest. At one moment they met with a water-spout, which seemed to advance to them directly. The sailors, despairing of human help, shouted passages from St. John, and to their efficacy ascribed their escape. It was not until the seventeenth that they found themselves safely in harbor. He gave to the whole coast the name of "the coast of contrasts," to preserve the memory of his disappointments.

The natives proved friendly, as he had found them before; but they told him that he would find no more gold upon the coast; that the mines were in the country of the Veragua. It was, on the tenth day of January that, after some delay, Columbus entered again the river of that name.

The people told him where he should find the mines, and were all ready to send guides with his own people to point them out. He gave to this river, the name of the River of Belen, and to the port in which he anchored he gave the name of Santa Maria de Belen, or Bethlehem.

His men discovered the mines, so called, at a distance of eight leagues from the port. The country between was difficult, being mountainous and crossed by many streams. They were obliged to pass the river of Veragua thirty-nine times. The Indians themselves were dexterous in taking out gold. Columbus added to their number seventy-five men.

In one day's work, they obtained "two or three *castellianos*" without much difficulty. A *castelliano* was a gold coin of the time, and the meaning of the text is probably that each man obtained this amount.

It was one of the "placers," such as have since proved so productive in different parts of the world.

Columbus satisfied himself that there was a much larger population inland. He learned from the Indians that the cacique, as he always calls the chief of these tribes, was a most important monarch in that region. His houses were larger than others, built handsomely of wood, covered with palm leaves.

The product of all the gold collected thus far is stated precisely in the official register. There were two hundred and twenty pieces of gold, large and small. Altogether they weighed seventy-two ounces, seven-eighths of an ounce and one grain. Besides these were twelve pieces, great and small, of an inferior grade of gold, which weighed fourteen ounces, three-eighths of an ounce, and six *tomienes*, a *tomiene* weighing one-third part of our drachm. In round numbers then, we will say that the result in gold of this cruising would be now worth $1,500.

Columbus collected gold in this way, to make his expedition popular at home, and he had, indeed, mortgaged the voyage, so to speak, by pledging the pecuniary results, as a fund to bear the expense of a new crusade. But, for himself, the prime desire was always discovery.

Eventually the Spaniards spent two months in that region, pressing their explorations in search of gold. And so promising did the tokens seem to him, that he determined to leave his brother, to secure the country and work the mines, while he should return to Spain, with the gold he had collected, and obtain reinforcements and supplies. But all these fond hopes were disappointed.

The natives, under a leader named Quibian, rallied in large numbers, probably intending to drive the colonists away. It was only by the boldest measures that their plans were met. When Columbus supposed that he had suppressed their enterprise, he took leave of his brother, as he had intended, leaving him but one of the four vessels.

Fortunately, as it proved, the wind did not serve. He sent back a boat to communicate with the settlement, but it fell into the hands of the savages. Doubtful as to the issue, a seaman, named Ledesma, volunteered to swim through the surf, and communicate with the settlement. The brave fellow succeeded. By passing through the surf again, he brought back the news that the little colony was closely besieged by the savages.

It seemed clear that the settlement must be abandoned, that Columbus's brother and his people must be taken back to Spain. This course was adopted. With infinite difficulty, the guns and stores which had been left with the colony were embarked on the vessels of the Admiral. The caravel which had been left for the colony could not be taken from the river. She was completely dismantled, and was left as the only memorial of this unfortunate colony.

At Puerto Bello he was obliged to leave another vessel, for she had been riddled by the teredo. The two which he had were in wretched condition. "They were as full of holes as a honey-comb." On the southern coast of Cuba, Columbus was obliged to supply them with cassava bread. The leaks increased. The ships' pumps were insufficient, and the men bailed out the water with buckets and kettles. On the twentieth of June, they were thankful to put into a harbor, called Puerto Bueno, on the coast of Jamaica, where, as it proved, they eventually left their worthless vessels, and where they were in exile from the world of civilization for twelve months.

Nothing in history is more pathetic than the memory that such a waste of a year, in the closing life of such a man as Columbus, should have been permitted by the jealousy, the cruelty, or the selfish ambition of inferior men.

He was not far from the colony at San Domingo. As the reader will see, he was able to send a message to his countrymen there. But those countrymen left him to take his chances against a strong tribe of savages. Indeed, they would not have been sorry to know that he was dead.

At first, however, he and his men welcomed the refuge of the harbor. It was the port which he had called Santa Gloria, on his first visit there. He was at once surrounded by Indians, ready to barter with them and bring them provisions. The poor Spaniards were hungry enough to be glad of this relief.

Mendez, a spirited sailor, had the oversight of this trade, and in one negotiation, at some distance from the vessels, he bought a good canoe of a friendly chief. For this he gave a brass basin, one of his two shirts, and a short jacket. On this canoe turned their after fortunes. Columbus refitted her, put on a false keel, furnished her with a mast and sail.

With six Indians, whom the chief had lent him, Diego Mendez, accompanied by only one Spanish companion, set sail in this little craft for San Domingo. Columbus sent by them a letter to the sovereigns, which gives the account of the voyage which the reader has been following.

When Mendez was a hundred miles advanced on his journey, he met a band of hostile savages. They had affected friendship until they had the adventurers in their power, when they seized them all. But while the savages were quarreling about the spoils, Mendez succeeded in escaping to his canoe, and returned alone to his master after fifteen days.

It was determined that the voyage should be renewed. But this time, another canoe was sent with that under the command of Mendez. He sailed again, storing his boats with cassava bread and calabashes of water. Bartholomew Columbus, with his armed band, marched along the coast, as the two canoes sailed along the shore.

Waiting then for a clear day, Mendez struck northward, on the passage, which was long for such frail craft, to San Domingo. It was eight months before Columbus heard of them. Of those eight months, the history is of dismal waiting, mutiny and civil war. It is pathetic, indeed, that a little body of men, who had been, once and again, saved from death in the most remarkable way, could not live on a fertile island, in a beautiful climate, without quarrelling with each other.

Two officers of Columbus, Porras and his brother, led the sedition. They told the rest of the crew that the Admiral's hope of relief from Mendez was a mere delusion. They said that he was an exile from Spain, and that he did not dare return to Hispaniola. In such ways they sought to rouse his people against him and his brother. As for Columbus, he was sick on board his vessel, while the two brothers Porras were working against him among his men.

On the second of January, 1504, Francesco de Porras broke into the cabin. He complained bitterly that they were kept to die in that desolate place, and accused the Admiral as if it were his fault. He told Columbus, that they had determined to go back to Spain; and then, lifting his voice, he shouted, "I am for Castile; who will follow me?" The mutinous crew instantly replied that they would do so. Voices were heard which threatened Columbus's life.

His brother, the Adelantado, persuaded Columbus to retire from the crowd and himself assumed the whole weight of the assault. The loyal part of the crew, however, persuaded him to put down his weapon, and on the other hand, entreated Porras and his companions to depart. It was clear enough that they had the power, and they tried to carry out their plans.

They embarked in ten canoes, and thus the Admiral was abandoned by forty-eight of his men. They followed, to the eastward, the route which Mendez had taken. In their lawless way they robbed the Indians of their provisions and of anything else that they needed. As Mendez had done, they waited at the eastern extremity of Jamaica for calm weather. They knew they could not manage the canoes, and they had several Indians to help them.

When the sea was smooth they started; but they had hardly gone four leagues from the land, when the waves began to rise under a contrary wind. Immediately they turned for shore, the canoes were overfreighted, and as the sea rose, frequently shipped water.

The frightened Spaniards threw overboard everything they could spare, retaining their arms only, and a part of their provisions. They even compelled the Indians to leap into the sea to lighten the boats, but, though they were skillful swimmers, they could not pretend to make land by swimming. They kept to the canoes, therefore, and would occasionally seize them to recover breath. The cruel Spaniards cut off their hands and stabbed them with their swords. Thus eighteen of their Indian comrades died, and they had none left, but such as were of most help in managing the canoes. Once on land, they doubted whether to make another effort or to return to Columbus.

Eventually they waited a month, for another opportunity to go to Hispaniola; but this failed as before, and losing all patience, they returned westward, to the commander whom they had insulted, living on the island "by fair means or foul," according as they found the natives friendly or unfriendly.

Columbus, meanwhile, with his half the crew, was waiting. He had established as good order as he could between his men and the natives, but he was obliged to keep a strict watch over such European food as he still had, knowing how necessary it was for the sick men in his number. On the other hand, the Indians, wholly unused to regular work, found it difficult to supply the food which so many men demanded.

The supplies fell off from day to day; the natives no longer pressed down to the harbor; the trinkets, with which food had been bought, had lost their charm; the Spaniards began to fear that they should starve on the shore of an island which, when Columbus discovered it, appeared to be the abode of plenty. It was at this juncture, when the natives were becoming more and more unfriendly, that Columbus justified himself by the tyrant's plea of necessity, and made use of his astronomical science, to obtain a supernatural power over his unfriendly allies.

He sent his interpreter to summon the principal caciques to a conference. For this conference he appointed a day when he knew that a total eclipse of the moon would take place. The chiefs met as they were requested. He told them that he and his followers worshipped a God who lived in the heavens; that that God favored such as did well, but punished all who displeased him.

He asked them to remember how this God had protected Mendez and his companions in their voyage, because they went obedient to the orders which had been given them by their chief. He asked them to remember that the same God had punished Porras and his companions with all sorts of affliction, because they were rebels. He said that now this great God was angry with the Indians, because they refused to furnish food to his faithful worshippers; that he proposed to chastise them with famine and pestilence.

He said that, lest they should disbelieve the warning which he gave, a sign would be given, in the heavens that night, of the anger of the great God. They would see that the moon would change its color and would lose its light. They might take this as a token of the punishment which awaited them.

The Indians had not that confidence in Columbus which they once had. Some derided what he said, some were alarmed, all waited with anxiety and curiosity. When the night came they saw a dark shadow begin to steal over the moon. As the eclipse went forward, their fears increased. At last the mysterious darkness covered the face of the sky and of the world, when they knew that they had a right to expect the glory of the full moon.

There were then no bounds to their terror. They, seized on all the provisions that they had, they rushed to the ships, they threw themselves at the feet of Columbus and begged him to intercede with his God, to withhold the calamity which he had threatened. Columbus would not receive them; he shut himself up in his cabin and remained there while the eclipse increased, hearing from within, as the narrator says, the howls and prayers of the savages.

It was not until he knew the eclipse was about to diminish, that he condescended to come forth, and told them that he had interceded with God, who would pardon them if they would fulfil their promises. In token of pardon, the darkness would be withdrawn from the moon.

The Indians saw the fulfilment of the promise, as they had seen the fulfilment of the threat. The moon reappeared in its brilliancy. They thanked the Admiral eagerly for his intercession, and repaired to their homes. From this time forward, having proved that he knew on earth what was passing in the heavens, they propitiated him with their gifts. The supplies came in regularly, and from this time there was no longer any want of provisions.

But no tales of eclipses would keep the Spaniards quiet. Another conspiracy was formed, as the eight remaining months of exile passed by, among the survivors. They meant to seize the remaining canoes, and with them make their way to Hispaniola. But, at the very point of the outbreak of the new mutiny, a sail was seen standing toward the harbor.

The Spaniards could see that the vessel was small. She kept the offing, but sent a boat on shore. As the boat drew near, those who waited so eagerly recognized Escobar, who had been condemned to death, in Isabella, when Columbus was in administration, and was pardoned by his successor Bobadilla. To see this man approaching for their relief was not hopeful, though he were called a Christian, and was a countryman of their own.

Escobar drew up to the ships, on which the Spaniards still lived, and gave them a letter from Ovando, the new governor of Hispaniola, with some bacon and a barrel of wine, which were sent as presents to the Admiral. He told Columbus, in a private interview, that the governor had sent him to express his concern at his misfortune, and his regret that he had not a vessel of sufficient size to bring off all the people, but that he would send one as soon as possible. He assured him that his concerns in Hispaniola were attended to faithfully in his absence; he asked him to write to the governor in reply, as he wished to return at once.

This was but scant comfort for men who had been eight months waiting to be relieved. But Escobar was master of the position. Columbus wrote a reply at once to Ovando, pointed out that the difficulties of his situation had been increased by the rebellion of the brothers Porras. He, however, expressed his reliance on his promise, and said he would remain patiently on his ships until relief came. Escobar took the letter, returned to his vessel, and she made sail at once, leaving the starving Spaniards in dismay, to the same fate which hung over them before.

Columbus tried to reassure them. He professed himself satisfied with the communications from Ovando, and told them that vessels large enough for them would soon arrive. He said that they could see that he believed this, because he had not himself taken passage with Escobar, preferring to share their lot with them. He had sent back the little vessel at once, so that no time might be lost in sending the necessary ships.

With these assurances he cheered their hearts. In truth, however, he was very indignant at Ovando's cool behavior. That he should have left them for months in danger and uncertainty, with a mere tantalizing message and a scanty present of food—all this naturally made the great leader indignant. He believed that Ovando hoped that he might perish on the island.

He supposed that Ovando thought that this would be favorable for his own political prospects, and he believed that Escobar was sent merely as a spy. This same impression is given by Las Casas, the historian, who was then at San Domingo. He says that Escobar was chosen simply because of his enmity to Columbus, and that he was ordered not to land, nor to hold conversation with any of the crew, nor to receive letters from any except the Admiral.

After Escobar's departure, Columbus sent an embassy on shore to communicate with the rebel party, who were living on the island. He offered to them free pardon, kind treatment, and a passage with him in the ships which he expected from Ovando, and, as a token of good will, he sent them a part of the bacon which Escobar had brought them.

Francesco de Porras met these ambassadors, and replied that they had no wish to return to the ships, but preferred living at large. They offered to engage that they would be peaceable, if the Admiral would promise them solemnly, that, in case two vessels arrived, they should have one to depart in; that if only one vessel arrived they should have half of it, and that the Admiral would now share with them the stores and articles of traffic, which he had left in the ship. But these demands Columbus refused to accept.

Porras had spoken for the rebels, but they were not so well satisfied with the answer. The incident gave occasion for what was almost an outbreak among them. Porras attempted to hold them in hand, by assuring them that there had been no real arrival of Escobar. He told them that there had been no vessel in port; that what had been seen was a mere phantasm conjured up by Columbus, who was deeply versed in necromancy.

He reminded them that the vessel arrived just in the edge of the evening; that it communicated with Columbus only, and then disappeared in the night.

Had it been a real vessel would he not have embarked, with his brother and his son? Was it not clear that it was only a phantom, which appeared for a moment and then vanished?

Not satisfied, however, with his control over his men, he marched them to a point near the ships, hoping to plunder the stores and to take the Admiral prisoner. Columbus, however, had notice of the approach of this marauding party, and his brother and fifty followers, of whose loyalty he was sure, armed themselves and marched to meet them. The Adelantado again sent ambassadors, the same whom he had sent before with the offer of pardon, but Porras and his companions would not permit them to approach.

They determined to offer battle to the fifty loyal men, thinking to attack and kill the Adelantado himself. They rushed upon him and his party, but at the first shock four or five of them were killed.

The Adelantado, with his own hand, killed Sanchez, one of the most powerful men among the rebels. Porras attacked him in turn, and with his sword cut his buckler and wounded his hand. The sword, however, was wedged in the shield, and before Porras could withdraw it, the Adelantado closed upon him and made him prisoner. When the rebels saw this result of the conflict, they fled in confusion.

The Indians, meanwhile, amazed at this conflict among men who had descended from heaven, gazed with wonder at the battle. When it was over, they approached the field, and looked with amazement on the dead bodies of the beings whom they had thought immortal. It is said, however, that at the mere sound of a groan from one of the wounded they fled in dismay.

The Adelantado returned in triumph to the ships. He brought with him his prisoners. Only two of his party had been wounded, himself and his steward. The next day the remaining fugitives sent in a petition to the Admiral, confessing their misdeeds and asking for pardon.

He saw that their union was broken; he granted their prayer, on the single condition that Francesco de Porras should remain a prisoner. He did not receive them on board the ships, but put them under the command of a loyal officer, to whom he gave a sufficient number of articles for trade, to purchase food of the natives.

This battle, for it was such, was the last critical incident in the long exile of the Spaniards, for, after a year of hope and fear, two vessels were seen standing into the harbor. One of them was a ship equipped, at Columbus's own expense, by the faithful Mendez; the other had been fitted out afterwards by Ovando, but had sailed in company with the first vessel of relief.

It would seem that the little public of Isabella had been made indignant by Ovando's neglect, and that he had been compelled, by public opinion to send another vessel as a companion to that sent by Mendez. Mendez himself, having seen the ships depart, went to Spain in the interest of the Admiral.

With the arrival at Puerto Bueno, in Jamaica, of the two relief vessels, Columbus's chief sufferings and anxiety were over. The responsibility, at least, was in other hands. But the passage to San Domingo consumed six tedious weeks. When he arrived, however, it was to meet one of his triumphs. He could hardly have expected it.

But his sufferings, and the sense of wrong that he had suffered, had, in truth, awakened the regard of the people of the colony. Ovando took him as a guest to his house. The people received him with distinction.

He found little to gratify him, however. Ovando, had ruled the poor natives with a rod of iron, and they were wretched. Columbus's own affairs had been neglected, and he could gain no relief from the governor. He spent only a month on the island, trying, as best he could, to bring some order into the administration of his own property; and then, on the twelfth of September, 1504, sailed for Spain.

Scarcely had the ship left harbor when she was dismasted in a squall. He was obliged to cross to another ship, under command of his brother, the Adelantado. She also was unfortunate. Her mainmast was sprung in a storm, and she could not go on until the mast was shortened.

In another gale the foremast was sprung, and it was only on the seventh of November that the shattered and storm-pursued vessel arrived at San Lucar. Columbus himself had been suffering, through the voyage, from gout and his other maladies. The voyage was, indeed, a harsh experience for a sick man, almost seventy years old.

He went at once to Seville, to find such rest as he might, for body and mind.

Chapter XIII: Two Sad Years

Columbus had been absent from Spain two years and six months. He returned broken in health, and the remaining two years of his life are only the sad history of his effort to relieve his name from dishonor and to leave to his sons a fair opportunity to carry forward his work in the world.

Isabella, alas, died on the twenty-sixth day of November, only a short time after his arrival. Ferdinand, at the least, was cold and hard toward him, and Ferdinand was now engaged in many affairs other than those of discovery. He was satisfied that Columbus did not know how to bring gold home from the colonies, and the promises of the last voyage, that they should strike the East, had not been fulfilled.

Isabella had testified her kindly memory of Columbus, even while he was in exile at Jamaica, by making him one of the body-guard of her oldest son, an honorary appointment which carried with it a handsome annual salary. After the return to Spain of Diego Mendez, the loyal friend who had cared for his interests so well in San Domingo, she had raised him to noble rank.

It is clear, therefore, that among her last thoughts came in the wish to do justice to him whom she had served so well. She had well done her duty which had been given her to do. She had never forgotten the new world to which it was her good fortune to send the discoverer, and in her death that discoverer lost his best friend.

On his arrival in Seville, where one might say he had a right to rest himself and do nothing else, Columbus engaged at once in efforts to see that the seamen who had accompanied him in this last adventure should be properly paid. Many of these men had been disloyal to him and unfaithful to their sovereign, but Columbus, with his own magnanimity, represented eagerly at court that they had endured great peril, that they brought great news, and that the king ought to repay them all that they had earned.

He says, in a letter to his son written at this period, "I have not a roof over my head in Castile. I have no place to eat nor to sleep excepting a tavern, and there I am often too poor to pay my scot." This passage has been quoted as if he were living as a beggar at this time, and the world has been asked to believe that a man who had a tenth of the revenue of the Indies due to him in some fashion, was actually living from hand to mouth from day to day. But this is a mere absurdity of exaggeration.

Undoubtedly, he was frequently pressed for ready money. He says to his son, in another letter, "I only live by borrowing." Still he had good credit with the Genoese bankers established in Andalusia. In writing to his son he begs him to economize, but at the same time he acknowledges the receipt of bills of exchange and considerable sums of money.

In the month of December, there is a single transaction in Hispaniola which amounts to five thousand dollars of our money. We must not, therefore, take literally his statement that he was too poor to pay for a night's lodging. On the other hand, it is observed in the correspondence that, on the fifteenth of April, 1505, the king ordered that everything which belonged to Columbus on account of his ten per cent should be carried to the royal treasury as a security for certain debts contracted by the Admiral.

The king had also given an order to the royal agent in Hispaniola that everything which he owned there should be sold. All these details have been carefully brought together by Mr. Harrisse, who says truly that we cannot understand the last order.

When at last the official proceedings relating to the affairs in Jamaica arrived in Europe, Columbus made an effort to go to court. A litter was provided for him, and all the preparations for his journey made. But he was obliged once more by his weakness to give up this plan, and he could only write letters pressing his claim. Of such letters the misfortune is, that the longer they are, and the more of the detail they give, the less likely are they to be read. Columbus could only write at night; in the daytime he could not use his hands.

He took care to show Ferdinand that his interests had not been properly attended to in the islands. He said that Ovando had been careless as to the king's service, and he was not unwilling to let it be understood that his own administration had been based on a more intelligent policy than that of either of the men who followed him.

But he was now an old man. He was unable to go to court in person. He had not succeeded in that which he had sailed for—a strait opening to the Southern Sea. He had discovered new gold mines on the continent, but he had brought home but little treasure. His answers from the court seemed to him formal and unsatisfactory. At court, the stories of the Porras brothers were told on the one side, while Diego Mendez and Carvajal represented Columbus.

In this period of the fading life of Columbus, we have eleven letters addressed by him to his son. These show that he was in Seville as late as February, 1505. From the authority of Las Casas, we know that he left that part of Spain to go to Segovia in the next May, and from that place he followed the court to Salamanca and Valladolid, although he was so weak and ill.

He was received, as he had always been, with professions of kindness; but nothing followed important enough to show that there was anything genuine in this cordiality. After a few days Columbus begged that some action might be taken to indemnify him for his losses, and to confirm the promises which had been made to him before. The king replied that he was willing to refer all points which had been discussed between them to an arbitration. Columbus assented, and proposed the Archbishop Diego de Deza as an arbiter.

The reader must remember that it was he who had assisted Columbus in early days when the inquiry was made at Salamanca. The king assented to the arbitration, but proposed that it should include questions which Columbus would not consider as doubtful. One of these was his restoration to his office of viceroy.

Now on the subject of his dignities Columbus was tenacious. He regarded everything else as unimportant in comparison. He would not admit that there was any question that he was the viceroy of the Indies, and all this discussion ended in the postponement of all consideration of his claims till, after his death, it was too late for them to be considered.

All the documents, when read with the interest which we take in his character and fortunes, are indeed pathetic; but they did not seem so to the king, if indeed they ever met his eye.

In despair of obtaining justice for himself, Columbus asked that his son Diego might be sent to Hispaniola in his place. The king would promise nothing, but seems to have attempted to make Columbus exchange the privileges which he enjoyed by the royal promise for a seignory in a little town in the kingdom of Leon, which is named not improperly "The Counts' Carrion."

It is interesting to see that one of the persons whom he employed, in pressing his claim at the court and in the management of his affairs, was Vespucci, the Florentine merchant, who in early life had been known as Alberigo, but had now taken the name of Americo.

The king was still engaged in the affairs of the islands. He appointed bishops to take charge of the churches in the colonies, but Columbus was not so much as consulted as to the persons who should be sent. When Philip arrived from Flanders, with his wife Juana, who was the heir of Isabella's fortunes and crown, Columbus wished to pay his court to them, but was too weak to do so in person.

There is a manly letter, written with dignity and pathos, in which he presses his claims upon them. He commissioned his brother, the Adelantado, to take this letter, and with it he went to wait upon the young couple. They received him most cordially, and gave flattering hopes that they would attend favorably to the suit. But this was too late for Columbus himself. Immediately after he had sent his brother away, his illness increased in violence.

The time for petitions and for answers to petitions had come to an end. His health failed steadily, and in the month of May he knew that he was approaching his death. The king and the court had gone to Villafranca de Valcacar.

On the nineteenth of May Columbus executed his will, which had been prepared at Segovia a year before. In this will he directs his son and his successors, acting as administrators, always to maintain "in the city of Genoa, some person of our line, who shall have a house and a wife in that place, who shall receive a sufficient income to live honorably, as being one of our relatives, having foot and root in the said city, as a native; since he will be able to receive from this city aid in favor of the things of his service; because from that city I came forth and in that city I was born." This clause became the subject of much litigation as the century went on.

Another clause which was much contested was his direction to his son Diego to take care of Beatriz Enriquez, the mother of Fernando. Diego is instructed to provide for her an honorable subsistence "as being a person to whom I have great obligation. What I do in this matter is to relieve my conscience, for this weighs much upon my mind. The reason of this cannot be written here."

The history of the litigation which followed upon this will and upon other documents which bear upon the fortunes of Columbus is curious, but scarcely interesting. The present representative of Columbus is Don Cristobal Colon de la Cerda, Duke of Veragua and of La Vega, a grandee of Spain of the first class, Marquis of Jamaica, Admiral and Seneschal Major of the Indies, who lives at Madrid.

Two days after the authentication of the will he died, on the twenty first of May, 1506, which was the day of Ascension. His last words were those of his Saviour, expressed in the language of the Latin Testament, "In manus tuas, Pater, commendo spiritum meum,"—"Father, into thy hands I commend my spirit." The absence of the court from Valladolid took with it, perhaps, the historians and annalists. For this or for some other reason, there is no mention whatever of Columbus's funeral in any of the documents of the time.

The body was laid in the convent of San Francisco at Valladolid. Such at least is the supposition of Navarrete, who has collected the original documents relating to Columbus.[40] He supposes that the funeral services were conducted in the church of the parish of Santa Maria de la Antigua. From the church of Saint Francis, not many months after, the body was removed to Seville. A new chapel had lately been built there, called Santa Maria de las Cuevas. In this chapel was the body of Columbus entombed. In a curious discussion of the subject, which has occupied much more space than it is worth, it is supposed that this was in the year 1513, but Mr. Harrisse has proved that this date is not accurate.

For at least twenty-eight years, the body was permitted to remain under the vaults of this chapel. Then a petition was sent to Charles V, for leave to carry the coffin and the body to San Domingo, that it might be buried in the larger chapel of the cathedral of that city. To this the emperor consented, in a decree signed June 2, 1537. It is not known how soon the removal to San Domingo was really made, but it took place before many years.

Mr. Harrisse quotes from a manuscript authority to show, that when William Penn besieged the city of San Domingo in 1655, all the bodies buried under the cathedral were withdrawn from view, lest the heretics should profane them, and that "the old Admiral's" body was treated like the rest.

Mr. Harrisse calls to mind the fact that the earthquake of the nineteenth of May, 1673,

---

[40] *Colección de los viages y descubrimientos que hicieron por mar los españoles desde fines del siglo XV" - Collection of the voyages and discoveries made by the Spaniards since the late 15th century (1825-1837)*

demolished the cathedral in part, and the tombs which it contained. He says, "the ruin of the colony, the climate, weather, and carelessness all contributed to the loss from sight and the forgetfulness of the bones of Columbus, mingled with the dust of his descendants"; and Mr. Harrisse does not believe that any vestige of them was ever found afterwards, in San Domingo or anywhere else. This remark, from the person who has given such large attention to the subject, is interesting. For it is generally stated and believed that the bones were afterwards removed to Havana in the island of Cuba. The opinion of Mr. Harrisse, as it has been quoted, is entitled to very great respect and authority.

A very curious question has arisen in later times as to the actual place where the remains now are. On this question there is great discussion among historians, and many reports, official and unofficial, have been published with regard to it.

In the year 1867, the proposal was made to the Holy Father at Rome, that Columbus should receive the honors known in the Roman Catholic Church as the honors of beatification. In 1877, De Lorgues,[41] the enthusiastic biographer of Columbus, represents that the inquiry had gone so far that these honors had been determined on. One who reads his book would be led to suppose that Columbus had already been recognized as on the way to be made a saint of the Church. But, in truth, though some such inquiry was

---

[41] *The life of Christopher Columbus. From authentic Spanish and Italian documents* by Roselly de Lorgues; 1870.

set on foot, he never received the formal honors of beatification.

We have one account by a contemporary of the appearance of Columbus.[42] We are told that he was a "robust man, quite tall, of florid complexion, with a long face."

In the next generation, Oviedo says Columbus was "of good aspect, and above the middle stature. His limbs were strong, his eyes quick, and all the parts of his body well proportioned. His hair was decidedly reddish, and the complexion of his face quite florid and marked with spots of red."

Bishop Las Casas knew the admiral personally, and describes him in these terms: "He was above the middle stature, his face was long and striking, his nose was aquiline, his eyes clear blue, his complexion light, tending towards a distinct florid expression, his beard and hair blonde in his youth, but they were blanched at an early age by care."

Las Casas says in another place, "he was rude in bearing, and careless as to his language. He was, however, gracious when he chose to be, but he was angry when he was annoyed."

Mr. Harrisse, who has collected these particulars from the different writers, says that this physical type may be frequently met now in the city and neighborhood of Genoa. He adds, "as for the portraits, whether painted, engraved, or in sculpture, which appear in collections, in private places, or as prints,

---

[42] In the first Decade of Peter Martyr.

there is not one which is authentic. They are all purely imaginary."

For the purpose of the illustration of this volume, we have used that which is best known, and for many reasons most interesting. It is preserved in the city of Florence, but neither the name of the artist nor the date of the picture is known. It is generally spoken of as the "Florentine portrait." The engraving follows an excellent copy, made by the order of Thomas Jefferson, and now in the possession of the Massachusetts Historical Society. We are indebted to the government of this society for permission to use it.[43]

A picture ascribed to Titian, and engraved and circulated by the geographer, Jomard, resembles closely the portraits of Philip III. The costume is one which Columbus never wore.

In his youth Columbus was affiliated with a religious brotherhood, that of Saint Catherine, in Genoa. In after times, on many occasions when it would have been supposed that he would be richly clothed, he appeared in a grave dress which recalled the recollections of the frock of the religious order of Saint Francis. According to Diego Columbus, he died, "dressed in the frock of this order, to which he had always been attached."

---

[43] The whole subject of the portraits of Columbus is carefully discussed in a learned paper presented to the Wisconsin Historical Society by Dr. James Davie Butler, and published in the Collections of that Society, Vol. IX, pp. 79-96.

The reader who has carefully followed the fortunes of the great discoverer understands from the history the character of the man. He would not have succeeded in his long suit at the court of Ferdinand and Isabella, had he not been a person of single purpose and iron will.

From the moment when he was in command of the first expedition, that expedition went prosperously to its great success, in precisely the way which he had foreseen and determined. True, he did not discover Asia, as he had hoped, but this was because America was in the way. He showed in that voyage all the attributes of a great discoverer; he deserved the honors which were paid to him on his return.

As has been said, however, this does not mean that he was a great organizer of cities, or that he was the right person to put in charge of a newly founded colony. It has happened more than once in the history of nations that a great general, who can conquer armies and can obtain peace, has not succeeded in establishing a colony or in governing a city.

On the other hand, it is fair to say that Columbus never had a chance to show what he would have been in the direction of his colonies had they been really left in his charge. This is true, that his heart was always on discovery; all the time that he spent in the wretched detail of the arrangement of a new-built town was time which really seemed to him wasted.

The great problem was always before him, how he should connect his discoveries with the knowledge which Europe had before of the coast of Asia. Always it seemed to him that the dominions of the Great Khan were within his reach. Always he was eager for that happy moment when he should find himself in personal communication with that great monarch, who had been so long the monarch of the East—who, as he thought, would prove to be the monarch of the West.

Columbus died with the idea that he had come close to Asia. Even a generation after his death, the companions of Cortes gave to the peninsula of California that name because it was the name given in romance to the farthest island of the eastern Indies.

Columbus met with many reverses, and died, one might almost say, a broken-hearted man. But history has been just to him, and has placed him in the foremost rank of the men who have set the world forward. And, outside of the technical study of history, those who like to trace the laws on which human progress advances have been proud and glad to see that here is a noble example of the triumph of faith.

The life of Columbus is an illustration constantly brought forward of the success which God gives to those who, having conceived of a great idea, bravely determine to carry it through.

His singleness of purpose, his unselfishness, his determination to succeed, have been cited for four centuries, and will be cited for centuries more, among the noblest illustrations which history has given, of success wrought out by the courage of one man.

Appendix A

(The following passages, from Admiral Fox's report, give his reasons for believing that Samana, or Atwood's Key, is the island where Columbus first touched land. The interest which attaches to this subject at the moment of the centennial, when many voyages will be made by persons following Columbus, induces me to copy Admiral Fox's reasonings in detail. I believe his conclusion to be correct.)

This method of applying Columbus's words in detail to refute each of the alleged tracks, and the study that I gave to the subject in the winter of 1878-79 in the Bahamas, which has been familiar cruising ground to me, has resulted in the selection of Samana or Atwood's Key for the first landing place.

It is a little island 8.8 miles east and west; 1.6 extreme breadth, and averaging 1.2 north and south. It has 8.6 square miles. The east end is in latitude 23 degrees 5' N.; longitude 73 degrees 37' west of Greenwich. The reef on which it lies is 15 by 2 1/2 miles.

On the southeast this reef stretches half a mile from the land, on the east four miles, on the west two, along the north shore one-quarter to one-half mile, and on the southwest scarcely one-quarter. Turk is smaller than Samana, and Cat very much larger.

The selection of two so unlike in size show that dimension has not been considered essential in choosing an island for the first landfall.[44]

The island is now uninhabited, but arrow heads and stone hatchets are sometimes found; and in places there are piles of stones supposed to have been made by the aborigines. Most of the growth is scrubby, with a few scattered trees.

The Nassau vessels enter an opening through the reef on the south side of the island and find a very comfortable little harbor with from two to two and a half fathoms of water. From here they send their boats on shore to "strip" guano, and cut satin, dye woods and bark.

When Columbus discovered Guanahani, the journal called it a "little island." After landing he speaks of it as *"bien grande,"* "very large," which some translate, tolerably, or pretty large. November 20, 1492 (Navarette, first edition, p. 61), the journal refers to Isabella, a larger island than Guanahani, as "little island," and the fifth of January following (p. 125) San Salvador is again called "little island."

The Bahamas have an area of about 37,000 square miles, six per cent of which may be land, enumerated as 36 islands, 687 keys, and 2,414 rocks. The submarine bank upon which these rest underlies Florida also. But this peninsula is wave-formed upon

---

[44] *I am indebted to T. J. McLain, Esq., United States consul at Nassau, for the following information given to him by the captains of this port, who visit Samana or Atwood's Key. The sub-sketch on this chart is substantially correct: Good water is only obtained by sinking wells. The two keys to the east are covered with guano; white boobies hold the larger one, and black boobies the other; neither intermingles.*

living corals, whose growth and gradual stretch toward the south has been made known by Agassiz.

I had an unsuccessful search for a similar story of the Bahamas, to learn whether there were any probable changes within so recent a period as four hundred years.

The common mind can see that all the rock there is coral, none of which is in position. The surface, the caves, the chinks, and the numerous pot-holes are compact limestone, often quite crystalline, while beneath it is oolitic, either friable or hard enough to be used for buildings. The hills are sand-blown, not upheaved. On a majority of the maps of the sixteenth century there were islands on Mouchoir, and on Silver Banks, where now are rocks "awash;" and the Dutch and the Severn Shoals, which lay to the east, have disappeared.

It is difficult to resist the impression that the shoal banks, and the reefs of the Bahamas, were formerly covered with land; and that for a geological age waste has been going on, and, perhaps, subsidence. The coral polyp seems to be doing only desultory work, and that mostly on the northeast or Atlantic side of the islands; everywhere else it has abandoned the field to the erosive action of the waves.

Columbus said that Guanahani had abundance of water and a very large lagoon in the middle of it. He used the word laguna—lagoon, not lago—lake. His arrival in the Bahamas was at the height of the rainy season. Governor Rawson's Report on the Bahamas, 1864, page 92, Appendix 4, gives the annual rainfall at Nassau for ten years, 1855—'64, as sixty-four inches. From May 1, to November 1 is the wet season, during which 44.7 inches fall; the other six months 19.3 only. The most is in October, 8.5 inches.

Andros, the largest island, 1,600 square miles, is the only one that has a stream of water. The subdivision of the land into so many islands and keys, the absence of mountains, the showery characteristic of the rainfall, the porosity of the rock, and the great heat reflected from the white coral, are the chief causes for the want of running water. During the rainy season the "abundance of water" collects in the low places, making ponds and lagoons, that afterward are soaked up by the rock and evaporated by the sun.

Turk and Watling have lagoons of a more permanent condition, because they are maintained from the ocean by permeation. The lagoon which Columbus found at Guanahani had certainly undrinkable water, or he would have gotten some for his vessels, instead of putting it off until he reached the third island.

There is nothing in the journal to indicate that the lagoon at Guanahani was aught but the flooding of the low grounds by excessive rains; and even if it was one communicating with the ocean, its absence now may be referred to the effect of those agencies which are working incessantly to reshape the soft structure of the Bahamas.

Samana has a range of hills on the southwest side about one hundred feet high, and on the northeast another, lower. Between them, and also along the north shore, the land is low, and during the season of rains there is a row of ponds parallel to the shore. On the south side a conspicuous white bluff looks to the southward and eastward.

The two keys, lying respectively half a mile and three miles east of the island, and possibly the outer breaker, which is four miles, all might have been connected with each other, and with the island, four hundred years ago. In that event the most convenient place for Columbus to anchor in the strong northeast trade-wind, was where I have put an anchor on the sub-sketch of Samana.

In a subsequent passage Admiral Fox says:—

There is a common belief that the first landing place is settled by one or another of the authors cited here. Nevertheless, I trust to have shown, paragraph by paragraph, wherein their several tracks are contrary to the journal, inconsistent with the true cartography of the neighborhood, and to the discredit, measurably, both of Columbus and of Las Casas. The obscurity and the carelessness which appear in part of the diary through the Bahamas offer no obstacle to this demonstration, provided that they do not extend to the "log," or nautical part.

Columbus went to sea when he was fourteen years of age, and served there almost continuously for twenty-three years. The strain of a sea-faring life, from so tender an age, is not conducive to literary exactness. Still, for the very reason of this sea experience, the "log" should be correct.

This is composed of the courses steered, distances sailed over, bearings of islands from one another, trend of shores, etc. The recording of these is the daily business of seamen, and here the entries were by Columbus himself, chiefly to enable him, on his return to Spain, to construct that nautical map, which is promised in the prologue of the first voyage.

In crossing the Atlantic the Admiral understated to the crew each day's run, so that they should not know how far they had gone into an unknown ocean. Las Casas was aware of this counterfeit "log," but his abridgment is from that one which Columbus kept for his own use.

If the complicated courses and distances in this were originally wrong, or if the copy of them is false, it is obvious that they cannot be "plotted" upon a correct chart. Conversely, if they ARE made to conform to a succession of islands among which he is known to have sailed, it is evident that this is a genuine transcript of the authentic "log" of Columbus, and, reciprocally, that we have the true track, the beginning of which is the eventful landfall of October 12, 1492.

The student or critical reader, and the seaman, will have to determine whether the writer has established this conformity. The public, probably, desires to have the question settled, but it will hardly take any interest in a discussion that has no practical bearing, and which, for its elucidation, leans so much upon the jargon or the sea.

It is not flattering to the English or Spanish speaking peoples that the four hundredth anniversary of this great event draws nigh, and is likely to catch us still floundering, touching the first landing place.

Summary

First. There is no objection to Samana in respect to size, position or shape. That it is a little island, lying east and west, is in its favor. The erosion at the east end, by which islets have been formed, recalls the assertion of Columbus that there it could be cut off in two days and made into an island.

The Nassau vessels still find a snug anchorage here during the northeast trades. These blew half a gale of wind at the time of the landfall; yet Navarette, Varnhagen, and Captain Becher anchored the squadron on the windward sides of the coral reefs of their respective islands, a "lee shore."

The absence of permanent lagoons at Samana I have tried to explain.

Second. The course from Samana to Crooked is to the southwest, which is the direction that the Admiral said he should steer "tomorrow evening." The distance given by him corresponds with the chart.

Third. The second island, Santa Maria, is described as having two sides which made a right angle, and the length of each is given. This points directly to Crooked and Acklin. Both form one island, so fitted to the words of the journal as cannot be done with any other land of the Bahamas.

Fourth. The course and distance from Crooked to Long Island is that which the Admiral gives from Santa Maria to Fernandina.

Fifth. Long Island, the third, is accurately described. The trend of the shores, "north-northwest and south-southeast;" the "marvelous port" and the "coast which runs east (and) west," can nowhere be found except at the southeast part of Long Island.

Sixth. The journal is obscure in regard to the fourth island. The best way to find it is to "plot" the courses FORWARD from the third island and the courses and distances BACKWARD from the fifth. These lead to Fortune for the fourth.

Seventh. The Ragged Islands are the fifth. These he named las islas de Arena—Sand Islands.

They lie west-southwest from the fourth, and this is the course the Admiral adhered to. He did not "log" all the run made between these islands; in consequence the "log" falls short of the true distance, as it ought to. These "seven or eight islands, all extending from north to south," and having shoal water "six leagues to the south" of them, are seen on the chart at a glance.

Eighth. The course and distance from these to Port Padre, in Cuba, is reasonable. The westerly current, the depth of water at the entrance of Padre, and the general description, are free of difficulties. The true distance is greater than the "logged," because Columbus again omits part of his run. It would be awkward if the true distances from the fourth to the fifth islands, and from the latter to Padre, had fallen short of the "log," since it would make the unexplainable situation which occurs in Irving's course and distance from Mucaras Reef to Boca de Caravela.

From end to end of the Samana track there are but three discrepancies. At the third island, two leagues ought to be two miles. At the fourth island twelve leagues ought to be twelve miles. The bearing between the third and fourth islands is not quite as the chart has it, nor does it agree with the courses he steered. These three are fairly explained, and I think that no others can be mustered to disturb the concord between this track and the journal.

Rev. Mr. Cronan, in his recent voyage, discovered a cave at Watling's island, where were many skeletons of the natives. It is thought that a study of the bones in these skeletons will give some new ethnological information as to the race which Columbus found, which is now, thanks to Spanish cruelty, entirely extinct.

Appendix B

The letter to the Lady Juana, which gives
Columbus's own statement of the indignities put
upon him in San Domingo, is written in his most
crabbed Spanish. He never wrote the Spanish
language accurately, and the letter, as printed from
his own manuscript, is even curious in its infelicities.
It is so striking an illustration of the character of the
man that we print here an abstract of it, with some
passages translated directly from his own language.

Columbus writes, towards the end of the year 1500,
to the former nurse of Don Juan, an account of the
treatment he has received. "If my complaint of the
world is new, its method of abuse is very old," he
says. "God has made me a messenger of the new
heaven and the new earth which is spoken of in the
Apocalypse by the mouth of St. John, after having
been spoken of by Isaiah, and he showed me the place
where it was." Everybody was incredulous, but the
queen alone gave the spirit of intelligence and zeal to
the undertaking. Then the people talked of obstacles
and expense. Columbus says "seven years passed in
talk, and nine in executing some noted acts which are
worthy of remembrance," but he returned reviled by
all.

"If I had stolen the Indies and had given them to
the Moors I could not have had greater enmity shown

to me in Spain." Columbus would have liked then to give up the business if he could have come before the queen. However he persisted, and he says he "undertook a new voyage to the new heaven and the new earth which before had been hidden, and if it is not appreciated in Spain as much as the other countries of India it is not surprising, because it is all owing to my industry." He "had believed that the voyage to Paria would reconcile all because of the pearls and gold in the islands of Espanola." He says, "I caused those of our people whom I had left there to come together and fish for pearls, and arranged that I should return and take from them what had been collected, as I understood, in measure a fanega (about a bushel). If I have not written this to their Highnesses it is because I wished also to have as much of gold. But that fled before me, as all other things; I would not have lost them and with them my honor, if I could have busied myself with my own affairs.

"When I went to San Domingo I found almost half of the colony uprising, and they made war upon me as a Moor, and the Indians on the other side were no less cruel.

"Hojida came and he tried to make order, and he said that their Highnesses had sent him with promises of gifts and grants and money. He made up a large company, for in all Espanola there were few men who were not vagabonds, and no one lived there who had wife or children." Hojida retired with threats.

"Then Vincente Ganez came with four ships. There were outbreaks and suspicions but no damage." He reported that six other ships under a brother of the Alcalde would arrive, and also the death of the queen, but these were rumors without foundation.

"Adrian (Mogica) attempted to go away as before, but our Lord did not permit him to carry out his bad plan." Here Columbus regrets that he was obliged to use force or ill-treat Adrian, but says he would have done the same had his brother wished to kill him or wrest from him the government which the king and queen had given him to guard.

"For six months I was ready to leave to take to their Highnesses the good news of the gold and to stop governing a dissolute people who feared neither king nor queen, full of meanness and malice. I would have been able to pay all the people with six hundred thousand maravedis and for that there were more than four millions of tithes without counting the third part of the gold."

Columbus says that he begged before his departure that they would send some one at his expense to take command, and yet again a subject with letters, for he says bitterly that he has such a singular reputation that if he "were building churches and hospitals they would say they were cells for stolen goods."

Then Bobadilla came to Santo Domingo while Columbus was at La Vega and the Adelantado at Jaragua. "The second day of his arrival he declared himself governor, created magistrates, made offices, published grants for gold and tithes, and everything else for a term of twenty years." He said he had come to pay the people, and declared he would send Columbus home in irons. Columbus was away. Letters with favors were sent to others, but none to him. Columbus resorted to methods to gain time so that their Highnesses could understand the state of things. But he was constantly maligned and persecuted by those who were jealous of him. He says:

"I think that you will remember that when the tempest threw me into the port of Lisbon, after having lost my sails, I was accused of having the intention to give India to that country. Afterwards their Highnesses knew to the contrary. Although I know but little, I cannot conceive that any one would suppose me so stupid as not to know that though India might belong to me, yet I could not keep it without the help of a prince."

Columbus complains that he has been judged as a governor who has been sent to a peaceful, well-regulated province. He says, "I ought to be judged as a captain sent from Spain to the Indies to conquer a warlike people, whose custom and religion are all opposed to ours, where the people live in the mountains without regular houses for themselves, and where, by the will of God, I have placed under the rule of the king and queen another world, and by which Spain, which calls itself poor, is today the richest empire. I ought to be judged as a captain who for many years bears arms incessantly.

"I know well that the errors that I have committed have not been with bad intentions, and I think that their Highnesses will believe what I say; but I know and see that they use pity for those who work against them."

"If, nevertheless, their Highnesses order that another shall judge me, which I hope will not be, and this ought to be on an examination made in India, I humbly beg of them to send there two conscientious and respectable people, at my expense, which may know easily that one finds five marcs of gold in four hours. However that may be, it is very necessary that they should go there."

Appendix C

It would have been so natural to give the name of Columbus to the new world which he gave to Castile and Leon, that much wonder has been expressed that America was not called Columbia, and many efforts have been made to give to the continent this name. The District of Columbia was so named at a time when American writers of poetry, were determined that "Columbia" should be the name of the continent. The ship Columbia, from which the great river of the West takes that name, had received this name under the same circumstances about the same time. The city of Columbia, which is the capital of South Carolina, was named with the same wish to do justice to the great navigator.

Side by side with the discussion as to the name, and sometimes making a part of it, is the question whether Columbus himself was really the first discoverer of the mainland. The reader has seen that he first saw the mainland of South America in the beginning of August, 1498. It was on the fifth, sixth or seventh day, according to Mr. Harrisse's accurate study of the letters. Was this the first discovery by a European of the mainland?

It is known that Ojeda, with whom the reader is familiar, also saw this coast. With him, as passenger on his vessel, was Alberico Vespucci, and at one time it was supposed that Vespucci had made some claim to be the discoverer of the continent, on account of this voyage. But in truth Ojeda himself says that before he sailed he had seen the map of the Gulf of Paria which Columbus had sent home to the sovereigns after he made that discovery. It also seems to be proved that Alberico Vespucci, as he was then called, never made for himself any claim to the great discovery.

Another question, of a certain interest to people proud of English maritime science, is the question whether the Cabots did not see the mainland before Columbus. It is admitted on all hands that they did not make their first voyage till they knew of Columbus's first discoveries; but it is supposed that in the first or second voyage of the Cabots, they saw the mainland of North America. The dates of the Cabots' voyages are unfortunately badly entangled. One of them is as early as 1494, but this is generally rejected. It is more probable that the king's letters patent, authorizing John Cabot and his three sons to go, with five vessels, under the English flag, for the discovery of islands and countries yet unknown, was dated the fifth of March, 1496. Whether, however, they sailed in that year or in the next year is a question. The first record of a discovery is in the account-book of the privy purse of Henry VII, in the words, "August 10th, 1497. To him who discovered the new island, ten pounds." This is clearly not a claim on which the discovery of the mainland can be based.

A manuscript known as the Cotton Manuscript says that John Cabot had sailed, but had not returned, at the moment when the manuscript was written. This period was "the thirteenth year of Henry VII." The thirteenth year of Henry began on the twenty-second of August, 1497, and ended in 1498. On the third of February, 1498, Henry VII granted permission to Cabot to take six English ships "to the lands and islands recently found by the said Cabot, in the name of the king and by his orders." Strictly speaking, this would mean that the mainland had then been discovered; but it is impossible to establish the claim of England on these terms.

What is, however, more to the point, is a letter from Pasqualigo, a Venetian merchant, who says, writing to Venice, on the twenty-third of August, 1497, that Cabot had discovered the mainland at seven hundred leagues to the west, and had sailed along it for a coast of three hundred leagues. He says the voyage was three months in length. It was made, then, between May and August, 1497. The evidence of this letter seems to show that the mainland of North America was really first discovered by Cabot. The discussion, however, does not in the least detract from the merit due to Columbus for the great discovery. Whether he saw an island or whether he saw the mainland, was a mere matter of what has been called landfall by the seamen. It is admitted on all hands that he was the leader in all these enterprises, and that it was on his success in the first voyage that all such enterprises followed.

BOOK II

Original Narratives of the Voyages of Christopher Columbus

From the work:
Original Narratives of Early American History

Reproduced under the auspices of the
American Historical Association

General editor, J. Franklin Jameson, Ph.D., LL.d.
Director of the Department of Historical Research in the
Carnegie Institution of Washington

Edited by
Edward Gaylord Bourne, PH.D.
Professor of history in Yale University

General preface to the original narratives of early American history

At its annual meeting in December, 1902, the American Historical Association approved and adopted the plan of the present series, and the undersigned was chosen as its general editor. The purpose of the series was to provide individual readers of history, and the libraries of schools and colleges, with a comprehensive and well-rounded collection of those classical narratives on which the early history of the United States is founded, or of those narratives which, if not precisely classical, hold the most important place as sources of American history anterior to 1700. The reasons for undertaking such a project are for the most part obvious. No modern history, however excellent, can give the reader all that he can get from the *ipsissima verba* of the first narrators, Argonauts or eyewitnesses, vivacious explorers or captains courageous. There are many cases in which secondary narrators have quite hidden from view these first authorities, whom it is therefore a duty to restore to their rightful position. In a still greater number of instances, the primitive narrations have become so scarce and expensive that no ordinary library can hope to possess anything like a complete set of the classics of early American history.

The series is to consist of such volumes as will illustrate the early history of all the chief parts of the country, with an additional volume of general index. The plan contemplates, not a body of extracts, but in general the publication or republication of whole works or distinct parts of works. In the case of narratives originally issued in some other language than English, the best available translations will be used, or fresh versions made. In a few instances, important narratives hitherto unprinted will be inserted. The English texts will be taken from the earliest editions, or those having the highest historical value, and will be reproduced with literal exactness. The maps will be such as will give real help toward understanding the events narrated in the volume. The special editors of the individual works will supply introductions, setting forth briefly the author's career and opportunities, when known, the status of the work in the literature of American history, and its value as a source, and indicating previous editions; and they will furnish such annotations, scholarly but simple, as will enable the intelligent reader to understand and to estimate rightly the statements of the text. The effort has been made to secure for each text the most competent editor.

The results of all these endeavors will be laid before the public in the confident hope that they will be widely useful in making more real and more vivid the apprehension of early American history. The general editor would not have undertaken the serious labors of preparation and supervision if he had not felt sure that it was a genuine benefit to American historical knowledge and American patriotism to make accessible, in one collection, so large a body of pioneer narrative. No subsequent sources can have quite the intellectual interest, none quite the sentimental value, which attaches to these early narrations, springing direct from the brains and hearts of the nation's founders.

Sacra recognosces annalibus eruta priscis.

J. FRANKLIN JAMESON.

CARNEGIE INSTITUTION, WASHINGTON, D.C.

NOTE

Special acknowledgments and thanks are due to the representatives of the late Arthur Middleton Reeves, who have kindly permitted the use of his translations of the Vinland sagas, originally printed in his *Finding of Wineland the Good*, published in London by the Clarendon Press in 1890; to the President and Council of the Hakluyt Society, for permission to use Sir Clements Markham's translation of the Journal of Columbus's first voyage, printed in Vol. LXXXVI. of the publications of that Society (London, 1893), and that of Dr. Chanca's letter and of the letter of Columbus respecting his fourth voyage, by the late Mr. R.H. Major, in their second and forty-third volumes, *Select Letters of Columbus* (London, 1847, 1870); to the Honorable John Boyd Thacher, of Albany, for permission to use his version of Las Casas's narrative of the third voyage, as printed by him in his *Christopher Columbus* (New York, 1904), published by Messrs. G.P. Putnam's Sons; to Messrs. Houghton, Mifflin and Company for permission to use, out of the third volume of Winsor's *Narrative and Critical History of America*, the late Dr. Charles Deane's translation, revised by Professor Bennet H. Nash, of the second letter of Raimondo de Soncino respecting John Cabot's expedition; and to George Philip and Son, Limited, of London, for permission to use the map in Markham's *Life of Christopher Columbus* as the basis for the map in the present volume [not available], showing the routes of Columbus's four voyages.

ORIGINAL NARRATIVES OF THE VOYAGES OF COLUMBUS

Articles of Agreement Between the Lords the Catholic Sovereigns and Crisobal Colon[45]

The things prayed for, and which Your Highnesses give and grant to Don Cristóbal Colon[46] as some recompense for what he is to discover in the Oceans, and for the voyage which now, with the help of God, he has engaged to make therein in the service of Your Highnesses, are the following:

---

[45] The Spanish text is that printed by Navarrete in his *Coleccion de los Viages y Descubrimientos*, etc. (Madrid, 1825), II. 7-8, and taken from the Archives of the Duke of Veragua. The translation is that of George F. Barwick printed by Benjamin Franklin Stevens in his *Christopher Columbus His Own Book of Privileges*, 1502, etc. (London, 1893), pp. 42-45, with such slight changes (chiefly of tenses) as were necessary to bring it into conformity with the text of Navarrete. This document is also given in English translation in *Memorials of Columbus* (London, 1823), pp. 40-43. That volume is a translation of G.B. Spotorno, *Codice Diplomatico Colombo-Americano* (Genoa, 1823).

[46] In this edition of the Narratives of the Voyages of Columbus his name in the translation of the original documents will be given in the form used in the originals. During his earlier years in Spain Columbus was known as Colomo, the natural Spanish form corresponding to the Italian Colombo. At some time prior to 1492 he adopted the form Colon, apparently to make more probable his claim to be descended from a Roman general, Colonius, and to be related to the French admiral, Coullon, called in contemporary Italian sources Colombo, and Columbus in Latin. In modern texts of Tacitus the Roman general's name is Cilonius, and modern research has shown that the French admiral's real name was Caseneuve and that Coullon was a sobriquet added for some unknown reason. On the two French naval commanders known as Colombo or Coullon and the baselessness of Columbus's alleged relationship see Vignaud, *Études Critiques sur la Vie de Colomb* pp. 131 ff.

Firstly, that Your Highnesses, as actual Lords of the said Oceans, appoint from this date the said Don Cristóbal Colon to be your Admiral in all those islands and mainlands which by his activity and industry shall be discovered or acquired in the said oceans, during his lifetime, and likewise, after his death, his heirs and successors one after another in perpetuity, with all the pre-eminences and prerogatives appertaining to the said office, and in the same manner as Don Alfonso Enriques, your High Admiral of Castile,[47] and his predecessors in the said office held it in their districts.--It so pleases their Highnesses. Juan de Coloma.

Likewise, that Your Highnesses appoint the said Don Cristóbal Colon to be your Viceroy and Governor General in all the said islands and mainlands and in the islands which, as aforesaid, he may discover and acquire[48] in the said seas; and that for the government of each and any of them he may make choice of three persons for each office,

---

[47] In 1497 Columbus at his own request was supplied with a copy of the ordinances establishing the admiralty of Castile so that he might have a documentary enumeration of his prerogatives in the Indies. This official copy he preserved in the collection of his papers known as the *Book of Privileges*, and the translation of the documents relating to the Admiralty of Castile is given in Stevens's edition of the *Book of Privileges*, pp. 14 ff. This dignity of Admiral comprised supreme or vice-regal authority on the sea and the general range of legal jurisdiction in determining suits of law that is enjoyed by modern courts of admiralty. A translation of Columbus's exposition of his rights derived from his admiralty of the islands in the Ocean may be found in P.L. Ford, *Writings of Columbus* (New York, 1892), pp. 177-198, taken from *Memorials of Columbus* (London, 1823), pp. 205-223. For a summary of these powers cf. the *Titulo* that follows.

[48] It is a remarkable fact that nothing is said in this patent of discovering a route to the Indies. It is often said that the sole purpose of Columbus was to discover such a route, yet it is clear that he expected to make some new discoveries, and that if he did not, the sovereigns were under no specified obligations to him. Patents are usually drawn on the lines indicated by the petitioner. Can we conclude that the complete silence of the articles as to the Indies means that Ferdinand and Isabella refused to make any promises if Columbus only succeeded in reaching the known East Indies and could gain for them no new possessions?

and that Your Highnesses may select and choose the one who shall be most serviceable to you; and thus the lands which our Lord shall permit him to discover and acquire for the service of Your Highnesses, will be the better governed.--It so pleases their Highnesses. Juan de Coloma.

Item, that of all and every kind of merchandise, whether pearls, precious stones, gold, silver, spices, and other objects and merchandise whatsoever, of whatever kind, name and sort, which may be bought, bartered, discovered, acquired and obtained within the limits of the said Admiralty, Your Highnesses grant from now henceforth to the said Don Cristóbal, and will that he may have and take for himself, the tenth part of the whole, after deducting all the expenses which may be incurred therein, so that of what shall remain clear and free he may have and take the tenth part for himself, and may do therewith as he pleases, the other nine parts being reserved for Your Highnesses.--It so pleases their Highnesses. Juan de Coloma.

Likewise, that if on account of the merchandise which he might bring from the said islands and lands which thus, as aforesaid, may be acquired or discovered, or of that which may be taken in exchange for the same from other merchants here, any suit should arise in the place where the said commerce and traffic shall be held and conducted; and if by the pre-eminence of his office of Admiral it appertains to him to take cognizance of such suit; it may please Your Highnesses that he or his deputy, and not another judge, shall take cognizance thereof and give judgment in the same from henceforth.-- It so pleases their Highnesses, if it appertains to the said office of Admiral, according as it was held by Admiral Don Alfonso Enriques, and others his successors in their districts, and if it be just. Juan de Coloma.

Item, that in all the vessels which may be equipped for
the said traffic and business, each time and whenever and
as often as they may be equipped, the said Don Cristóbal
Colon may, if he chooses, contribute and pay the eighth
part of all that may be spent in the equipment, and that
likewise he may have and take the eighth part of the
profits that may result from such equipment.--It so
pleases their Highnesses. Juan de Coloma.

These are granted and despatched, with the replies of
Your Highnesses at the end of each article, in the town of
Santa Fe de la Vega of Granada, on the seventeenth day
of April in the year of the nativity of our Saviour Jesus
Christ, one thousand four hundred and ninety-two. I the
King. I the Queen. By command of the King and of the
Queen. Juan de
Coloma. Registered, Calcena.

Title granted by the Catholic Sovereigns to Cristobal Colon of Admiral, Viceroy, and Governor of the islands and mainland that may be discovered[49]

Don Ferdinand and Donna Isabella, by the grace of God King and Queen of Castile, Leon, Aragon, Sicily, Granada, Toledo, Valencia, Galicia, Majorca, Seville, Sardinia, Cordova, Corsica, Murcia, Jaen, Algarbe, Algeciras, Gibraltar, and the Canary Islands; Count and Countess of Barcelona; Lords of Biscay and Molina; Dukes of Athens and Neopatria; Counts of Roussillon and Cerdagne, Marquises of Oristano and Goziano; Forasmuch as you, Cristóbal Colon, are going by our command, with some of our ships and with our subjects, to discover and acquire certain islands and mainland in the ocean, and it is hoped that, by the help of God, some of the said islands and mainland in the said ocean will be discovered and acquired by your pains and industry; and as it is a just and reasonable thing that since you incur the said danger for our service you should be rewarded for it, and since we desire to honor and favor you on account of what is aforesaid, it is our will and pleasure that you, the said Cristóbal Colon, after you have discovered and acquired

---

[49] Spanish text in Navarrete, II. 9-11. We omit the long preamble. Spanish text and facsimile of Paris Codex in Stevens, *Christopher Columbus His Own Book of Privileges*, pp. 49 ff. The translation is that of George F. Barwick. This document is also to be found in English in *Memorials of Columbus* (London, 1823), pp. 52-57.

the said islands and mainland in the said ocean, or any of
them whatsoever, shall be our Admiral of the said islands
and mainland which you may thus discover and acquire,
and shall be our Admiral and Viceroy and Governor
therein, and shall be empowered from that time forward
to call and entitle yourself Don Cristóbal Colon, and that
your sons and successors in the said office and charge
may likewise entitle and call themselves Don, and
Admiral and Viceroy and Governor thereof; and that you
may have power to use and exercise the said office of
Admiral, together with the said office of Viceroy and
Governor of the said islands and mainland which you may
thus discover and acquire, by yourself or by your
lieutenants, and to hear and determine all the suits and
causes civil and criminal appertaining to the said office of
Admiralty, Viceroy, and Governor according as you shall
find by law, and as the Admirals of our kingdoms are
accustomed to use and exercise it; and may have power to
punish and chastise delinquents, and exercise the said
offices of Admiralty, Viceroy, and Governor, you and your
said lieutenants, in all that concerns and appertains to
the said offices and to each of them; and that you shall
have and levy the fees and salaries annexed, belonging
and appertaining to the said offices and to each of them,
according as our High Admiral in the Admiralty of our
kingdoms levies and is accustomed to levy them. And by
this our patent, or by the transcript thereof signed by a
public scrivener, we command Prince Don Juan, our very
dear and well beloved son, and the Infantes, dukes,
prelates, marquises, counts, masters of orders, priors,
commanders, and members of our council, and auditors of
our audiencia, alcaldes, and other justices whomsoever of
our household, court, and chancery, and sub-commanders,
alcaldes of castles and fortified and unfortified houses,
and all councillors, assistants, regidores, alcaldes, bailiffs,
judges, veinticuatros, jurats, knights, esquires, officers,

and liege men[50] of all the cities, towns, and places of our kingdoms and dominions, and of those which you may conquer and acquire, and the captains, masters, mates, officers, mariners, and seamen, our natural subjects who now are or hereafter shall be, and each and any of them, that upon the said islands and mainland in the said ocean being discovered and acquired by you, and the oath and formality requisite in such case having been made and done by you or by him who may have your procuration,[51] they shall have and hold you from thenceforth for the whole of your life, and your son and successor after you, and successor after successor for ever and ever, as our Admiral of the said ocean, and as Viceroy and Governor of the said islands and mainland, which you, the said Don Cristóbal Colon, may discover and acquire; and they shall treat with you, and with your said lieutenants whom you may place in the said offices of Admiral, Viceroy, and Governor, about everything appertaining thereto, and shall pay and cause to be paid to you the salary, dues and other things annexed and appertaining to the said offices, and shall observe and cause to be observed toward you all the honors, graces, favors, liberties, pre-eminences, prerogatives, exemptions, immunities, and all other things, and each of them, which in virtue of the said offices of Admiral, Viceroy, and Governor you shall be entitled to have and enjoy, and which ought to be observed towards you in every respect fully and completely so that nothing may be diminished

---

[50] Audiencia means the king's court of justice; regidores are roughly equivalent to members of a town council. The Navarrete text has corregidores, town governors appointed by the king. Veinticuatros were town councillors, so called because commonly 24 in number. Jurats were municipal executive officers in Aragon. The original which is translated "liege men" is Homes-Buenos. Further explanations of these offices may be found in Hume, Spain, Its Greatness and Decay, pp. 18 ff., and in The Cambridge Modern History, I. 348 ff.

[51] Procuration=power of attorney.

therefrom; and that neither therein nor in any part thereof shall they place or consent to place hindrance or obstacle against you; for we by this our patent from now henceforth grant to you the said offices of Admiralty, Viceroy, and Governor, by right of inheritance for ever and ever, and we give you actual and prospective possession thereof, and of each of them, and power and authority to use and exercise it, and to collect the dues and salaries annexed and appertaining to them and to each of them, according to what is aforesaid. Concerning all that is aforesaid, if it should be necessary and you should require it of them, we command our chancellor and notaries and the other officers who are at the board of our seals to give, deliver, pass, and seal for you our patent of privilege with the circle of signatures, in the strongest, firmest, and most sufficient manner that you may request and may find needful, and neither one nor the other of you or them shall do contrary hereto in any manner, under penalty of our displeasure and of ten thousand maravedis[52] to our chamber, upon every one who shall do to the contrary. And further we command the man who shall show them this our patent, to cite them to appear before us in our court, wheresoever we may be, within fifteen days from the day of citation, under the said penalty, under which we command every public scrivener who may be summoned for this purpose, to give to the person who shall show it to him a certificate thereof signed with his signature, whereby we may know in what manner our command is executed.

Given in our city of Granada, on the thirtieth day of the month of April, in the year of the nativity of our Lord Jesus Christ one thousand four hundred and ninety-two. I

---

[52] The maravedi at this time was equal in coin value to about two-thirds of a cent.

the King. I the Queen. I, Juan de Coloma, Secretary of the King and of the Queen, our Lords, caused this to be written by their command. Granted in form, Roderick, Doctor. Registered, Sebastian de Olano. Francisco de Madrid, Chancellor.

JOURNAL OF THE FIRST
VOYAGE OF COLUMBUS

Introduction

The contents of Columbus's Journal of his first voyage were first made known to the public in the epitome incorporated in Ferdinand Columbus's life of the Admiral, which has come down to us only in the Italian translation of Alfonso Ulloa, the *Historie del S.D. Fernando Colombo nelle quali s'ha particolare e vera relazione della vita e de' fatti dell' Ammiraglio D. Christoforo Colombo suo padre*, etc. (Venice, 1571).

This account is accessible in English in Churchill's *Voyages*, Vol. II.[53], and in Pinkerton's *Voyages*,[54] Vol. XII.

Another epitome was prepared by Bartolomé de Las Casas and inserted in his *Historia de las Indias*. This account was embodied in the main by Antonio de Herrera in his *Historia General de las Indias Occidentales* (Madrid, 1601). It is accessible in English in John Stevens's translation of Herrera (London, 1725-1726).

These independent epitomes of the original were supplemented in 1825 by the publication by the Spanish archivist Martin Fernandez de Navarrete in his *Coleccion de los Viages y Descubrimientos que hicieron por mar los*

---

[53] *A Collection of voyages and travels: some now first printed from original manuscripts, others now first published in English: in six volumes with a general preface giving an account of the progress of navigation from its first beginning...1732* Compiled by Awnsham and John Churchill, London. [54] *Voyages and Travels in All Parts of the World*, by John Pinkerton, 1812, Michigan.

Españoles desde fines del siglo XV. of a considerably more detailed narrative (likewise independently abridged from the original) which existed in two copies in the archives of the Duke del Infantado. Navarrete says that the handwriting of the older copy is that of Las Casas and that Las Casas had written some explanatory notes in the margin. This longer narrative, here reprinted, was first translated by Samuel Kettell of Boston and published in 1827 under the title *Personal Narrative of the First Voyage of Columbus.* The next translation was that of Clements R. Markham for the Hakluyt Society in 1893. A third and very exact rendering appeared in 1903 in John Boyd Thacher's *Christopher Columbus*, Vol. I.

The translation given here is that of Sir Clements R. Markham with some slight revisions. When we recall the very scanty and fragmentary knowledge which we have of the Cabot voyages, and how few in fact of the great discoverers of this era left personal narratives of their achievements, we realize our singular good fortune in possessing so full a daily record from the hand of Columbus himself which admits us as it were "into the very presence of the Admiral to share his thoughts and impressions as the strange panorama of his experiences unfolded before him."[55] Sir Clements R. Markham declares the Journal "the most important document in the whole range of the history of geographical discovery, because it is a record of the enterprise which changed the whole face, not only of that history, but of the history of mankind."[56]

EDWARD G. BOURNE.

---

[55] Bourne, *Spain in America*, p. 22.
[56] *Journal of Christopher Columbus*, p. viii.

Journal of the first voyage of Columbus

This is the first voyage and the routes and direction taken by the Admiral Don Cristóbal Colon when he discovered the Indies, summarized; except the prologue made for the Sovereigns, which is given word for word and commences in this manner.

In the name of our Lord Jesus Christ

Because, O most Christian, and very high, very excellent, and puissant Princes, King and Queen of the Spains and of the islands of the Sea, our Lords, in this present year of 1492, after your Highnesses had given an end to the war with the Moors who reigned in Europe, and had finished it in the very great city of Granada, where in this present year, on the second day of the month of January, by force of arms, I saw the royal banners of your Highnesses placed on the towers of Alfambra,[57] which is the fortress of that city, and I saw the Moorish King come forth from the gates of the city and kiss the royal hands of your Highnesses, and of the Prince my Lord, and presently in that same month, acting on the information that I had given to your Highnesses touching the lands of India, and

---

[57] The Alhambra.

respecting a Prince who is called Gran Can, which means in our language King of Kings, how he and his ancestors had sent to Rome many times to ask for learned men[58] of our holy faith to teach him, and how the Holy Father had never complied, insomuch that many people believing in idolatries were lost by receiving doctrine of perdition:

YOUR HIGHNESSES, as Catholic Christians and Princes who love the holy Christian faith, and the propagation of it, and who are enemies to the sect of Mahoma and to all idolatries and heresies, resolved to send me, Cristóbal Colon, to the said parts of India to see the said princes, and the cities and lands, and their disposition, with a view that they might be converted to our holy faith;[59] and ordered that I should not go by land to the eastward, as had been customary, but that I should go by way of the west, whither up to this day, we do not know for certain that any one has gone.

Thus, after having turned out all the Jews from all your kingdoms and lordships, in the same month of January,[60] your Highnesses gave orders to me that with a sufficient fleet I should go to the said parts of India, and for this

---

[58] This information Columbus is ordinarily supposed to have derived from Toscanelli's letter which may be found in Fiske, *Discovery of America*, I. 356 ff. and II. App. The original source of the information, however, is Marco Polo, and Columbus summarized the passage on the margin in his copy of *Marco Polo*, Lib. I., ch. IV., as follows: "Magnus Kam misit legatos ad pontificem:" *Raccolta Colombiana*, Part I, Tomo 2, p. 446. That he read and annotated these passages before 1492 seems most probable. See Bourne, _*Spain in America*, pp. 10-15, and Vignaud, *Toscanelli and Columbus*, p. 284.

[59] It is interesting to notice the emphasis of the missionary motive in this preamble. Nothing is said in regard to the search for a new route to the Indies for commercial reasons. Nor is reference made to the expectation of new discoveries which is prominent in the royal patent granted to Columbus, see above p. 78.

[60] The edict of expulsion bears the date of March 30.

they made great concessions to me, and ennobled me, so that henceforward I should be called Don, and should be Chief Admiral of the Ocean Sea, perpetual Viceroy and Governor of all the islands and continents that I should discover and gain, and that I might hereafter discover and gain in the Ocean Sea, and that my eldest son should succeed, and so on from generation to generation for ever.

I left the city of Granada on the 12th day of May, in the same year of 1492, being Saturday, and came to the town of Palos, which is a seaport; where I equipped three vessels well suited for such service; and departed from that port, well supplied with provisions and with many sailors, on the 3d day of August of the same year, being Friday, half an hour before sunrise, taking the route to the islands of Canaria, belonging to your Highnesses, which are in the said Ocean Sea, that I might thence take my departure for navigating until I should arrive at the Indies, and give the letters of your Highnesses to those princes, so as to comply with my orders. As part of my duty I thought it well to write an account of all the voyage very punctually, noting from day to day all that I should do and see, and that should happen, as will be seen further on. Also, Lords Princes, I resolved to describe each night what passed in the day, and to note each day how I navigated at night. I propose to construct a new chart for navigating, on which I shall delineate all the sea and lands of the Ocean in their proper positions under their bearings; and further, I propose to prepare a book, and to put down all as it were in a picture, by latitude from the equator, and western longitude. Above all, I shall have accomplished much, for I shall forget sleep, and shall work at the business of navigation, that so the service may be performed; all which will entail great labor.

Friday, 3d of August

We departed on Friday, the 3d of August, in the year
1492, from the bar of Saltes, at 8 o'clock, and proceeded
with a strong sea breeze until sunset, towards the south,
for 60 miles, equal to 15 leagues;[61] afterwards S.W. and
W.S.W., which was the course for the Canaries.

Saturday, 4th of August

They steered S.W. 1/4 S.

Sunday, 5th of August

They continued their course day and night more than 40
leagues.

Monday, 6th of August

The rudder of the caravel *Pinta* became unshipped, and
Martin Alonso Pinzon, who was in command, believed or
suspected that it was by contrivance of Gomes Rascon and
Cristóbal Quintero, to whom the caravel belonged, for
they dreaded to go on that voyage. The Admiral says that,
before they sailed, these men had been displaying a
certain backwardness, so to speak. The Admiral was
much disturbed at not being able to help the said caravel
without danger, and he says that he was eased of some
anxiety when he reflected that Martin Alonso Pinzon was
a man of energy and ingenuity. They made, during the
day and night, 29 leagues.

---

[61] Columbus reckoned in Italian miles, four of which make a league.
(Navarrete.)

Tuesday, 7th of August

The rudder of the *Pinta* was shipped and secured, and they proceeded on a course for the island of Lanzarote, one of the Canaries. They made, during the day and night, 25 leagues.

Wednesday, 8th of August

Opinions respecting their position varied among the pilots of the three caravels; but that of the Admiral proved to be nearer the truth. He wished to go to Gran Canaria, to leave the caravel *Pinta*, because she was disabled by the faulty hanging of her rudder, and was making water. He intended to obtain another there if one could be found. They could not reach the place that day.

Thursday, 9th of August

The Admiral was not able to reach Gomera until the night of Sunday, while Martin Alonso remained on that coast of Gran Canaria by order of the Admiral, because his vessel could not be navigated. Afterwards the Admiral took her to Canaria, and they repaired the *Pinta* very thoroughly through the pains and labor of the Admiral, of Martin Alonso, and of the rest. Finally they came to Gomera. They saw a great fire issue from the mountain of the island of Tenerife, which is of great height. They rigged the *Pinta* with square sails, for she was lateen rigged; and the Admiral reached Gomera on Sunday, the 2nd of September, with the *Pinta* repaired.

The Admiral says that many honorable Spanish gentlemen who were at Gomera with Doña Ines Peraza, mother of Guillen Peraza (who was afterwards the first Count of Gomera), and who were natives of the island of Hierro, declared that every year they saw land to the west of the Canaries; and others, natives of Gomera, affirmed the same on oath. The Admiral here says that he remembers, when in Portugal in the year 1484, a man came to the King from the island of Madeira, to beg for a caravel to go to this land that was seen, who swore that it could be seen every year, and always in the same way.[62] He also says that he recollects the same thing being affirmed in the islands of the Azores; and all these lands were described as in the same direction, and as being like each other, and of the same size. Having taken in water, wood, and meat, and all else that the men had who were left at Gomera by the Admiral when he went to the island of Canaria to repair the caravel *Pinta*, he finally made sail from the said island of Gomera, with his three caravels, on Thursday, the 6th day of September.

Thursday, 6th of September

He departed on that day from the port of Gomera in the morning, and shaped a course to go on his voyage; having received tidings from a caravel that came from the island of Hierro that three Portuguese caravels were off that island with the object of taking him. (This must have been the result of the King's annoyance that Colon should have gone to Castile.) There was a calm all that day and night, and in the morning he found himself between Gomera and Tenerife.

---

[62] On June 30, 1484, King John II. of Portugal granted to Fernam Domimguez do Arco, "resident in the island of Madeyra, if he finds it, an island which he is now going in search of." *Alguns Documentos do Archivo Nacional da Torre do Tombo*, p. 56.

Friday, 7th of September

The calm continued all Friday and Saturday, until the third hour of the night.

Saturday, 8th of September

At the third hour of Saturday night[63] it began to blow from the N.E., and the Admiral shaped a course to the west. He took in much sea over the bows, which retarded progress, and 9 leagues were made in that day and night.

Sunday, 9th of September

This day the Admiral made 19 leagues, and he arranged to reckon less than the number run, because if the voyage was of long duration, the people would not be so terrified and disheartened. In the night he made 120 miles, at the rate of 12 miles an hour, which are 30 leagues. The sailors steered badly, letting the ship fall off to N.E., and even more, respecting which the Admiral complained many times.[64]

Monday, 10th of September

In this day and night he made 60 leagues, at the rate of 10 miles an hour, which are 2-1/2 leagues; but he only

---

[63] *Tres horas de noche* means three hours after sunset.
[64] "On this day [Sunday, Sept. 9] they lost sight of land; and many, fearful of not being able to return for a long time to see it, sighed and shed tears. But the admiral, after he had comforted all with big offers of much land and wealth to keep them in hope and to lessen their fear which they had of the long way, when that day the sailors reckoned the distance 18 leagues, said he had counted only 15, having decided to lessen the record so that the crew would not think they were as far from Spain as in fact they were." *Historie del Signor Don Fernando Colombo* (London ed., 1867), pp. 61-62.

counted 48 leagues, that the people might not be alarmed if the voyage should be long.

Tuesday, 11th of September

That day they sailed on their course, which was west, and made 20 leagues and more. They saw a large piece of the mast of a ship of 120 tons, but were unable to get it. In the night they made nearly 20 leagues, but only counted 16, for the reason already given.

Wednesday, 12th of September

That day, steering their course, they made 33 leagues during the day and night, counting less.

Thursday, 13th of September

That day and night, steering their course, which was west, they made 33 leagues, counting 3 or 4 less. The currents were against them. On this day, at the commencement of the night, the needles turned a half point to north-west, and in the morning they turned somewhat more north-west.[65]

---

[65] Las Casas in his *Historia*, I. 267, says "on that day at nightfall the needles northwested that is to say the fleur de lis which marks the north was not pointing directly at it but verged somewhat to the left of north and in the morning northeasted that is to say the fleur de lis pointed to right of the north until sunset." The *Historie* agrees with the text of the Journal that the needle declined more to the west, instead of shifting to an eastern declination. The author of the *Historie* remarks: "This variation no one had ever observed up to this time," p. 62. "Columbus had crossed the point of no variation, which was then near the meridian of Flores, in the Azores, and found the variation no longer easterly, but more than a point westerly. His explanation that the pole-star, by means of which the change was detected, was not itself stationary, is very plausible. For the pole-star really does describe a circle round the pole of the earth, equal in diameter to about six times that of the sun; but this is not equal to the change observed in the direction of the needle." (Markham.)

Friday, 14th of September

That day they navigated, on their westerly course, day and night, 20 leagues, counting a little less. Here those of the caravel *Niña* reported that they had seen a tern[66] and a boatswain bird,[67] and these birds never go more than 25 leagues from the land.[68]

Saturday, 15th of September

That day and night they made 27 leagues and rather more on their west course; and in the early part of the night there fell from heaven into the sea a marvellous flame of fire, at a distance of about 4 or 5 leagues from them.

Sunday, 16th of September

That day and night they steered their course west, making 39 leagues, but the Admiral only counted 36. There were some clouds and small rain. The Admiral says that on that day, and ever afterwards, they met with very temperate breezes, so that there was great pleasure in enjoying the mornings, nothing being wanted but the song

---

[66] *Garjao*. This word is not in the Spanish dictionaries that I have consulted. The translator has followed the French translators MM. Chalumeau de Verneuil and de la Roquette who accepted the opinion of the naturalist Cuvier that the *Garjao* was the *hirondelle de mer*, the *Sterna maxima* or royal tern.

[67] *Rabo de junco*, literally, reedtail, is the tropic bird or Phaethon. The name "boatswain-bird" is applied to some other kinds of birds, besides the tropic bird. Cf. *Alfred Newton, Dictionary of Birds* (London, 1896). Ferdinand Columbus says: *rabo di giunco*, "a bird so called because it has a long feather in its tail," p. 63.

[68] This remark is, of course, not true of the tropic bird or *rabo de junco*, as was abundantly proved on this voyage.

of nightingales. He says that the weather was like April in Andalusia. Here they began to see many tufts of grass which were very green, and appeared to have been quite recently torn from the land. From this they judged that they were near some island, but not the main land, according to the Admiral, "because," as he says, "I make the main land to be more distant."

Monday, 17th of September

They proceeded on their west course, and made over 50 leagues in the day and night, but the Admiral only counted 47. They were aided by the current. They saw much very fine grass and herbs from rocks, which came from the west. They, therefore, considered that they were near land. The pilots observed the north point, and found that the needles turned a full point to the west of north. So the mariners were alarmed and dejected, and did not give their reason. But the Admiral knew, and ordered that the north should be again observed at dawn. They then found that the needles were true. The cause was that the star makes the movement, and not the needles. At dawn, on that Monday, they saw much more weed appearing, like herbs from rivers, in which they found a live crab, which the Admiral kept. He says that these crabs are certain signs of land. The sea-water was found to be less salt than it had been since leaving the Canaries. The breezes were always soft. Every one was pleased, and the best sailors went ahead to sight the first land. They saw many tunny-fish, and the crew of the *Niña* killed one. The Admiral here says that these signs of land came from the west, "in which direction I trust in that high God in whose hands are all victories that very soon we shall sight land." In that morning he says that a white bird was seen which has not the habit of sleeping on the sea, called *rabo de junco* (boatswain-bird).

Tuesday, 18th of September

This day and night they made over 55 leagues, the Admiral only counting 48. In all these days the sea was very smooth, like the river at Seville. This day Martin Alonso, with the *Pinta* which was a fast sailer, did not wait, for he said to the Admiral, from his caravel, that he had seen a great multitude of birds flying westward, that he hoped to see land that night, and that he therefore pressed onward. A great cloud appeared in the north, which is a sign of the proximity of land.

Wednesday, 19th of September

The Admiral continued on his course, and during the day and night he made but 25 leagues because it was calm. He counted 22. This day, at 10 o'clock, a booby[69] came to the ship, and in the afternoon another arrived, these birds not generally going more than 20 leagues from the land. There was also some drizzling rain without wind, which is a sure sign of land. The Admiral did not wish to cause delay by beating to windward to ascertain whether land was near, but he considered it certain that there were islands both to the north and south of his position, (as indeed there were, and he was passing through the middle of them). For his desire was to press onwards to the Indies, the weather being fine. For on his return, God willing, he could see all. These are his own words. Here the pilots found their positions. He of the *Niña* made the Canaries 440 leagues distant, the *Pinta* 420. The pilot of the Admiral's ship made the distance exactly 400 leagues.

---

[69] *Alcatraz.* The rendering "booby" follows Cuvier's note to the French translation. The "booby" is the "booby gannet." The Spanish dictionaries give pelican as the meaning of *Alcatraz.* The gannets and the pelicans were formerly classed together. The word *Alcatraz* was taken over into English and corrupted to *Albatros.* Alfred Newton, *Dictionary of Birds* (London, 1896), art. "Albatros."

Thursday, 20th of September

This day the course was W. b. N., and as her head was all round the compass owing to the calm that prevailed,[70] the ship made only 7 or 8 leagues. Two boobies came to the ship, and afterwards another, a sign of the proximity of land. They saw much weed, although none was seen on the previous day. They caught a bird with the hand, which was like a tern. But it was a river-bird, not a sea-bird, the feet being like those of a gull. At dawn two or three land-birds came singing to the ship, and they disappeared before sunset. Afterwards a booby came from W.N.W., and flew to the S.W., which was a sign that it left land in the W.N.W.; for these birds sleep on shore, and go to sea in the mornings in search of food, not extending their flight more than 20 leagues from the land.

Friday, 21st September

Most of the day it was calm, and later there was a little wind. During the day and night they did not make good more than 13 leagues. At dawn they saw so much weed that the sea appeared to be covered with it, and it came from the west. A booby was seen. The sea was very smooth, like a river, and the air the best in the world. They saw a whale, which is a sign that they were near land, because they always keep near the shore.

---

[70] More exactly, "He sailed this day toward the West a quarter northwest and half the division [i.e., west by north and west by one eighth northwest] because of the veering winds and calm that prevailed."

Saturday, 22nd of September

They shaped a course W.N.W. more or less, her head turning from one to the other point, and made 30 leagues. Scarcely any weed was seen. They saw some sandpipers and another bird. Here the Admiral says: "This contrary wind was very necessary for me, because my people were much excited at the thought that in these seas no wind ever blew in the direction of Spain." Part of the day there was no weed, and later it was very thick.

Sunday, 23rd of September

They shaped a course N.W., and at times more northerly; occasionally they were on their course, which was west, and they made about 22 leagues. They saw a dove and a booby, another river-bird, and some white birds. There was a great deal of weed, and they found crabs in it. The sea, being smooth and calm, the crew began to murmur, saying that here there was no great sea, and that the wind would never blow so that they could return to Spain. Afterwards the sea rose very much, without wind, which astonished them. The Admiral here says: "Thus the high sea was very necessary to me, such as had not appeared but in the time of the Jews when they went out of Egypt and murmured against Moses who delivered them out of captivity."[71]

---

[71] The abridger of the original journal missed the point here and his epitome is unintelligible. Las Casas says in his *Historia*, I. 275: "The Admiral says in this place that the adverseness of the winds and the high sea were very necessary to him since they freed the crew of their erroneous idea that there would be no favorable sea and winds for their return and thereby they received some relief of mind or were not in so great despair, yet even then some objected, saying that that wind would not last, up to the Sunday following, when they had nothing to answer when they saw the sea so high. By which means, Cristóbal Colon says here, God dealt with him and with them as he dealt with Moses and the Jews when he

Monday, 24th of September

The Admiral went on his west course all day and night, making 14 leagues. He counted 12. A booby came to the ship, and many sandpipers.[72]

Tuesday, 25th of September

This day began with a calm, and afterwards there was wind. They were on their west course until night. The Admiral conversed with Martin Alonso Pinzon, captain of the other caravel *Pinta*, respecting a chart which he had sent to the caravel three days before, on which, as it would appear, the Admiral had certainis lands depicted in that sea.[73] Martin Alonso said that the ships were in the position on which the islands were placed, and the Admiral replied that so it appeared to him: but it might be that they had not fallen in with them, owing to the currents which had always set the ships to the N.E., and that they had not made so much as the pilots reported. The Admiral then asked for the chart to be returned, and it was sent back on a line.[74] The Admiral then began to

---

drew them from Egypt showing signs to favor and aid him and to their confusion."

[72] Las Casas, *Historia*, I. 275-276, here describes with detail the discontent of the sailors and their plots to put Columbus out of the way. The passage is translated in Thacher, *Christopher Columbus*, I. 524. The word rendered "sandpipers" is *pardelas*, petrels. The French translation has *petrels tachetes*, *i.e.*, "pintado petrels," or cape pigeons.

[73] More exactly, "On which it seems the Admiral had painted certain islands." The Spanish reads: "*donde segun parece tenia pintadas el Almirante ciertas islas*," etc. The question is whether Columbus made the map or had it made. The rendering of the note is supported by the French translators and by Harrisse.

[74] Las Casas, I. 279, says: "This map is the one which Paul, the physician, the Florentine, sent, which I have in my possession with other articles which belonged to the Admiral himself who discovered these Indies, and writings in his own hand which came into my possession. In it he depicted many

plot the position on it, with the pilot and mariners. At sunset Martin Alonso went up on the poop of his ship, and with much joy called to the Admiral, claiming the reward as he had sighted land. When the Admiral heard this positively declared, he says that he gave thanks to the Lord on his knees while Martin Alonso said the *Gloria in excelsis* with his people. The Admiral's crew did the same. Those of the *Niña* all went up on the mast and into the rigging, and declared that it was land. It so seemed to the

---

islands and the main land which were the beginning of India and in that region the realms of the Grand Khan," etc. Las Casas does not tell us how he knew that the Toscanelli map which he found in Columbus's papers was the map that the Admiral used on the first voyage. That is the general assumption of scholars, but there is no positive evidence of the fact. The Toscanelli map is no longer extant, and all reconstructions of it are based on the globe of Martin Behaim constructed in 1492. The reconstruction by H. Wagner which may be seen in S. Ruge, *Columbus*, 2te aufl. (Berlin, 1902) is now accepted as the most successful.

According to the reckoning of the distances in the Journal, Columbus was now about 550 leagues or 2200 Italian miles west of the Canaries. The Toscanelli map was divided off into spaces each containing 250 miles. Columbus was therefore nine spaces west of the Canaries. No reconstruction of Toscanelli's map puts any islands at nine spaces from the Canaries except so far as the reconstructors insert the island of Antilia on the basis of Behaim's globe. The Antilia of Behaim according to Wagner was eight spaces west of the Canaries. Again Ferdinand Columbus, in his _Historie_ under date of October 7 (p. 72), says the sailors "had been frequently told by him that he did not look for land until they had gone 750 leagues west from the Canaries, at which distance he had told them he would have found Española then called Cipango." 750 leagues or 3000 Italian miles would be 12 spaces on the Toscanelli map.

But according to the Toscanelli letter Cipango was 10 spaces west of Antilia, and therefore 18 spaces or 4500 miles west of the Canaries. Columbus then seems to have expected to find Cipango some 1500 miles to the east of where it was placed on the Toscanelli map. These considerations justify a very strong doubt whether Columbus was shaping his course and basing his expectations on the data of the Toscanelli letter and map, or whether the fact that Las Casas found what he took to be the Toscanelli map in the Admiral's papers proves that it was that map which he had on his first voyage.

Admiral, and that it was distant 25 leagues. They all continued to declare it was land until night. The Admiral ordered the course to be
altered from W. to S.W., in which direction the land had appeared. That day they made 4 leagues on a west course, and 17 S.W. during the night, in all 21; but the people were told that 13 was the distance made good: for it was always feigned to them that the distances were less, so that the voyage might not appear so long. Thus two reckonings were kept on this voyage, the shorter being feigned, and the longer being the true one. The sea was very smooth, so that many sailors bathed alongside. They saw many *dorados*[75] and other fish.

Wednesday, 26th of September

The Admiral continued on the west course until afternoon. Then he altered course to S.W., until he made out that what had been said to be land was
only clouds. Day and night they made 31 leagues, counting 24 for the people. The sea was like a river, the air pleasant and very mild.

Thursday, 27th of September

The course west, and distance made good during day and night 24 leagues, 20 being counted for the people. Many *dorados* came. One was killed. A
boatswain-bird came.

Friday, 28th of September

The course was west, and the distance, owing to calms, only 14 leagues in day and night, 13 leagues being

---

[75] *Dorado* is defined by Stevens as the dory or gilt head.

counted. They met with little weed; but caught two *dorados*, and more in the other ships.

Saturday, 29th of September

The course was west, and they made 24 leagues, counting 21 for the people. Owing to calms, the distance made good during day and night was not much. They saw a bird called *rabiforcado*[76] (man-o'-war bird), which makes the boobies vomit what they have swallowed, and eats it, maintaining itself on nothing else. It is a sea-bird, but does not sleep on the sea, and does not go more than 20 leagues from the land. There are many of them at the Cape Verde Islands. Afterwards they saw two boobies. The air was very mild and agreeable, and the Admiral says that nothing was wanting but to hear the nightingale. The sea smooth as a river. Later, three boobies and a man-o'-war bird were seen three times. There was much weed.

Sunday, 30th of September

The western course was steered, and during the day and night, owing to calms, only 14 leagues were made, 11 being counted. Four boatswain-birds came to the ship, which is a great sign of land, for so many birds of this kind together is a sign that they are not straying or lost. They also twice saw four boobies. There was much weed. Note that the stars which are called *Las Guardias* (the

---

[76] *Rabiforcado*, Portuguese. The Spanish form is *rabihorcado*. It means "forked tail." The modern English equivalent is "frigate bird." It is "the Fregata aquila of most ornithologists, the Frégate of French and the Rabihorcado of Spanish mariners." Newton, *Dictionary of Birds*, art. "Frigate-Bird." Newton says that the name "man-of-war bird" has generally passed out of use in books.

Pointers[77]), when night comes on, are near the western point, and when dawn breaks they are near the N.E. point; so that, during the whole night, they do not appear to move more than three lines or 9 hours, and this on each night. The Admiral says this, and also that at nightfall the needles vary a point westerly, while at dawn they agree exactly with the star. From this it would appear that the north star has a movement like the other stars, while the needles always point correctly.

Monday, 1st of October

Course west, and 25 leagues made good, counted for the crew as 20 leagues. There was a heavy shower of rain. At dawn the Admiral's pilot made the distance from Hierro 578 leagues to the west. The reduced reckoning which the Admiral showed to the crew made it 584 leagues; but the truth which the Admiral observed and kept secret was 707.

Tuesday, 2nd of October

Course west, and during the day and night 39 leagues were made good, counted for the crew as 30. The sea always smooth. Many thanks be given to God, says the Admiral, that the weed is coming from east to west, contrary to its usual course. Many fish were seen, and one was killed. A white bird was also seen that appeared to be a gull.

---

[77] Rather, the Guards, the name given to the two brightest stars in the constellation of the Little Bear. The literal translation is: "the Guards, when night comes on, are near the arm on the side to the west, and when dawn breaks they are on the line under the arm to the northeast," etc. What Columbus meant I cannot explain. Neither Navarrete nor the French translators offer any suggestions.

Wednesday, 3rd of October

They navigated on the usual course, and made good 47 leagues, counted as 40. Sandpipers appeared, and much weed, some of it very old and some quite fresh and having fruit. They saw no birds. The Admiral, therefore, thought that they had left the islands behind them which were depicted on the charts. The Admiral here says that he did not wish to keep the ships beating about during the last week, and in the last few days when there were so many signs of land, although he had information of certain islands in this region. For he wished to avoid delay, his object being to reach the Indies. He says that to delay would not be wise.[78]

Thursday, 4th of October

Course west, and 63 leagues made good during the day and night, counted as 46. More than forty sandpipers came to the ship in a flock, and two boobies, and a ship's boy hit one with a stone. There also came a man-o'-war bird and a white bird like a gull.

---

[78] Las Casas, I. 282, adds to the foregoing under date of October 3: "He says here that it would not have been good sense to beat about and in that way to be delayed in search of them [i.e., the islands] since he had favorable weather and his chief intention was to go in search of the Indies by way of the west, and this was what he proposed to the King and Queen, and they had sent him for that purpose. Because he would not turn back to beat up and down to find the islands which the pilots believed to be there, particularly Martin Alonzo by the chart which, as was said, Cristóbal Colon had sent to his caravel for him to see, and it was their opinion that he ought to turn, they began to stir up a mutiny, and the disagreement would have gone farther if God had not stretched out his arm as he was wont, showing immediately new signs of their being near land since now neither soft words nor entreaties nor prudent reasoning of Cristóbal Colon availed to quiet them and to persuade them to persevere." Ferdinand Columbus says simply, "For this reason the crew began to be mutinous, persevering in their complaints and plots," p. 71. See page 108, note 1.

Friday, 5th of October

The Admiral steered his course, going 11 miles an hour, and during the day and night they made good 57 leagues, as the wind increased somewhat during the night: 45 were counted. The sea was smooth and quiet. "To God," he says, "be many thanks given, the air being pleasant and temperate, with no weed, many sandpipers, and flying-fish coming on the deck in numbers."

Saturday, 6th of October

The Admiral continued his west course, and during day and night they made good 40 leagues, 33 being counted. This night Martin Alonso said that it would be well to steer south of west,[79] and it appeared to the Admiral that Martin Alonso did not say this with respect to the island of Cipango.[80] He saw that if an error was made the land would not be reached so quickly, and that consequently it would be better to go at once to the continent and afterwards to the islands.

Sunday, 7th of October

The west course was continued; for two hours they went at the rate of 12 miles an hour, and afterwards 8 miles an hour. They made good 23 leagues, counting 18 for the people. This day, at sunrise, the caravel *Niña*, which went ahead, being the best sailer, and pushed forward as much as possible to sight the land first, so as to enjoy the

---

[79] *Á la cuarta del Oueste, á la parte del Sudueste*, at the quarter from the west toward the southwest, *i.e.*, west by south.

[80] Las Casas, in the *Historia de las Indias*, I. 283, writes, "That night Martin Alonso said that it would be well to sail west by south for the island of Cipango which the map that Cristóbal Colon showed him represented." *Cf.* page 101, note 2.

reward which the Sovereigns had promised to whoever should see it first, hoisted a flag at the mast-head and fired a gun, as a signal that she had sighted land, for such was the Admiral's order. He had also ordered that, at sunrise and sunset, all the ships should join him; because those two times are most proper for seeing the greatest distance, the haze clearing away. No land was seen during the afternoon, as reported by the caravel _Niña_, and they passed a great number of birds flying from N. to S.W. This gave rise to the belief that the birds were either going to sleep on land, or were flying from the winter which might be supposed to be near in the land whence they were coming. The Admiral was aware that most of the islands held by the Portuguese were discovered by the flight of birds. For this reason he resolved to give up the west course, and to shape a course W.S.W. for the two following days.[81] He began the new course one hour before sunset. They made good, during the night, about 5 leagues, and 23 in the day, altogether 28 leagues.

Monday, 8th of October

The course was W.S.W., and 11-1/2 or 12 leagues were made good in the day and night; and at times it appears that they went at the rate of 15 miles an hour during the night (if the handwriting is not deceptive).[82] The sea was

---

[81] Las Casas remarks, I. 285, "If he had kept up the direct westerly course and the impatience of the Castilians had not hindered him, there is no doubt that he would have struck the main land of Florida and from there to New Spain, although the difficulties would have been unparalleled and the losses unbearable that they would have met with, and it would have been a divine miracle if he had ever returned to Castile."

[82] Grajaos. The translator assumed this to be the same as garjao; the French translators, on the other hand, took it to be the same as grajos, crows. In Portuguese dictionaries the word grajão is found as the name of "an Indian bird."

like the river at Seville. "Thanks be to God," says the Admiral, "the air is very soft like the April at Seville; and it is a pleasure to be here, so balmy are the breezes." The weed seemed to be very fresh. There were many land-birds, and they took one that was flying to the S.W. Terns,[83] ducks, and a booby were also seen.

Tuesday, 9th of October

The course was S.W., and they made 5 leagues. The wind then changed, and the Admiral steered W. by N. 4 leagues. Altogether, in day and night, they made 11 leagues by day and 20-1/2 leagues by night; counted as 17 leagues altogether. Throughout the night birds were heard passing.

Wednesday, 10th of October

The course was W.S.W., and they went at the rate of 10 miles an hour, occasionally 12 miles, and sometimes 7. During the day and night they made 59 leagues, counted as no more than 44. Here the people could endure no longer. They complained of the length of the voyage. But the Admiral cheered them up in the best way he could, giving them good hopes of the advantages they might gain from it. He added that, however much they might complain, he had to go to the Indies, and that he would go on until he found them, with the help of our Lord.[84]

---

[84] The trouble with the captains and the sailors is told in greatest detail by Oviedo, *Historia de las Indias*, lib. II., cap. V. He is the source of the story that the captains finally declared they would go on three days longer and not another hour. Oviedo does not say that Columbus acquiesced in this arrangement. Modern critics have been disposed to reject Oviedo's account, but strictly interpreted, it is not inconsistent with our other sources. Columbus recalls in his Journal, February 14, 1493, the terror of the situation which was evidently more serious than the entry of October 10 would imply. Peter Martyr too says that the sailors plotted to throw

Thursday, 11th of October

The course was W.S.W., and there was more sea than there had been during the whole of the voyage. They saw sandpipers, and a green reed near the ship. Those of the caravel _Pinta_ saw a cane and a pole, and they took up another small pole which appeared to have been worked with iron; also another bit of cane, a land-plant, and a small board. The crew of the caravel *Niña* also saw signs of land, and a small branch covered with berries.[85] Every one breathed afresh and rejoiced at these signs. The run until sunset was 27 leagues.

After sunset the Admiral returned to his original west course, and they went along at the rate of 12 miles an hour. Up to two hours after midnight they had gone 90 miles, equal to 22-1/2 leagues. As the caravel *Pinta* was a better sailer, and went ahead of the Admiral, she found the land, and made the signals ordered by the Admiral. The land was first seen by a sailor named Rodrigo de Triana.[86] But the Admiral, at ten o'clock, being on the castle of the poop,[87] saw a light, though it was so

---

Columbus overboard and adds: "After the thirtieth day roused by madness they declared they were going back," but that Columbus pacified them. *De Rebus Oceanicis*, Dec. lib. I., fol. 2, ed. of 1574. Oviedo says that he derived information from Vicente Yañez Pinzon, "since with him I had a friendship up to the year 1514 when he died." *Historia de las Indias*, II., cap. XIII.

[85] *Escaramojos*. Wild roses.

[86] It was full moon on October 5. On the night of the 11th the moon rose at 11 P.M. and at 2 A.M. on the morning of the 12th it was 39° above the horizon. It would be shining brightly on the sandy shores of an island some miles ahead, being in its third quarter, and a little behind Rodrigo de Triana, when he sighted land at 2 A.M. (Markham.)

[87] The high decks fore and aft were called castles. The name survives in the English forecastle. Stevens gives poop alone as the English for *Castilla de popa*.

uncertain that he could not affirm it was land. He called Pero Gutierrez, a gentleman of the King's bed-chamber, and said that there seemed to be a light, and that he should look at it. He did so, and saw it.[88] The Admiral said the same to Rodrigo Sanchez of Segovia, whom the King and Queen had sent with the fleet as inspector, but he could see nothing, because he was not in a place whence anything could be seen. After the Admiral had spoken he saw the light once or twice, and it was like a wax candle rising and falling. It seemed to few to be an indication of land; but the Admiral made certain that land was close.

When they said the *Salve,* which all the sailors were accustomed to sing in their way, the Admiral asked and admonished the men to keep a good look-out on the forecastle, and to watch well for land; and to him who should first cry out that he saw land, he would give a silk doublet, besides the other rewards promised by the Sovereigns, which were 10,000 maravedis to him who should first see it.[89] At two hours after midnight the land was sighted at a distance of two leagues. They shortened sail, and lay by under the mainsail without the bonnets.

---

[88] Oviedo, lib. II., cap. V., says that, as they were sailing along, a sailor, a native of Lepe, cried out, "Light," "Land," but was immediately told that the admiral had already seen it and remarked upon it.

[89] Columbus received this award. His claiming or accepting it under the circumstances has been considered discreditable and a breach of faith by many modern writers. Oviedo says the native of Lepe was so indignant at not getting the reward that "he went over into Africa and denied the faith," _i.e._, became a Mohammedan. Las Casas seems to have seen no impropriety in Columbus' accepting the award. He tells us, l. 289, that this annuity was paid to Columbus throughout his life and was levied from the butcher shops of Seville. A maravedi was equal to two-thirds of a cent.

Friday, 12th of October

The vessels were hove to, waiting for daylight; and on Friday they arrived at a small island of the Lucayos, called in the language of the Indians, Guanahani.[90] Presently they saw naked people. The Admiral went on shore in the armed boat, and Martin Alonso Pinzon, and Vicente Yañez, his brother, who was captain of the *Niña*. The Admiral took the royal standard, and the captains went with two banners of the green cross, which the Admiral took in all the ships as a sign, with an F and a Y[91] and a crown over each letter, one on one side of the cross and the other on the other. Having landed, they saw trees very green, and much water, and fruits of diverse kinds. The Admiral called to the two captains, and to the others who leaped on shore, and to Rodrigo Escovedo, secretary of the whole fleet, and to Rodrigo Sanchez of Segovia,[92] and said that they should bear faithful testimony that he, in presence of all, had taken, as he now took, possession of the said island[93] for the King and for the Queen his Lords, making the declarations that are required, as is now largely set forth in the testimonies which were then made in writing.

Presently many inhabitants of the island assembled. What follows is in the actual words of the Admiral in his book of the first navigation and discovery of the Indies.[94]

---

[90] Pronounced originally, according to Las Casas, I. 291, with the accent on the last syllable. Guanahani is now generally accepted to have been Watling Island. See Markham, *Christopher Columbus*, pp. 89-107, for a lucid discussion of the landfall.

[91] Fernando and Ysabel.

[92] The royal inspector.

[93] Las Casas adds, I. 293, "To which he gave the name Sant Salvador."

[94] We have here perhaps the original title of what in its abridged form we now call the Journal.

"I," he says, "that we might form great friendship, for I knew that they were a people who could be more easily freed and converted to our holy faith by love than by force, gave to some of them red caps, and glass beads to put round their necks, and many other things of little value, which gave them great pleasure, and made them so much our friends that it was a marvel to see. They afterwards came to the ship's boats where we were, swimming and bringing us parrots, cotton threads in skeins, darts, and many other things; and we exchanged them for other things that we gave them, such as glass beads and small bells. In fine, they took all, and gave what they had with good will. It appeared to me to be a race of people very poor in everything. They go as naked as when their mothers bore them, and so do the women, although I did not see more than one young girl. All I saw were youths, none more than thirty years of age. They are very well made, with very handsome bodies, and very good countenances. Their hair is short and coarse, almost like the hairs of a horse's tail. They wear the hairs brought down to the eyebrows, except a few locks behind, which they wear long and never cut. They paint themselves black, and they are the color of the Canarians, neither black nor white. Some paint themselves white, others red, and others of what color they find. Some paint their faces, others the whole body, some only round the eyes, others only on the nose.

They neither carry nor know anything of arms, for I showed them swords, and they took them by the blade and cut themselves through ignorance. They have no iron, their darts being wands without iron, some of them having a fish's tooth at the end, and others being pointed in various ways. They are all of fair stature and size, with good faces, and well made. I saw some with marks of wounds on their bodies, and I made signs to ask what it was, and they gave me to understand that people from other adjacent islands came with the intention of seizing them, and that they defended themselves. I believed, and still believe, that they come here from the mainland to take them prisoners. They should be good servants and intelligent, for I observed that they quickly took in what was said to them, and I believe that they would easily be made Christians, as it appeared to me that they had no religion. I, our Lord being pleased, will take hence, at the time of my departure, six natives for your Highnesses, that they may learn to speak. I saw no beast of any kind except parrots, on this island." The above is in the words of the Admiral.

Saturday, 13th of October

"As soon as dawn broke many of these people came to the beach, all youths, as I have said, and all of good stature, a very handsome people. Their hair is not curly, but loose and coarse, like horse hair. In all the forehead is broad, more so than in any other people I have hitherto seen. Their eyes are very beautiful and not small, and themselves far from black, but the color of the Canarians. Nor should anything else be expected, as this island is in a line east and west from the island of Hierro in the Canaries. Their legs are very straight, all in one line, and no belly, but very well formed. They came to the ship in small canoes, made out of the trunk of a tree like a long boat, and all of one piece, and wonderfully worked, considering the country. They are large, some of them holding 40 to 45 men, others smaller, and some only large enough to hold one man. They are propelled with a paddle like a baker's shovel, and go at a marvellous rate. If the canoe capsizes, they all promptly begin to swim, and to bale it out with calabashes that they take with them. They brought skeins of cotton thread, parrots, darts, and other small things which it would be tedious to recount, and they give all in exchange for anything that may be given to them. I was attentive, and took trouble to ascertain if there was gold. I saw that some of them had a small piece fastened in a hole they have in the nose, and by signs I was able to make out that to the south, or going from the island to the south, there was a king who had great cups full, and who possessed a great quantity. I tried to get them to go there, but afterwards I saw that they had no inclination. I resolved to wait until to-morrow in the afternoon and then to depart, shaping a course to the S.W., for, according to what many of them told me, there was land to the S., to the S.W., and N.W., and that the natives from the N.W. often came to attack them, and went on to the S.W. in search of gold and precious stones.

"This island is rather large and very flat, with bright green trees, much water, and a very large lake in the centre, without any mountain, and the whole land so green that it is a pleasure to look on it. The people are very docile, and for the longing to possess our things, and not having anything to give in return, they take what they can get, and presently swim away. Still, they give away all they have got, for whatever may be given to them, down to broken bits of crockery and glass. I saw one give 16 skeins of cotton for three *ceotis*[95] of Portugal, equal to one *blanca* of Spain, the skeins being as much as an *arroba* of cotton thread. I shall keep it, and shall allow no one to take it, preserving it all for your Highnesses, for it may be obtained in abundance. It is grown in this island, though the short time did not admit of my ascertaining this for a certainty. Here also is found the

---

[95] The Portuguese *ceitil* (pl. *ceitis*) was a small coin deriving its name from Ceuta, opposite Gibraltar, in Africa, a Portuguese possession. The *blanca* was one-half a maravedi, or about one-third of a cent.

gold they wear fastened in their noses. But, in order not to lose time, I intend to go and see if I can find the island of Cipango.[96] Now, as it is night, all the natives have gone on shore with their canoes."

Sunday, 14th of October

"At dawn I ordered the ship's boat and the boats of the caravels to be got ready, and I went along the coast of the island and to the N.N.E., to see the other side, which was on the other side to the east, and also to see the villages. Presently I saw two or three, and the people all came to the shore, calling out and giving thanks to God. Some of them brought us water, others came with food, and when they saw that I did want to land, they got into the sea, and came swimming to us. We understood that they asked us if we had come from heaven. One old man came into the boat, and others cried out, in loud voices, to all the men and women, to come and see the men who had come from heaven, and to bring them to eat and drink. Many came, including women, each bringing something, giving thanks to God, throwing themselves on the ground and shouting to us to come on shore. But I was afraid to land, seeing an extensive reef of rocks which surrounded the island, with deep water between it and the shore forming a port large enough for as many ships as there are in Christendom, but with a very narrow entrance. It is true that within this reef there are some sunken rocks, but the sea has no more motion than the water in a well. In order to see all this I went this morning, that I might be able to give a full account to your Highnesses, and also where a fortress might be established. I saw a piece of land which appeared like an island, although it is not one, and on it there were six houses. It might be converted into an

---

[96] Cipango. Marco Polo's name for Japan.

island in two days, though I do not see that it would be necessary, for these people are very simple as regards the use of arms, as your Highnesses will see from the seven that I caused to be taken, to bring home and learn our language and return; unless your Highnesses should order them all to be brought to Castile, or to be kept as captives on the same island; for with fifty men they can all be subjugated and made to do what is required of them. Close to the above peninsula there are gardens of the most beautiful trees I ever saw, and with leaves as green as those of Castile in the month of April and May, and much water. I examined all that port, and afterwards I returned to the ship and made sail. I saw so many islands that I hardly knew how to determine to which I should go first. Those natives I had with me said, by signs, that there were so many that they could not be numbered, and they gave the names of more than a hundred. At last I looked out for the largest, and resolved to shape a course for it, and so I did. It will be distant five leagues from this of *San Salvador*, and the others some more, some less. All are very flat, and all are inhabited. The natives make war on each other, although these are very simple-minded and handsomely-formed people."

Monday, 15th of October

"I had laid by during the night, with the fear of reaching the land to anchor before daylight,[97] not knowing whether the coast was clear of rocks, and at dawn I made sail. As the island was more than 5 leagues distant and nearer 7, and the tide checked my way, it was noon when we arrived at the said island. I found that side facing towards the island of San Salvador trended north and south with a length of 5 leagues, and the other which I followed ran

---

[97] Rather, "I had lain to during the night for fear of reaching the land," etc.

east and west for more than 10 leagues.[98] As from this
island I saw another larger one to the west, I clued up[99]
the sails, after having run all that day until night,
otherwise I could not have reached the western cape. I
gave the name of Santa Maria de la Concepcion[100] to the
island, and almost as the sun set I anchored near the said
cape to ascertain if it contained gold. For the people I had
taken from the island of San Salvador told me that here
they wore very large rings of gold on their arms and legs.
I really believed that all they said was nonsense, invented
that they might escape. My desire was not to pass any
island without taking possession, so that, one having been
taken, the same may be said of all. I anchored, and
remained until to-day, Tuesday, when I went to the shore
with the boats armed, and landed. The people, who were
numerous, went naked, and were like those of the other
island of San Salvador. They let us go over the island, and
gave us what we required. As the wind changed to the
S.E., I did not like to stay, and returned to the ship. A
large canoe was alongside the *Niña*, and one of the men of
the island of San Salvador, who was on board, jumped
into the sea and got into the canoe. In the middle of the
night before, another swam away behind the canoe, which
fled, for there never was boat that could have overtaken
her, seeing that in speed they have a great advantage.[101]
So they reached the land and left the canoe. Some of my

---

[98] These lengths are exaggerated.

[99] The word is *cargué* and means "raised" or "hoisted." The same word
seven lines above was translated "made sail." Las Casas in the
corresponding passage in his *Historia* uses *alzar*.

[100] Identified as Rum Cay.

[101] A line is missing in the original. The text may be restored as follows,
beginning with the end of the preceding sentence, "jumped into the sea
and got into the canoe; in the middle of the night before the other threw
[himself into the sea and swam off. The boat was lowered] and put after
the canoe which escaped since there never was a boat which could
have overtaken him, since we were far behind him."

people went on shore in chase of them, but they all fled like fowls and the canoe they had left was brought alongside the caravel *Niña*, whither, from another direction, another small canoe came, with a man who wished to barter with skeins of cotton.

Some sailors jumped into the sea, because he would not come on board the caravel, and seized him. I was on the poop of my ship, and saw everything. So I sent for the man, gave him a red cap, some small beads of green glass, which I put on his arms, and small bells, which I put in his ears, and ordered his canoe, which was also on board, to be returned to him. I sent him on shore, and presently made sail to go to the other large island which was in sight to the westward. I also ordered the other large canoe, which the caravel *Niña* was towing astern, to be cast adrift; and I soon saw that it reached the land at the same time as the man to whom I had given the above things. I had not wished to take the skein of cotton that he offered me. All the others came round him and seemed astonished, for it appeared clear to them that we were good people. The other man who had fled might do us some harm, because we had carried him off, and for that reason I ordered this man to be set free and gave him the above things, that he might think well of us, otherwise, when your Highnesses again send an expedition, they might not be friendly. All the presents I gave were not worth four maravedis. At 10 we departed with the wind S.W., and made for the south, to reach that other island, which is very large, and respecting which all the men that I bring from San Salvador make signs that there is much gold, and that they wear it as bracelets on the arms, on the legs, in the ears and nose, and round the neck. The distance of this island from that of Santa Maria is 9 leagues on a course east to west. All this part of the island trends N.W. and S.E., and it appeared that this coast must have length of 28 leagues. It is very flat, without any mountain, like San Salvador and Santa Maria, all being beach without rocks, except that there are some sunken rocks near the land, whence it is necessary to keep a good lookout when it is desired to anchor, and not to come to very near the land; but the water is always very clear, and the bottom is visible. At a distance of two shots of a lombard, there is, off all these islands, such a depth that the bottom cannot be reached. These islands are very green and fertile, the climate very mild. They may contain many things of which I have no knowledge, for I do not wish to stop, in discovering and visiting many islands, to find gold. These people make signs that it is worn on the arms and legs; and it must be gold, for they point to some pieces that I have. I cannot err, with the help of our Lord, in finding out where this gold has its origin. Being in the middle of the channel between these two islands, that is to say, that of Santa Maria and this large one, to which I give the name of Fernandina,[102] I came upon a man alone in a canoe going from Santa Maria to Fernandina. He had a little of their bread, about the size of a fist, a calabash of water, a piece of brown earth powdered and then kneaded, and some dried leaves, which must be a thing highly valued by them,[103] for they bartered with it at San Salvador. He also had with him a native basket with a string of glass beads, and two *blancas*, by which I knew that he had come from the island of San Salvador, and had been to Santa Maria, and thence to Fernandina. He came alongside the ship, and I made him come on board as he desired, also getting the canoe inboard, after taking care of all his property. I ordered him to be given to eat bread and treacle, and also to drink: and so I shall take him on to Fernandina, where I shall return everything to him, order that he may give a

---

[102] Long Island. (Markham.)
[103] Possibly a reference to tobacco.

good account of us, that, our Lord pleasing, when your Highnesses shall send here, those who come may receive honor, and that the natives may give them all they require."

Tuesday, 16th of October

"I sailed from the island of Santa Maria de la Concepcion at about noon, to go to Fernandina Island, which appeared very large to the westward, and I navigated all that day with light winds. I could not arrive in time to be able to see the bottom, so as to drop the anchor on a clear place, for it is necessary to be very careful not to lose the anchors. So I stood off and on all that night until day, when I came to an inhabited place where I anchored, and whence that man had come that I found yesterday in the canoe in mid channel. He had given such a good report of us that there was no want of canoes alongside the ship all that night, which brought us water and what they had to offer. I ordered each one to be given something, such as a few beads, ten or twelve of those made of glass on a thread, some timbrels made of brass such as are worth a maravedi in Spain, and some straps, all which they looked upon as most excellent. I also ordered them to be given treacle to eat when they came on board. At three o'clock[104] I sent the ship's boat on shore for water, and the natives with good will showed my people where the water was, and they themselves brought the full casks down to the boat, and did all they could to please us.

"This island is very large, and I have determined to sail round it, because, so far as I can understand, there is a mine in or near it. The island is eight leagues from Santa

---

[104] It should be "about nine o'clock." The original is *á horas de tercia*, which means "at the hour of tierce," *i.e.*, the period between nine and twelve.

Maria, nearly east and west; and this point I had reached, as well as all the coast, trends N.N.W. and S.S.E. I saw at least 20 leagues of it, and then it had not ended. Now, as I am writing this, I made sail with the wind at the south, to sail round the island, and to navigate until I find Samaot, which is the island or city where there is gold, as all the natives say who are on board, and as those of San Salvador and Santa Maria told us. These people resemble those of the said islands, with the same language and customs, except that these appear to me a rather more domestic and tractable people, yet also more subtle. For I observed that those who brought cotton and other trifles to the ship, knew better than the others how to make a bargain. In this island I saw cotton cloths made like mantles. The people were better disposed, and the women wore in front of their bodies a small piece of cotton which scarcely covered them.

"It is a very green island, level and very fertile, and I have no doubt that they sow and gather corn[105] all the year round, as well as other things. I saw many trees very unlike those of our country. Many of them have their branches growing in different ways and all from one trunk, and one twig is one form, and another in a different shape, and so unlike that it is the greatest wonder in the world to see the great diversity; thus one branch has leaves like those of a cane, and others like those of a mastick tree: and on a single tree there are five or six different kinds. Nor are these grafted, for it may be said that grafting is unknown, the trees being wild, and untended by these people. They do not know any religion, and I believe they could easily be converted to

---

[105] *Panizo*, literally "panic grass." Here Columbus seems to use the word as descriptive of maize or Indian corn, and later the word came to have this meaning. On the different species of panic grass, see Candolle, *Origin of Cultivated Plants* (index under *panicum*.)

Christianity, for they are very intelligent. Here the fish are so unlike ours that it is wonderful. Some are the shape of dories, and of the finest colors in the world, blue, yellow, red, and other tints, all painted in various ways, and the colors are so bright that there is not a man who would not be astonished, and would not take great delight in seeing them. There are also whales. I saw no beasts on the land of any kind, except parrots and lizards. A boy told me that he saw a large serpent. I saw neither sheep, nor goats, nor any other quadruped. It is true I have been here a short time, since noon,[106] yet I could not have failed to see some if there had been any. I will write respecting the circuit of this island after I have been round it."

Wednesday, 17th of October

"At noon I departed from the village off which I was anchored, and where I took in water, to sail round this island of Fernandina. The wind was S.W. and South. My wish was to follow the coast of this island to the S.E., from where I was, the whole coast trending N.N.W. and S.S.E.; because all the Indians I bring with me, and others, made signs to this southern quarter, as the direction of the island they call Samoet, where the gold is. Martin Alonso Pinzon, captain of the caravel *Pinta*, on board of which I had three of the Indians, came to me and said that one of them had given him to understand very positively that the island might be sailed round much quicker by shaping a N.N.W. course. I saw that the wind would not help me to take the course I desired, and that it was fair for the other, so I made sail to the N.N.W. When I was two leagues from the cape of the island, I discovered a very wonderful harbor.[107] It has one mouth, or, rather, it may

---

[106] Rather, "since it is noon.
[107] Port Clarence in Long Island. (Markham.)

be said to have two, for there is an islet in the middle. Both are very narrow, and within it is wide enough for a hundred ships, if there was depth and a clean bottom, and the entrance was deep enough. It seemed desirable to explore it and take soundings, so I anchored outside, and went in with all the ship's boats, when we saw there was insufficient depth. As I thought, when I first saw it, that it was the mouth of some river, I ordered the water-casks to be brought. On shore I found eight or ten men, who presently came to us and showed us the village, whither I sent the people for water, some with arms, and others with the casks; and, as it was some little distance, I waited two hours for them.

"During that time I walked among the trees, which was the most beautiful thing I had ever seen, beholding as much verdure as in the month of May in Andalusia. The trees are unlike ours as night from day, as are the fruits, the herbs, the stones, and everything. It is true that some of the trees bore some resemblance to those in Castile, but most of them are very different, and some were so unlike that no one could compare them to anything in Castile. The people were all like those already mentioned: like them naked, and the same size. They give what they possess in exchange for anything that may be given to them. I here saw some of the ship's boys bartering broken bits of glass and crockery for darts. The men who went for water told me that they had been in the houses of the natives, and that they were very plain and clean inside. Their beds and bags for holding things[108] were like nets of cotton.[109] The houses are like booths, and very high, with

---

[108] Rather, "beds and hangings." The original is *paramentos de cosas*, but in the corresponding passage in his *Historia*, I. 310, Las Casas has *paramentos de casa*, which is almost certainly the correct reading.
[109] "These are called Hamacas in Española." Las Casas, I. 310, where will be found an elaborate description of them.

good chimneys.[110] But, among many villages that I saw, there was none that consisted of more than from twelve to fifteen houses. Here they found that the married women wore clouts of cotton, but not the young girls, except a few who were over eighteen years of age. They had dogs, mastiffs, and hounds;[111] and here they found a man who had a piece of gold in his nose, the size of half a castellano,[112] on which they saw letters. I quarrelled with these people because they would not exchange or give what was required; as I wished to see what and whose this money was; and they replied that they were not accustomed to barter.

"After the water was taken I returned to the ship, made sail, and shaped a course N.W., until I had discovered all the part of the coast of the island which trends east to west. Then all the Indians turned round and said that this island was smaller than Samoet, and that it would be well to return back so as to reach it sooner. The wind presently went down and then sprang up from W.N.W., which was contrary for us to continue on the previous course. So I turned back, and navigated all that night to E.S.E., sometimes to east and to S.E. This course was steered to keep me clear of the land, for there were very heavy clouds and thick weather, which did not admit of my approaching the land to anchor. On that night it rained very heavily from midnight until nearly dawn, and

---

[110] For ornament. Las Casas calls them caps or crowns, I. 311.

[111] Rather: "mastiffs and beagles." Las Casas, I. 311, says the Admiral called these dogs mastiffs from the report of the sailors. "If he had seen them, he would not have called them so but that they resembled hounds. These and the small ones would never bark but merely a grunt in the throat."

[112] The *castellano* was one-sixth of an ounce. Las Casas, I. 311, remarks: "They were deceived in believing the marks to be letters since those people are wont to work it in their fashion, since never anywhere in all the Indies was there found any trace of money of gold or silver or other metal."

even afterwards the clouds threatened rain. We found ourselves at the S.W. end
of the island, where I hoped to anchor until it cleared up, so as to see the other island whither I have to go. On all these days, since I arrived in these Indies, it has rained more or less. Your Highnesses may believe that this land is the best and most fertile, and with a good climate, level, and as good as there is in the world."

Thursday, 18th of October

"After it had cleared up I went before the wind, approaching the island as near as I could, and anchored when it was no longer light enough to
keep under sail. But I did not go on shore, and made sail at dawn...."

Friday, 19th of October

"I weighed the anchors at daylight, sending the caravel *Pinta* on an E.S.E. course, the caravel *Niña* S.S.E., while I shaped a S.E. course, giving orders that these courses were to be steered until noon, and that then the two caravels should alter course so as to join company with me. Before we had sailed for three hours we saw an island to the east, for which we steered, and all three vessels arrived at the north point before noon. Here there is an islet, and a reef of rocks to seaward of it, besides one between the islet and the large island. The men of San Salvador, whom I bring with me, called it Saomete, and I gave it the name of Isabella.[113] The wind was north and the said islet bore from the island of Fernandina, whence I had taken my departure, east and west. Afterwards we ran along the coast of the island, westward from the islet,

---

[113] Crooked Island (Markham.)

and found its length to be 12 leagues as far as a cape, which I named Cabo Hermoso, at the western end. The island is beautiful, and the coast very deep, without sunken rocks off it. Outside the shore is rocky, but further in there is a sandy beach, and here I anchored on that Friday night until morning. This coast and the part of the island I saw is almost flat, and the island is very beautiful; for if the other islands are lovely, this is more so. It has many very green trees, which are very large. The land is higher than in the other islands, and in it there are some hills, which cannot be called mountains: and it appears that there is much water inland. From this point to the N.E. the coast makes a great angle, and there are many thick and extensive groves. I wanted to go and anchor there, so as to go on shore and see so much beauty; but the water was shallow, and we could only anchor at a distance from the land. The wind also was fair for going to this cape, where I am now anchored, to which I gave the name of Cabo Hermoso, [114] because it is so. Thus it was that I do not anchor in that angle, but as I saw this cape so green and so beautiful, like all the other lands of these islands, I scarcely knew which to visit first; for I can never tire my eyes in looking at such lovely vegetation, so different from ours. I believe that there are many herbs and many trees that are worth much in Europe for dyes and for medicines; but I do not know them, and this causes me great sorrow. Arriving at this cape, I found the smell of the trees sand flowers so delicious that it seemed the pleasantest thing in the world. To-morrow, before I leave this place, I shall go on shore to see what there is at this cape. There are no people, but there are villages in the interior, where, the Indians I bring with me say, there is a king who has much gold. To-morrow I intend to go so far inland as to find the village, and see and have some

---

[114] Cape Beautiful.

speech with this king, who, according to the signs they make, rules over all the neighboring islands, goes about clothed, and wears much gold on his person. I do not give much faith to what they say, as well because I do not understand them well as because they are so poor in gold that even a little that this king may have would appear much to them. This cape, to which I have given the name of Cabo Fermoso, is, I believe, on an island separated from Saometo, and there is another small islet between them. I did not try to examine them in detail, because it could not be done in 50 years. For my desire is to see and discover as much as I can before returning to your Highnesses, our Lord willing, in April. It is true that in the event of finding places where there is gold or spices in quantity I should stop until I had collected as much as I could. I, therefore, proceed in the hope of coming across such places."

Saturday, 20th of October

"To-day, at sunrise, I weighed the anchors from where I was with the ship, and anchored off the S.W. point of the island of Saometo, to which I gave the name of Cabo de la Laguna, and to the island Isabella. My intention was to navigate to the north-east and east from the south-east and south, where, I understood from the Indians I brought with me, was the village of the king. I found the sea so shallow that I could not enter nor navigate in it, and I saw that to follow a route by the south-east would be a great round. So I determined to return by the route that I had taken from the N.N.E. to the western part, and to sail round this island to [reconnoitre it].

"I had so little wind that I never could sail along the coast, except during the night. As it was dangerous to anchor off these islands except in the day, when one can see where to let the anchor, for the bottom is all in patches, some clear and some rocky, I lay to all this Sunday night. The caravels anchored because they found themselves near the shore, and they thought that, owing to the signals that they were in the habit of making, I would come to anchor, but I did not wish to do so."

Sunday, 21st of October

"At ten o'clock I arrived here, off this islet, and anchored, as well as the caravels. After breakfast I went on shore, and found only one house, in which there was no one, and I supposed they had fled from fear, because all their property was left in the house. I would not allow anything to be touched, but set out with the captains and people to explore the island. If the others already seen are very beautiful, green, and fertile, this is much more so, with large trees and very green. Here there are large lagoons with wonderful vegetation on their banks. Throughout the island all is green, and the herbage like April in Andalusia. The songs of the birds were so pleasant that it seemed as if a man could never wish to leave the place. The flocks of parrots concealed the sun; and the birds were so numerous, and of so many different kinds, that it was wonderful. There are trees of a thousand sorts, and all have their several fruits; and I feel the most unhappy man in the world not to know them, for I am well assured that they are all valuable. I bring home specimens of them, and also of the land. Thus walking along round one of the lakes I saw a serpent, which we killed, and I bring home the skin for your Highnesses. As soon as it saw us it went into the lagoon, and we followed, as the water was not very deep, until we killed it with lances. It is 7 spans long, and I believe that there are many like it in these lagoons.[115] Here I came upon some aloes, and I have

---

[115] "The Indians of this island of Española call it *iguana*." Las Casas I. 314. He gives a minute description of it.

determined to take ten quintals on board to-morrow, for they tell me that they are worth a good deal. Also, while in search of good water, we came to a village about half a league from our anchorage. The people, as soon as they heard us, all fled and left their houses, hiding their property in the wood. I would not allow a thing to be touched, even the value of a pin. Presently some men among them came to us, and one came quite close. I gave him some bells and glass beads, which made him very content and happy. That our friendship might be further increased, I resolved to ask him for something; I requested him to get some water. After I had gone on board, the natives came to the beach with calabashes full of water, and they delighted much in giving it to us. I ordered another string of glass beads to be presented to them, and they said they would come again to-morrow. I wished to fill up all the ships with water at this place, and, if there should be time, I intended to search the island until I had had speech with the king, and seen whether he had the gold of which I had heard. I shall then shape a course for another much larger island, which I believe to be Cipango, judging from the signs made by the Indians I bring with me. They call it Cuba, and they say that there are ships and many skilful sailors there. Beyond this island there is another called Bosio,[116] which they also say is very large, and others we shall see as we pass, lying between. According as I obtain tidings of gold or spices I shall settle what should be done. I am still

---

[116] The names in the Spanish text are Colba and Bosio, errors in transcription for Cuba and Bohio. Las Casas, I. 315, says in regard to the latter: "To call it Bohio was to misunderstand the interpreters, since throughout all these islands, where the language is practically the same, they call the huts in which they live *bohio* and this great island Española they called Hayti, and they must have said that in Hayti there were great *bohios*."

resolved to go to the mainland and the city of Guisay,[117] and to deliver the letters of your Highnesses to the Gran Can, requesting a reply and returning with it."

Monday, 22nd of October

"All last night and to-day I was here, waiting to see if the king or other person would bring gold or anything of value. Many of these people came, like those of the other islands, equally naked, and equally painted, some white, some red, some black, and others in many ways. They brought darts and skeins of cotton to barter, which they exchanged with the sailors for bits of glass, broken crockery, and pieces of earthenware. Some of them had pieces of gold fastened in their noses, which they willingly gave for a hawk's bell and glass beads. But there was so little that it counts for nothing. It is true that they looked upon any little thing that I gave them as a wonder, and they held our arrival to be a great marvel, believing that we came from heaven. We got water for the ships from a lagoon which is near the Cabo del Isleo (Cape of the Islet), as we named it. In the said lagoon Martin Alonso Pinzon, captain of the *Pinta*, killed another serpent 7 *spans* long, like the one we got yesterday. I made them gather here as much of the aloe as they could find."

Tuesday, 23rd of October

"I desired to set out to-day for the island of Cuba, which I think must be Cipango, according to the signs these people make, indicative of its size and riches, and I did not delay any more here nor [attempt to sail] ...[118] round this island to the residence of this king or lord, and have

---

[117] The name is spelled Quinsay in the Latin text of Marco Polo which Columbus annotated.
[118] One or two words are missing in the original.

speech with him, as I had intended. This would cause me much delay, and I see that there is no gold mine here. To sail round would need several winds, for it does not blow here as men may wish. It is better to go where there is great entertainment, so I say that it is not reasonable to wait, but rather to continue the voyage and inspect much land, until some very profitable country is reached, my belief being that it will be rich in spices. That I have no personal knowledge of these products causes me the greatest sorrow in the world, for I see a thousand kinds of trees, each one with its own special fruit, all green now as in Spain during the months of May and June, as well as a thousand kinds of herbs with their flowers; yet I know none of them except this aloe, of which I ordered a quantity to be brought on board to bring to your Highnesses. I have not made sail for Cuba because there is no wind, but a dead calm with much rain. It rained a great deal yesterday without causing any cold. On the contrary, the days are hot and the nights cool, like May in Andalusia."

Wednesday, 24th of October

"At midnight I weighed the anchors and left the anchorage at Cabo del Isleo, in the island of Isabella.[119] From the northern side, where I was, I intended to go to the island of Cuba, where I heard of the people who were very great, and had gold, spices, merchandise, and large ships. They showed me that the course thither would be W.S.W., and so I hold. For I believe that it is so, as all the Indians of these islands, as well as those I brought with me in the ships, told me by signs. I cannot understand

---

[119] The translation here should be, "raised the anchors at the island of Isabella at Cabo del Isleo, which is on the northern side where I tarried to go to the island of Cuba, which I heard from this people is very great and has gold," etc.

their language, but I believe that it is of the island of Cipango that they recount these wonders.[120] On the spheres I saw, and on the delineations of the map of the world,[121] Cipango is in this region. So I shaped a course W.S.W. until daylight, but at dawn it fell calm and began to rain, and went on nearly all night. I remained thus, with little wind, until the afternoon, when it began to blow fresh. I set all the sails in the ship, the mainsail with two bonnets, the foresail, spritsail, mizzen, main topsail, and the boat's sail on the poop. So I proceeded until nightfall, when the Cabo Verde of the island of Fernandina, which is at the S.W. end, bore N.W. distant 7 leagues. As it was now blowing hard, and I did not know how far it was to this island of Cuba, I resolved not to go in search of it during the night; all these islands being very steep-to, with no bottom round them for a distance of two shots of a lombard. The bottom is all in patches, one bit of sand and another of rock, and for this reason it is not safe to anchor without inspection with the eye. So I determined to take in all the sails except the foresail, and to go on under that reduced canvas. Soon the wind increased, while the route was doubtful, and there was very thick weather, with rain. I ordered the foresail to be furled, and we did not make two leagues during that night."

---

[120] These two lines should read, "I believe that it is the island of Cipango of which marvellous things are related."

[121] The exact translation is, "On the spheres that I saw and on the paintings of world-maps it is this region." The plural number is used in both cases. Of the globes of this date, i.e., 1492 or earlier, that of Behaim is the only one that has come down to us. Of the world maps Toscanelli's, no longer extant, may have been one, but it is to be noted that Columbus uses the plural.

Thursday, 25th of October

"I steered W.S.W. from after sunset until 9 o'clock, making 5 leagues. Afterwards I altered course to west, and went 8 miles an hour until one in the afternoon; and from that time until three made good 44 miles. Then land was sighted, consisting of 7 or 8 islands, the group running north and south, distant from us 5 leagues."

Friday, 26th of October

"The ship was on the south side of the islands, which were all low, distant 5 or 6 leagues. I anchored there. The Indians[122] on board said that thence to Cuba was a voyage in their canoes of a day and a half; these being small dug-outs without a sail. Such are their canoes. I departed thence for Cuba, for by the signs the Indians made of its greatness, and of its gold and pearls, I thought that it must be Cipango."

Saturday, 27th of October

"I weighed from these islands at sunrise, and gave them the name of Las Islas de Arena, owing to the little depth the sea had for a distance of 6 leagues to the southward of them. We went 8 miles an hour on a S.S.W. course until one o'clock having made 40 miles. Until night we had run 28 miles on the same course, and before dark the land was sighted. At night there was much rain. The vessels, on Saturday until sunset, made 17 leagues on a S.S.W. course."

---

[122] Columbus's conviction that he has reached the Indies is registered by his use from now on of the word "Indians" for the people.

Sunday, 28th of October

"I went thence in search of the island of Cuba on a S.S.W. course, making for the nearest point of it, and entered a very beautiful river without danger of sunken rocks or other impediments. All the coast was clear of dangers up to the shore. The mouth of the river was 12 *brazas* across, and it is wide enough for a vessel to beat in.[123] I anchored about a lombard-shot inside." The Admiral says that "he never beheld such a beautiful place, with trees bordering the river, handsome, green, and different from ours, having fruits and flowers each one according to its nature. There are many birds, which sing very sweetly. There are a great number of palm trees of a different kind from those in Guinea and from ours, of a middling height, the trunks without that covering, and the leaves very large, with which they thatch their houses. The country is very level." The Admiral jumped into his boat and went on shore. He came to two houses, which he believed to belong to fishermen who had fled from fear. In one of them he found a kind of dog that never barks, and in both there were nets of palm-fibre and cordage, as well as horn fish-hooks, bone harpoons, and other apparatus "for fishing, and several hearths. He believed that many people lived together in one house. He gave orders that nothing in the houses should be touched, and so it was done." The herbage was as thick as in Andalusia during April and May. He found much purslane and wild amaranth.[124] He returned to the boat and went up the river for some distance, and he says it was great pleasure to see the bright verdure, and the birds, which he could not leave to

---

[123] This should be, "The mouth of the river is 12 fathoms deep and it is wide enough," etc.

[124] *Bledos.* The French translators give *cresson sauvage*, wild cress, as the equivalent.

go back. He says that this island is the most beautiful that eyes have seen, full of good harbors and deep rivers, and the sea appeared as if it never rose; for the herbage on the beach nearly reached the waves, which does not happen where the sea is rough. (Up to that time they had not experienced a rough sea among all those islands.) He says that the island is full of very beautiful mountains, although they are not very extensive as regards length, but high; and all the country is high like Sicily. It is abundantly supplied with water, as they gathered from the Indians they had taken with them from the island of Guanahani. These said by signs that there are ten great rivers, and that they cannot go round the island in twenty days. When they came near land with the ships, two canoes came out; and, when they saw the sailors get into a boat and row about to find the depth of the river where they could anchor, the canoes fled. The Indians say that in this island there are gold mines and pearls, and the Admiral saw a likely place for them and mussel-shells, which are signs of them. He understood that large ships of the Gran Can came here, and that from here to the mainland was a voyage of ten days.[125] The Admiral called this river and harbor San Salvador.[126]

Monday, 29th of October

The Admiral weighed anchor from this port and sailed to the westward, to go to the city, where, as it seemed, the Indians said that there was a king. They doubled a point six leagues to the N.W.,[127] and then another point,[128] then

---

[125] Las Casas, I. 320, says Columbus understood "that from these to the mainland would be a sail of ten days by reason of the notion he had derived from the chart or picture which the Florentine sent him."

[126] Baracoa (Las Casas); Puerto Naranjo (Markham); Nipe (Navarrete); Nuevitas (Thacher).

[127] Punta de Mulas. (Navarrete.)

[128] Punta de Cabañas. (Navarrete.

east ten leagues. After another league he saw a river with no very large entrance, to which he gave the name of Rio de la Luna.[129] He went on until the hour of vespers. He saw another river much larger than the others, as the Indians told him by signs, and near he saw goodly villages of houses. He called the river Rio de Mares.[130] He sent two boats on shore to a village to communicate, and one of the Indians he had brought with him, for now they understood a little, and show themselves content with Christians. All the men, women, and children fled, abandoning their houses with all they contained. The Admiral gave orders that nothing should be touched. The houses were better than those he had seen before, and he believed that the houses would improve as he approached the mainland. They were made like booths, very large, and looking like tents in a camp without regular streets, but one here and another there. Within they were clean and well swept, with the furniture well made. All are of palm branches beautifully constructed. They found many images in the shape of women, and many heads like masks,[131] very well carved. It was not known whether these were used as ornaments, or to be worshipped. They had dogs which never bark, and wild birds tamed in their houses. There was a wonderful supply of nets and other fishing implements, but nothing was touched. He believed that all the people on the coast were fishermen, who took the fish inland, for this island is very large, and so beautiful, that he is never tired of praising it. He says that he found trees and fruits of very marvellous taste; and adds that they must have cows or other cattle, for he saw skulls which were like those of cows.[132] The songs of

---

[129] Puerto de Banes. (Navarrete.)

[130] Puerto de las Nuevitas del Principe. (Navarrete.)

[131] Las Casas, I. 321, has "many heads well carved from wood." Possibly these were totems.

[132] Las Casas, I. 321, comments, "These must have been skulls of the

the birds and the chirping of crickets throughout the night lulled everyone to rest, while the air was soft and healthy, and the nights neither hot nor cold. On the voyage through the other islands there was great heat but here it is tempered like the month of May. He attributed the heat of the other islands to their flatness, and to the wind coming from the east, which is hot. The water of the rivers was salt at the mouth, and they did not know whence the natives got their drinking-water, though they have sweet water in their houses. Ships are able to turn in this river, both entering and coming out, and there are very good leading-marks. He says that all this sea appears to be constantly smooth, like the river at Seville, and the water suitable for the growth of pearls. He found large shells unlike those of Spain. Remarking on the position of the river and port, to which he gave the name of San Salvador,[133] he describes its mountains as lofty and beautiful, like the Peña de las Enamoradas,[134] and one of them has another little hill on its summit, like a graceful mosque. The other river and port, in which he now was,[135] has two round mountains to the S.W., and a fine low cape running out to the W.S.W.

Tuesday, 30th of October

He left the Rio de Mares and steered N.W., seeing a cape covered with palm trees, to which he gave the name of Cabo de Palmas,[136] after having made good 15 leagues. The Indians on board the caravel *Pinta* said that beyond

---

manati, a very large fish, like large calves, which has a skin with no scales like a whale and its head is like that of a cow."

[133] "I believe that this port was Baracoa, which name Diego Velasquez, the first of the Spaniards to settle Cuba, gave to the harbor of Asumpcion." Las Casas, I. 322.

[134] Near Granada in Spain.

[135] Nuevitas del Principe. (Navarrete.)

[136] "Alto de Juan Dañue." (Navarrete.)

that cape there was a river,[137] and that from the river to Cuba it was four days' journey. The captain of the *Pinta* reported that he understood from that, that this Cuba was a city, and that the land was a great continent trending far to the north. The king of that country, he gathered, was at war with the Gran Can, whom they called Cami, and his land or city Fava, with many other names. The Admiral resolved to proceed to that river, and to send a present, with the letter of the Sovereigns, to the king of that land. For this service there was a sailor who had been to Guinea, and some of the Indians of Guanahani wished to go with him, and afterwards to return to their homes. The Admiral calculated that he was forty-two degrees to the north of the equinoctial line (but the handwriting is here illegible).[138] He says that he must attempt to reach the Gran Can, who he thought was here or at the city of Cathay,[139] which belongs to him, and is very grand, as he was informed before leaving Spain. All this land, he adds, is low and beautiful, and the sea deep.

Wednesday, 31st of October

All Tuesday night he was beating to windward, and he saw a river, but could not enter it because the entrance was narrow. The Indians fancied that the ships could

---

[137] Rio Maximo. (Navarrete.)

[138] Rather, "The text here is corrupt." Las Casas, I. 324, gives the same figures and adds, "yet I think the text is erroneous." Navarrete says the quadrants of that period measured the altitude double and so we should take half of forty-two as the real altitude. If so, one wonders why there was no explanation to this effect in the original journal which Las Casas saw or why Las Casas was not familiar with this fact and did not make this explanation. Ruge, *Columbus*, pp. 144, 145, says there were no such quadrants, and regards these estimates as proofs of Columbus's ignorance as a scientific navigator.

[139] In Toscanelli's letter Cathay is a province in one place and a city in another.

enter wherever their canoes could go. Navigating onwards, he came to a cape running out very far, and surrounded by sunken rocks,[140] and he saw a bay where small vessels might take shelter. He could not proceed because the wind had come round to the north, and all the coast runs N.W. and S.E. Another cape further on ran out still more.[141] For these reasons, and because the sky showed signs of a gale, he had to return to the Rio de Mares.

Thursday, November the 1st

At sunrise the Admiral sent the boats on shore to the houses that were there, and they found that all the people had fled. After some time a man made his appearance. The Admiral ordered that he should be left to himself, and the sailors returned to the boats. After dinner, one of the Indians on board was sent on shore. He called out from a distance that there was nothing to fear, because the strangers were good people and would do no harm to anyone, nor were they people of the Gran Can, but they had given away their things in many islands where they had been. The Indian then swam on shore, and two of the natives took him by the arms and brought him to a house, where they heard what he had to say. When they were certain that no harm would be done to them they were reassured, and presently more than sixteen canoes came to the ships with cotton-thread and other trifles. The Admiral ordered that nothing should be taken from them, that they might understand that he sought for nothing but gold, which they call nucay.[142] Thus they went to and

---

[140] Boca de Carabelas grandes. (Navarrete.)

[141] Punta del Maternillo. (Navarrete.)

[142] Las Casas says, I. 326. "I think the Christians did not understand, for the language of all these islands is the same, and in this island of Española gold is called caona."

fro between the ships and the shore all day, and they came to the Christians on shore with confidence. The Admiral saw no gold whatever among them, but he says that he saw one of them with a piece of worked silver fastened to his nose. They said, by signs, that within three days many merchants from inland would come to buy the things brought by the Christians, and would give information respecting the king of that land. So far as could be understood from their signs, he resided at a distance of four days' journey. They had sent many messengers in all directions, with news of the arrival of the Admiral. "These people," says the Admiral, "are of the same appearance and have the same customs as those of the other islands, without any religion so far as I know, for up to this day I have never seen the Indians on board say any prayer; though they repeat the *Salve* and *Ave Maria* with their hands raised to heaven, and they make the sign of the cross. The language is also the same, and they are all friends; but I believe that all these islands are at war with the Gran Can, whom they called Cavila, and his province Bafan. They all go naked like the others." This is what the Admiral says.

"The river," he adds, "is very deep, and the ships can enter the mouth, going close to the shore. The sweet water does not come within a league of the mouth. It is certain," says the Admiral, "that this is the mainland, and that I am in front of Zayto and Guinsay, a hundred leagues, a little more or less, distant the one from the other.[143] It is

---

[143] The last words should be, "distant from the one and from the other." Las Casas, I. 327, says: "Zayton and Quisay are certain cities or provincias of the mainland which were depicted on the map of Paul the physician as mentioned above." These Chinese cities were known from Marco Polo's description of them. This passage in the Journal is very perplexing if it assumes that Columbus was guided by the Toscanelli letter. Again a few days earlier Columbus was sure that Cuba was Cipango, and now he is equally certain that it is the mainland of Asia asserted by Toscanelli to be 26 spaces or 6500 Italian miles west of Lisbon, but the next day his estimate

very clear that no one before has been so far as this by sea. Yesterday, with wind from the N.W., I found it cold."

Friday, 2nd of November

The Admiral decided upon sending two Spaniards, one named Rodrigo de Jerez, who lived in Ayamonte, and the other Luis de Torres, who had served in the household of the Adelantado of Murcia, and had been a Jew, knowing Hebrew, Chaldee, and even some Arabic. With these men he sent two Indians, one from among those he had brought from Guanahani and another a native of the houses by the river-side. He gave them strings of beads with which to buy food if they should be in need, and ordered them to return in six days. He gave them specimens of spices, to see if any were to be found. Their instructions were to ask for the king of that land, and they were told what to say on the part of the Sovereigns of Castile, how they had sent the Admiral with letters and a present, to inquire after his health and establish friendship, favoring him in what he might desire from them. They were to collect information respecting certain provinces, ports, and rivers of which the Admiral had notice, and to ascertain their distances from where he was.

This night the Admiral took an altitude with a quadrant, and found that the distance from the equinoctial line was 42 degrees.[144] He says that, by his reckoning, he finds that he has gone over 1142 leagues from the island of

---

of his distance from Lisbon is 4568 miles. It would seem as if Columbus attached no importance to the estimate of distances on the Toscanelli map which was the only original information in it.

Hierro.[145] He still believes that he has reached the mainland.

Saturday, 3rd of November

In the morning the Admiral got into the boat, and, as the river is like a great lake at the mouth, forming a very excellent port, very deep, and clear of rocks, with a good beach for careening ships, and plenty of fuel, he explored it until he came to fresh water at a distance of two leagues from the mouth. He ascended a small mountain to obtain a view of the surrounding country, but could see nothing, owing to the dense foliage of the trees, which were very fresh and odoriferous, so that he felt no doubt that there were aromatic herbs among them. He said that all he saw was so beautiful that his eyes could never tire of gazing upon such loveliness, nor his ears of listening to the songs of birds. That day many canoes came to the ships, to barter with cotton threads and with the nets in which they sleep, called *hamacas*.

Sunday, 4th of November

At sunrise the Admiral again went away in the boat, and landed to hunt the birds he had seen the day before. After a time, Martin Alonso Pinzon came to him with two pieces of cinnamon, and said that a Portuguese, who was one of his crew, had seen an Indian carrying two very large bundles of it; but he had not bartered for it, because of the penalty imposed by the Admiral on any one who bartered. He further said that this Indian carried some brown things like nutmegs. The master of the *Pinta* said that he had found the cinnamon trees. The Admiral went to the place, and found that they were not cinnamon trees. The Admiral showed the Indians some specimens of cinnamon

---

[145] The true distance was 1105 leagues. (Navarrete.)

and pepper he had brought from Castile, and they knew it, and said, by signs, that there was plenty in the vicinity, pointing to the S.E. He also showed them gold and pearls, on which certain old men said that there was an infinite quantity in a place called *Bohio*,[146] and that the people wore it on their necks, ears, arms, and legs, as well as pearls. He further understood them to say that there were great ships and much merchandise, all to the S.E. He also understood that, far away, there were men with one eye, and others with dogs' noses[147] who were cannibals, and that when they captured an enemy, they beheaded him and drank his blood, and cut off his private parts.

The Admiral then determined to return to the ship and wait the return of the two men he had sent, intending to depart and seek for those lands, if his envoys brought some good news touching what he desired. The Admiral further says: "These people are very gentle and timid; they go naked, as I have said without arms and without law. The country is very fertile. The people have plenty of *mames* which are like carrots and have the flavor of chestnuts; and they have *faxones* and beans of kinds very different from ours.[148] They also have much cotton, which

---

[146] "*Bohio* means in their language 'house,' and therefore it is to be supposed that they did not understand the Indians, but that it was Hayti, which is this island of Española where they made signs there was gold." Las Casas, I. 329.

[147] Columbus understood the natives to say these things because of his strong preconceptions as to what he would find in the islands off the coast of Asia based on his reading of the Book of Sir John Maundeville. Cf. ch. XVIII. of that work, *e.g.*, "a great and fair isle called Nacumera.... And all the men and women have dogs' heads," and ch. XIX., *e.g.*, "In one of these isles are people of great stature, like giants, hideous to look upon; and they have but one eye in the middle of the forehead."

[148] Las Casas, I. 329, identifies the *mames* as *ajes* and *batatas*. The batatas, whence our word "potato," is the sweet potato. *Mames* is more commonly written *ñames* or *ignames*. This is the Guinea Negro name of the *Dioscorea sativa*, in English "Yam." *Ajes* is the native West Indies name.

they do not sow, as it is wild in the mountains, and I believe they collect it throughout the year, because I saw pods empty, others full, and flowers all on one tree. There are a thousand other kinds of fruits, which it is impossible for me to write about, and all must be profitable." All this the Admiral says.

Monday, 5th of November

This morning the Admiral ordered the ship to be careened, afterwards the other vessels, but not all at the same time. Two were always to be at the anchorage, as a precaution; although he says that these people were very safe, and that without fear all the vessels might have been careened at the same time. Things being in this state, the master[149] of the *Niña* came to claim a reward from the Admiral because he had found mastic, but he did not bring the specimen, as he had dropped it. The Admiral promised him a reward, and sent Rodrigo Sanchez and master Diego to the trees. They collected some, which was kept to present to the Sovereigns, as well as the tree. The Admiral says that he knew it was mastic, though it ought to be gathered at the proper season. There is enough in that district for a yield of 1000 *quintals* every year. The Admiral also found here a great deal of the plant called aloe. He further says that the *Puerto de Mares* is the best in the world, with the finest

---

See Peschel, *Zeitalter der Entdeckungen*, p. 139, and Columbus's journal, Dec. 13 and Dec. 16. *Faxones* are the common haricot kidney beans or string beans, *Phaseolus vulgaris*. This form of the name seems a confusion of the Spanish *fásoles* and the Portuguese *feijões*. That Columbus, an Italian by birth who had lived and married in Portugal and removed to Spain in middle life, should occasionally make slips in word-forms is not strange. More varieties of this bean are indigenous in America than were known in Europe at the time of the discoveries. Cf. De Candolle, *Origi of Cultivated Plants*, pp. 338 ff.

[149] The word is *contramaestre*, boatswain.

climate and the most gentle people. As it has a high, rocky cape, a fortress might be built, so that, in the event of the place becoming rich and important, the merchants would be safe from any other nations. He adds: "The Lord, in whose hands are all victories, will ordain all things for his service. An Indian said by signs that the mastic was good for pains in the stomach."

Tuesday, 6th of November

Yesterday, at night, says the Admiral, the two men came back who had been sent to explore the interior. They said that after walking 12 leagues they came to a village of 50 houses, where there were a thousand inhabitants, for many live in one house. These houses are like very large booths. They said that they were received with great solemnity, according to custom, and all, both men and women, came out to see them. They were lodged in the best houses, and the people touched them, kissing their hands and feet, marvelling and believing that they came from heaven, and so they gave them to understand. They gave them to eat of what they had. When they arrived, the chief people conducted them by the arms to the principal house, gave them two chairs on which to sit, and all the natives sat round them on the ground. The Indian who came with them described the manner of living of the Christians, and said that they were good people.

Presently the men went out, and the women came sitting round them in the same way, kissing their hands and feet, and looking to see if they were of flesh and bones like themselves. They begged the Spaniards to remain with them at least five days. The Spaniards showed the natives specimens of cinnamon, pepper and other spices which the Admiral had given them, and they said, by signs, that there was plenty at a short distance from thence to S.E., but that there they did not know whether there was

any.[150] Finding that they had no information respecting
cities, the Spaniards returned; and if they had desired to
take those who wished to accompany them, more than 500
men and women would have come, because they thought
the Spaniards were returning to heaven. There came,
however, a principal man of the village and his son, with
a servant. The Admiral conversed with them, and showed
them much honor. They made signs respecting many
lands and islands in those parts. The Admiral thought of
bringing them to the Sovereigns. He says that he knew
not what fancy took them; either from fear, or owing to
the dark night, they wanted to land. The ship was at the
time high and dry, but, not wishing to make them angry,
he let them go on their saying that they would return at
dawn, but they never came back. The two Christians met
with many people on the road going home, men and
women with a half-burnt weed in their hands, being
the herbs they are accustomed to smoke.[151] They did not
find villages on the road of more than five houses all

---

[150] The last line should read, "but that they did not know whether there
was any in the place where they were."

[151] The last line should read, "with a brand in their hand, [and] herbs to
smoke as they are accustomed to do." This is the earliest reference to
smoking tobacco. Las Casas, I. 332, describes the process as the natives
practised it: "These two Christians found on their way many people, men
and women, going to and from their villages and always the men with a
brand in their hands and certain herbs to take their smoke, which are dry
herbs placed in a certain leaf, also dry like the paper muskets which boys
make at Easter time. Having lighted one end of it, they suck at the other
end or draw in with the breath that smoke which they make themselves
drowsy and as if drunk, and in that way, they say, cease to feel fatigue.
These muskets, or whatever we call them, they call *tabacos*. I knew
Spaniards in this island of Española who were accustomed to take them,
who, when they were rebuked for it as a vice, replied they could not give
it up. I do not know what pleasant taste or profit they found in them." Las
Casas' last remarks show that smoking was not yet common in his later life
in Spain. The paper muskets of Las Casas are blow-pipes. Oviedo, lib. V.,
cap. II., gives a detailed description of the use of tobacco. He says that
the Indians smoked by inserting these tubes in the nostrils and that after
two or three inhalations they lost consciousness. He knew some Christians
who used it as an anesthetic when in great pain.

receiving them with the same reverence. They saw many kinds of trees, herbs, and sweet-smelling flowers; and birds of many different kinds, unlike those of Spain, except the partridges, geese, of which there are many, and singing nightingales.

They saw no quadrupeds except the dogs that do not bark.[152] The land is very fertile, and is cultivated with yams and several kinds of beans different from ours, as well as corn.[153] There were great quantities of cotton gathered, spun, and worked up. In a single house they saw more than 500 *arrobas*,[154] and as much as 4000 *quintals* could be yielded every year. The Admiral said that "it did not appear to be cultivated, and that it bore all the year round. It is very fine, and has a large boll. All that was possessed by these people they gave at a very low price, and a great bundle of cotton was exchanged for the point of a needle or other trifle. They are a people," says the Admiral, "guileless and unwarlike. Men and women go as naked as when their mothers bore them.

It is true that the women wear a very small piece of cotton-cloth which covers their private parts and no more, and they are of very good appearance, not very dark, less so than the Canarians. I hold, most serene Princes, that if devout religious persons were here, knowing the language, they would all turn Christians. I trust in our

---

[152] On this indigenous species of dumb dogs, *cf.* Oviedo, lib. XII. cap. V. They have long been extinct in the Antilles. Oviedo says there were none in Española when he wrote. He left the island in 1546.

[153] This last part of this sentence should read, "and is cultivated with *mames*, kidney beans, other beans, this same panic [*i.e.*, Indian corn], etc." The corresponding passage in the *Historie* of Ferdinand Columbus reads, "and another grain like panic called by them *mahiz* of very excellent flavor cooked or roasted or pounded in porridge (polenta)," p. 87

[154] The *arroba* was 25 pounds and the *quintal* one hundred weight.

Lord that your Highnesses will resolve upon this with much diligence, to bring so many great nations within the Church, and to convert them; as you have destroyed those who would not confess the Father, the Son, and the Holy Ghost. And after your days, all of us being mortal, may your kingdoms remain in peace, and free from heresy and evil, and may you be well received before the eternal Creator, to whom I pray that you may have long life and great increase of kingdoms and lordships, with the will and disposition to increase the holy Christian religion as you have done hitherto. Amen!"

"To-day I got the ship afloat, and prepared to depart on Thursday, in the name of God, and to steer S.E. in search of gold and spices, and to discover land."

These are the words of the Admiral, who intended to depart on Thursday, but, the wind being contrary, he could not go until the 12th of November.

Monday, 12th of November

The Admiral left the port and river of Mares before dawn to visit the island called Babeque, so much talked of by the Indians on board, where, according to their signs, the people gather the gold on the beach at night with candles, and afterwards beat it into bars with hammers.[155]
To go thither it was necessary to shape a course E. b. S. After having made 8 leagues along the coast, a river was sighted, and another 4 leagues brought them to another river, which appeared to be of great volume, and larger than any they had yet seen. The Admiral did not wish to stop nor to enter any of these rivers, for two reasons: the

---

[155] In Las Casas, I. 339, Bohio is mentioned with Babeque, and it is in Bohio that the people were reported to gather gold on the beach.

first and principal one being that wind and weather were favorable for going in search of the said island of Babeque; the other, that, if there was a populous and famous city near the sea, it would be visible, while, to go up the rivers, small vessels are necessary, which those of the expedition were not. Much time would thus be lost; moreover, exploration of such rivers is a separate enterprise, that coast was peopled near the river, to which the name of Rio del Sol was given.

The Admiral says that, on the previous Sunday, the 11th of November, it seemed good to take some persons from amongst those at Rio de Mares, to bring to the Sovereigns, that they might learn our language, so as to be able to tell us what there is in their lands. Returning, they would be the mouthpieces of the Christians, and would adopt our customs and the things of the faith. "I saw and knew" (says the Admiral) "that these people are without any religion, not idolaters, but very gentle, not knowing what is evil, nor the sins of murder and theft, being without arms, and so timid that a hundred would fly before one Spaniard, although they joke with them.[156] They, however, believe and know that there is a God in heaven and say that we have come from Heaven. At any prayer that we say, they repeat, and make the sign of the cross. Thus your Highnesses should resolve to make them Christians, for I believe that, if the work was begun, in a little time a multitude of nations would be converted to our faith, with the acquisition of great lordships, peoples, and riches for Spain. Without doubt, there is in these lands a vast quantity of gold, and the Indians I have on board do not speak without reason when they say that in these islands there are places where they dig out gold, and wear it on their necks, ears, arms, and legs, the rings

---

[156] I.e., although the Spaniards may be only fooling with them.

being very large. There are also precious stones, pearls, and an infinity of spices.

In this river of Mares, whence we departed to-night, there is undoubtedly a great quantity of mastic, and much more could be raised, because the trees may be planted, and will yield abundantly. The leaf and fruit are like the mastic, but the tree and leaf are larger. As Pliny describes it, I have seen it on the island of Chios in the Archipelago. I ordered many of these trees to be tapped, to see if any of them would yield resin; but, as it rained all the time I was in that river, I could not get any, except a very little, which I am bringing to your Highnesses. It may not be the right season for tapping, which is, I believe, when the trees come forth after winter and begin to flower. But when I was there the fruit was nearly ripe. Here also there is a great quantity of cotton, and I believe it would have a good sale here without sending it to Spain, but to the great cities of the Gran Can,[157] which will be discovered without doubt, and many others ruled over by other lords, who will be pleased to serve our Highnesses, and whither will be brought other commodities of Spain and of the Eastern lands; but these are to the west as regards us. There is also here a great yield of aloes,[158] though this is not a commodity that will yield great profit. The mastic, however, is important, for it is only obtained from the said island of Chios, and I believe the harvest is

---

[157] An interesting forecast of the future which may be compared with John Cabot's; see one of the last pages of this volume.

[158] *Linaloe*. Lignaloes or agallochum, to be distinguished from the medicinal aloes. Both were highly prized articles of mediaeval Oriental trade. Lignaloes is mentioned by Marco Polo as one of the principal commodities exchanged in the market of Zaitun. It is also frequently mentioned in the Bible. *Cf.* numbers xxiv, 6, or Psalm xlv. 8. The aloes of Columbus were probably the Barbadoes aloes of commerce, and the mastic the produce of the *Bursera gummifera*. The last did not prove to be a commercial resin like the mastic of Scio. See *Encyclopædia Britannica* under Aloes and Mastic, and Heyd, *Histoire du Commerce du Levant au Moyen Age*, II. 581, 633.

worth 50,000 ducats, if I remember right.[159] There is here, in the mouth of the river, the best port I have seen up to this time, wide, deep, and clear of rocks. It is an excellent site for a town and fort, for any ship could come close up to the walls; the land is high, with a temperate climate, and very good water.

"Yesterday a canoe came alongside the ship, with six youths in it. Five came on board, and I ordered them to be detained. They are now here. I afterwards sent to a house on the western side of the river, and seized seven women, old and young, and three children. I did this because the men would behave better in Spain if they had women of their own land, than without them. For on many occasions the men of Guinea have been brought to learn the language in Portugal, and afterwards, when they returned, and it was expected that they would be useful in their land, owing to the good company they had enjoyed and the gifts they had received, they never appeared after arriving. Others may not act thus. But having women, they have the wish to perform what they are required to do; besides, the women would teach our people their language, which is the same in all these islands, so that those who make voyages in their canoes are understood everywhere. On the other hand, there are a thousand different languages in Guinea, and one native does not understand another.

"The same night the husband of one of the women came alongside in a canoe, who was father of the three children--one boy and two girls. He asked me to let him come with them, and besought me much. They are now all consoled

---

[159] The ducat being 9s. 2d. In the seventeenth century the value of the mastic exported from Chios (Scio) was 30,000 ducats. Chios belonged to Genoa from 1346 to 1566. (Markham.)

at being with one who is a relation of them all. He is a man of about 45 years of age." All these are the words of the Admiral. He also says that he had felt some cold, and that it would not be wise to continue discoveries in a northerly direction in the winter. On this Monday, until sunset, he steered a course E. b. S., making 18 leagues, and reaching a cape, to which he gave the name of Cabo de Cuba.

Tuesday, 13th of November

This night the ships were on a bowline, as the sailors say, beating to windward without making any progress. At sunset they began to see an opening in the mountains, where two very high peaks[160] were visible. It appeared that here was the division between the land of Cuba and that of Bohio, and this was affirmed by signs, by the Indians who were on board. As soon as the day had dawned, the Admiral made sail toward the land, passing a point which appeared at night to be distant two leagues. He then entered a large gulf, 5 leagues to the S.S.E., and there remained 5 more, to arrive at the point where, between two great mountains, there appeared to be an opening; but it could not be made out whether it was an inlet of the sea. As he desired to go to the island called Babeque, where according to the information he had received, there was much gold; and as it bore east, and as no large town was in sight the wind freshening more than ever, he resolved to put out to sea, and work to the east with a northerly wind. The ship made 8 miles an hour, and from ten in the forenoon, when that course was taken, until sunset, 56 miles, which is 14 leagues to the eastward from the Cabo de Cuba. The other land of Bohio

---

[160] *Las Sierras del Cristal* and *Las Sierras de Moa.* (Navarrete.)

294

was left to leeward. Commencing from the cape of the said gulf, he discovered, according to his reckoning, 80 miles, equal to 20 leagues, all that coast running E.S.E. and W.N.W.

Wednesday, 14th of November

All last night the Admiral was beating to windward (he said that it would be unreasonable to navigate among those islands during the night, until they had been explored), for the Indians said yesterday that it would take three days to go from Rio de Mares to the island of Babeque, by which should be understood days' journeys in their canoes equal to about 7 leagues. The wind fell, and, the course being east, she could not lay her course nearer than S.E., and, owing to other mischances, he was detained until the morning. At sunrise he determined to go in search of a port, because the wind had shifted from north to N.E., and, if a port could not be found, it would be necessary to go back to the ports in the island of Cuba, whence they came. The Admiral approached the shore, having gone over 28 miles E.S.E. that night. He steered south ... miles to the land, where he saw many islets and openings. As the wind was high and the sea rough, he did not dare to risk an attempt to enter, but ran along the coast W.N.W., looking out for a port, and saw many, but none very clear of rocks. After having proceeded for 64 miles, he found a very deep opening, a quarter of a mile wide, with a good port and river. He ran in with her head S.S.W., afterwards south to S.E. The port[161] was spacious and very deep, and he saw so many islands that he could not count them all, with very high land covered with trees of many kinds, and an infinite number of palms. He was much astonished to see so many

---

[161] Puerto de Taxamo, in Cuba. (Navarrete.)

lofty islands; and assured the Sovereigns that the mountains and isles he had seen since yesterday seemed to him to be second to none in the world; so high and clear of clouds and snow, with the sea at their bases so deep. He believes that these islands are those innumerable ones that are depicted on the maps of the world in the Far East.[162] He believed that they yielded very great riches in precious stones and spices and that they extend much further to the south, widening out in all directions. He gave the name of La Mar de Nuestra Señora, and to the haven, which is near the mouth of the entrance to these islands, Puerto del Principe. He did not enter it, but examined it from outside, until another time, on Saturday of the next week, as will there appear. He speaks highly of the fertility, beauty, and height of the islands which he found in this gulf, and he tells the Sovereigns not to wonder at his praise of them, for that he has not told them the hundredth part. Some of them seemed to reach to heaven, running up into peaks like diamonds. Others rising to a great height have a flat top like a table. At their bases the sea is of a great depth, with enough water for a very large carrack. All are covered with foliage and without rocks.

Thursday, 15th of November

The Admiral went to examine these islands in the ships' boats, and speaks marvels of them, how he found mastic, and aloes without end. Some of them were cultivated with the roots of which the Indians make bread; and he found that fires had been lighted in several places. He saw no fresh water. There were some natives, but they fled. In all

---

[162] Cf. Fra Mauro's Map (1457-1459), Bourne, *Spain in America*, 14, and Behaim's Globe, Winsor's *Columbus*, p. 186, or Fiske's *Discovery of America*, I. 422.

parts of the sea where the vessels were navigated he found a depth of 15 or 16 fathoms, and all *basa*, by which he means that the ground is sand and not rocks; a thing much desired by sailors, for the rocks cut their anchor cables.

Friday, 16th of November

As in all parts, whether islands or mainlands, that he visited, the Admiral always left a cross; so, on this occasion, he went in a boat to the entrance of these havens, and found two very large trees on a point of land, one longer than the other. One being placed over the other, made a cross, and he said that a carpenter could not have made it better. He ordered a very large and high cross to be made out of these timbers. He found canes on the beach, and did not know where they had grown, but thought they must have been brought down by some river, and washed up on the beach (in which opinion he had reason). He went to a creek on the south-east side of the entrance to the port. Here, under a height of rock and stone like a cape, there was depth enough for the largest carrack in the world close in shore, and there was a corner where six ships might lie without anchors as in a room. It seemed to the Admiral that a fortress might be built here at small cost, if at any time any famous trade should arise in that sea of islands.

Returning to the ship, he found that the Indians who were on board had fished up very large shells found in those seas. He made the people examine them, to see if there was mother-o'-pearl, which is in the shells where pearls grow. They found a great deal, but no pearls, and their absence was attributed to its not being the season, which is May and June. The sailors found an animal which seemed to be a *taso*, or *taxo*.[163] They also fished with nets, and, among many others, caught a fish which was exactly like a pig, not like a tunny, but all covered with a very hard shell, without a soft place except the tail and the eyes, and a hole underneath to discharge its superfluities. It was ordered to be salted, to bring home for the Sovereigns to see.[164]

Saturday, 17th of November

The Admiral got into the boat, and went to visit the islands he had not yet seen to the S.W. He saw many more very fertile and pleasant islands, with a great depth between them. Some of them had springs of fresh water, and he believed that the water of those streams came from some sources at the summits of the mountains. He went on, and found a beach bordering on very sweet water, which was very cold. There was a beautiful meadow, and many very tall palms. They found a large nut of the kind belonging to India, great rats,[165] and enormous crabs. He saw many birds, and there was a strong smell of musk, which made him think it must be there. This day the two eldest of the six youths brought from the Rio de Mares, who were on board the caravel *Niña*, made their escape.

Sunday, 18th of November

The Admiral again went away with the boats, accompanied by many of the sailors, to set up the cross which he had ordered to be made out of the two large trees at the entrance to the Puerto del Principe, on a fair

---

[163] Las Casas did not know the meaning of this word. In all probability it is the Italian *tasso*, badger. Cf. p. 139, note 1. The animal, Cuvier suggested was probably the coati.
[164] Cuvier conjectured this to be the trunk fish.
[165] The agouti.

site cleared of trees, whence there was an extensive and very beautiful view. He says that there is a greater rise and fall of the sea there than in any other port he has seen, and that this is no marvel, considering the numerous islands. The tide is the reverse of ours, because here, when the moon is S.S.W., it is low water in the port. He did not get under way, because it was Sunday.

Monday, 19th of November

The Admiral got under way before sunrise, in a calm. In the afternoon there was some wind from the east, and he shaped a N.N.E. course. At sunset the Puerto del Principe bore S.S.W. 7 leagues. He saw the island of Babeque bearing due east about 60 miles. He steered N.E. all that night, making 60 miles, and up to ten o'clock of Tuesday another dozen; altogether 18 leagues N.E. b. W.

Tuesday, 20th of November

They left Babeque, or the islands of Babeque, to the E.S.E., the wind being contrary; and, seeing that no progress was being made, and the sea was getting rough, the Admiral determined to return to the Puerto del Principe, whence he had started, which was 25 leagues distant. He did not wish to go to the island he had called Isabella, which was twelve leagues off, and where he might have anchored that night, for two reasons: one was that he had seen two islands to the south which he wished to explore; the other, because the Indians he brought with him, whom he had taken at the island of Guanahani, which he named San Salvador, eight leagues from Isabella, might get away, and he said that he wanted them to take to Spain. They thought that, when the Admiral had found gold, he would let them return to their homes. He came near the Puerto del Principe, but could not reach it, because it was night, and because the current drifted them to the N.W. He turned her head to N.E. with a light wind. At three o'clock in the morning the wind changed, and a course was shaped E.N.E., the wind being S.S.W., and changing at dawn to south and S.E. At sunset Puerto del Principe bore nearly S.W. by W. 48 miles, which are 12 leagues.

Wednesday, 21st of November

At sunrise the Admiral steered east, with a southerly wind, but made little progress, owing to a contrary sea. At vespers he had gone 24 miles. Afterwards the wind changed to east and he steered S. b. E., at sunset having gone 12 miles. Here he found himself forty-two degrees north of the equinoctial line, as in the port of Mares, but he says that he kept the result from the quadrant in suspense until he reached the shore, that it might be adjusted (as it would seem that he thought this distance was too great, and he had reason, it not being possible, as these islands are only in ... degrees).[166] To believe the quadrant was right he was led by seeing the north star as high as in Castile ...Reinforcing this was the great heat which he says he found there.... From this heat which the Admiral says he endured there he argued that in these Indies and where he was going there must be much gold.[167]

---

[166] See p. 134, note 3. The words following "Port of Mares" should be translated "but here he says that he has the quadrant hung up (or not in use) until he reaches land to repair it. Since it seemed to him that this distance," etc. Las Casas omitted to insert the number of degrees in his comment.

[167] The sentences omitted are comments of Las Casas on these reflections of Columbus.

This day Martin Alonso Pinzon parted company with the caravel *Pinta*, in disobedience to and against the wish of the Admiral, and out of avarice, thinking that an Indian who had been put on board his caravel could show him where there was much gold. So he parted company, not owing to bad weather, but because he chose. Here the Admiral says: "He had done and said many other things to me."

Thursday, 22nd of November

On Wednesday night the Admiral steered S.S.E., with the wind east, but it was nearly calm. At 3 it began to blow from N.N.E.; and he continued to steer south to see the land he had seen in that quarter. When the sun rose he was as far off as the day before, owing to adverse currents, the land being 40 miles off. This night Martin Alonso shaped a course to the east, to go to the island of Babeque, where the Indians say there is much gold. He did this in sight of the Admiral, from whom he was distant 16 miles. The Admiral stood towards the land all night. He shortened sail, and showed a lantern, because Pinzon would thus have an opportunity of joining him, the night being very clear, and the wind fair to come, if he had wished to do so.

Friday, 23rd of November

The Admiral stood towards the land all day, always steering south with little wind, but the current would never let them reach it, being as far off at sunset as in the morning. The wind was E.N.E., and they could shape a southerly course, but there was little of it. Beyond this cape there stretched out another land or cape, also trending east, which the Indians on board called Bohio. They said that it was very large, and that there were people in it who had one eye in their foreheads, and others who were cannibals, and of whom they were much afraid. When they saw that this course was taken, they said that they could not talk to these people because they would be eaten, and that they were very well armed. The Admiral says that he well believes that there were such people, and that if they are armed they must have some ability. He thought that they may have captured some of the Indians, and because they did not return to their homes, the others believed that they had been eaten. They thought the same of the Christians and of the Admiral when some of them first saw the strangers.

Saturday, 24th of November

They navigated all night, and at 3[168] they reached the level island[169] at the very same point they had come to the week before, when they started for the island of Babeque. At first the Admiral did not dare to approach the shore, because it seemed that there would be a great surf in that mountain-girded bay. Finally he reached the sea of Nuestra Señora, where there are many islands, and entered a port near the mouth of the opening to the islands. He says that if he had known of this port before he need not have occupied himself in exploring the islands, and it would not have been necessary to go back. He, however, considered that the time was well spent in examining the islands. On nearing the land he sent in the boat to sound, finding a good sandy bottom in 6 to 20 fathoms. He entered the haven, pointing the ship's head S.W. and then west, the flat island bearing north. This, with another island near it, forms a harbor which would hold all the ships of Spain safe from all winds. This entrance on the S.W. side is passed by steering S.S.W., the outlet being to the west very deep and wide. Thus a

---

[168] *A la hora de tercia*, about 9 A.M..
[169] Cayo de Moa. (Navarrete.)

vessel can pass amidst these islands, and he who approaches from the north, with a knowledge of them can pass along the coast. These islands are at the foot of a great mountain-chain running east and west, which is longer and higher than any others on this coast, where there are many. A reef of rocks outside runs parallel with the said mountains, like a bench, extending to the entrance. On the side of the flat island, and also to the S.E., there is another small reef, but between them there is great width and depth. Within the port, near the S.E. side of the entrance, they saw a large and very fine river,[170] with more volume than any they had yet met with, and fresh water could be taken from it as far as the sea. At the entrance there is a bar, but within it is very deep, 19 fathoms. The banks are lined with palms and many other trees.

Sunday, 25th of November

Before sunrise the Admiral got into the boat, and went to see a cape or point of land[171] to the S.E. of the flat island, about a league and a half distant, because there appeared to be a good river there. Presently, near to the S.E. side of the cape, at a distance of two cross-bow shots, he saw a large stream of beautiful water falling from the mountains[172] above, with a loud noise. He went to it, and saw some stones shining in its bed like gold.[173] He remembered that in the river Tagus, near its junction with the sea, there was gold; so it seemed to him that this should contain gold, and he ordered some of these stones to be collected, to be brought to the Sovereigns. Just

---

[170] Rio de Moa. (Navarrete.)

[171] Punta del Mangle or del Guarico. (Navarrete.)

[172] Sierras de Moa. (Navarrete.)

[173] "These must have been *margaseta* stones which look like gold in streams and of which there is an abundance in the rivers of these islands." Las Casas, I. 346.

then the sailor boys called out that they had found large
pines. The Admiral looked up the hill, and saw that they
were so wonderfully large that he could not exaggerate
their height and straightness, like stout yet fine spindles.
He perceived that here there was material for great
store of planks and masts for the largest ships in Spain.
He saw oaks and arbutus trees,[174] with a good river, and
the means of making water-power.[175] The climate was
temperate, owing to the height of the mountains. On the
beach he saw many other stones of the color of iron, and
others that some said were like silver ore, all brought
down by the river. Here he obtained a new mast and yard
for the mizzen of the caravel *Niña*. He came to the mouth
of the river, and entered a creek which was deep and
wide, at the foot of that S.E. part of the cape, which would
accommodate a hundred ships without any anchor or
hawsers. Eyes never beheld a better harbor. The
mountains are very high, whence descend many limpid
streams, and all the hills are covered with pines, and an
infinity of diverse and beautiful trees. Two or three other
rivers were not visited.

The Admiral described all this, in much detail, to the
Sovereigns, and declared that he had derived unspeakable
joy and pleasure at seeing it, more especially the pines,
because they enable as many ships as is desired to be
built here, bringing out the rigging, but finding here
abundant supplies of wood and provisions. He affirms
that he has not enumerated a hundredth part of what
there is here, and that it pleased our Lord always to show
him one thing better than another, as well on the ground
and among the trees, herbs, fruits, and flowers, as in the

---

[174] *Madroños. Arbutus unedo* or the Strawberry tree. The California
Madroña is the *Arbutus Menziesii.*
[175] Rather, "for making sawmills."

people, and always something different in each place. It had been the same as regards the havens and the waters. Finally, he says that if it caused him who saw it so much wonder, how much more will it affect those who hear about it; yet no one can believe until he sees it.

Monday, 26th of November

At sunrise the Admiral weighed the anchors in the haven of Santa Catalina, where he was behind the flat island, and steered along the coast in the direction of Cabo del Pico, which was S.E. He reached the cape late, because the wind failed and then saw another cape, S.E. b. E. 60 miles, which, when 20 miles off, was named Cabo de Campana, but it could not be reached that day. They made good 32 miles during the day, which is 8 leagues. During this time the Admiral noted nine remarkable ports,[176] which all the sailors thought wonderfully good, and five large rivers; for they sailed close along the land, so as to see everything. All along the coast there are very high and beautiful mountains, not arid or rocky, but all accessible, and very lovely. The valleys, like the mountains, were full of tall and fine trees, so that it was a glory to look upon them, and there seemed to be many pines. Also, beyond the said Cabo de Pico to the S.E. there are two islets, each about two leagues round, and inside them three excellent havens and two large rivers. Along the whole coast no inhabited places were visible from the sea. There may have been some, and there were indications of them, for, when the men landed, they found signs of people and numerous remains of fires. The Admiral conjectured that the land he saw to-day S.E. of the Cabo de Campana was the island called by the Indians Bohio: it looked as if this cape was separated from

---

[176] Among these were the Bay of Yamanique, and the ports of Jaragua, Taco, Cayaganueque, Nava, and Maravi. (Navarrete.)

the mainland. The Admiral says that all the people he has
hitherto met with have very great fear of
those of Caniba or Canima. They affirm that they live in
the island of Bohio, which must be very large, according to
all accounts. The Admiral understood that those of
Caniba come to take people from their homes, they being
very cowardly, and without knowledge of arms. For this
use it appears that these Indians do not settle on the sea-
coast owing to being near the land of Caniba. When the
natives who were on board saw a course shaped for that
land, they feared to speak, thinking they were going to
be eaten; nor could they rid themselves of their fear. They
declared that the Canibas[177] had only one eye and dogs'
faces. The Admiral thought they lied, and was inclined to
believe that it was people from the dominions of the Gran
Can who took them into captivity.

Tuesday, 27th of November

Yesterday, at sunset, they arrived near a cape named
Campana by the Admiral; and, as the sky was clear and
the wind light, he did not wish to run in close to the land
and anchor, although he had five or six singularly good
havens under his lee. The Admiral was attracted on the
one hand by the longing and delight he felt to gaze upon
the beauty and freshness of those lands, and on the other
by a desire to complete the work he had undertaken. For
these reasons he remained close hauled, and stood off and
on during the night. But, as the currents had set him
more than 5 or 6 leagues to the S.E. beyond where he had
been at nightfall, passing the land of Campana, he came
in sight of a great opening beyond that cape, which
seemed to divide one land from another, leaving an
island between them. He decided to go back, with the
wind S.E., steering to the point where the opening had

---

[177] The original of the words Cannibal and Carib and Caribbean.

appeared, where he found that it was only a large bay,[178] and at the end of it, on the S.E. side, there was a point of land on which was a high and square-cut hill,[179] which had looked like an island. A breeze sprang up from the north, and the Admiral continued on a S.E. course, to explore the coast and discover all that was there. Presently he saw, at the foot of the Cabo de Campana, a wonderfully good port[180], and a large river, and, a quarter of a league on, another river, and a third, and a fourth to a seventh at similar distances, from the furthest one to Cabo de Campana being 20 miles S.E. Most of these rivers have wide and deep mouths, with excellent havens for large ships, without sandbanks or sunken rocks. Proceeding onwards from the last of these rivers, on a S.E. course, they came to the largest inhabited place they had yet seen, and a vast concourse of people came down to the beach with loud shouts, all naked, with their darts in their hands. The Admiral desired to have speech with them, so he furled sails and anchored. The boats of the ship and the caravel were sent on shore, with orders to do no harm whatever to the Indians, but to give them presents. The Indians made as if they would resist the landing, but, seeing that the boats of the Spaniards continued to advance without fear, they retired from the beach. Thinking that they would not be terrified if only two or three landed, three Christians were put on shore, who told them not to be afraid, in their own language, for they had been able to learn a little from the natives who were on board. But all ran away, neither great nor small remaining. The Christians went to the houses, which were of straw, and built like the others they had seen, but found no one in any of them. They returned to the ships, and made sail at noon in the

---

[178] The port of Baracoa. (Navarrete.)

[179] Monte del Yunque. (Navarrete.)

[180] Punta de Maici. (Id)

direction of a fine cape to the eastward, about 8 leagues distant. Having gone about half a league, the Admiral saw, on the south side of the same bay, a very remarkable harbor[181], and to the S.E. some wonderfully beautiful country like a valley among the mountains, whence much smoke arose, indicating a large population, with signs of much cultivation. So he resolved to stop at this port, and see if he could have any speech or intercourse with the inhabitants. It was so that, if the Admiral had praised the other havens, he must praise this still more for its lands, climate, and people. He tells marvels of the beauty of the country and of the trees, there being palms and pine trees; and also of the great valley which is not flat, but diversified by hill and dale, the most lovely scene in the world. Many streams flow from it, which fall from the mountains.

As soon as the ship was at anchor the Admiral jumped into the boat, to get soundings in the port, which is the shape of a hammer. When he was facing the entrance he found the mouth of a river on the south side of sufficient width for a galley to enter it, but so concealed that it is not visible until close to. Entering it for the length of the boat, there was a depth of from 5 to 8 fathoms. In passing up it the freshness and beauty of the trees, the clearness of the water, and the birds, made it all so delightful that he wished never to leave them. He said to the men who were with him that to give a true relation to the Sovereigns of the things they had seen, a thousand tongues would not suffice, nor his hand to write it, for that it was like a scene of enchantment. He desired that many other prudent and credible witnesses might see it, and he was sure that they would be as unable to exaggerate the scene as he was.

---

[181] Puerto de Baracoa. (*Id.*)

The Admiral also says: "How great the benefit that is to be derived from this country would be, I cannot say. It is certain that where there are such lands there must be an infinite number of things that would be profitable. But I did not remain long in one port, because I wished to see as much of the country as possible, in order to make a report upon it to your Highnesses; and besides, I do not know the language, and these people neither understand me nor any other in my company; while the Indians I have on board often misunderstand. Moreover, I have not been able to see much of the natives, because they often take to flight. But now, if our Lord pleases, I will see as much as possible, and will proceed by little and little, learning and comprehending; and I will make some of my followers learn the language. For I have perceived that there is only one language up to this point. After they understand the advantages, I shall labor to make all these people Christians. They will become so readily, because they have no religion nor idolatry, and your Highnesses will send orders to build a city and fortress, and to convert the people. I assure your Highnesses that it does not appear to me that there can be a more fertile country nor a better climate under the sun, with abundant supplies of water. This is not like the rivers of Guinea, which are all pestilential. I thank our Lord that, up to this time, there has not been a person of my company who has had so much as a headache, or been in bed from illness, except an old man who has suffered from the stone all his life, and he was well again in two days. I speak of all three vessels. If it will please God that your Highnesses should send learned men out here, they will see the truth of all I have said. I have related already how good a place Rio de Mares would be for a town and fortress, and this is perfectly true; but it bears no comparison with this place, nor with the Mar de Nuestra Señora. For here there must be a large population, and very valuable productions, which I hope to discover before I return to Castile. I say that if Christendom will find profit among these people, how much more will Spain, to whom the whole country should be subject. Your Highnesses ought not to consent that any stranger should trade here, or put his foot in the country, except Catholic Christians, for this was the beginning and end of the undertaking; namely, the increase and glory of the Christian religion, and that no one should come to these parts who was not a good Christian."[182]

All the above are the Admiral's words. He ascended the river for some distance, examined some branches of it, and, returning to the mouth, he found some pleasant groves of trees, like a delightful orchard. Here he came upon a boat or _canoa_, dug out of one tree as big as a *fusta*[183] of twelve benches, fastened under a boat-house or bower made of wood, and thatched with palm-leaves, so that it could be neither injured by sun nor by the water. He says that here would be the proper site for a town and fort, by reason of the good port, good water, good land, and abundance of fuel.

Wednesday, 28th of November

The Admiral remained during this day, in consequence of the rain and thick weather, though he might have run along the coast, the wind being S.W., but he did not weigh, because he was unacquainted with the coast

---

[182] With these suggestions for a colonial policy cf. Columbus's more detailed programme in his letter to Ferdinand and Isabella, below. In the Spanish policy of exclusion of foreigners from the colonies the religious motive, as here, was quite as influential as the spirit of trade monopoly. Las Casas, in making the same quotation from the Journal, remarks, I. 351: "All these are his exact words, although some of them are not perfect Castilian, since that was not the Admiral's mother tongue."

[183] The *fusta* was a long, low boat propelled by oars or a sail. It is represented in earlier English by "foist" and "fuste."

beyond, and did not know what danger there might be for the vessels. The sailors of the two vessels went on shore to wash their clothes, and some of them walked inland for a short distance. They found indications of a large population, but the houses were all empty, everyone having fled. They returned by the banks of another river, larger than that which they knew of, at the port.

Thursday, 29th of November

The rain and thick weather continuing, the Admiral did not get under way. Some of the Christians went to another village to the N.W., but found no one, and nothing in the houses. On the road they met an old man who could not run away, and caught him. They told him they did not wish to do him any harm, gave him a few presents, and let him go. The Admiral would have liked to have had speech with him, for he was exceedingly satisfied with the delights of that land, and wished that a settlement might be formed there, judging that it must support a large population. In one house they found a cake of wax,[184] which was taken to the Sovereigns, the Admiral saying that where there was wax there were also a thousand other good things. The sailors also found, in one house, the head of a man in a basket, covered with another basket, and fastened to a post of the house. They found the same things in another village. The Admiral believed that they must be the heads of some founder, or principal ancestor of a lineage, for the houses are built to contain a great number of people in each; and these should be relations, and descendants of a common

---

[184] Las Casas, I. 353, remarks, "This wax was never made in the island of Cuba, and this cake that was found came from the kingdom and provinces of Yucatan, where there is an immense amount of very good yellow wax." He supposes that it might have come from the wrecks of canoes engaged in trade along the coast of Yucatan.

ancestor.

Friday, 30th of November

They could not get under way to-day because the wind
was east, and dead against them. The Admiral sent 8 men
well armed, accompanied by two of the Indians he had on
board, to examine the villages inland, and get speech with
the people. They came to many houses, but found no one
and nothing, all having fled. They saw four youths who
were digging in their fields, but, as soon as they saw the
Christians, they ran away, and could not be overtaken.
They marched a long distance, and saw many villages and
a most fertile land, with much cultivation and many
streams of water. Near one river they saw a canoe dug out
of a single tree, 95 *palmos*[185] long, and capable of carrying
150 persons.

Saturday, 1st of December

They did not depart, because there was still a foul wind,
with much rain. The Admiral set up a cross at the
entrance of this port, which he called Puerto Santo, on
some bare rocks. The point is that which is on[186]
the S.E. side of the entrance; but he who has to enter
should make more over to the N.W.; for at the foot of both,
near the rock, there are 12 fathoms and a very clean
bottom. At the entrance of the port, toward the

---

[185] About 70 feet. Las Casas adds the words, "it was most beautiful," and
continues, "it is no wonder for there are in that island very thick and very
long and tall fragrant red cedars and commonly all their canoes are
made from these valuable trees."
[186] *Puerto de Baracoa. (Navarrete.)*

S.E. point, there is a reef of rocks above water,[187] sufficiently far from the shore to enable one to pass between if it is necessary, for both on the side of the rock and the shore there is a depth of 12 to 15 fathoms; and, on entering, a ship's head should be turned S.W.

Sunday, 2nd of December

The wind was still contrary, and they could not depart. Every night the wind blows on the land, but no vessel need be alarmed at all the gales in the world, for they cannot blow home by reason of a reef of rocks at the opening to the haven, etc. A sailor-boy found, at the mouth of the river, some stones which looked as if they contained gold; so they were taken to be shown to the Sovereigns. The Admiral says that there are great rivers at the distance of a lombard shot.[188]

Monday, 3rd of December

By reason of the continuance of an easterly wind the Admiral did not leave this port. He arranged to visit a very beautiful headland a quarter of a league to the S.E. of the anchorage. He went with the boats and some armed men. At the foot of the cape there was the mouth of a fair river, and on entering it they found the width to be a hundred paces, with a depth of one fathom. Inside they found 12, 5, 4, and 2 fathoms, so that it would hold all the

---

[187] This reef actually exists on the S.E. side of the entrance to this port, which is described with great accuracy by Columbus. (Navarrete.)
[188] Lombarda is the same as bombarda, bombard, the earliest type of cannon. The name has nothing to do with Lombardy, but is simply the form which was used in Castile in the fifteenth century while bombarda was used elsewhere in the peninsula and in Europe. The average-sized bombard was a twenty-five pounder. Diccionario Enciclopedico Hispano-Americano, art. lombardo, based on Aráutegui, Apuntes Históricos sobre la Artilleria Española en los Siglos XIV y XV.

ships there are in Spain. Leaving the river, they came to a cove in which were five very large canoes,[189] so well constructed that it was a pleasure to look at them. They were under spreading trees, and a path led from them to a very well-built boat-house, so thatched that neither sun nor rain could do any harm. Within it there was another canoe made out of a single tree like the others, like a *fusta* with 17 benches. It was a pleasant sight to look upon such goodly work. The Admiral ascended a mountain, and afterwards found the country level, and cultivated with many things of that land, including such calabashes, as it was a glory to look upon them.[190] In the middle there was a large village, and they came upon the people suddenly; but, as soon as they were seen, men and women took to flight. The Indian from on board, who was with the Admiral, cried out to them that they need not be afraid, as the strangers were good people. The Admiral made him give them bells, copper ornaments, and glass beads, green and yellow, with which they were well content. He saw that they had no gold nor any other precious thing, and that it would suffice to leave them in peace. The whole district was well peopled, the rest having fled from fear. The Admiral assures the Sovereigns that ten thousand of these men would run from ten, so cowardly and timid are they. No arms are carried by them, except wands,[191] on the point of which a short piece of wood is fixed, hardened

---

[189] This line should be, "in which he saw five very large *almadias* [low, light boats] which the Indians call *canoas*, like *fustas*, very beautiful and so well constructed," etc. "Canoe" is one of the few Arawak Indian words to have become familiar English.

[190] Rather, "He went up a mountain and then he found it all level and planted with many things of the country and gourds so that it was glorious to see it." De Candolle believes the calabash or gourd to have been introduced into America from Africa. *Cf.* his *Origin of Cultivated Plants*, pp. 245 ff. Oviedo, however, in his *Historia General y Natural de Indias*, lib. VIII., cap. VIII., says that the *calabaças* of the Indies were the same as those in Spain and were cultivated not to eat but to use the shells as vessels.

[191] Rather, "rods."

by fire, and these they are very ready to exchange.
returning to where he had left the boats, he sent back
some men up the hill, because he fancied he had seen a
large apiary. Before those he had sent could return, they
were joined by many Indians, and they went to the boats,
where the Admiral was waiting with all his people. One
of the natives advanced into the river near the stern of
the boat, and made a long speech, which the Admiral did
not understand. At intervals the other Indians raised
their hands to Heaven, and shouted. The Admiral
thought he was assuring him that he was pleased at his
arrival; but he saw the Indian who came from the ship
change the color of his face, and turn as yellow as wax,
trembling much, and letting the Admiral know by
signs that he should leave the river, as they were going to
kill him. He pointed to a cross-bow which one of the
Spaniards had, and showed it to the Indians, and the
Admiral let it be understood that they would all be
slain, because that cross-bow carried far and killed
people. He also took a sword and drew it out of the
sheath, showing it to them, and saying the same, which,
when they had heard, they all took to flight; while the
Indian from the ship still trembled from cowardice,
though he was a tall, strong man. The Admiral did not
want to leave the river, but pulled towards the place
where the natives had assembled in great numbers, all
painted, and as naked as when their mothers bore them.
Some had tufts of feathers on their heads, and all had
their bundles of darts.

The Admiral says: "I came to them, and gave them some
mouthfuls of bread, asking for the darts, for which I gave
in exchange copper ornaments, bells, and glass beads.
This made them peaceable, so that they came to the boats
again, and gave us what they had. The sailors had killed a
turtle, and the shell was in the boat in pieces. The sailor-
boys gave them some in exchange for a bundle of darts.

These are like the other people we have seen, and with the same belief that we came from Heaven. They are ready to give whatever thing they have in exchange for any trifle without saying it is little; and I believe they would do the same with gold and spices if they had any. I saw a fine house, not very large, and with two doors, as all the rest have. On entering, I saw a marvellous work, there being rooms made in a peculiar way, that I scarcely know how to describe it. Shells and other things were fastened to the ceiling. I thought it was a temple, and I called them and asked, by signs, whether prayers were offered up there. They said that they were not, and one of them climbed up and offered me all the things that were there, of which I took some."

Tuesday, 4th of December

The Admiral made sail with little wind, and left that port, which he called Puerto Santo. After going two leagues, he saw the great river[192] of which he spoke yesterday. Passing along the land, and beating to windward on S.E. and W.N.W. courses, they reached Cabo Lindo,[193] which is E.S.E. 5 leagues from Cabo del Monte. A league and a half from Cabo del Monte there is an important but rather narrow river, which seemed to have a good entrance, and to be deep. Three-quarters of a league further on, the Admiral saw another very large river, and he thought it must have its source at a great distance. It had a hundred paces at its mouth, and no bar, with a depth of 8 fathoms. The Admiral sent the boat in, to take soundings, and they found the water fresh until it enters the sea.

This river had great volume, and must have a large population on its banks. Beyond Cabo Lindo there is a

---

[192] Rio Boma. (Navarrete.)
[193] Punta del Fraile. (*Id.*)

great bay, which would be open for navigation to E.N.E. and S.E. and S.S.W.

Wednesday, 5th of December

All this night they were beating to windward off Cape Lindo, to reach the land to the east, and at sunrise the Admiral sighted another cape,[194] two and a half leagues to the east. Having passed it, he saw that the land trended S. and S.W., and presently saw a fine high cape in that direction, 7 leagues distant.[195] He would have wished to go there, but his object was to reach the island of Babeque, which, according to the Indians, bore N.E.; so he gave up the intention. He could not go to Babeque either, because the wind was N.E. Looking to the S.E., he saw land, which was a very large island, according to the information of the Indians, well peopled, and called by them Bohio.[196] The Admiral says that the inhabitants of Cuba, or Juana,[197] and of all the other islands, are much afraid of the inhabitants of Bohio, because they say that they eat people. The Indians relate other things, by signs, which are very wonderful; but the Admiral did not believe them. He only inferred that those of Bohio must have more cleverness and cunning to be able to capture the others, who, however, are very poor-spirited. The wind veered from N.E. to North, so the Admiral determined to

---

[194] Punta de los Azules. (*Id.*)

[195] Las Casas, I. 359, says, "This high and beautiful cape whither he would have liked to go I believe was Point Maycí, which is the extreme end of Cuba toward the east." According to the modern maps of Cuba it must have been one of the capes to the southwest of Point Maicí.

[196] *Cf.* note 57. Las Casas, I. 359, remarks, "Its real name was Haytí, the last syllable long and accented." He thinks it possible that the cape first sighted may have been called Bohio.

[197] Columbus gave Cuba the name Juana "in memory of Prince Juan the heir of Castile." *Historie*, p. 83.

leave Cuba, or Juana, which, up to this time, he had supposed to be the mainland, on account of its size, having coasted along it for 120 leagues.[198] He shaped a course S.E. b. E., the land he had sighted bearing S.E.; taking this precaution because the wind always veered from N. to N.E. again, and thence to east and S.E. The wind increased, and he made all sail, the current helping them; so that they were making 8 miles an hour from the morning until one in the afternoon (which is barely 6 hours, for they say that the nights were nearly 15 hours). Afterwards they went 10 miles an hour, making good 88 miles by sunset, equal to 22 leagues, all to the S.E. As night was coming on, the Admiral ordered the caravel *Niña*, being a good sailer, to proceed ahead, so as to sight a harbor at daylight. Arriving at the entrance of a port which was like the Bay of Cadiz, while it was still dark, a boat was sent in to take soundings, which showed a light from a lantern. Before the Admiral could beat up to where the caravel was, hoping that the boat would show a leading-mark for entering the port, the candle in the lantern went out. The caravel, not seeing the light, showed a light to the Admiral, and, running down to him, related what had happened. The boat's crew then showed another light, and the caravel made for it; but the Admiral could not do so, and was standing off and on all night.

Thursday, 6th of December

When daylight arrived the Admiral found himself four leagues from the port, to which he gave the name of

---

[198] "In leaving the cape or eastern point of Cuba he gave it the name Alpha and Omega, which means beginning and end, for he believed that this cape was the end of the mainland in the Orient." Las Casas, I. 360.

Puerto Maria,[199] and to a fine cape bearing S.S.W. he gave the name of Cabo de la Estrella.[200] It seemed to be the furthest point of the island towards the south, distant 28 miles. Another point of land, like an island, appeared about 40 miles to the east. To another fine point, 54 miles to the east, he gave the name of Cabo del Elefante,[201] and he called another, 28 miles to the S.E., Cabo de Cinquin. There was a great opening or bay, which might be the mouth of a river,[202] distant 20 miles. It seemed that between Cabo del Elefante and that of Cinquin there was a great opening,[203] and some of the sailors said that it formed an island, to which the name of Isla de la Tortuga[204] was given. The island appeared to be very high land, not closed in with mountains, but with beautiful valleys, well cultivated, the crops appearing like the wheat on the plain of Cordova in May. That night they saw many fires, and much smoke, as if from workshops,[205] in the day time; it appeared to be a signal made by people who were at war. All the coast of this land trends to the east.

At the hour of vespers the Admiral reached this port, to which he gave the name of Puerto de San Nicolas, in honor of St. Nicholas, whose day it was;[206] and on entering it he was astonished at its beauty and

---

[199] The port of St. Nicholas Mole, in Hayti. (Navarrete.)

[200] Cape of St. Nicholas. (*Id.*)

[201] Punta Palmista. (*Id.*)

[202] Puerto Escudo. (*Id.*)

[203] *The channel between Tortuga Island and the main.*

[204] Tortoise.

[205] *Atalayas,* "watchtowers."

[206] This method of giving names in honor of the saint on whose day a new cape or river was discovered was very commonly followed during the period of discoveries, and sometimes the date of a discovery, or the direction of a voyage, or other data can be verified by comparing the names given with the calender.

excellence. Although he had given great praise to the ports of Cuba, he had no doubt that this one not only equalled, but excelled them, and none of them are like it. At the entrance it is a league and a half wide, and a vessel's head should be turned S.S.E., though, owing to the great width, she may be steered on any bearing that is convenient; proceeding on this course for two leagues.[207] On the south side of the entrance the coast forms a cape, and thence the course is almost the same as far as a point where there is a fine beach, and a plain covered with fruit-bearing trees of many kinds; so that the Admiral thought there must be nutmegs and other spices among them, but he did not know them, and they were not ripe. There is a river falling into the harbor, near the middle of the beach. The depth of this port is surprising, for, until reaching the land, for a distance of ...[208] the lead did not reach the bottom at 40 fathoms; and up to this length there are 15 fathoms with a very clean bottom. Throughout the port there is a depth of 15 fathoms, with a clean bottom, at a short distance from the shore; and all along the coast there are soundings with clean bottom, and not a single sunken rock. Inside, at the length of a boat's oar from the land, there are 5 fathoms. Beyond the limit of the port to the S.S.E. a thousand carracks could beat up. One branch of the port to the N.E. runs into the land for a long half league, and always the same width, as if it had been measured with a cord. Being in this creek, which is 25 paces wide, the principal entrance to the harbor is not in sight, so that it appears land-locked.[209] The depth of this creek is 11 fathoms throughout, all with clean bottom; and close to the land,

---

[207] This clause should be "It extends in this manner to the south-south-east two leagues."

[208] A gap in the manuscript.

[209] This is the "Carenero," within the port of St. Nicholas. (Navarrete.)

where one might put the gangboards on the grass, there are eight fathoms. The whole port is open to the air, and clear of trees. All the island appeared to be more rocky than any that had been discovered. The trees are smaller, and many of them of the same kinds as are found in Spain, such as the ilex, the arbutus and others, and it is the same with the herbs. It is a very high country, all open and clear, with a very fine air, and no such cold has been met with elsewhere, though it cannot be called cold except by comparison. Towards the front of the haven there is a beautiful valley, watered by a river; and in that district there must be many inhabitants, judging from the number of large canoes, like galleys, with 15 benches. All the natives fled as soon as they saw the ships. The Indians who were on board had such a longing to return to their homes that the Admiral considered whether he should not take them back when he should depart from here. They were already suspicious, because he did not shape a course towards their country; whence he neither believed what they said, nor could he understand them, nor they him, properly. The Indians on board had the greatest fear in the world of the people of this island. In order to get speech of the people it would be necessary to remain some days in harbor; but the Admiral did not do so, because he had to continue his discoveries, and because he could not tell how long he might be detained. He trusted in our Lord that the Indians he brought with him would understand the language of the people of this island; and afterwards he would communicate with them, trusting that it might please God's Majesty that he might find trade in gold before he returned.

Friday, 7th of December

At daybreak the Admiral got under way, made sail, and left the port of St. Nicholas. He went on with the wind in the west for two leagues, until he reached the point which forms the Carenero, when the angle in the coast bore S.E., and the Cabo de la Estrella was 24 miles to the S.W. Thence he steered along the coast eastward to Cabo Cinquin about 48 miles, 20 of them being on an E.N.E. coast. All the coast is very high, with a deep sea. Close in shore there are 20 to 30 fathoms, and at the distance of a lombard-shot there is no bottom; all which the Admiral discovered that day, as he sailed along the coast with the wind S.W., much to his satisfaction. The cape, which runs out in the port of St. Nicholas the length of a shot from a lombard, could be made an island by cutting across it, while to sail round it is a circuit of 3 or 4 miles. All that land is very high, not clothed with very high trees, but with ilex, arbutus, and others proper to the land of Castile. Before reaching Cape Cinquin by two leagues, the Admiral discovered a small roadstead[210] like an opening in the mountains, through which he could see a very large valley, covered with crops like barley, and he therefore judged that it must sustain a large population. Behind there was a high range of mountains. On reaching Cabo Cinquin, the Cabo de la Tortuga bore N.E. 32 miles.[211] Off Cabo Cinquin, at the distance of a lombard-shot, there is a high rock, which is a good landmark. The Admiral being there, he took the bearing of Cabo del Elefante, which was E.S.E. about 70 miles,[212] the intervening land being very high. At a distance of 6 leagues there was a conspicuous cape,[213] and he saw many large valleys and plains, and high mountains inland, all reminding him of Spain. After 8 leagues he came to a very deep but narrow river, though a carrack might easily enter it, and the mouth without bar or rocks.

---

[210] Accepting Navarrete's conjecture of *abrezuela* or *anglezuela* for the reading *agrezuela* of the text.

[211] It should be north 11 miles. (Navarrete.)

[212] This is an error. It should be 15 miles. (Navarrete.) The direction *al Leste cuarta del Sueste* is East by South.

[213] Puerto Escudo. (Navarrete.)

After 16 miles there was a wide and deep harbor,[214] with on bottom at the entrance, nor, at 3 paces from the shore, less than 15 fathoms; and it runs inland a quarter of a league. It being yet very early, only one o'clock in the afternoon, and the wind being aft and blowing fresh, yet, as the sky threatened much rain, and it was very thick, which is dangerous even on a known coast, how much more in an unknown country, the Admiral resolved to enter the port, which he called Puerto de la Concepcion. He landed near a small river at the point of the haven, flowing from valleys and plains, the beauty of which was a marvel to behold. He took fishing-nets with him; and, before he landed, a mullet, like those of Spain, jumped into the boat, this being the first time they had seen fish resembling the fish of Castile. The sailors caught and killed others and soles and other fish like those of Castile. Walking a short distance inland, the Admiral found much land under cultivation, and heard the singing of nightingales and other birds of Castile. Five men were seen, but they would not stop, running away. The Admiral found myrtles and other trees and plants, like those of Castile, and so also were the land and mountains.[215]

Saturday, 8th of December

In this port there was heavy rain, with a fresh breeze from the north. The harbor is protected from all winds except the north; but even this can do no harm whatever, because there is a great surf outside, which prevents such a sea within the river as would make a ship work on her cables. After midnight the wind veered to N.E., and then

---

[214] Bahia Mosquito. (Navarrete.)
[215] Cuvier notes that neither the nightingale proper nor the Spanish myrtle are found in America.

to east, from which winds this port is well sheltered by the island of Tortuga, distant 36 miles.[216]

Sunday, 9th of December

To-day it rained, and the weather was wintry, like October Castile. No habitations had been seen except a very beautiful house in the Puerto de S. Nicolas, which was better built than any that had been in other parts. "The island is very large" says the Admiral: "it would not be much if it has a circumference of 200 leagues. All the parts he had seen were well cultivated. He believed that the villages must be at a distance from the sea, whither they went when the ships arrived; for they all took to flight, taking everything with them, and they made smoke-signals, like a people at war." This port has a width of a thousand paces at its entrance, equal to a quarter of a league. There is neither bank nor reef within, and there are scarcely soundings close in shore. Its length, running inland, is 3000 paces, all clean, and with a sandy bottom; so that any ship may anchor in it without fear, and enter it without precaution. At the upper end there are the mouths of two rivers, with the most beautiful champaign country, almost like the lands of Spain: these even have the advantage; for which seasons the Admiral gave the name of the said island Isla Española.[217]

---

[216] It should be 11 miles. (Navarrete.)

[217] I.e., Spanish Isle, not "Little Spain," which is sometimes erroneously given in explanation of the Latin Hispaniola. This last is a Latinized form of Española and not a diminutive. Las Casas, I. 367, in the corresponding passage, has "Seeing the greatness and beauty of this island and its resemblance to Spain although much superior and that they had caught fish in it like the fish of Castile and for other similar reasons he decided on December 9 when in the harbor of Concepcion to name this island Spanish Island."

At a period some time later than his first voyage Columbus decided that

Monday, 10th of December

It blew hard from the N.E., which made them drag their anchors half a cable's length. This surprised the Admiral, who had seen that the anchors had taken good hold of the ground. As he saw that the wind was foul for the direction in which he wanted to steer, he sent six men on shore, well armed to go two or three leagues inland, and endeavor to open communications with the natives. They came and returned without having seen either people or houses. But they found some hovels, wide roads, and some places where many fires had been made. They saw excellent lands, and many mastic trees, some specimens of which they took; but this is not the time for collecting it, as it does not coagulate.

Tuesday, 11th of December

The Admiral did not depart, because the wind was still east and S.E. In front of this port, as has been said, is the island of La Tortuga. It appears to be a large island, with the coast almost like that of Española, and the distance between them is about ten leagues.[218] It is well to know that from the Cabo de Cinquin, opposite Tortuga, the coast trends to the south. The Admiral had a great desire to see that channel between these two islands, and to examine the island of Española, which is the most beautiful thing in the world. According to what the Indians said who were on board, he would have to go to the island of Babeque. They declared that it was very

---

Española and Cipango were the same and also identical with the Ophir of the Bible. *Cf.* his marginal note to Landino's Italian translation of Pliny's *Natural History*, "la isola de Feyti, vel de Ofir, vel de Cipango, a la quale habio posto nome Spagnola." *Raccolta Colombiana*, pt. I., vol. II., p. 472.

[218] The distance is 11 miles. (Navarrete.)

large, with great mountains, rivers, and valleys; and that
the island of Bohio was larger than Juana, which they call
Cuba, and that it is not surrounded by water. They seem
to imply that there is mainland behind Española, and
they call it Caritaba, and say it is of vast extent. They
have reason in saying that the inhabitants are a clever
race, for all the people of these islands are in great fear of
those of Caniba. So the Admiral repeats, what he has
said before, that Caniba is nothing else but the Gran Can,
who ought now to be very near. He sends ships to capture
the islanders; and as they do not return, their countrymen
believe that they have been eaten. Each day we
understand better what the Indians say, and they us, so
that very often we are intelligible to each other. The
Admiral sent people on shore, who found a great deal of
mastic, but did not gather it. He says that the rains make
it, and that in Chios they collect it in March. In these
lands, being warmer, they might take it in January. They
caught many fish like those of Castile--dace, salmon,
hake, dory, gilt heads, mullets, *corbinas*, shrimps,[219] and
they saw sardines. They found many aloes.[220]

Wednesday, 12th of December

The Admiral did not leave the port to-day, for the same
reason: a contrary wind. He set up a great cross on the
west side of the entrance, on a very picturesque height,
"in sign," he says, "that your Highnesses hold this land for

---

[219] Camarones.

[220] The proper English equivalents for these names in the original are hard
to find. The *corbina* was a black fish and the name is found in both
Spanish and Portuguese. *Pámpanos* is translated "giltheads," but the
name is taken over into English as "pompano." It must be remembered
that in many cases the names of European species were applied to
American species which resembled them but which were really distinct
species of the same genus.

your own, but chiefly as a sign of our Lord Jesus Christ."
This being done, three sailors strolled into the woods to
see the trees and bushes. Suddenly they came upon a
crowd of people, all naked like the rest. They called to
them, and went towards them, but they ran away. At last
they caught a woman; for I had ordered that some should
be caught, that they might be treated well, and made to
lose their fear. This would be a useful event, for it could
scarcely be otherwise, considering the beauty of the
country. So they took the woman, who was very young
and beautiful, to the ship, where she talked to the Indians
on board; for they all speak the same language. The
Admiral caused her to be dressed, and gave her glass
beads, hawks' bells, and brass ornaments; then he sent
her back to the shore very courteously, according to his
custom. He sent three of the crew with her, and three of
the Indians he had on board, that they might open
communications with her people. The sailors in the boat,
who took her on shore, told the Admiral that she did not
want to leave the ship, but would rather remain with the
other women he had seized at the port of Mares, in the
island of Juana or Cuba. The Indians who went to put the
woman on shore said that the natives came in a canoe,
which is their caravel, in which they navigate from one
place to another; but when they came to the entrance of
the harbor, and saw the ships, they turned back, left the
canoe, and took the road to the village. The woman
pointed out the position of the village. She had a piece of
gold in her nose, which showed that there was gold in that
island.

Thursday, 13th of December

The three men who had been sent by the Admiral with
the woman returned at 3 o'clock in the morning, not
having gone with her to the village, because the distance
appeared to be long, or because they were afraid. They

said that next day many people would come to the ships, as they would have been reassured by the news brought them by the woman. The Admiral, with the desire of ascertaining whether there were any profitable commodities in that land, being so beautiful and fertile, and of having some speech with the people, and being desirous of serving the Sovereigns, determined to send again to the village, trusting in the news brought by the woman that the Christians were good people. For this service he selected nine men well armed, and suited for such an enterprise, with whom an Indian went from those who were on board. They reached the village, which is 4-1/2 leagues to the S.E., and found that it was situated in a very large and open valley. As soon as the inhabitants saw the Christians coming they all fled inland, leaving all their goods behind them. The village consisted of a thousand houses, with over three thousand inhabitants. The Indian whom the Christians had brought with them ran after the fugitives, saying that they should have no fear, for the Christians did not come from Cariba, but were from Heaven, and that they gave many beautiful things to all the people they met. They were so impressed with what he said, that upwards of two thousand came close up to the Christians, putting their hands on their heads, which was a sign of great reverence and friendship; and they were all trembling until they were reassured. The Christians related that, as soon as the natives had cast off their fear, they all went to the houses, and each one brought what he had to eat, consisting of yams,[221] which are roots like large radishes, which they sow and cultivate in all their lands, and is their staple food. They make bread of it, and roast it. The yam has the smell of a chestnut, and anyone would think he was eating chestnuts. They gave their guests bread and fish, and all they had. As the Indians who came in the ship had

---

[221] Rather, "bread of *niames*." Cf. note, p. 139.

understood that the Admiral wanted to have some parrots, one of those who accompanied the Spaniards mentioned this, and the natives brought out parrots, and gave them as many as they wanted, without asking anything for them. The natives asked the Spaniards not to go that night, and that they would give them many other things that they had in the mountains. While all these people were with the Spaniards, a great multitude was seen to come, with the husband of the woman whom the Admiral had honored and sent away. They wore hair over their shoulders, and came to give thanks to the Christians for the honor the Admiral had done them, and for the gifts. The Christians reported to the Admiral that this was a handsomer and finer people than any that had hitherto been met with. But the Admiral says that he does not see how they can be a finer people than the others, giving to understand that all those he had found in the other islands were very well conditioned. As regards beauty, the Christians said there was no comparison, both men and women, and that their skins are whiter than the others. They saw two girls whose skins were as white as any that could be seen in Spain. They also said, with regard to the beauty of the country they saw, that the best land in Castile could not be compared with it. The Admiral also, comparing the lands they had seen before with these, said that there was no comparison between them, nor did the plain of Cordova come near them, the difference being as great as between night and day. They said that all these lands were cultivated, and that a very wide and large river passed through the centre of the valley, and could irrigate all the fields. All the trees were green and full of fruit, and the plants tall and covered with flowers. The roads were broad and good. The climate was like April in Castile; the nightingale and other birds sang as they do in Spain during that month, and it was the most pleasant place in the world. Some birds sing sweetly at night. The crickets and frogs are heard a good deal. The fish are like those of Spain. They saw much aloe and mastic, and cotton-fields. Gold was not found, and it is not wonderful that it should not have been found in so short a time.

Here the Admiral calculated the number of hours in the day and night, and from sunrise to sunset. He found that twenty half-hour glasses passed, though he says that here there may be a mistake, either because they were not turned with equal quickness, or because some sand may not have passed. He also observed with a quadrant, and found that he was 34 degrees from the equinoctial line.[222]

Friday, 14th of December

The Admiral left the Puerto de la Concepcion with the land-breeze, but soon afterwards it fell calm (and this is experienced every day by those who are on this coast). Later an east wind sprang up, so he steered N.N.E., and arrived at the island of Tortuga. He sighted a point which he named Punta Pierna, E.N.E. of the end of the island 12 miles; and from thence another point was seen and named Punta Lanzada, in the same N.E. direction 16 miles. Thus from the end of Tortuga to Punta Aguda the distance is 44 miles, which is 11 leagues E.N.E. Along this route there are several long stretches of beach. The island of Tortuga is very high, but not mountainous, and is very beautiful and populous, like Española, and the land is cultivated, so that it looked like the plain of Cordova. Seeing that the wind was foul, and that he could not steer for the island

---

[222] Las Casas, I. 373, says that at that season the length of the day in Española is somewhat over eleven hours. The correct latitude is 20°.

of Baneque,[223] he determined to return to the Puerto de la Concepcion whence he had come; but he could not fetch a river which is two leagues to the east of that port.

Saturday, 15th of December

Once more the Admiral left the Puerto de la Concepcion, but, on leaving the port, he was again met by a contrary east wind. He stood over to Tortuga, and then steered with the object of exploring the river he had been unable to reach yesterday; nor was he able to fetch the river this time, but he anchored half a league to leeward of it, where there was clean and good anchoring ground. As soon as the vessels were secured, he went with the boats to the river, entering an arm of the sea, which proved not to be the river. Returning, he found the mouth, there being only one, and the current very strong. He went in with the boats to find the villagers that had been seen the day before. He ordered a tow-rope to be got out and manned by the sailors, who hauled the boats up for a distance of two lombard-shots. They could not get further owing to the strength of the current. He saw some houses, and the large valley where the villages were, and he said that a more beautiful valley he had never seen, this river flowing through the centre of it. He also saw people at the entrance, but they all took to flight. He further says that these people must be much hunted, for they live in such a state of fear. When the ships arrived at any port, they presently made signals by fires on heights throughout the country; and this is done more in this island of Española and in Tortuga, which is also a large island, than in the others that were visited before. He called this valley Valle del Paraiso,[224] and the river Guadalquivir; because he

---

[223] Elsewhere called Babeque. (Navarrete.)
[224] Paradise Valley.

says that it is the size of the Guadalquivir at Cordova. The banks consist of shingle, suitable for walking.[225]

Sunday, 16th of December

At midnight the Admiral made sail with the land-breeze to get clear of that gulf. Passing along the coast of Española on a bowline, for the wind had veered to the east, he met a canoe in the middle of the gulf, with a single Indian in it. The Admiral was surprised how he could have kept afloat with such a gale blowing. Both the Indian and his canoe were taken on board, and he was given glass beads, bells, and brass trinkets, and taken in the ship, until she was off a village 17 miles from the former anchorage, where the Admiral came to again. The village appeared to have been lately built, for all the houses were new. The Indian then went on shore in his canoe, bringing the news that the Admiral and his companions were good people; although the intelligence had already been conveyed to the village from the place where the natives had their interview with the six Spaniards. Presently more than five hundred natives with their king came to the shore opposite the ships, which were anchored very close to the land. Presently one by one, then many by many, came to the ship without bringing anything with them, except that some had a few grains of very fine gold in their ears and noses, which they readily gave away. The Admiral ordered them all to be well treated; and he says: "for they are the best people in the world, and the gentlest; and above all I entertain the hope in our Lord that your Highnesses will make them all Christians, and that they will be all your subjects, for as yours I hold them." He also saw that they

---

[225] Rather, "There are on the edges or banks of the shore many beautiful stones and it is all suitable for walking." The Spanish text seems to be defective.

all treated the king with respect, who was on the sea-shore. The Admiral sent him a present, which he received in great state. He was a youth of about 21 years of age, and he had with him an aged tutor, and other councillors who advised and answered him, but he uttered very few words. One of the Indians who had come in the Admiral's ship spoke to him, telling him how the Christians had come from Heaven, and how they came in search of gold, and wished to find the island of Baneque. He said that it was well and that there was much gold in the said island. He explained to the alguazil of the Admiral[226] that the way they were going was the right way, and that in two days they would be there; adding, that if they wanted anything from the shore he would give it them with great pleasure. This king, and all the others, go naked as their mothers bore them, as do the women without any covering, and these were the most beautiful men and women that had yet been met with. They are fairly white, and if they were clothed and protected from the sun and air, they would be almost as fair as people in Spain. This land is cool, and the best that words can describe. It is very high, yet the top of the highest mountain could be ploughed with bullocks; and all is diversified with plains and valleys. In all Castile there is no land that can be compared with this for beauty and fertility. All this island, as well as the island of Tortuga, is cultivated like the plain of Cordova. They raise on these lands crops of yams,[227] which are small branches, at the foot of which grow roots like carrots, which serve as bread. They powder and knead them, and make them into bread; then they plant the same branch in another part, which again sends out four or five of the same roots, which are very

---

[226] Diego de Arana of Cordova, a near relation of Beatriz Henriquez, the mother of the Admiral's son Fernando. (Markham.) Alguazil means constable.

[227] Ajes. The same as mames.

nutritious, with the taste of chestnuts. Here they have the largest the Admiral had seen in any part of the world, for he says that they have the same plant in Guinea. At this place they were as thick as a man's leg. All the people were stout and lusty, not thin, like the natives that had been seen before, and of a very pleasant manner, without religious belief. The trees were so luxuriant that the leaves left off being green, and were dark colored with verdure. It was a wonderful thing to see those valleys, and rivers of sweet water, and the cultivated fields, and land fit for cattle, though they have none, for orchards, and for anything in the world that a man could seek for.

In the afternoon the king came on board the ship, where the Admiral received him in due form, and caused him to be told that the ships belonged to the Sovereigns of Castile, who were the greatest princes in the world. But neither the Indians who were on board, who acted as interpreters, nor the king, believed a word of it. They maintained that the Spaniards came from Heaven, and that the Sovereigns of Castile must be in Heaven, and not in this world. They placed Spanish food before the king to eat, and he ate a mouthful, and gave the rest to his councillors and tutor, and to the rest who came with him.

"Your Highnesses may believe that these lands are so good and fertile, especially these of the island of Española, that there is no one who would know how to describe them, and no one who could believe if he had not seen them. And your Highnesses may believe that this island, and all the others, are as much yours as Castile. Here there is only wanting a settlement and the order to the people to do what is required. For I, with the force I have under me, which is not large, could march over all these islands without opposition. I have seen only three sailors land, without wishing to do harm, and a multitude of Indians fled before them. They have no arms, and are without warlike instincts; they all go naked, and are so timid that a thousand would not stand before three of our men. So that they are good to be ordered about, to work and sow, and do all that may be necessary, and to build towns, and they should be taught to go about clothed and to adopt our customs."

Monday, 17th of December

It blew very hard during the night from E.N.E., but there was not much sea, as this part of the coast is enclosed and sheltered by the island of Tortuga. The sailors were sent away to fish with nets. They had much intercourse with the natives, who brought them certain arrows of the Caniba or Canibales. They are made of reeds, pointed with sharp bits of wood hardened by fire, and are very long. They pointed out two men who wanted certain pieces of flesh on their bodies, giving to understand that the Canibales had eaten them by mouthfuls. The Admiral did not believe it. Some Christians were again sent to the village, and, in exchange for glass beads, obtained some pieces of gold beaten out into fine leaf. They saw one man, whom the Admiral supposed to be Governor of that province, called by them Cacique,[228] with a piece of gold leaf as large as a hand, and it appears that he wanted to barter with it. He went into his house, and the other remained in the open space outside. He cut the leaf into small pieces, and each time he came out he brought a piece and exchanged it. When he had no more left, he said by signs that he had sent for more, and that he would bring it another day. The Admiral says that all these things, and the manner of doing them, with their gentleness and the information they gave, showed these

---

[228] This Indian word survives in modern Spanish with the meaning political boss.

people to be more lively and intelligent than any that had hitherto been met with. In the afternoon a canoe arrived from the island of Tortuga with a crew of forty men; and when they arrived on the beach, all the people of the village sat down in sign of peace, and nearly all the crew came on shore. The cacique rose by himself, and, with words that appeared to be of a menacing character, made them go back to the canoe and shove off. He took up stones from the beach and threw them into the water, all having obediently gone back into the canoe. He also took a stone and put it in the hands of my Alguazil,[229] that he might throw it. He had been sent on shore with the Secretary[230] to see if the canoe had brought anything of value. The alguazil did not wish to throw the stone. That cacique showed that he was well disposed to the Admiral. Presently the canoe departed, and afterwards they said to the Admiral that there was more gold in Tortuga than in Española, because it is nearer to Baneque. The Admiral did not think that there were gold mines either in Española or Tortuga, but that the gold was brought from Baneque in small quantities, there being nothing to give in return. That land is so rich that there is no necessity to work much to sustain life, nor to clothe themselves, as they go naked. He believed that they were very near the source, and that our Lord would point out where the gold has its origin. He had information that from here to Baneque was four days' journey, about 34 leagues, which might be traversed with a fair wind in a single day.

Tuesday, 18th of December

The Admiral remained at the same anchorage, because there was no wind, and also because the cacique had said that he had sent for gold. The Admiral did not expect

---

[229] Diego de Arana.
[230] Rodrigo de Escobedo.

much from what might be brought, but he wanted to understand better whence it came. Presently he ordered the ship and caravel to be adorned with arms and dressed with flags, in honor of the feast of Santa Maria de la O,[231] or commemoration of the Annunciation, which was on that day, and many rounds were fired from the lombards. The king of that island of Española had got up very early and left his house, which is about five leagues away, reaching the village at three in the morning. There were several men from the ship in the village, who had been sent by the Admiral to see if any gold had arrived. They said that the king came with two hundred men; that he was carried in a litter by four men; and that he was a youth, as has already been said. To-day, when the Admiral was dining under the poop, the king came on board with all his people.

The Admiral says to the Sovereigns: "Without doubt, his state, and the reverence with which he is treated by all his people, would appear good to your Highnesses, though they all go naked. When he came on board, he found that I was dining at a table under the poop, and, at a quick walk, he came to sit down by me, and did not wish that I should give place by coming to receive him or rising from the table, but that I should go on with my dinner. I thought that he would like to eat of our viands, and ordered them to be brought for him to eat. When he came under the poop, he made signs with his hand that all the rest should remain outside, and so they did, with the

---

[231] In Spain in earlier times the Annunciation was celebrated on December 18 to avoid having it come in Lent. When the Roman usage in regard to Annunciation was adopted in Spain they instituted the Feast of our Lady's Expectation on December 18. It was called "The Feast of O because the first of the greater antiphons is said in the vespers of its vigil." Addis and Arnold, *Catholic Dictionary*, under "Mary." The series of anthems all begin with "O."

greatest possible promptitude and reverence. They all sat on the deck, except the men of mature age, whom I believe to be his councillors and tutor, who came and sat at his feet. Of the viands which I put before him, he took of each as much as would serve to taste it, sending the rest to his people, who all partook of the dishes. The same thing in drinking: he just touched with his lips, giving the rest to his followers. They were all of fine presence and very few words. What they did say, so far as I could make out, was very clear and intelligent. The two at his feet watched his mouth, speaking to him and for him, and with much reverence. After dinner, an attendant brought a girdle, made like those of Castile, but of different material, which he took and gave to me, with pieces of worked gold, very thin. I believe they get very little here, but they say that they are very near the place where it is found, and where there is plenty. I saw that he was pleased with some drapery I had over my bed, so I gave it him, with some very good amber beads I wore on my neck, some colored shoes, and a bottle of orange-flower water. He was marvellously well content, and both he and his tutor and councillors were very sorry that they could not understand me, nor I them. However, I knew that they said that, if I wanted anything, the whole island was at my disposal. I sent for some beads of mine, with which, as a charm, I had a gold excelente,[232] on which your Highnesses were stamped. I showed it to him, and said as I had done yesterday, that your Highnesses ruled the best part of the world, and that there were no princes so great. I also showed him the royal standards, and the others with a cross, of which he thought much. He said to his councillors what great lords your Highnesses must be to have sent me from so far, even from Heaven to this country, without fear. Many other things passed between

---

[232] The excelente was worth two castellanos or about $6 in coin value.

them which I did not understand, except that it was easy to see that they held everything to be very wonderful."

When it got late, and the king wanted to go, the Admiral sent him on shore in his boat very honorably, and saluted him with many guns. Having landed, he got into his litter, and departed with his 200 men, his son being carried behind on the shoulders of an Indian, a man highly respected. All the sailors and people from the ships were given to eat, and treated with much honor wherever they liked to stop. One sailor said that he had stopped in the road and seen all the things given by the Admiral. A man carried each one before the king, and these men appeared to be among those who were most respected. His son came a good distance behind the king, with a similar number of attendants, and the same with a brother of the king, except that the brother went on foot, supported under the arms by two honored attendants. This brother came to the ship after the king, and the Admiral presented him with some of the things used for barter. It was then that the Admiral learnt that a king was called Cacique in their language. This day little gold was got by barter, but the Admiral heard from an old man that there were many neighboring islands, at a distance of a hundred leagues or more, as he understood, in which much gold is found; and there is even one island that was all gold. In the others there was so much that it was said they gather it with sieves, and they fuse it and make bars, and work it in a thousand ways.

They explained the work by signs. This old man pointed out to the Admiral the direction and position, and he determined to go there, saying that if the old man had not been a principal councillor of the king he would detain him, and make him go, too; or if he knew the language he would ask him, and he believed, as the old man was friendly with him and the other Christians, that he would go of his own accord. But as these people were now subjects of the King of Castile, and it would not be right to injure them, he decided upon leaving him. The Admiral set up a very large cross in the centre of the square of that village, the Indians giving much help; they made prayers and worshipped it, and, from the feeling they show, the Admiral trusted in our Lord that all the people of those islands would become Christians.

Wednesday, 19th of December

This night the Admiral got under way to leave the gulf formed between the islands of Tortuga and Española, but at dawn of day a breeze sprang up from the east, against which he was unable to get clear of the strait between the two islands during the whole day. At night he was unable to reach a port which was in sight.[233] He made out four points of land, and a great bay with a river, and beyond he saw a large bay,[234] where there was a village, with a valley behind it among high mountains covered with trees, which appeared to be pines. Over the Two Brothers there is a very high mountain-range running N.E. and S.W., and E.S.E. from the Cabo de Torres is a small island to which the Admiral gave the name of Santo Tomas, because to-morrow was his vigil. The whole circuit of this island alternates with capes and excellent harbors, so far as could be judged from the sea. Before coming to the island on the west side, there is a cape which runs far into the sea, in part high, the rest low; and for this reason the Admiral named it Cabo Alto y Bajo.[235] From the road[236] of Torres East by South 60 miles, there is a mountain higher

---

[233] El Puerto de la Granja. (Navarrete.)
[234] The bay of Puerto Margot. (Id.)
[235] Point and Island of Margot. (Navarrete.)
[236] Camino for Cabo (?). (Markham.)

than any that reaches the sea,[237] and from a distance it looks like an island, owing to a depression on the land side. It was named Monte Caribata, because that province was called Caribata. It is very beautiful, and covered with green trees, without snow or clouds. The weather was then, as regards the air and temperature, like March in Castile, and as regards vegetation, like May. The nights lasted 14 hours.

Thursday, 20th of December

At sunrise they entered a port between the island of Santo Tomas and the Cabo de Carabata,[238] and anchored. This port is very beautiful, and would hold all the ships in Christendom. The entrance appears impossible from the sea to those who have never entered, owing to some reefs of rocks which run from the mountainous cape almost to the island. They are not placed in a row, but one here, another there, some towards the sea, others near the land. It is therefore necessary to keep a good look-out for the entrances, which are wide and with a depth of 7 fathoms, so that they can be used without fear. Inside the reefs there is a depth of 12 fathoms. A ship can lie with a cable made fast, against any wind that blows. At the entrance of this port there is a channel on the west side of a sandy islet with 7 fathoms, and many trees on its shore. But there are many sunken rocks in that direction, and a look-out should be kept up until the port is reached. Afterwards there is no need to fear the greatest storm in the world. From this port a very beautiful cultivated valley is in sight, descending from the S.E., surrounded by such lofty mountains that they appear to reach the sky, and covered with green trees. Without doubt there are mountains here which are higher than the island of

---

[237] Mountain over Guarico. (Navarrete.)
[238] Bahia de Acúl. (Navarrete.)

Tenerife, in the Canaries, which is held to be the highest yet known.[239] On this side of the island of Santo Tomas, at a distance of a league, there is another islet, and beyond it another, forming wonderful harbors; though a good look-out must be kept for sunken rocks.

The Admiral also saw villages, and smoke made by them.

Friday, 21st of December

To-day the Admiral went with the ship's boats to examine this port, which he found to be such that it could not be equalled by any he had yet seen; but, having praised the others so much, he knew not how to express himself, fearing that he will be looked upon as one who goes beyond the truth. He therefore contents himself with saying that he had old sailors with him who say the same. All the praises he has bestowed on the other ports are true, and that this is better than any of them is equally true. He further says: "I have traversed the sea for 23 years,[240] without leaving it for any time worth counting, and I saw all the east and the west, going on the route of the north, which is England, and I have been to Guinea, but in all those parts there will not be found the perfection of harbors ...[241] always found ...[242] better than another, that I, with good care, saw written; and I again affirm it was well written, that this one is better

---

[239] This conjecture proved to be wrong. The Peak of Teneriffe is over 12,000 ft. high, while 10,300 ft. (Mt. Tina) is the highest elevation in Santo Domingo.

[240] This is one of the passages used to determine the date of Columbus's birth. By combining his statement quoted in the *Historie* of Ferdinand, ch. IV., that he went to sea at 14, and this assertion that he followed the sea steadily for 23 years, we find that he was 37 years old in 1484 or 1485, when he left Portugal and ceased sea-faring till 1492.

[241] A gap of a line and a half in the manuscript.

[242] Another gap in the manuscript.

than all others, and will hold all the ships of the world, secured with the oldest cables." From the entrance to the end is a distance of five leagues.[243] The Admiral saw some very well cultivated lands, although they are all so, and he sent two of the boat's crew to the top of a hill to see if any village was near, for none could be seen from the sea. At about ten o'clock that night, certain Indians came in a canoe to see the Admiral and the Christians, and they were given presents, with which they were much pleased. The two men returned, and reported that they had seen a very large village at a short distance from the sea.[244] The Admiral ordered the boat to row towards the place where the village was until they came near the land, when he saw two Indians, who came to the shore apparently in a state of fear. So he ordered the boats to stop, and the Indians that were with the Admiral were told to assure the two natives that no harm whatever was intended to them. Then they came nearer the sea, and the Admiral nearer the land. As soon as the natives had got rid of their fear, so many came that they covered the ground, with women and children, giving a thousand thanks. They ran hither and thither to bring us bread made of *niames*, which they call *ajes*, which is very white and good, and water in calabashes, and in earthen jars made like those of Spain, and everything else they had and that they thought the Admiral could want, and all so willingly and cheerfully that it was wonderful. "It cannot be said that, because what they gave was worth little, therefore they gave liberally, because those who had pieces of gold gave as freely as those who had a calabash of water; and it is easy to know when a thing is given with a hearty desire to give." These are the Admiral's words. "These people have no spears nor any other arms, nor

---

[243] The distance is six miles. (Navarrete.)
[244] Acúl. (Id.)

have any of the inhabitants of the whole island, which I believe to be very large. They go naked as when their mothers bore them, both men and women. In Juana and the other islands the women wear a small clout of cotton in front, with which to cover their private parts, as large as the flap of a man's breeches, especially after they have passed the age of twelve years, but here neither old nor young do so. Also, the men in the other islands jealously hide their women from the Christians, but here they do not." The women have very beautiful bodies, and they were the first to come and give thanks to Heaven, and to bring what they had, especially things to eat, such as bread of *ajes*, nuts,[245] and four or five kinds of fruits, some of which the Admiral ordered to be preserved, to be taken to the Sovereigns. He says that the women did not do less in other ports before they were hidden; and he always gave orders that none of his people should annoy them; that nothing should be taken against their wills, and that everything that was taken should be paid for. Finally, he says that no one could believe that there could be such good-hearted people, so free to give, anxious to let the Christians have all they wanted, and, when visitors arrived, running to bring everything to them.

Afterwards the Admiral sent six Christians to the village to see what it was like, and the natives showed them all the honor they could devise, and gave them all they had; for no doubt was any longer entertained that the Admiral and all his people had come from Heaven; and the same was believed by the Indians who were brought from the other islands, although they had now been told what they ought to think. When the six Christians had gone, some *canoas* came with people to ask the Admiral to come to

---

[245] *Gonze avellanada.* The interpretation of the French translators is followed. The word *gonze* is not given in the dictionaries.

their village when he left the place where he was. *Canoa* is a boat in which they navigate, some large and others small. Seeing that this village of the chief was on the road, and that many people were waiting there for him, the Admiral went there; but, before he could depart, an enormous crowd came to the shore, men, women, and children, crying out to him not to go, but to stay with them. The messengers from the other chief, who had come to invite him, were waiting with their canoes, that he might not go away, but come to see their chief, and so he did. On arriving where the chief was waiting for him with many things to eat, he ordered that all the people should sit down, and that the food should be taken to the boats, where the Admiral was, on the sea-shore. When he saw that the Admiral had received what he sent, all or most of the Indians ran to the village, which was near, to bring more food, parrots, and other things they had, with such frankness of heart that it was marvellous. The Admiral gave them glass beads, brass trinkets, and bells: not because they asked for anything in return, but because it seemed right, and, above all, because he now looked upon them as future Christians, and subjects of the Sovereigns, as much as the people of Castile. He further says that they want nothing except to know the language and be under governance; for all they may be told to do will be done without any contradiction. The Admiral left this place to go to the ships, and the people, men, women, and children, cried out to him not to go, but remain with them. After the boats departed, several canoes full of people followed after them to the ship, who were received with much honor, and given to eat. There had also come before another chief from the west, and many people even came swimming, the ship being over a good half-league from the shore. I sent certain persons to the chief, who had gone back, to ask him about these islands. He received them very well, and took them to his village, to give them some large pieces of gold. They arrived at a large river, which the Indians crossed by swimming. The Christians were unable, so they turned back. In all this district there are very high mountains which seem to reach the sky, so that the mountain in the island of Tenerife appears as nothing in height and beauty, and they are all green with trees. Between them there are very delicious valleys, and at the end of this port, to the south, there is a valley so large that the end of it is not visible, though no mountains intervene, so that it seems to be 15 or 20 leagues long. A river flows through it, and it is all inhabited and cultivated, and as green as Castile in May or June; but the night contains 14 hours, the land being so far north. This port is very good for all the winds that can blow, being enclosed and deep, and the shores peopled by a good and gentle race without arms or evil designs. Any ship may lie within it without fear that other ships will enter at night to attack her, because, although the entrance is over two leagues wide, it is protected by reefs of rocks which are barely awash; and there is only a very narrow channel through the reef, which looks as if it had been artificially made, leaving an open door by which ships may enter. In the entrance there are 7 fathoms of depth up to the shore of a small flat island, which has a beach fringed with trees. The entrance is on the west side, and a ship can come without fear until she is close to the rock. On the N.W. side there are three islands, and a great river a league from the cape on one side of the port. It is the best harbor in the world, and the Admiral gave it the name of Puerto de la Mar de Santo Tomas, because to-day it was that Saint's day. The Admiral called it a sea, owing to its size.

Saturday, 22nd of December

At dawn the Admiral made sail to shape a course in search of the islands which the Indians had told him contained much gold, some of them having more gold than earth. But the weather was not favorable, so he anchored again, and sent away the boat to fish with a net. The lord of that land,[246] who had a place near there, sent a large canoe full of people, including one of his principal attendants, to invite the Admiral to come with the ships to his land, where he would give him all he wanted. The chief sent, by this servant, a girdle which, instead of a purse,[247] had attached to it a mask with two large ears made of beaten gold, the tongue, and the nose. These people are very open-hearted, and whatever they are asked for they give most willingly; while, when they themselves ask for anything, they do so as if receiving a great favor. So says the Admiral. They brought the canoe alongside the boat, and gave the girdle to a boy; then they came on board with their mission. It took a good part of the day before they could be understood. Not even the Indians who were on board understood them well, because they have some differences of words for the names of things. At last their invitation was understood by signs. The Admiral determined to start to-morrow, although he did not usually sail on a Sunday, owing to a devout feeling, and not on account of any superstition whatever. But in the hope that these people would become Christians through the willingness they show, and that they will be subjects of the Sovereigns of Castile, and because he now holds them to be so, and that they may serve with love, he wished and endeavored to please them. Before leaving, to-day, the Admiral sent six men to a large village three leagues to the westward, because the

[246] "This king was a great lord and king Guacanagarí, one of the five great kings and lordships of this island." Las Casas, I. 389.

[247] "This girdle was of fine jewellery work, like misshapen pearls, made of fish-bones white and colored interspersed, like embroidery, so sewed with a thread of cotton and by such delicate skill that on the reverse side it looked like delicate embroidery, although all white, which it was a pleasure to see." Las Casas, I. 389. From this we learn that wampum belts were in use among the Indians of Española.

chief had come the day before and said that he had some pieces of gold. When the Christians arrived, the secretary of the Admiral, who was one of them, took the chief by the hand. The Admiral had sent him, to prevent the others from imposing upon the Indians. As the Indians are so simple, and the Spaniards so avaricious and grasping, it does not suffice that the Indians should give them all they want in exchange for a bead or a bit of glass, but the Spaniards would take everything without any return at all. The Admiral always prohibits this, although, with the exception of gold, the things given by the Indians are of little value. But the Admiral, seeing the simplicity of the Indians, and that they will give a piece of gold in exchange for six beads, gave the order that nothing should be received from them unless something had been given in exchange. Thus the chief took the secretary by the hand and led him to his house, followed by the whole village, which was very large. He made his guests eat, and the Indians brought them many cotton fabrics, and spun-cotton in skeins. In the afternoon the chief gave them three very fat geese and some small pieces of gold. A great number of people went back with them, carrying all the things they had got by barter, and they also carried the Spaniards themselves across streams and muddy places. The Admiral ordered some things to be given to the chief, and both he and his people were very well satisfied, truly believing that the Christians had come from Heaven, so that they considered themselves fortunate in beholding them. On this day more than 120 canoes came to the ships, all full of people, and all bringing something, especially their bread and fish, and fresh water in earthen jars. They also brought seeds of good kinds, and there was a grain which they put into a porringer of water and drank it. The Indians who were on board said that this was very wholesome.

Sunday, 23rd of December

The Admiral could not go with the ships to that land whither he had been invited by the chief, because there was no wind. But he sent, with the three messengers who were waiting for the boats, some people, including the secretary. While they were gone, he sent two of the Indians he had on board with him to the villages which were near the anchorage. They returned to the ship with a chief, who brought the news that there was a great quantity of gold in that island of Española, and that people from other parts came to buy it. They said that here the Admiral would find as much as he wanted. Others came, who confirmed the statement that there was much gold in the island, and explained the way it was collected. The Admiral understood all this with much difficulty; nevertheless, he concluded that there was a very great quantity in those parts, and that, if he could find the place whence it was got, there would be abundance; and, if not, there would be nothing. He believed there must be a great deal, because during the three days that he had been in that port, he had got several pieces of gold, and he could not believe that it was brought from another land. "Our Lord, who holds all things in his hands, look upon me, and grant what shall be for his service." These are the Admiral's words. He says that, according to his reckoning, a thousand people had visited the ship, all of them bringing something. Before they come alongside, at a distance of a crossbow-shot, they stand up in the canoe with what they bring in their hands, crying out, "Take it! Take it!" He also reckoned that 500 came to the ship swimming, because they had no canoes, the ship being near a league from the shore. Among the visitors, five chiefs had come, sons of chiefs, with all their families of wives and children, to see the Christians. The Admiral ordered something to be given to all, because such gifts were all well employed. "May our

349

Lord favor me by his clemency, that I may find this gold, I mean the mine of gold, which I hold to be here, many saying that they know it." These are his words. The boats arrived at night, and said that there was a grand road as far as they went, and they found many canoes, with people who went to see the Admiral and the Christians, at the mountain of Caribatan. They held it for certain that, if the Christmas festival was kept in that port,[248] all the people of the island would come, which they calculated to be larger than England.[249] All the people went with them to the village,[250] which they said was the largest, and the best laid out with streets, of any they had seen. The Admiral says it is part of the Punta Santa,[251] almost three leagues S.E. The canoes go very fast with paddles; so they went ahead to apprise the *Cacique*, as they call the chief. Up to that time the Admiral had not been able to understand whether Cacique meant king or governor. They also have another name for a great man--*Nitayno*;[252] but it was not clear whether they used it for lord, or governor, or judge. At last the cacique came to them, and joined them in the square, which was clean-swept, as was all the village. The population numbered over 2,000 men. This king did great honor to the people from the ship, and every inhabitant brought them something to eat and drink. Afterwards the king gave each of them cotton cloths such as women wear, with parrots for the Admiral, and some pieces of gold. The people also gave cloths and other things from their houses to the sailors; and as for the trifles they got in return, they seemed to look upon

---

[248] Port of Guarico. (Navarrete.)

[249] This estimate was far too great. The island is about one-third the size of Great Britain and one-half the size of England.

[250] Guarico.

[251] It is now called San Honorato. (Navarrete.)

[252] "The fact is that *Cacique* was the word for king, and *Nitayno* for knight and principal lord." Las Casas, I. 394.

350

them as relics. When they wanted to return in the afternoon, he asked them to stay until the next day, and all the people did the same. When they saw that the Spaniards were determined to go, they accompanied them most of the way, carrying the gifts of the cacique on their backs as far as the boats, which had been left at the mouth of the river.

Monday, 24th of December

Before sunrise the Admiral got under way with the land-breeze. Among the numerous Indians who had come to the ship yesterday, and had made signs that there was gold in the island, naming the places whence it was collected, the Admiral noticed one who seemed more fully informed, or who spoke with more willingness, so he asked him to come with the Christians and show them the position of the gold mines. This Indian has a companion or relation with him, and among other places they mentioned where gold was found, they named Cipango, which they called Civao.[253] Here they said that there was a great quantity of gold, and that the cacique carried banners of beaten gold. But they added that it was very far off to the eastward.

Here the Admiral addresses the following words to the Sovereigns: "Your Highnesses may believe that there is no better nor gentler people in the world. Your Highnesses ought to rejoice that they will soon become Christians, and that they will be taught the good customs of your kingdom. A better race there cannot be, and both the people and the lands are in such quantity that I know not how to write it. I have spoken in the superlative degree of

---

[253] The similarity between the names and the report of gold made Columbus particularly confident of the identification.

the country and people of Juana which they call Cuba, but there is as much difference between them and this island and people as between day and night. I believe that no one who should see them could say less than I have said, and I repeat that the things and the great villages of this island of Española, which they call Bohio, are wonderful. All here have a loving manner and gentle speech, unlike the others, who seem to be menacing when they speak. Both men and women are of good stature, and not black. It is true that they all paint, some with black, others with other colors, but most with red. I know that they are tanned by the sun, but this does not affect them much. Their houses and villages are pretty, each with a chief, who acts as their judge, and who is obeyed by them. All these lords use few words, and have excellent manners. Most of their orders are given by a sign with the hand, which is understood with surprising quickness." All these are the words of the Admiral.

He who would enter the sea of Santo Tomé[254] ought to stand for a good league across the mouth to a flat island in the middle, which was named La Amiga,[255] pointing her head towards it. When the ship is within a stone's-throw of it the course should be altered to make for the eastern shore, leaving the west side, and this shore, and not the other, should be kept on board, because a great reef runs out from the west, and even beyond that there are three sunken rocks. This reef comes within a lombard-shot of the Amiga island. Between them there are seven fathoms at least, with a gravelly bottom. Within, a harbor will be found large enough for all the ships in the world, which would be there without need of cables. There is another reef with sunken rocks, on the east side of the island of Amiga, which are extensive and

---

[254] Entrance of the Bay of Acúl. (Navarrete.)
[255] Isla de Ratos. (Id.)

run out to sea, reaching within two leagues of the cape. But it appeared that between them there was an entrance, within two lombard-shots of Amiga, on the west side of Monte Caribatan, where there was a good and very large port.[256]

Tuesday, 25th of December. Christmas

Navigating yesterday, with little wind, from Santo Tomé to Punta Santa, and being a league from it, at about eleven o'clock at night the Admiral went down to get some sleep, for he had not had any rest for two days and a night. As it was calm, the sailor who steered the ship thought he would go to sleep, leaving the tiller in charge of a boy.[257] The Admiral had forbidden this throughout the voyage, whether it was blowing or whether it was calm. The boys were never to be entrusted with the helm. The Admiral had no anxiety respecting sand-banks and rocks, because, when he sent the boats to that king on Sunday, they had passed to the east of Punta Santa at least three leagues and a half, and the sailors had seen all the coast, and the rocks there are from Punta Santa, for a distance of three leagues to the E.S.E. They saw the course that should be taken, which had not been the case before, during this voyage. It pleased our Lord that, at twelve o'clock at night, when the Admiral had retired to rest, and when all had fallen asleep, seeing that it was a dead calm and the sea like glass, the tiller being in the hands of a boy, the current carried the ship on one of the sand-banks. If it had not been night the bank could have been seen, and the surf on it could be heard for a good league. But the ship ran upon it so gently that it could scarcely be felt. The boy, who felt the helm and heard the

---

[256] Puerto Frances. (Navarrete.)
[257] Perhaps better "a young common sailor."

rush of the sea, cried out. The Admiral at once came up, and so quickly that no one had felt that the ship was aground. Presently the master of the ship,[258] whose watch it was, came on deck. The Admiral ordered him and others to launch the boat, which was on the poop, and lay out an anchor astern. The master, with several others, got into the boat, and the Admiral thought that they did so with the object of obeying his orders. But they did so in order to take refuge with the caravel, which was half a league to leeward. The caravel would not allow them to come on board acting judiciously, and they therefore returned to the ship; but the caravel's boat arrived first. When the Admiral saw that his own people fled in this way, the water rising and the ship being across the sea, seeing no other course, he ordered the masts to be cut away and the ship to be lightened as much as possible, to see if she would come off. But, as the water continued to rise, nothing more could be done. Her side fell over across the sea, but it was nearly calm. Then the timbers opened, and the ship was lost.[259] The Admiral went to the caravel to arrange about the reception of the ship's crew, and as a light breeze was blowing from the land, and continued during the greater part of the night, while it was unknown how far the bank extended, he hove her to until daylight. He then went back to the ship, inside the reef; first having sent a boat on shore with Diego de Arana of Cordova, alguazil of the fleet, and Pedro Gutierrez, gentleman of the king's bedchamber, to inform the king, who had invited the ships to come on the previous

---

[258] The master, who was also the owner, of the Admiral's ship was Juan de la Cosa of Santoña, afterwards well known as a draughtsman and Pilot. (Markham.)

[259] Rather, "Then the seams opened but not the ship." That is, the ship was not stove. The word translated "seams" is *conventos*, which Las Casas, I. 398, defines as *los vagos que hay entre costillas y costillas*. In this passage he is using *costillas* not in the technical sense of *costillas de nao*, "ribs," but in the sense of "planks," as in *costillas de cuba*, "barrel staves."

Saturday. His town was about a league and a half from the sand-bank. They reported that he wept when he heard the news, and he sent all his people with large canoes to unload the ship. This was done, and they landed all there was between decks in a very short time. Such was the great promptitude and diligence shown by that king. He himself, with brothers and relations, was actively assisting as well in the ship as in the care of the property when it was landed, that all might be properly guarded. Now and then he sent one of his relations weeping to the Admiral, to console him, saying that he must not feel sorrow or annoyance, for he would supply all that was needed. The Admiral assured the Sovereigns that there could not have been such good watch kept in any part of Castile, for that there was not even a needle missing. He ordered that all the property should be placed by some houses which the king placed at his disposal, until they were emptied, when everything would be stowed and guarded in them. Armed men were placed round the stores to watch all night. "The king and all his people wept [says the Admiral]. They are a loving people, without covetousness, and fit for anything; and I assure your Highnesses that there is no better land nor people. They love their neighbors as themselves, and their speech is the sweetest and gentlest in the world, and always with a smile. Men and women go as naked as when their mothers bore them. Your Highnesses should believe that they have very good customs among themselves. The king is a man of remarkable presence, and with a certain self-contained manner that is a pleasure to see. They have good memories, wish to see everything, and ask the use of what they see." All this is written by the Admiral.

Wednesday, 26th of December

To-day, at sunrise, the king of that land came to the caravel Niña where the Admiral was, and said to him, almost weeping, that he need not be sorry, for that he would give him all he had; that he had placed two large houses at the disposal of the Christians who were on shore, and that he would give more if they were required, and as many canoes as could load from the ship and discharge on shore, with as many people as were wanted. This had all been done yesterday, without so much as a needle being missed. "So honest are they," says the Admiral, "without any covetousness for the goods of others, and so above all was that virtuous king." While the Admiral was talking to him, another canoe arrived from a different place, bringing some pieces of gold, which the people in the canoe wanted to exchange for a hawk's bell; for there was nothing they desired more than these bells. They had scarcely come alongside when they called and held up the gold, saying *Chuq chuq* for the bells, for they are quite mad about them. After the king had seen this, and when the canoes which came from other places had departed, he called the Admiral and asked him to give orders that one of the bells was to be kept for another day, when he would bring four pieces of gold the size of a man's hand. The Admiral rejoiced to hear this, and afterwards a sailor, who came from the shore, told him that it was wonderful what pieces of gold the men on shore were getting in exchange for next to nothing. For a needle they got a piece of gold worth two *castellanos*, and that this was nothing to what it would be within a month. The king rejoiced much when he saw that the Admiral was pleased. He understood that his friend wanted much gold, and he said, by signs, that he knew where there was, in the vicinity, a very large quantity; so that he must be in good heart, for he should have as much as he wanted. He gave some account of it, especially saying that in Cipango, which they call Cibao,[260] it is so abundant that it is of no value, and that they will bring it, although there

---

[260] In reality Cibao was a part of Española.

is also much more in the island of Española, which they call Bohio, and in the province of Caritaba. The king dined on board the caravel with the Admiral and afterwards went on shore, where he received the Admiral with much honor. He gave him a collation consisting of three or four kinds of *ajes*, with shrimps and game, and other viands they have, besides the bread they call *cazavi*.[261] He then took the Admiral to see some groves of trees near the houses, and they were accompanied by at least a thousand people, all naked. The lord had on a shirt and a pair of gloves, given to him by the Admiral, and he was more delighted with the gloves than with anything else. In his manner of eating, both as regards the high-bred air and the peculiar cleanliness he clearly showed his nobility. After he had eaten, he remained some time at table, and they brought him certain herbs, with which he rubbed his hands. The Admiral thought that this was done to make them soft, and they also gave him water for his hands. After the meal he took the Admiral to the beach. The Admiral then sent for a Turkish bow and a quiver of arrows, and took a shot at a man of his company, who had been warned. The chief, who knew nothing about arms, as they neither have them nor use them, thought this a wonderful thing. He, however, began to talk of those of Caniba, whom they call Caribes. They come to capture the natives, and have bows and arrows without iron, of which there is no memory in any of these lands, nor of steel, nor any other metal except gold and copper. Of copper the Admiral had only seen very little. The Admiral said, by signs, that the Sovereigns of Castile would order the Caribs to be destroyed, and that all should be taken with their hands tied together. He ordered a Lombard and a hand-gun to

---

[261] Made from the manioc roots or *ajes*. Cassava biscuit can be got to-day at fancy grocery stores. It is rather insipid.

be fired off, and seeing the effect caused by its force and what the shots penetrated, the king was astonished. When his people heard the explosion they all fell on the ground. They brought the Admiral a large mask, which had pieces of gold for the eyes and ears and in other parts, and this they gave, with other trinkets of gold that the same king had put on the head and round the neck of the Admiral, and of other Christians, to whom they also gave many pieces. The Admiral received much pleasure and consolation from these things, which tempered the anxiety and sorrow he felt at the loss of the ship. He knew our Lord had caused the ship to stop here, that a settlement might be formed. "From this," he says, "originated so many things that, in truth, the disaster was really a piece of good fortune. For it is certain that, if I had not lost the ship, I should have gone on without anchoring in this place, which is within a great bay, having two or three reefs of rock. I should not have left people in the country during this voyage, nor even if I had desired to leave them, should I have been able to obtain so much information, nor such supplies and provisions for a fortress. And true it is that many people had asked me to give them leave to remain. Now I have given orders for a tower and a fort, both well built, and a large cellar, not because I believe that such defences will be necessary. I believe that with the force I have with me I could subjugate the whole island, which I believe to be larger than Portugal, and the population double.[262] But they are naked and without arms and hopelessly timid. Still, it is advisable to build this tower being so far from your Highnesses. The people may thus know the skill of the subjects of your Highnesses, and what they can do; and will obey them with love and fear. So they make preparations to build the fortress, with provision of bread and wine for more than a year, with seeds for sowing, the

---

[262] In reality, three-quarters the size of Portugal.

ship's boat, a caulker and carpenter, a gunner and cooper. Many among these men have a great desire to serve your Highnesses and to please me, by finding out where the mine is whence the gold is brought. Thus everything is got in readiness to begin the work. Above all, it was so calm that there was scarcely wind or wave when the ship ran aground." This is what the Admiral says; and he adds more to show that it was great good luck, and the settled design of God, that the ship should be lost in order that people might be left behind. If it had not been for the treachery of the master and his boat's crew, who were all or mostly his countrymen,[263] in neglecting to lay out the anchor so as to haul the ship off in obedience to the Admiral's orders, she would have been saved. In that case, the same knowledge of the land as has been gained in these days would not have been secured, for the Admiral always proceeded with the object of discovering, and never intended to stop more than a day at any one place, unless he was detained by the wind. Still the ship was very heavy and unsuited for discovery. It was the people of Palos who obliged him to take such a ship, by not complying "with what they had promised to the King and Queen, namely, to supply suitable vessels for this expedition. This they did not do. Of all that there was on board the ship, not a needle, nor a board, nor a nail was lost, for she remained as whole as when she sailed, except that it was necessary to cut away and level down in order to get out the jars and merchandise, which were landed and carefully guarded." He trusted in God that, when he returned from Spain, according to his intention, he would find a tun of gold collected by barter by those he was to leave behind, and that they would have found the mine,

---

[263] Juan de la Cosa, the master, was a native of Santoña, on the north coast of Spain. There were two other Santoña men on board and several from the north coast. (Markham.)

and spices in such quantities that the Sovereigns would, in three years, be able to undertake and fit out an expedition to go and conquer the Holy Sepulchre. "With this in view," he says, "I protested to your Highnesses that all the profits of this my enterprise should be spent in the conquest of Jerusalem, and your Highnesses laughed and said that it pleased them, and that, without this, they entertained that desire." These are the Admiral's words.

Thursday, 27th of December

The king of that land came alongside the caravel at sunrise, and said that he had sent for gold, and that he would collect all he could before the Admiral departed; but he begged him not to go. The king and one of his brothers, with another very intimate relation, dined with the Admiral, and the two latter said they wished to go to Castile with him. At this time the news came that the caravel *Pinta* was in a river at the end of this island. Presently the cacique sent a canoe there, and the Admiral sent a sailor in it. For it was wonderful how devoted the cacique was to the Admiral. The necessity was now evident of hurrying on preparations for the return to Castile.

Friday, 28th of December

The Admiral went on shore to give orders and hurry on the work of building the fort, and to settle what men should remain behind.[264] The king, it would seem, had

------

[264] "He ordered then all his people to make great haste and the king ordered his vassals to help him and as an immense number joined with the Christians they managed so well and with such diligence that in a matter of ten days our stronghold was well made and as far as could be then constructed. He named it the City of Christmas (Villa de la Navidad) because he had arrived there on that day, and so to-day that harbor is

watched him getting into the boat, and quickly went into his house dissimulating, sending one of his brothers to receive the Admiral and conduct him to one of the houses that had been set aside for the Spaniards, which was the largest and best in the town. In it there was a couch made of palm matting, where they sat down. Afterward the brother sent an attendant to say that the Admiral was there, as if the king did not know that he had come. The Admiral, however, believed that this was a feint in order to do him honor more. The attendant gave the message, and the cacique came in great haste, and put a large soft piece of gold he had in his hand round the Admiral's neck. They remained together until the evening, arranging what had to be done.

Saturday, 29th of December

A very youthful nephew of the king came to the caravel at sunrise, who showed a good understanding and disposition. As the Admiral was always working to find out the origin of the gold, he asked everyone, for he could now understand somewhat by signs. This youth told him that, at a distance of four days' journey, there was an island to the eastward called Guarionex, and others called Macorix, Mayonic, Fuma, Cibao, and Coroay,[265] in which there was plenty of gold. The Admiral wrote these names down, and now understood what had been said by a brother of the king, who was annoyed with him, as the Admiral understood. At other times the Admiral had suspected that the king had worked against his knowing where the gold had its origin and was collected, that he

---

called Navidad, although there is no memory that there even has been a fort or any building there, since it is overgrown with trees as large and tall as if fifty years had passed, and I have seen them." Las Casas, I. 408.
[265] These were not islands, but districts whose chiefs were called by the same names. Cf. Las Casas, I. 410.

might not go away to barter in another part of the island. For there are such a number of places in this same island that it is wonderful. After nightfall the king sent a large mask of gold, and asked for a washhand basin and jug. The Admiral thought he wanted them for patterns to copy from, and therefore sent them.

Sunday, 30th of December

The Admiral went on shore to dinner, and came at a time when five kings had arrived, all with their crowns, who were subject to this king, named Guacanagari. They represented a very good state of affairs, and the Admiral says to the Sovereigns that it would have given them pleasure to see the manner of their arrival. On landing, the Admiral was received by the king, who led him by the arms to the same house where he was yesterday, where there were chairs, and a couch on which the Admiral sat. Presently the king took the crown off his head and put it on the Admiral's head, and the Admiral took from his neck a collar of beautiful beads of several different colors, which looked very well in all its parts, and put it on the king. He also took off a cloak of fine material, in which he had dressed himself that day, and dressed the king in it, and sent for some colored boots, which he put on his feet, and he put a large silver ring on his finger, because he had heard that he had admired greatly a silver ornament worn by one of the sailors. The king was highly delighted and well satisfied, and two of those kings who were with him came with him to where the Admiral was, and each gave him a piece of gold. At this time an Indian came and reported that it was two days since he left the caravel *Pinta* in a port to the eastward. The Admiral returned to the caravel and

Vincent Anes,[266] the captain, said that he had seen the rhubarb plant, and that they had it on the island Amiga, which is at the entrance of the sea of Santo Tomé, six leagues off, and that he had recognized the branches and roots. They say that rhubarb forms small branches above ground, and fruit like green mulberries, almost dry, and the stalk, near the root, is as yellow and delicate as the best color for painting, and underground the root grows like a large pear.

Monday, 31st of December

To-day the Admiral was occupied in seeing that water and fuel were taken on board for the voyage to Spain, to give early notice to the Sovereigns, that they might despatch ships to complete the discoveries. For now the business appeared to be so great and important that the Admiral was astonished.[267] He did not wish to go until he had examined all the land to the eastward, and explored the coast, so as to know the route to Castile, with a view to sending sheep and cattle.[268] But as he had been left with only a single vessel, it did not appear prudent to encounter the dangers that are inevitable in making discoveries. He complained that all this inconvenience had been caused by the caravel *Pinta* having parted company.

Tuesday, 1st of January, 1493

At midnight the Admiral sent a boat to the island Amiga to bring the rhubarb. It returned at vespers with a bundle of it. They did not bring more because they had no spade

---

[266] For Yañez. Vincent Yañez Pinzon.

[267] Rather, "For now the business appeared to be so great and important that it was wonderful (said the Admiral) and he said he did not wish," etc.

[268] The first suggestion of systematic colonization in the New World.

to dig it up with; it was taken to be shown to the Sovereigns. The king of that land said that he had sent many canoes for gold. The canoe returned that had been sent for tidings of the *Pinta*, without having found her. The sailor who went in the canoe said that twenty leagues from there he had seen a king who wore two large plates of gold on his head, but when the Indians in the canoe spoke to him he took them off. He also saw much gold on other people. The Admiral considered that the King Guacanagari ought to have prohibited his people from selling gold to the Christians, in order that it might all pass through his hands. But the king knew the places, as before stated, where there was such a quantity that it was not valued. The supply of spices also is extensive, and is worth more than pepper or manegueta. He left instructions to those who wished to remain that they were to collect as much as they could.

Wednesday, 2nd of January

In the morning the Admiral went on shore to take leave of the King Guacanagari, and to depart from him in the name of the Lord. He gave him one of his shirts. In order to show him the force of the lombards, and what effect they had, he ordered one to be loaded and fired into the side of the ship that was on shore, for this was apposite to the conversation respecting the Caribs, with whom Guacanagari was at war. The king saw whence the lombard-shot came, and how it passed through the side of the ship and went far away over the sea. The Admiral also ordered a skirmish of the crews of the ships, fully armed, saying to the cacique that he need have no fear of the Caribs even if they should come. All this was done that the king might look upon the men who were left behind as friends, and that he might also have a proper fear of them. The king took the Admiral to dinner at the house where he was established, and the others who came with him. The Admiral strongly recommended to his friendship Diego de Arana, Pedro Gutierrez, and Rodrigo Escovedo, whom he left jointly as his lieutenants over the people who remained behind, that all might be well regulated and governed for service of their Highnesses. The cacique showed much love for the Admiral, and great sorrow at his departure, especially when he saw him go on board. A relation of that king said to the Admiral that he had ordered a statue of pure gold to be made, as big as the Admiral, and that it would be brought within ten days. The Admiral embarked with the intention of sailing presently, but there was no wind.

He left on that island of Española, which the Indians called Bohio, 39 men[269] with the fortress, and he says that they were great friends of Guacanagari. The lieutenants placed over them were Diego de Arana of Cordova, Pedro Gutierrez, keeper of the king's drawing-room, and servant of the chief butler, and Rodrigo de Escovedo, a native of Segovia, nephew of Fray Rodrigo Perez, with all the powers he himself received from the Sovereigns. He left behind all the merchandise which had been provided for bartering, which was much, that they might trade for gold. He also left the ship's boat, that they, most of them being sailors, might go, when the time seemed convenient, to discover the gold mine, in order that the Admiral, on his return, might find much gold. They were also to find a good site for a town, for this was not altogether a desirable port; especially as the gold the natives brought came from the east; also, the farther to the east the

---

[269] The actual number was 44, according to the official list given in a document printed by Navarrete, which is a notice to the next of kin to apply for wages due, dated Burgos, December 20, 1507. Markham reproduces this list in his edition of Columbus's Journal.

nearer to Spain. He also left seeds for sowing, and his officers, the alguazil and secretary, as well as a ship's carpenter, a caulker, a good gunner familiar with engineering (*que sabe bien de ingenios*), a cooper, a physician, and a tailor, all being seamen as well.[270]

Thursday, 3rd of January

The Admiral did not go to-day, because three of the Indians whom he had brought from the islands, and who had staid behind, arrived, and said that the others with their women would be there at sunrise.[271] The sea also was rather rough, so that they could not land from the boat. He determined to depart to-morrow, with the grace of God. The Admiral said that if he had the caravel *Pinta* with him he could make sure of shipping a tun of gold, because he could then follow the coasts of these islands, which he would not do alone, for fear some accident might impede his return to Castile, and prevent him from reporting all he had discovered to the Sovereigns. If it was certain that the caravel *Pinta* would arrive safely in Spain with Martin Alonso Pinzon, he would not hesitate to act as he desired; but as he had no certain tidings of him, and as he might return and tell lies to the Sovereigns, that he might not receive the punishment he deserved for having done so much harm in having parted company without permission, and impeded the good service that might have been done, the Admiral could only trust in our Lord that he would grant favorable weather, and remedy all things.

---

[270] Las Casas gives the farewell speech of the Admiral to those who were left behind at Navidad, I. 415. It is translated in Thacher's *Columbus*, I. 632.
[271] "It is not known how many he took from this island but I believe he took some, altogether he carried ten or twelve Indians to Castile according to the Portuguese History [Barros] and I saw them in Seville yet I did not notice nor do I recollect that I counted them." Las Casas, I. 419.

Friday, 4th of January

At sunrise the Admiral weighed the anchor, with little wind, and turned her head N.W. to get clear of the reef, by another channel wider than the one by which he entered, which, with others, is very good for coming in front of the Villa de la Navidad, in all which the least depth is from 3 to 9 fathoms. These two channels run N.W. and S.E., and the reefs are long, extending from the Cabo Santo to the Cabo de Sierpe for more than six leagues, and then a good three leagues out to sea. At a league outside Cabo Santo there are not more than 8 fathoms of depth, and inside that cape, on the east side, there are many sunken rocks, and channels to enter between them. All this coast trends N.W. and S.E., and it is all beach, with the land very level for about a quarter of a league inland. After that distance there are very high mountains, and the whole is peopled with a very good race, as they showed themselves to the Christians. Thus the Admiral navigated to the east, shaping a course for a very high mountain, which looked like an island, but is not one, being joined to the mainland by a very low neck. The mountain has the shape of a very beautiful tent. He gave it the name of Monte Cristi. It is due east of Cabo Santo, at a distance of 18 leagues.[272] That day, owing to the light wind, they could not reach within six leagues of Monte Cristi. He discovered four very low and sandy islets,[273] with a reef extending N.W. and S.E. Inside, there is a large gulf,[274] which extends from this mountain to the S.E. at least twenty leagues,[275] which must all be shallow, with many sandbanks, and inside numerous rivers which are not

---

[272] It is N. 80° E. 70 leagues. (Navarrete.)

[273] Los siete Hermanos. (Id.)

[274] Bahia de Manzanillo. (Id.)

[275] Should be S.W. three leagues.

navigable. At the same time the sailor who was sent in the canoe to get tidings of the *Pinta* reported that he saw a river[276] into which ships might enter. The Admiral anchored at a distance of 6 leagues[277] from Monte Cristi, in 19 fathoms, and so kept clear of many rocks and reefs. Here he remained for the night. The Admiral gives notice to those who would go to the Villa de la Navidad that, to make Monte Cristi, he should stand off the land two leagues, etc. (But as the coast is now known it is not given here.) The Admiral concluded that Cipango was in that island, and that it contained much gold, spices, mastic, and rhubarb.

Saturday, 5th of January

At sunrise the Admiral made sail with the land-breeze, and saw that to the S.S.E.[278] of Monte Cristi, between it and an island, there seemed to be a good port to anchor in that night. He shaped an E.S.E. course, afterward S.S.E., for six leagues round the high land, and found a depth of 17 fathoms, with a very clean bottom, going on for three leagues with the same soundings. Afterwards it shallowed to 12 fathoms up to the promontory of the mountain, and off the promontory, at one league, the depth of 9 fathoms was found, the bottom clean, and all fine sand. The Admiral followed the same course until he came between the mountain and the island,[279] where he found 3-1/2 fathoms at low water, a very good port, and here he anchored.[280] He went in the boat to the islet, where he found remains of fire and footmarks, showing that fishermen had been there. Here they saw many stones

---

[276] Rio Tapion, in the Bahia de Manzanillo. (*Id.*)

[277] A mistake for three leagues. (*Id.*)

[278] Should be W.S.W. (*Id.*)

[279] Isla Cabra. (Navarrete.)

[280] Anchorage of Monte Cristi. (*Id.*)

painted in colors, or a quarry of such stones, very beautifully worked by nature, suited for the building of a church or other public work, like those he found on the island of San Salvador. On this islet he also found many plants of mastic. He says that this Monte Cristi is very fine and high, but accessible, and of a very beautiful shape, all the land round it being low, a very fine plain, from which the height rises, looking at a distance like an island disunited from other land. Beyond the mountain, to the east, he saw a cape at a distance of 24 miles, which he named Cabo del Becerro,[281] whence to the mountain for two leagues there are reefs of rocks, though it appeared as if there were navigable channels between them. It would, however, be advisable to approach in daylight, and to send a boat ahead to sound. From the mountain eastward to Cabo del Becerro, for four leagues, there is a beach, and the land is low, but the rest is very high, with beautiful mountains and some cultivation. Inland, a chain of mountains runs N.E. and S.W., the most beautiful he had seen, appearing like the hills of Cordova. Some other very lofty mountains appear in the distance toward the south and S.E., and very extensive green valleys with large rivers: all this in such quantity that he did not believe he had exaggerated a thousandth part. Afterwards he saw, to the eastward of the mountain, a land which appeared like that of Monte Cristi in size and beauty. Further to the east and N.E. there is land which is not so high, extending for some hundred miles or near it.

Sunday, 6th of January

That port is sheltered from all winds, except north and N.W., and these winds seldom blow in this region. Even when the wind is from those quarters, shelter may be

---

281 Punta Rucia. (Id.)

found near the islet in 3 or 4 fathoms. At sunrise the
Admiral made sail to proceed along the coast, the course
being east, except that it is necessary to look out for
several reefs of stone and sand, within which there are
good anchorages, with channels leading to them. After
noon it blew fresh from the east. The Admiral ordered a
sailor to go to the mast-head to look out for reefs, and he
saw the caravel *Pinta* coming, with the wind aft, and she
joined the Admiral.[282] As there was no place to anchor,
owing to the rocky bottom, the Admiral returned for ten
leagues to Monte Cristi, with the *Pinta* in company.
Martin Alonso Pinzon came on board the caravel *Niña*,
where the Admiral was, and excused himself by saying
that he had parted company against his will, giving
reasons for it. But the Admiral says that they were all
false; and that on the night when Pinzon parted company
he was influenced by pride and covetousness. He could not
understand whence had come the insolence and disloyalty
with which Pinzon had treated him during the voyage.
The Admiral had taken no notice, because he did not wish
to give place to the evil works of Satan, who desired to
impede the voyage. It appeared that one of the Indians,
who had been put on board the caravel by the Admiral
with others, had said that there was much gold in an
island called Baneque, and, as Pinzon's vessel was light
and swift, he determined to go there, parting company
with the Admiral, who wished to remain and explore the
coasts of Juana and Española, with an easterly course.
When Martin Alonso arrived at the island of Baneque[283]
he found no gold. He then went to the coast of Española,
on information from the Indians that there was a great
quantity of gold and many mines in that island of
Española, which the Indians call Bohio. He thus arrived

---

[282] Martin Alonso Pinzon had slipped away during the night of November
21.
[283] Here probably the island of Iguana Grande.

near the Villa de Navidad, about 15 leagues from it, having then been absent more than twenty days, so that the news brought by the Indians was correct, on account of which the King Guacanagari sent a canoe, and the Admiral put a sailor on board; but the *Pinta* must have gone before the canoe arrived. The Admiral says that the *Pinta* obtained much gold by barter, receiving large pieces the size of two fingers in exchange for a needle. Martin Alonso took half, dividing the other half among the crew. The Admiral then says: "Thus I am convinced that our Lord miraculously caused that vessel to remain here, this being the best place in the whole island to form a settlement, and the nearest to the gold mines." He also says that he knew of another great island, to the south of the island of Juana, in which there is more gold than in this island, so that they collect it in bits the size of beans, while in Española they find the pieces the size of grains of wheat. They call that island Yamaye.[284] The Admiral also heard of an island further east, in which there were only women, having been told this by many people.[285] He was also informed that Yamaye and the island of Española were ten days' journey in a canoe from the mainland, which would be about 70 or 80 leagues, and that there the people wore clothes.[286]

---

[284] Jamaica.

[285] On this myth see below under January 15.

[286] It is remarkable that this report, which refers probably to Yucatan and to the relatively high state of culture of the Mayas, drew no further comment from Columbus. From our point of view it ought to have made a much greater impression than we have evidence that it did; from his point of view that he was off Asia it was just what was to be expected and so is recorded without comment.

Monday, 7th of January

This day the Admiral took the opportunity of calking the caravel, and the sailors were sent to cut wood. They found mastic and aloes in abundance.

Tuesday, 8th of January

As the wind was blowing fresh from the east and S.E., the Admiral did not get under way this morning. He ordered the caravel to be filled up with wood and water and with all other necessaries for the voyage. He wished to explore all the coast of Española in this direction. But those he appointed to the caravels as captains were brothers, namely, Martin Alonso Pinzon and Vicente Anes. They also had followers who were filled with pride and avarice, considering that all now belonged to them, and unmindful of the honor the Admiral had done them. They had not and did not obey his orders, but did and said many unworthy things against him; while Martin Alonso had deserted him from the 21st of November until the 6th of January without cause or reason, but from disaffection. All these things had been endured in silence by the Admiral in order to secure a good end to the voyage. He determined to return as quickly as possible, to get rid of such an evil company, with whom he thought it necessary to dissimulate, although they were a mutinous set, and though he also had with him many good men; for it was not a fitting time for dealing out punishment.

The Admiral got into the boat and went up the river[287] which is near, toward the S.S.W. of Monte Cristi, a good league. This is where the sailors went to get fresh water

---

[287] This is the large river Yaqui, which contains much gold in its sand. It was afterwards called the Santiago. (Navarrete.)

for the ships. He found that the sand at the mouth of the river, which is very large and deep, was full of very fine gold, and in astonishing quantity. The Admiral thought that it was pulverized in the drift down the river, but in a short time he found many grains as large as lentils, while there was a great deal of the fine powder.

As the fresh water mixed with the salt when it entered the sea, he ordered the boat to go up for the distance of a stone's-throw. They filled the casks from the boat, and when they went back to the caravel they found small bits of gold sticking to the hoops of the casks and of the barrel. The Admiral gave the name of Rio del Oro to the River.[288] Inside the bar it is very deep, though the mouth is shallow and very wide. The distance to the Villa de la Navidad is 17 leagues,[289] and there are several large rivers on the intervening coast, especially three which probably contain much more gold than this one, because they are larger. This river is nearly the size of the Guadalquivir at Cordova, and from it to the gold mines the distance is not more than 20 leagues.[290] The Admiral further says that he did not care to take the sand containing gold, because their Highnesses would have it all as their property at their town of Navidad; and because his first object was now to bring the news and to get rid of the evil company that was with him, whom he had always said were a mutinous set.

Wednesday, 9th of January

The Admiral made sail at midnight, with the wind S.E., and shaped an E.N.E. course, arriving at a point named

---

[288] Afterwards called the Rio de Santiago. (Navarrete.)

[289] This should be 8 leagues. (Id.)

[290] Las Casas, I. 429, says the distance to the mines was not 4 leagues.

Punta Roja,[291] which is 60 miles[292] east of Monte Cristi, and anchored under its lee three hours before nightfall. He did not venture to go out at night, because there are many reefs, until they are known. Afterwards, if, as will probably be the case, channels are found between them, the anchorage, which is good and well sheltered, will be profitable. The country between Monte Cristi and this point where the Admiral anchored is very high land, with beautiful plains, the range running east and west, all green and cultivated, with numerous streams of water, so that it is wonderful to see such beauty. In all this country there are many turtles, and the sailors took several when they came on shore to lay their eggs at Monte Cristi, as large as a great wooden buckler.

On the previous day, when the Admiral went to the Rio del Oro, he saw three mermaids,[293] which rose well out of the sea; but they are not so beautiful as they are painted, though to some extent they have the form of a human face. The Admiral says that he had seen some, at other times, in Guinea, on the coast of the Manequeta.[294]

---

[291] Punta Isabelica. (*Id.*)

[292] The distance is 10-1/2 leagues, or 42 of the Italian miles used by Columbus. (*Id.*)

[293] The mermaids [Spanish, "sirens"] of Columbus are the *manatis*, or sea-cows, of the Caribbean Sea and great South American rivers. They are now scarcely ever seen out at sea. Their resemblance to human beings, when rising in the water, must have been very striking. They have small rounded heads, and cervical vertebrae which form a neck, enabling the animal to turn its head about. The fore limbs also, instead of being pectoral fins, have the character of the arm and hand of the higher mammalia. These peculiarities, and their very human way of suckling their young, holding it by the forearm, which is movable at the elbow-joint, suggested the idea of mermaids. The congener of the *manati*, which had been seen by Columbus on the coast of Guinea, is the *dugong*. (Markham.)

[294] Las Casas has "on the coast of Guinea where manequeta is gathered" (I. 430). *Amomum Melequeta*, an herbaceous, reedlike plant, three to five feet high, is found along the coast of Africa, from Sierra Leone to the Congo. Its seeds were called "Grains of Paradise," or *maniguetta*, and the

The Admiral says that this night, in the name of our Lord, he would set out on his homeward voyage without any further delay whatever, for he had found what he sought, and he did not wish to have further cause of offence with Martin Alonso until their Highnesses should know the news of the voyage and what had been done. Afterwards he says, "I will not suffer the deeds of evil-disposed persons, with little worth, who, without respect for him to whom they owe their positions, presume to set up their own wills with little ceremony."

Thursday, 10th of January

He departed from the place where he had anchored, and at sunset he reached a river, to which he gave the name of Rio de Gracia, three leagues to the S.E. He came to at the mouth,[295] where there is good anchorage on the east side. There is a bar with no more than two fathoms of water, and very narrow across the entrance. It is a good and well-sheltered port, except that there are many shipworms,[296] owing to which the caravel *Pinta*, under Martin Alonso, received a good deal of damage. He had been here bartering for 16 days, and got much gold, which was what Martin Alonso wanted. As soon as he heard from the Indians that the Admiral was on the coast

---

coast alluded to by Columbus, between Liberia and Cape Palmas, was hence called the Grain Coast. The grains were used as a condiment, like pepper, and in making the spiced wine called *hippocras*. (Markham.)

[295] Rio Chuzona chica. (Navarrete.)

[296] Reading *broma* ("ship worm") for *bruma* ("mist") in the sentence: *sino que tiene mucha bruma*. De la Roquette in the French translation gives *bruma* the meaning of "shipworm," supposing it to be a variant form of *broma*. The Italian translator of the letter on the fourth voyage took *broma* to be *bruma*, translated it *pruina e bruma*, and consequently had Columbus's ship injured by frost near Panama in April! Cf. Thacher, *Christopher Columbus*, II. 625, 790.

of the same island of Española, and that he could not
avoid him, Pinzon came to him. He wanted all the people
of the ship to swear that he had not been there more than
six days. But his treachery was so public that it could not
be concealed. He had made a law that half of all the gold
that was collected was his. When he left this port he took
four men and two girls by force. But the Admiral ordered
that they should be clothed and put on shore to return to
their homes. "This," the Admiral says, "is a service of your
Highnesses. For all the men and women are subjects of
your Highnesses, as well in this island as in the others.
Here, where your Highnesses already have a settlement,
the people ought to be treated with honor and favor,
seeing that this island has so much gold and such good
spice-yielding lands."

Friday, 11th of January

At midnight the Admiral left the Rio de Gracia with the
land-breeze, and steered eastward until he came to a cape
named Belprado, at a distance of four leagues. To the S.E.
is the mountain to which he gave the name of Monte de
Plata,[297] eight leagues distant. Thence from the cape
Belprado to E.S.E. is the point named Angel, eighteen
leagues distant; and from this point to the Monte de Plata
there is a gulf, with the most beautiful lands in the world,
all high and fine lands which extend far inland. Beyond
there is a range of high mountains running east and west,
very grand and beautiful. At the foot of this mountain
there is a very good port,[298] with 14 fathoms in the

---

[297] So called because the summit is always covered with white or silver
clouds. Las Casas, I. 432. A monastery of Dominicans was afterwards built
on Monte de Plata, in which Las Casas began to write his history of the
Indies in the year 1527. Las Casas, IV. 254. (Markham.)

[298] Puerto de Plata, where a flourishing seaport town was afterwards
established; founded by Ovando in 1502. It had fallen to decay in 1606.
(Markham.)

entrance. The mountain is very high and beautiful, and all the country is well peopled. The Admiral believed there must be fine rivers and much gold. At a distance of 4 leagues E.S.E. of Cabo del Angel there is a cape named Punta del Hierro,[299] and on the same course, 4 more leagues, a point is reached named Punta Seca.[300] Thence, 6 leagues further on, is Cabo Redondo,[301] and further on Cabo Frances, where a large bay[302] is formed, but there did not appear to be anchorage in it. A league further on is Cabo del Buen Tiempo, and thence, a good league S.S.E., is Cabo Tajado.[303] Thence, to the south, another cape was sighted at a distance of about 15 leagues. To-day great progress was made, as wind and tide were favorable. The Admiral did not venture to anchor for fear of the rocks, so he was hove-to all night.

Saturday, 12th of January

Towards dawn the Admiral filled and shaped a course to the east with a fresh wind, running 20 miles before daylight, and in two hours afterwards 24 miles. Thence he saw land to the south,[304] and steered towards it, distant 48 miles. During the night he must have run 28 miles N.N.E., to keep the vessels out of danger. When he saw the land, he named one cape that he saw Cabo de Padre y Hijo, because at the east point there are two rocks, one larger than the other.[305] Afterwards, at two leagues to the eastward, he saw a very fine bay between two grand

---

[299] Punta Macuris. The distance is 3, not 4 leagues. (Navarrete.)

[300] Punta Sesua. The distance is only one league. (*Id.*)

[301] Cabo de la Roca. It should be 5, not 6 leagues. (*Id.*)

[302] Bahia Escocesa. (*Id.*)

[303] Las Casas says that none of these names remained even in his time. I. 432.

[304] This was the Peninsula of Samana. (Navarrete.)

[305] Isla Yazual. (*Id.*)

mountains. He saw that it was a very large port with a very good approach; but, as it was very early in the morning, and as the greater part of the time it was blowing from the east, and then they had a N.N.W. breeze, he did not wish to delay any more. He continued his course to the east as far as a very high and beautiful cape, all of scarped rock, to which he gave the name of Cabo del Enamorado,[306] which was 32 miles to the east of the port named Puerto Sacro.[307] On rounding the cape, another finer and loftier point came in sight,[308] like Cape St. Vincent in Portugal, 12 miles east of Cabo del Enamorado. As soon as he was abreast of the Cabo del Enamorado, the Admiral saw that there was a great bay[309] between this and the next point, three leagues across, and in the middle of it a small island.[310] The depth is great at the entrance close to the land. He anchored here in twelve fathoms, and sent the boat on shore for water, and to see if intercourse could be opened with the natives, but they all fled. He also anchored to ascertain whether this was all one land with the island of Española, and to make sure that this was a gulf and not a channel, forming another island. He remained astonished at the great size of Española.

Sunday, 13th of January

The Admiral did not leave the port, because there was no land-breeze with which to go out. He wished to shift to another better port, because this was rather exposed. He

---

[306] Cabo Cabron, or Lover's Cape; the extreme N.E. point of the island, rising nearly 2000 feet above the sea. (Markham.)

[307] Puerto Yaqueron. (Navarrete.)

[308] Cabo Samana; called Cabo de San Theramo afterwards by Columbus (Markham.)

[309] The Bay of Samana. (Navarrete.)

[310] Cayo de Levantados. (Id.)

also wanted to wait, in that haven, the conjunction of the sun and moon, which would take place on the 17th of this month, and the opposition of the moon with Jupiter and conjunction with Mercury, the sun being in opposition to Jupiter, which is the cause of high winds. He sent the boat on shore to a beautiful beach to obtain yams for food. They found some men with bows and arrows, with whom they stopped to speak, buying two bows and many arrows from them. They asked one of them to come on board the caravel and see the Admiral; who says that he was very wanting in reverence, more so than any native he had yet seen.[311] His face was all stained with charcoal,[312] but in all parts there is the custom of painting the body different colors. He wore his hair very long, brought together and fastened behind, and put into a small net of parrots' feathers. He was naked, like all the others. The Admiral supposed that he belonged to the Caribs, who eat men,[313] and that the gulf he had seen yesterday formed this part of the land into an island by itself. The Admiral asked about the Caribs, and he pointed to the east, near at hand, which means that he saw the Admiral yesterday before he entered the bay. The Indian said there was much gold to the east, pointing to the poop of the caravel, which was a good size, meaning that there were pieces as large. He called gold *tuob*, and did not understand *caona*, as they call it in the first part of the island that was visited, nor *nozay*, the name in San Salvador and the other islands.

---

[311] This should be, "who says that he was very ugly of countenance, more so than the others that he had seen."

[312] Las Casas says, I. 433, "Not charcoal but a certain dye they make from a certain fruit."

[313] Las Casas, I. 434, says there never were any cannibals in Española.

Copper or a base gold is called *tuob* in Española.[314] Of the island of Matinino this Indian said that it was peopled by women without men, and that in it there was much *tuob*, which is gold or copper, and that it is more to the east of Carib.[315] He also spoke of the island of Goanin,[316] where there was much *tuob*. The Admiral says that he had received notices of these islands from many persons; that in the other islands the natives were in great fear of the Caribs, called by some of them Caniba, but in Española Carib. He thought they must be an audacious race, for they go to all these islands and eat the people they can capture. He understood a few words, and the Indians who were on board comprehended more, there being a difference in the languages owing to the great distance between the various islands. The Admiral ordered that the Indian should be fed, and given pieces of green and red cloth, and glass beads, which they like very much, and then sent on shore. He was told to bring gold if he had any, and it was believed that he had, from some small things he brought with him. When the boat reached the shore there were fifty-five men behind the trees, naked, and with very long hair, as the women wear it in Castile. Behind the head they wore plumes of feathers of parrots and other birds, and each man carried a bow. The Indian landed, and signed to the others to put down their bows and arrows, and a piece of a staff, which

---

[314] Las Casas, I. 434, says that a section in the northeastern part of Española "was inhabited by a tribe which called themselves *Mazariges* and others *Ciguayos* and that they spoke different languages from the rest of the island. I do not remember if they differed from each other in speech since so many years have passed, and to-day there is no one to inquire of, although I have talked many times with both generations; but more than fifty years have gone by." The Ciguayos, he adds, were called so because they wore their hair long as women do in Castile. This passage shows that Las Casas was writing this part of his history a half-century after he went first to Española, which was in 1502, with Ovando.

[315] Porto Rico. (Navarrete.)

[316] Las Casas, I. 434, says that Guanin was not the name of an island, but the word for a kind of base gold.

is like...,[317] very heavy, carried instead of a sword.[318] As soon as they came to the boat the crew landed, and began to buy the bows and arrows and other arms, in accordance with an order of the Admiral. Having sold two bows, they did not want to give more, but began to attack the Spaniards, and to take hold of them. They were running back to pick up their bows and arrows where they had laid them aside, and took cords in their hands to bind the boat's crew. Seeing them rushing down, and being prepared—for the Admiral always warned them to be on their guard--the Spaniards attacked the Indians, and gave one a slash with a knife in the buttocks, wounding another in the breast with an arrow. Seeing that they could gain little, although the Christians were only seven and they numbered over fifty, they fled, so that none were left, throwing bows and arrows away.[319] The Christians would have killed many, if the pilot, who was in command, had not prevented them. The Spaniards presently returned to the caravel with the boat. The Admiral regretted the affair for one reason, and was pleased for another. They would have fear of the Christians, and they were no doubt an ill-conditioned people, probably Caribs, who eat men. But the Admiral felt alarm lest they should do some harm to the 39 men left in the fortress and town of Navidad, in the event of their coming here in their boat. Even if they are not Caribs, they are a neighboring people, with similar habits, and fearless, unlike the other inhabitants of the island,

---

[317] A gap in the original manuscript.

[318] Las Casas, I. 435, has, "and as word of a palm-tree board which is very hard and very heavy, not sharp but blunt, about two fingers thick everywhere, with which as it is hard and heavy like iron, although a man has a helmet on his head they will crush his skull to the brain with one blow."

[319] "This was the first fight that there was in all the Indies and when the blood of the Indians was shed." Las Casas, I. 436.

who are timid, and without arms. The Admiral says all this, and adds that he would have liked to have captured some of them. He says that they lighted many smoke signals, as is the custom in this island of Española.

Monday, 14th of January

This evening the Admiral wished to find the houses of the Indians and to capture some of them, believing them to be Caribs. For, owing to the strong east and north-east winds and the heavy sea, he had remained during the day. Many Indians were seen on shore. The Admiral, therefore, ordered the boat to be sent on shore, with the crew well armed. Presently the Indians came to the stern of the boat, including the man who had been on board the day before, and had received presents from the Admiral. With him there came a king, who had given to the said Indian some beads in token of safety and peace for the boat's crew. This king, with three of his followers, went on board the boat and came to the caravel. The Admiral ordered them to be given biscuit and treacle to eat, and gave the chief a red cap, some beads, and a piece of red cloth. The others were also given pieces of cloth. The chief said that next day he would bring a mask made of gold, affirming that there was much here, and in Carib[320] and Matinino.[321] They afterwards went on shore well satisfied.

The Admiral here says that the caravels were making much water, which entered by the keel; and he complains of the caulkers at Palos, who caulked the vessels very badly, and ran away when they saw that the Admiral had detected the badness of their work, and intended to oblige

---

[320] Porto Rico. Navarrete says it is certain that the Indians called Porto Rico Isla de Carib.
[321] Probably Martinique or Guadeloupe. (Navarrete.)

them to repair the defect. But, notwithstanding that the caravels were making much water, he trusted in the favor and mercy of our Lord, for his high Majesty well knew how much controversy there was before the expedition could be despatched from Castile, that no one was in the Admiral's favor save Him alone who knew his heart, and after God came your Highnesses, while all others were against him without any reason. He further says: "And this has been the cause that the royal crown of your Highnesses has not a hundred millions of revenue more than after I entered your service, which is seven years ago in this very month, the 20th of January.[322] The increase will take place from now onwards. For the almighty God will remedy all things,"[323] These are his words.

Tuesday, 15th of January

The Admiral now wished to depart, for there was nothing to be gained by further delay, after these occurrences and the tumult with the Indians. To-day he had heard that all the gold was in the district of the town of Navidad, belonging to their Highnesses; and that in the island of Carib[324] there was much copper, as well as in Matinino. The intercourse at Carib would, however, be difficult, because the natives are said to eat human flesh. Their island would be in sight from thence, and the Admiral determined to go there, as it was on the route, and thence to Matinino, which was said to be entirely peopled by women, without men.[325] He would thus see both islands,

---

[322] By this calculation the Admiral entered the service of the Catholic Sovereigns on January 20, 1486. (Navarrete.)

[323] "What would he have said if he had seen the millions and millions (cuentos y millones) that the sovereigns have received from his labors since his death?" Las Casas, I. 437.

[324] Porto Rico.

[325] Columbus had read in Marco Polo of the islands of MASCULIA and FEMININA in the Indian Seas and noted the passage in his copy. See ch.

and might take some of the natives. The Admiral sent the boat on shore, but the king of that district had not come, for his village was distant. He, however, sent his crown of gold, as he had promised; and many other natives came with cotton, and bread made from yams, all with their bows and arrows. After the bartering was finished, four youths came to the caravel. They appeared to the Admiral to give such a clear account of the islands to the eastward, on the same route as the Admiral would have to take, that he determined to take them to Castile with him. He says that they had no iron nor other metals; at least none was seen, but it was impossible to know much of the land in so short a time, owing to the difficulty with the language, which the Admiral could not understand except by guessing, nor could they know what was said to them, in such a few days. The bows of these people are as large as those of France or England. The arrows are similar to the darts of the natives who have been met with previously, which are made of young canes, which grow very straight, and a yard and a half or two yards in length. They point them with a piece of sharp wood, a span and a half long, and at the end some of them fix a fish's tooth, but most of

---

XXXIII. of pt. III. of Marco Polo. On the other hand there is evidence for an indigenous Amazon myth in the New World. The earliest sketch of American folk-lore ever made, that of the Friar Ramon Pane in 1497, preserved in Ferdinand Columbus's *Historie* and in a condensed form in Peter Martyr's *De Rebus Oceanicis* (Dec. I., lib. IX.), tells the story of the culture-hero Guagugiona, who set forth from the cave, up to that time the home of mankind, "with all the women in search of other lands and he came to Matinino, where at once he left the women and went away to another country," etc., *Historie* (London ed., 1867), p. 188. Ramon's name is erroneously given as Roman in the *Historie*. On the Amazons in Venezuela, see Oviedo, lib. XXV., cap. XIV. It may be accepted that the Amazon myth as given by Oviedo, from which the great river derived its name, River of the Amazons, is a composite of an Arawak folk-tale like that preserved by Ramon Pane overlaid with the details of the Marco Polo myth, which in turn derives from the classical myth.

them anoint it with an herb.[326] They do not shoot as in other parts, but in a certain way which cannot do much harm. Here they have a great deal of fine and long cotton, and plenty of mastic. The bows appeared to be of yew, and there is gold and copper. There is also plenty of *aji*,[327] which is their pepper, which is more valuable than pepper, and all the people eat nothing else, it being very wholesome. Fifty caravels might be annually loaded with it from Española. The Admiral says that he found a great deal of weed in this bay, the same as was met with at sea when he came on this discovery. He therefore supposed that there were islands to the eastward, in the direction of the position where he began to meet with it; for he considers it certain that this weed has its origin in shallow water near the land, and, if this is the case, these Indies must be very near the Canary Islands. For this reason he thought the distance must be less than 400 leagues.

Wednesday, 16th of January

They got under way three hours before daylight, and left the gulf, which was named Golfo de las Flechas,[328] with the land-breeze. Afterwards there was a west wind, which was fair to go to the island of Carib on an E.N.E. course. This was where the people live of whom all the natives of the other islands are so frightened, because they roam over the sea in canoes without number, and eat the men they can capture. The Admiral steered the course

---

[326] *Y los mas le ponen allí yerba*, "and the most of them put on poison." The description of these arrows corresponds exactly with that given by Sir E. im Thurn of the poisoned arrows of the Indians of Guiana, which still have "adjustable wooden tips smeared with poison, which are inserted in the socket at the end of a reed shaft." *Among the Indians of Guiana*, p. 242.

[327] Capsicum. (Markham.)

[328] Gulf of the Arrows. This was the Bay of Samana, into which the river Yuna flows. (Navarrete.)

indicated by one of the four Indians he took yesterday in the Puerto de las Flechas. After having sailed about 64 miles, the Indians made signs that the island was to the S.E.[329] The Admiral ordered the sails to be trimmed for that course, but, after having proceeded on it for two leagues, the wind freshened from a quarter which was very favorable for the voyage to Spain. The Admiral had noticed that the crew were downhearted when he deviated from the direct route home, reflecting that both caravels were leaking badly, and that there was no help but in God. He therefore gave up the course leading to the islands, and shaped a direct course for Spain E.N.E. He sailed on this course, making 48 miles, which is 12 leagues, by sunset. The Indians said that by that route they would fall in with the island of Matinino, peopled entirely by women without men, and the Admiral wanted very much to take five or six of them to the Sovereigns. But he doubted whether the Indians understood the route well, and he could not afford to delay, by reason of the leaky condition of the caravels. He, however, believed the story and that, at certain seasons, men came to them from the island of Carib, distant ten or twelve leagues. If males were born, they were sent to the island of the men; and if females, they remained with their mothers.[330] The Admiral says that these two islands cannot have been more than 15 or 20 leagues to the S.E. from where he altered course, the Indians not understanding how to point out the direction. After losing sight of the cape, which was named San Theramo,[331] which was left 16 leagues to the west, they went for 12 leagues E.N.E. The weather was very fine.

---

[329] Porto Rico. It would have been distant about 30 leagues. (Navarrete.)

[330] "The sons remain with their mothers till the age of fourteen when they go to join their fathers in their separate abode." Marco Polo, pt. III., ch. XXXIII.

[331] Now called Cabod el Engaño,[TN-4] the extreme eastern point of Española. It had the same name when Las Casas wrote. (Markham.)

Thursday, 17th of January

The wind went down at sunset yesterday, the caravels having sailed 14 glasses, each a little less than half-an-hour, at 4 miles an hour, making 28 miles. Afterwards the wind freshened, and they ran all that watch, which was 10 glasses. Then another six until sunrise at 8 miles an hour, thus making altogether 84 miles, equal to 21 leagues, to the E.N.E., and until sunset 44 miles, or 11 leagues, to the east. Here a booby[332] came to the caravel, and afterwards another. The Admiral saw a great deal of gulf-weed.

Friday, 18th of January

During the night they steered E.S.E., with little wind, for 40 miles, equal to 10 leagues, and then 30 miles, or 7-1/2 leagues, until sunrise. All day they proceeded with little wind to E.N.E. and N.E. by E., more or less, her head being sometimes north and at others N.N.E., and, counting one with the other they made 60 miles, or 15 leagues. There was little weed, but yesterday and to-day the sea appeared to be full of tunnies. The Admiral believed that from there they must go to the tunny-fisheries of the Duke, of Conil and Cadiz.[333] He also thought they were near some islands, because a frigate-bird[334] flew round the caravel, and afterwards went away to the S.S.E. He said that to the S.E. of the island

---

[332] Alcatraz.

[333] The *almadrabas*, or tunny fisheries of Rota, near Cadiz, were inherited by the Duke, as well as those of Conil, a little fishing town 6 leagues east of Cadiz. (Markham.)

[334] *Un pescado* (a fish), called the *rabiforcado*. For *un pescado*, we should probably read *una ave pescadora*, and translate: a fishing bird, called *rabiforcado*. See entry for September 29 and note.

of Española were the islands of Carib, Matinino, and many others.

Saturday, 19th of January

During the night they made good 56 miles N.N.E., and 64 N.E. by N. After sunrise they steered N.E. with the wind fresh from S.W., and afterwards W.S.W. 84 miles, equal to 21 leagues. The sea was again full of small tunnies. There were boobies, frigate-birds, and terns.[335]

Sunday, 20th of January

It was calm during the night, with occasional slants of wind, and they only made 20 miles to the N.E. After sunrise they went 11 miles S.E., and then 36 miles N.N.E., equal to 9 leagues. They saw an immense quantity of small tunnies, the air very soft and pleasant, like Seville in April or May, and the sea, for which God be given many thanks, always very smooth. Frigate-birds, sandpipers,[336] and other birds were seen.

Monday, 21st of January

Yesterday, before sunset, they steered N.E. b. E., with the wind east, at the rate of 8 miles an hour until midnight, equal to 56 miles. Afterwards they steered N.N.E. 8 miles

---

[335] *Alcatraces, rabos de juncos*, and *rabiforcados*: boobies, boatswain-birds, and frigate-birds. The translator has not been consistent in selecting English equivalents for these names. In the entry of January 18 *rabiforcado* is frigate-bird; in that of January 19 *rabo de junco* is frigate-bird; in that of January 21 *rabo de junco* is *boatswain-bird*. September 14 *garjao* is the tern, while on January 19 the *rabiforcado* is the tern. On these birds, see notes 11, 12, 13, and 20. See also Oviedo, *Historia General y natural de las Indias*, lib. XIV., cap. I., for descriptions of these birds.

[336] *Rabiforcados y pardelas*. Las Casas, I. 440, has *aves pardelas*. Talhausen, *Neues Spanisch-deutsches Wörterbuch*, defines *pardelas* as *Peters-vogel*, i.e., petrel.

an hour, so that they made 104 miles, or 26 leagues, during the night N.E. by N. After sunrise they steered N.N.E. with the same wind, which at times veered to N.E., and they made good 88 miles in the eleven hours of daylight, or 21 leagues: except one that was lost by delay caused by closing with the *Pinta* to communicate. The air was colder, and it seemed to get colder as they went further north, and also that the nights grew longer owing to the narrowing of the sphere. Many *boatswain-birds* and terns[337] were seen, as well as other birds but not so many fish, perhaps owing to the water being colder. Much weed was seen.

Tuesday, 22nd of January

Yesterday, after sunset, they steered N.N.E. with an east wind. They made 8 miles an hour during five glasses, and three before the watch began, making eight glasses, equal to 72 miles, or 18 leagues. Afterwards they went N.E. by N. for six glasses, which would be another 18 miles. Then, during four glasses of the second watch N.E. at six miles an hour, or three leagues. From that time to sunset, for eleven glasses, E.N.E. at 6 leagues an hour,[338] equal to seven leagues. Then E.N.E. until 11 o'clock, 32 miles. Then the wind fell, and they made no more during that day. The Indians swam about. They saw boatswain-birds and much weed.

---

[337] *Rabos de juncos y pardelas*. The translator vacillates between sandpipers and terns in rendering *pardelas*. Cf. January 28 and 31, but as has just been noted "petrels" is the proper word.

[338] An error of the transcriber for miles. Each glass being half-an-hour, going six miles an hour, they would have made 33 miles or 8-1/4 leagues in five hours and a half. (Navarrete.)

Wednesday, 23rd of January

To-night the wind was very changeable, but, making the allowances applied by good sailors, they made 84 miles or 21 leagues, N.E. by N. Many times the caravel *Niña* had to wait for the *Pinta*, because she sailed badly when on a bowline the mizzen being of little use owing to the weakness of the mast. He says that if her captain, that is, Martin Alonso Pinzon, had taken the precaution to provide her with a good mast in the Indies, where there are so many and such excellent spars, instead of deserting his commander from motives of avarice, he would have done better. They saw many boatswain-birds and much weed. The heavens have been clouded over during these last days, but there has been no rain. The sea has been as smooth as a river, for which many thanks be given to God. After sunrise they went free, and made 30 miles, or 7-1/2 leagues N.E. During the rest of the day E.N.E. another 30 miles.

Thursday, 24th of January

They made 44 miles, or 11 leagues, during the night, allowing for many changes in the wind, which was generally N.E. After sunrise until sunset E.N.E. 14 leagues.

Friday, 25th of January

They steered during part of the night E.N.E. for 13 glasses, making 9-1/2 leagues. Then N.N.E. 6 miles. The wind fell, and during the day they only made 28 miles E.N.E., or 7 leagues. The sailors killed a tunny and a very large shark, which was very welcome, as they now had nothing but bread and wine, and some yams from the Indies.

Saturday, 26th of January

This night they made 56 miles, or 14 leagues, E.S.E. After sunrise they steered E.S.E., and sometimes S.E., making 40 miles up to 11 o'clock. Afterwards they went on another tack, and then on a bowline, 24 miles, or 6 leagues, to the north, until night.

Sunday, 27th of January

Yesterday, after sunset, they steered N.E. and N.E. by N. at the rate of five miles an hour, which in thirteen hours would be 65 miles, or 16-1/2 leagues. After sunrise they steered N.E. 24 miles, or 6 leagues, until noon, and from that time until sunset 3 leagues E.N.E.

Monday, 28th of January

All night they steered E.N.E. 36 miles, or 9 leagues. After sunrise until sunset E.N.E. 20 miles, or 5 leagues. The weather was temperate and pleasant. They saw boatswain-birds, sandpipers,[339] and much weed.

Tuesday, 29th of January

They steered E.N.E. 39 miles, or 9-1/2 leagues, and during the whole day 8 leagues. The air was very pleasant, like April in Castile, the sea smooth, and fish they call d*orados*[340] came on board.

---

[339] Petrels.
[340] The English equivalent is dory, or gilthead.

Wednesday, 30th of January

All this night they made 6 leagues E.N.E., and in the day
S.E. by S. 13-1/2 leagues. Boatswain-birds, much weed,
and many tunnies.

Thursday, 31st of January

This night they steered N.E. by N. 30 miles, and
afterwards N.E. 35 miles, or 16 leagues. From sunrise to
night E.N.E. 13-1/2 leagues. They saw boatswain-birds
and terns.[341]

Friday, 1st of February

They made 16-1/2 leagues E.N.E. during the night, and
went on the same course during the day 29-1/4 leagues.
The sea very smooth, thanks be to God.

Saturday, 2nd of February

They made 40 miles, or 10 leagues, E.N.E. this night. In
the daytime, with the same wind aft, they went 7 miles an
hour, so that in eleven hours they had gone 77 miles, or 9-
1/4 leagues. The sea was very smooth, thanks be to God,
and the air very soft. They saw the sea so covered with
weed that, if they had not known about it before, they
would have been fearful of sunken rocks. They saw terns.

Sunday, 3rd of February

This night, the wind being aft and the sea very smooth,
thanks be to God, they made 29 leagues. The North Star
appeared very high, as it does off Cape St. Vincent. The

---

[341] Petrels.

Admiral was unable to take the altitude, either with the astrolabe or with the quadrant, because the rolling caused by the waves prevented it. That day he steered his course E.N.E., going 10 miles an hour, so that in eleven hours he made 27 leagues.

Monday, 4th of February

During the night the course was N.E. by E., going twelve miles an hour part of the time, and the rest ten miles. Thus they made 130 miles, or 32 leagues and a half. The sky was very threatening and rainy, and it was rather cold, by which they knew that they had not yet reached the Azores. After sunrise the course was altered to east. During the whole day they made 77 miles, or 19-1/4 leagues.

Tuesday, 5th of February

This night they steered east, and made 55 miles, or 13-1/2 leagues. In the day they were going ten miles an hour, and in eleven hours made 110 miles, or 27-1/2 leagues. They saw sandpipers, and some small sticks, a sign that they were near land.

Wednesday, 6th of February

They steered east during the night, going at the rate of eleven miles an hour, so that in the thirteen hours of the night they made 143 miles, or 35-1/4 leagues. They saw many birds. In the day they went 14 miles an hour, and made 154 miles, or 38-1/2 leagues; so that, including night and day, they made 74 leagues, more or less. Vicente Anes[342] said that they had left the island of Flores to the

---

[342] Vicente Yañez Pinzon.

north and Madeira to the east. Roldan[343] said that the island of Fayal, or San Gregorio, was to the N.N.E. and Puerto Santo to east. There was much weed.

Thursday, 7th of February

This night they steered east, going ten miles an hour, so that in thirteen hours they made 130 miles, or 32-1/2 leagues. In the daytime the rate was eight miles an hour, in eleven hours 88 miles, or 22 leagues.
This morning the Admiral found himself 65 leagues south of the island of Flores, and the pilot Pedro Alonso,[344] being further north, according to his reckoning, passed between Terceira and Santa Maria to the east, passing to windward of the island of Madeira, twelve leagues further north. The sailors saw a new kind of weed, of which there is plenty in the islands of the Azores.

Friday, 8th of February

They went three miles an hour to the eastward for some time during the night, and afterwards E.S.E., going twelve miles an hour. From sunrise to noon they made 27 miles, and the same distance from noon till sunset, equal to 13 leagues S.S.E.

---

[343] Later a rich citizen of the city of Santo Domingo, Española, where he was known as Roldan the pilot. Las Casas, I. 443.

[344] The name is also written Peralonso Niño. He made one of the first voyages to the mainland of South America after the third voyage of Columbus. See Irving, *Companions of Columbus*. Bourne, *Spain in America*, p. 69.

Saturday, 9th of February

For part of this night they went 3 leagues S.S.E., and afterwards S. by E., then N.E. 5 leagues until ten o'clock in the forenoon, then 9 leagues east until dark.

Sunday, 10th of February

From sunset they steered east all night, making 130 miles, or 32-1/2 leagues. During the day they went at the rate of nine miles an hour, making 99 miles, or 24-1/2 leagues, in eleven hours.

In the caravel of the Admiral, Vicente Yañez and the two pilots, Sancho Ruiz and Pedro Alonso Niño, and Roldan, charted or plotted the route.
They all made the position a good deal beyond the islands of the Azores to the east, and, navigating to the north, none of them touched Santa Maria, which is the last of all the Azores. They made the position five leagues beyond it, and were in the vicinity of the islands of Madeira and Puerto Santo. But the Admiral was very different from them in his reckoning, finding the position very much in rear of theirs. This night he found the island of Flores to the north, and to the east he made the direction to be towards Nafe in Africa, passing to leeward of the island of Madeira to the north ... leagues.[345] So that the pilots were nearer to Castile than the Admiral by 150 leagues. The Admiral says that, with the grace of God, when they reach the land they will find out whose reckoning was most correct. He also says that he went 263 leagues from the island of Hierro to the place where he first saw the gulf-weed.

---

[345] A gap in the original manuscript.

Monday, 11th of February

This night they went twelve miles an hour on their course, and during the day they ran 16-1/2 leagues. They saw many birds, from which they judged that land was near.

Tuesday, 12th of February

They went six miles an hour on an east course during the night, altogether 73 miles, or 18-1/4 leagues. At this time they began to encounter bad weather with a heavy sea; and, if the caravel had not been very well managed, she must have been lost. During the day they made 11 or 12 leagues with much difficulty and danger.

Wednesday, 13th of February

From sunset until daylight there was great trouble with the wind, and the high and tempestuous sea. There was lightning three times to the N.N.E.--a sign of a great storm coming either from that quarter or its opposite. They were lying-to most of the night, afterwards showing a little sail, and made 52 miles, which is 13 leagues. In the day the wind moderated a little, but it soon increased again. The sea was terrific, the waves crossing each other, and straining the vessels. They made 55 miles more, equal to 13-1/2 leagues.

Thursday, 14th of February

This night the wind increased, and the waves were terrible, rising against each other, and so shaking and straining the vessel that she could make no headway, and was in danger of being stove in. They carried the mainsail very closely reefed, so as just to give her steerage-way, and proceeded thus for three hours, making 20 miles. Meanwhile, the wind and sea increased, and, seeing the great danger, the Admiral began to run before it, there being nothing else to be done. The caravel *Pinta* began to run before the wind at the same time, and Martin Alonso ran her out of sight,[346] although the Admiral kept showing lanterns all night, and the other answered. It would seem that she could do no more, owing to the force of the tempest, and she was taken far from the route of the Admiral. He steered that night E.N.E., and made 54 miles, equal to 13 leagues. At sunrise the wind blew still harder, and the cross sea was terrific. They continued to show the closely-reefed mainsail, to enable her to rise from between the waves, or she would otherwise have been swamped. An E.N.E. course was steered, and afterwards N.E. by E. for six hours, making 7-1/2 leagues. The Admiral ordered that a pilgrimage should be made to Our Lady of Guadalupe,[347] carrying a candle of 6 lbs. of weight in wax, and that all the crew should take an oath that the pilgrimage should be made by the man on whom the lot fell. As many chick-peas were got as there were persons on board, and on one a cross was cut with a knife. They were then put into a cap and shaken up. The first who put in his hand was the Admiral, and he drew out the chick-pea with a cross, so the lot fell on him; and he was bound to go on the pilgrimage and fulfil the vow. Another lot was drawn, to go on pilgrimage to Our Lady of Loreto, which is in the march of Ancona, in the Papal

---

[346] Martin Alonso Pinzon succeeded in bringing the caravel *Pinta* into port at Bayona in Galicia. He went thence to Palos, arriving in the evening of the same day as the *Niña* with the Admiral. Pinzon died very soon afterwards. Oviedo [I. 27] says: "He went to Palos to his own house and died after a few days since he went there very ill." (Markham.)

[347] Virgin of Guadalupe was the patroness of Estremadura. As many of the early colonists went from Estremadura there came to be a good number of her shrines in Mexico. Cf. R. Ford, *Handbook for Spain*, index under "Guadalupe."

territory, a house where Our Lady works many and great miracles.[348] The lot fell on a sailor of the port of Santa Maria, named Pedro de Villa, and the Admiral promised to pay his travelling expenses. Another pilgrimage was agreed upon, to watch for one night in Santa Clara at Moguer,[349] and have a mass said, for which they again used the chick-peas, including the one with a cross. The lot again fell on the Admiral. After this the Admiral and all the crew made a vow that, on arriving at the first land, they would all go in procession, in their shirts, to say their prayers in a church dedicated to Our Lady.

Besides these general vows made in common, each sailor made a special vow; for no one expected to escape, holding themselves for lost, owing to the fearful weather from which they were suffering. The want of ballast increased the danger of the ship, which had become light, owing to the consumption of the provisions and water. On account of the favorable weather enjoyed among the islands, the Admiral had omitted to make provision for this need, thinking that ballast might be taken on board at the island inhabited by women, which he had intended to visit. The only thing to do was to fill the barrels that had contained wine or fresh water with water from the sea, and this supplied a remedy.

Here the Admiral writes of the causes which made him fear that he would perish, and of others that gave him hope that God would work his salvation, in order that such news as he was bringing to the Sovereigns might not be lost. It seemed to him that the strong desire he felt to

---

[348] A full account of the shrine at Loreto may be found in Addis and Arnold, *Catholic Dictionary*, under "Loreto."

[349] "This is the house where the sailors of the country particularly have their devotions." Las Casas, I. 446. Moguer was a village near Palos.

bring such great news, and to show that all he had said and offered to discover had turned out true, suggested the fear that he would not be able to do so, and that each stinging insect would be able to thwart and impede the work. He attributes this fear to his little faith, and to his want of confidence in Divine Providence.

He was comforted, on the other hand, by the mercies of God in having vouchsafed him such a victory, in the discoveries he had made, and in that God had complied with all his desires in Castile, after much adversity and many misfortunes. As he had before put all his trust in God, who had heard him and granted all he sought, he ought now to believe that God would permit the completion of what had been begun, and ordain that he should be saved. Especially as he had freed him on the voyage out, when he had still greater reason to fear, from the trouble caused by the sailors and people of his company, who all with one voice declared their intention to return, and protested that they would rise against him. But the eternal God gave him force and valor to withstand them all, and in many other marvellous ways had God shown his will in this voyage besides those known to their Highnesses. Thus he ought not to fear the present tempest, though his weakness and anxiety prevent him from giving tranquillity to his mind. He says further that it gave him great sorrow to think of the two sons he left at their studies in Cordova, who would be left orphans, without father or mother,[350] in a strange land;

---

[350] As Beatriz Enriquez, the mother of Ferdinand, was still living, this passage has occasioned much perplexity. A glance at the corresponding passage, quoted in direct discourse from this entry in the Journal, in the *Historie* of Ferdinand, shows that the words "orphans without father or mother" were not in the original Journal, if we can trust this transcript. On the other hand, Las Casas, in his *Historia*, I. 447, where he used the original Journal and not the abridgment that has come down to us, has the words "*huerfanos de padre y madre en tierra estraña*." It may be that Ferdinand noted the error of the original Journal and quietly corrected it.

while the Sovereigns would not know of the services he had performed in this voyage, nor would they receive the prosperous news which would move them to help the orphans. To remedy this, and that their Highnesses might know how our Lord had granted a victory in all that could be desired respecting the Indies,[351] and that they might understand that there were no storms in those parts, which may be known by the herbs and trees which grow even within the sea;[352] also that the Sovereigns might still have information, even if he perished in the storm, he took a parchment and wrote on it as good an account as he could of all he had discovered, entreating any one who might pick it up to deliver it to the Sovereigns. He rolled this parchment up in waxed cloth, fastened it very securely, ordered a large wooden barrel to be brought, and put it inside, so that no one else knew what it was. They thought that it was some act of devotion, and so he ordered the barrel to be thrown into the sea. Afterwards, in the showers and squalls, the wind veered to the west, and they went before it, only with the foresail, in a very confused sea, for five hours. They made 2-1/2 leagues N.E. They had taken in the reefed mainsail, for fear some wave of the sea should carry all away.

Friday, 15th of February

Last night, after sunset, the sky began to clear toward the west, showing that the wind was inclined to come from

---

[351] In Ferdinand's text nothing is said explicitly about the Indies.

[352] There is nothing corresponding to this in Ferdinand's extract from the Journal. Was this omission also a case of pious revision? The Admiral thought that there could be no great storms in the countries he had discovered, because trees (mangroves) actually grew with their roots in the sea. The herbage on the beach nearly reached the waves, which does not happen when the sea is rough. (Markham.)

that quarter. The admiral added the bonnet[353] to the mainsail. The sea was still very high, although it had gone down slightly. They steered E.N.E., and went four miles an hour, which made 13 leagues during the eleven hours of the night. After sunrise they sighted land. It appeared from the bows to bear E.N.E. Some said it was the island of Madeira, others that it was the rock of Cintra, in Portugal, near Lisbon. Presently the wind headed to E.N.E., and a heavy sea came from the west, the caravel being 5 leagues from the land. The Admiral found by his reckoning that he was close to the Azores, and believed that this was one of them. The pilots and sailors thought it was the land of Castile.[354]

Saturday, 16th of February

All that night the Admiral was standing off and on to keep clear of the land, which they now knew to be an island, sometimes standing N.E., at others N.N.E., until sunrise, when they tacked to the south to reach the island, which was now concealed by a great mist. Another island was in sight from the poop, at a distance of eight leagues. Afterwards, from sunrise until dark, they were tacking to reach the land against a strong wind and head-sea. At the time of repeating the *Salve*, which is just before dark, some of the men saw a light to leeward, and it seemed that it must be on the island they first saw yesterday. All night they were beating to windward, and going as near as they could, so as to see some way to the island at sunrise. That night the Admiral got a little rest,

---

[353] The bonnet was a small sail usually cut to a third the size of the mizzen, or a fourth of the mainsail. It was secured through eyelet-holes to the leech of the mainsail, in the manner of a studding sail. (Navarrete.)
[354] On this day the Admiral dated the letter to Santangel, the *escribano de racion*, which is given below on pp. 263-272.

for he had not slept nor been able to sleep since Wednesday, and he had lost the use of his legs from long exposure to the wet and cold. At sunrise[355] he steered S.S.W., and reached the island at night, but could not make out what island it was, owing to the thick weather.

Monday, 18th of February

Yesterday, after sunset, the Admiral was sailing round the island, to see where he could anchor and open communications. He let go one anchor, which he presently lost, and then stood off and on all night. After sunrise he again reached the north side of the island, where he anchored, and sent the boat on shore. They had speech with the people, and found that it was the island of Santa Maria, one of the Azores. They pointed out the port[356] to which the caravel should go. They said that they had never seen such stormy weather as there had been for the last fifteen days, and they wondered how the caravel could have escaped. They gave many thanks to God, and showed great joy at the news that the Admiral had discovered the Indies. The Admiral says that his navigation had been very certain, and that he had laid his route down on the chart. Many thanks were due to our Lord, although there had been some delay. But he was sure that he was in the region of the Azores, and that this was one of them. He pretended to have gone over more ground, to mislead the pilots and mariners who pricked off the charts, in order that he might remain master of that route to the Indies, as, in fact, he did. For none of the others kept an accurate reckoning, so that no one but himself could be sure of the route to the Indies.

---

[355] This was on Sunday, 17th of February. (Navarrete.)
[356] The port of San Lorenzo. (Id.).

Tuesday, 19th of February

After sunset three natives of the island came to the beach and hailed. The Admiral sent the boat, which returned with fowls and fresh bread. It was carnival time, and they brought other things which were sent by the captain of the island, named Juan de Castañeda, saying that he knew the Admiral very well, and that he did not come to see him because it was night but that at dawn he would come with more refreshments, bringing with him three men of the boat's crew, whom he did not send back owing to the great pleasure he derived from hearing their account of the voyage. The Admiral ordered much respect to be shown to the messengers, and that they should be given beds to sleep in that night, because it was late, and the town was far off. As on the previous Thursday, when they were in the midst of the storm, they had made a vow to go in procession to church of Our Lady as soon as they came to land, the Admiral arranged that half the crew should go to comply with their obligation to a small chapel, like a hermitage, near the shore; and that he would himself go afterwards with the rest. Believing that it was a peaceful land, and confiding in the offers of the captain of the island, and in the peace that existed between Spain and Portugal, he asked the three men to go to the town and arrange for a priest to come and say mass. The half of the crew then went in their shirts, in compliance with their vow. While they were at their prayers, all the people of the town, horse and foot, with the captain at their head, came and took them all prisoners. The Admiral, suspecting nothing, was waiting for the boat to take him and the rest to accomplish the vow. At 11 o'clock, seeing that they did not come back, he feared that they had been detained, or that the boat had been swamped, all the island being surrounded by high rocks. He could not see what had taken place, because the hermitage was round a point. He got up the anchor, and

made sail until he was in full view of the hermitage, and
he saw many of the horsemen dismount and get into the
boat with arms. They came to the caravel to seize the
Admiral. The captain stood up in the boat, and asked for
an assurance of safety from the Admiral, who replied
that he granted it; but, what outrage was this, that he
saw none of his people in the boat? The Admiral added
that they might come on board, and that he would do all
that might be proper. The Admiral tried, with fair words,
to get hold of this captain, that he might recover his own
people, not considering that he broke faith by giving him
security, because he had offered peace and security, and
had then broken his word. The captain, as he came with
an evil intention, would not come on board. Seeing that he
did not come alongside, the Admiral asked that he might
be told the reason for the detention of his men, an act
which would displease the King of Portugal, because the
Portuguese received much honor in the territories of the
King of Castile, and were as safe as if they were in
Lisbon. He further said that the Sovereigns had given
him letters of recommendation to all the Lords and
Princes of the world, which he would show the captain if
he would come on board; that he was the Admiral of the
Ocean Sea, and Viceroy of the Indies, which belonged
to their Highnesses,[357] and that he would show the
commissions signed with their signatures, and attested by
their seals, which he held up from a distance. He added
that his Sovereigns were in friendship and amity with the
King of Portugal, and had ordered that all honor should
be shown to ships that came from Portugal. Further, that
if the captain did not surrender his people, he would still
go on to Castile, as he had quite sufficient to navigate as

---

[357] The incredulity of the Portuguese governor as to these assertions was
natural. The title Admiral of the Ocean Sea was novel and this was the first
time it was announced that Spain or any other European power had
possessions in the Indies.

far as Seville, in which case the captain and his followers would be severely punished for their offence. Then the captain and those with him replied that they did not know the King and Queen of Castile there, nor their letters, nor were they afraid of them, and they would give the Admiral to understand that this was Portugal, almost menacing him. On hearing this the Admiral was much moved, thinking that some cause of disagreement might have arisen between the two kingdoms during his absence, yet he could not endure that they should not be answered reasonably. Afterwards he turned to the captain, and said that he should go to the port with the caravel, and that all that had been done would be reported to the King his Lord. The Admiral made those who were in the caravel bear witness to what he said, calling to the captain and all the others, and promising that he would not leave the caravel until a hundred Portuguese had been taken to Castile, and all that island had been laid waste. He then returned to anchor in the port where he was first, the wind being very unfavorable for doing anything else.

Wednesday, 20th of February

The Admiral ordered the ship to be repaired, and the casks to be filled alongside for ballast. This was a very bad port, and he feared he might have to cut the cables. This was so, and he made sail for the island of San Miguel; but there is no good port in any of the Azores for the weather they then experienced, and there was no other remedy but to go to sea.

Thursday, 21st of February

Yesterday the Admiral left that island of Santa Maria for that of San Miguel, to see if a port could be found to shelter his vessel from the bad weather. There was much wind and a high sea, and he was sailing until night without being able to see either one land or the other, owing to the thick weather caused by wind and sea. The Admiral says he was in much anxiety, because he only had three sailors who knew their business, the rest knowing nothing of seamanship.[358] He was lying-to all that night, in great danger and trouble. Our Lord showed him mercy in that the waves came in one direction, for if there had been a cross sea they would have suffered much more. After sunrise the island of San Miguel was not in sight, so the Admiral determined to return to Santa Maria, to see if he could recover his people and boat, and the anchors and cables he had left there.

The Admiral says that he was astonished at the bad weather he encountered in the region of these islands. In the Indies he had navigated throughout the winter without the necessity for anchoring, and always had fine weather, never having seen the sea for a single hour in such a state that it could not be navigated easily. But among these islands he had suffered from such terrible storms. The same had happened in going out as far as the Canary Islands, but as soon as they were passed there was always fine weather, both in sea and air. In concluding these remarks, he observes that the sacred theologians and wise men[359] said well when they placed the terrestrial paradise in the Far East, because it is a most temperate region. Hence these lands that he had now discovered must, he says, be in the extreme East.

---

[358] Half the crew were still detained on shore.

[359] That the site of the Garden of Eden was to be found in the Orient was a common belief in the Middle Ages and later. Cf. the *Book of Sir John Mandeville*, ch. XXX.

Friday, 22nd of February

Yesterday the Admiral anchored off Santa Maria, in the place or port where he had first anchored. Presently a man came down to some rocks at the edge of the beach, signalling that they were not to go away. Soon afterwards the boat came with five sailors, two priests, and a scrivener. They asked for safety, and when it was granted by the Admiral, they came on board, and as it was night they slept on board, the Admiral showing them all the civility he could. In the morning they asked to be shown the authority of the Sovereigns of Castile, by which the voyage had been made. The Admiral felt that they did this to give some color of right to what they had done, and to show that they had right on their side. As they were unable to secure the person of the Admiral, whom they intended to get into their power when they came with the boat armed, they now feared that their game might not turn out so well, thinking, with some fear, of what the Admiral had threatened, and which he proposed to put into execution. In order to get his people released, the Admiral displayed the general letter of the Sovereigns to all Princes and Lords, and other documents, and having given them of what he had, the Portuguese went on shore satisfied, and presently released all the crew and the boat. The Admiral heard from them that if he had been captured also, they never would have been released, for the captain said that those were the orders of the King his Lord.

Saturday, 23rd of February

Yesterday the weather began to improve, and the Admiral got under way to seek a better anchorage, where he could take in wood and stones for ballast; but he did not find one until the hour of compline.[360]

Sunday, 24th of February

He anchored yesterday in the afternoon, to take in wood and stones, but the sea was so rough that they could not land from the boat, and during the first watch it came on to blow from the west and S.W. He ordered sail to be made, owing to the great danger there is off these islands in being at anchor with a southerly gale, and as the wind was S.W. it would go round to south. As it was a good wind for Castile, he gave up his intention of taking in wood and stones, and shaped an easterly course until sunset, going seven miles an hour for six hours and a half, equal to 45-1/2 miles. After sunset he made six miles an hour, or 66 miles in eleven hours, altogether 111 miles, equal to 28 leagues.

Monday, 25th of February

Yesterday, after sunset, the caravel went at the rate of five miles an hour on an easterly course, and in the eleven hours of the night she made 65 miles, equal to 16-1/4 leagues. From sunrise to sunset they made another 16-1/2 leagues with a smooth sea, thanks be to God. A very large bird, like an eagle, came to the caravel.

Tuesday, 26th of February

Yesterday night the caravel steered her course in a smooth sea, thanks be to God. Most of the time she was going eight miles an hour, and made a hundred miles, equal to 25 leagues. After sunrise there was little wind

---

[360] The last of the canonical hours of prayer, about nine in the evening.

and some rain-showers. They made about 8 leagues
E.N.E.

Wednesday, 27th of February

During the night and day she was off her course, owing to
contrary winds and a heavy sea. She was found to be 125
leagues from Cape St. Vincent, and 80 from the island of
Madeira, 106 from Santa Maria. It was very troublesome
to have such bad weather just when they were at the very
door of their home.

Thursday, 28th of February

The same weather during the night, with the wind from
south and S.E., sometimes shifting to N.E. and E.N.E.,
and it was the same all day.

Friday, 1st of March

To-night the course was E.N.E., and they made twelve
leagues. During the day, 23-1/2 leagues on the same
course.

Saturday, 2nd of March

The course was E.N.E., and distance made good 28
leagues during the night, and 20 in the day.

Sunday, 3rd of March

After sunset the course was east; but a squall came down,
split all the sails, and the vessel was in great danger; but
God was pleased to deliver them. They drew lots for
sending a pilgrim in a shirt to Santa Maria de la Cinta at
Huelva, and the lot fell on the Admiral. The whole crew
also made a vow to fast on bread and water during the

first Saturday after their arrival in port. They had made 60 miles before the sails were split. Afterwards they ran under bare poles, owing to the force of the gale and the heavy sea. They saw signs of the neighborhood of land, finding themselves near Lisbon.

Monday, 4th of March

During the night they were exposed to a terrible storm, expecting to be overwhelmed by the cross-seas, while the wind seemed to raise the caravel into the air, and there was rain and lightning in several directions. The Admiral prayed to our Lord to preserve them, and in the first watch it pleased our Lord to show land, which was reported by the sailors. As it was advisable not to reach it before it was known whether there was any port to which he could run for shelter, the Admiral set the mainsail, as there was no other course but to proceed, though in great danger. Thus God preserved them until daylight, though all the time they were in infinite fear and trouble. When it was light, the Admiral knew the land, which was the rock of Cintra, near the river of Lisbon, and he resolved to run in because there was nothing else to be done. So terrible was the storm, that in the village of Cascaes, at the mouth of the river, the people were praying for the little vessel all that morning. After they were inside, the people came off, looking upon their escape as a miracle. At the third hour they passed Rastelo, within the river of Lisbon, where they were told that such a winter, with so many storms, had never before been known, and that 25 ships had been lost in Flanders, while others had been wind-bound in the river for four months. Presently the Admiral wrote to the king of Portugal, who was then at a distance of nine leagues, to state that the Sovereigns of Castile had ordered him to enter the ports of his Highness, and ask for what he required for payment, and requesting that the king would give permission for the caravel to come to

410

Lisbon, because some ruffians hearing that he had much gold on board, might attempt a robbery in an unfrequented port, knowing that they did not come from Guinea, but from the Indies.

Tuesday, 5th of March

To-day the great ship of the King of Portugal was also at anchor off Rastelo, with the best provision of artillery and arms that the Admiral had ever seen. The master of her, named Bartolomé Diaz, of Lisbon, came in an armed boat to the caravel, and ordered the Admiral to get into the boat, to go and give an account of himself to the agents of the king and to the captain of that ship. The Admiral replied that he was the Admiral of the Sovereigns of Castile, and that he would not give an account to any such persons, nor would he leave the ship except by force, as he had not the power to resist. The master replied that he must then send the master of the caravel. The Admiral answered that neither the master nor any other person should go except by force, for if he allowed anyone to go, it would be as if he went himself; and that such was the custom of the Admirals of the Sovereigns of Castile, rather to die than to submit, or to let any of their people submit. The master then moderated his tone, and told the Admiral that if that was his determination he might do as he pleased. He, however, requested that he might be shown the letters of the Kings of Castile, if they were on board. The Admiral readily showed them, and the master returned to the ship and reported what had happened to the captain, named Alvaro Dama. That officer, making great festival with trumpets and drums, came to the caravel to visit the Admiral, and offered to do all that he might require.[361]

---

[361] Modern scholars have too hastily identified this Bartolomé Diaz with the discoverer of the Cape of Good Hope. There is no evidence for this

Wednesday, 6th of March

As soon as it was known that the Admiral came from the Indies, it was wonderful how many people came from Lisbon to see him and the Indians, giving thanks to our Lord, and saying that the heavenly Majesty had given all this to the Sovereigns of Castile as a reward for their faith and their great desire to serve God.

Thursday, 7th of March

To-day an immense number of people came to the caravel, including many knights, and amongst them the agents of the king, and all gave infinite thanks to our Lord for so wide an increase of Christianity granted by our Lord to the Sovereigns of Castile; and they said that they received it because their Highnesses had worked and labored for the increase of the religion of Christ.

Friday, 8th of March

To-day the Admiral received a letter from the king of Portugal,[362] brought by Don Martin de Noroña, asking him to visit him where he was, as the weather was not suitable for the departure of the caravel. He complied, to prevent suspicion, although he did not wish to go, and went to pass the night at Sacanben. The king had given orders to his officers that all that the Admiral, his crew, and the caravel were in need of should be given without

---

except the identity of the name. Against the supposition are the facts that neither Columbus, Las Casas, nor Ferdinand remark upon this meeting with the most eminent Portuguese navigator of the time, and that this Diaz is a subordinate officer on this ship who is sent to summon Columbus to report to the captain. That the great admiral of 1486-1487 would in 1493 be a simple *Patron* on a single ship is incredible.

[362] João II.

payment, and that all the Admiral wanted should be complied with.

Saturday, 9th of March

To-day the Admiral left Sacanben, to go where the king was residing, which was at Valparaiso, nine leagues from Lisbon. Owing to the rain, he did not arrive until night. The king caused him to be received very honorably by the principal officers of his household; and the king himself received the Admiral with great favor, making him sit down, and talking very pleasantly. He offered to give orders that everything should be done for the service of the Sovereigns of Castile, and said that the successful termination of the voyage had given him great pleasure. He said further that he understood that, in the capitulation between the Sovereigns and himself, that conquest belonged to him.[363] The Admiral replied that he had not seen the capitulation, nor knew more than that the Sovereigns had ordered him not to go either to La Mina[364] or to any other port of Guinea, and that this had been ordered to be proclaimed in all the ports of Andalusia before he sailed. The king graciously replied that he held it for certain that there would be no necessity for any arbitrators. The Admiral was assigned as a guest to the Prior of Clato, who was the principal person in that place, and from whom he received many favors and civilities.

---

[363] The treaty of Alcaçovas signed by Portugal September 8, 1479, and by Spain March 6, 1480. In it Ferdinand and Isabella relinquished all rights to make discoveries along the coast of Africa and retained of the African islands only the Canaries. The Spanish text is printed in *Alguns Documentos da Torre do Tombo* (Lisbon, 1892), pp. 45-46. See also Vignaud, *Toscanelli and Columbus*, pp. 61-64.

[364] "The Mine," more commonly El Mina, a station established on the Gold Coast by Diogo de Azambuja in 1482. The full name in Portuguese was S. Jorge da Mina, St. George of the Mine.

Sunday, 10th of March

To-day, after mass, the king repeated that if the Admiral wanted anything he should have it. He conversed much with the Admiral respecting his voyage, always ordering him to sit down, and treating him with great favor.

Monday, 11th of March

To-day the Admiral took leave of the king, who entrusted him with some messages to the Sovereigns, and always treating him with much friendliness.[365] He departed after

[365] The Portuguese historian Ruide Pina, in his *Cronica D'El Rey João*, gives an account of Columbus's meeting with the king which is contemporary. From his official position as chief chronicler and head of the national archives and from the details which he mentions it is safe to conclude that he was an eye-witness.

"In the following year, 1493, while the king was in the place of the Val do Paraiso which is above the Monastery of Sancta Maria das Vertudes, on account of the great pestilences which prevailed in the principal places in this district, on the sixth of March there arrived at Restello in Lisbon Christovam Colombo, an Italian who came from the discovery of the islands of Cipango and Antilia which he had accomplished by the command of the sovereigns of Castile from which land he brought with him the first specimens of the people, gold and some other things that they have; and he was entitled Admiral of them. And the king being informed of this, commanded him to come before him and he showed that he felt disgusted and grieved because he believed that this discovery was made within the seas and bounds of his lordship of Guinea which was prohibited and likewise because the said Admiral was somewhat raised from his condition and in the account of his affairs always went beyond the bounds of the truth and made this thing in gold, silver, and riches much greater than it was. The king was accused of negligence in withdrawing from him for not giving him credit and authority in regard to this discovery for which he had first come to make request of him. And although the king was urged to consent to have him slain there, since with his death the prosecution of this enterprise so far as the sovereigns of Castile were concerned would cease on account of the decease of the discoverer; and that this could be done without suspicion if he consented and ordered it, since as he was discourteous and greatly elated they could get involved with him in such a way that each one of these his faults would seem to be the true cause of his death; yet the king

414

dinner, Don Martin de Noroña being sent with him, and all the knights set out with him, and went with him some distance, to do him honor. Afterwards he came to a monastery of San Antonio, near a place called Villafranca, where the Queen was residing. The Admiral went to do her reverence and to kiss her hand, because she had sent to say that he was not to go without seeing her. The Duke[366] and the Marquis were with her, and the Admiral was received with much honor. He departed at night, and went to sleep at Llandra.

Tuesday, 12th of March

To-day, as he was leaving Llandra to return to the caravel, an esquire of the king arrived, with an offer that if he desired to go to Castile by land, that he should be supplied with lodgings, and beasts, and all that was necessary. When the Admiral took leave of him, he ordered a mule to be supplied to him, and another for his pilot, who was with him, and he says that the pilot received a present of twenty *espadines*.[367] He said this

---

like a most God-fearing prince not only forbade this but on the contrary did him honor and showed him kindness and therewith sent him away." *Collecçaõ de Livros Ineditos de Historia Portugueza*, II. 178-179. It will be noted that according to this account Columbus said he had discovered Cipango and Antilia, a mythical island which is represented on the maps of the fifteenth century, and that Columbus is called Colombo his Italian name, and not Colom or Colon.

[366] This may have been her brother, the Duke of Bejar, afterwards King Manoel.

[367] *Espadim*: a Portuguese gold piece coined by João II. Las Casas, I. 466, says: "20 *Espadinos*, a matter of 20 ducats." The Espadim contained 58 to 65 grains of gold. W.C. Hazlitt, *Coinage of European Nations, sub voce.* King João II. gave Columbus's pilot almost exactly the sum which Henry VII. gave to John Cabot, which was £10. In the French translation and the translation in J.B. Thacher's *Christopher Columbus* the word *espadines* is erroneously taken to be Spanish and rendered "*Épées*," and "small short swords."

that the Sovereigns might know all that was done. He arrived on board the caravel that night.

Wednesday, 13th of March

To-day, at 8 o'clock, with the flood tide, and the wind N.N.W., the Admiral got under way and made sail for Seville.

Thursday, 14th of March

Yesterday, after sunset, a southerly course was steered, and before sunrise they were off Cape St. Vincent, which is in Portugal. Afterwards he shaped a course to the east for Saltes, and went on all day with little wind, "until now that the ship is off Furon."

Friday, 15th of March

Yesterday, after sunset, she went on her course with little wind, and at sunrise she was off Saltes. At noon, with the tide rising, they crossed the bar of Saltes, and reached the port which they had left on the 3rd of August of the year before.[368] The Admiral says that so ends this journal, unless it becomes necessary to go to Barcelona by sea, having received news that their Highnesses are in that city, to give an account of all his voyage which our Lord had permitted him to make, and saw fit to set forth in him. For, assuredly, he held with a firm and strong knowledge that His High Majesty made all things good, and that all is good except sin. Nor can he value or think of anything being done without His consent. "I know respecting this voyage," says the Admiral, "that he has miraculously shown his will, as may be seen from this

---

[368] Having been absent 225 days.

journal, setting forth the numerous miracles that have been displayed in the voyage, and in me who was so long at the court of your Highnesses, working in opposition to and against the opinions of so many chief persons of your household, who were all against me, looking upon this enterprise as folly. But I hope in our Lord, that it will be a great benefit to Christianity, for so it has ever appeared." These are the final words of the Admiral Don Cristoval Colon respecting his first voyage to the Indies and their discovery.

Letter from Columbus to Luis de Santangel

Introduction

This letter, the earliest published narrative of Columbus's first voyage, was issued in Barcelona in April, 1493, not far from the time when the discoverer was received in state by the King and Queen. The *Escribano de Racion*, to whom it was addressed, was Luis de Santangel, who had deeply interested himself in the project of Columbus and had advanced money to enable Queen Isabella to meet the expenses of the voyage. He, no doubt, placed a copy in the hands of the printer. Only two printed copies of this Spanish letter, as it is called, have come down to us. One is a folio of the first imprint, discovered and reproduced in 1889. Of this the unique copy is in the Lenox Library in New York; its first page is reproduced in facsimile in this volume, by courteous permission of the authorities of the library. The other is a quarto of the second and slightly corrected imprint, first made known in 1852 and first reproduced in 1866. Facsimiles of both are given in Thacher's *Christopher Columbus*, II. 17-20 and 33-40.

Columbus sent a duplicate of this letter with some slight changes to Gabriel Sanxis (Spanish form, Sanchez), the treasurer of Aragon, from whose hands a copy came into the possession of Leander de Cosco, who translated it into Latin, April 29, 1493.

This Latin version was published in Rome, probably in May, 1493, and this issue was rapidly followed by reprints in Rome, Basel, Paris, and Antwerp. It is to this Latin version that the European world outside of Spain was indebted for its first knowledge of the new discoveries.

A poetical paraphrase in Italian by Giuliano Dati was published in Rome in June, 1493. This is reprinted in Major's *Select Letters of Columbus*. The first German edition of the letter was published in Strassburg in 1497.

In the years 1493-1497 the Santangel letter was printed twice in Spanish, and the duplicate of it, the Sanchez letter, was printed nine times in Latin, five times in Dati's Italian paraphrase, and once in German. Until the publication in 1571 of the *Historie*, the Italian translation of Ferdinand Columbus's biography of his father, which contains an abridgment of Columbus's *Journal*, these letters and the account in Peter Martyr's *Decades de Rebus Oceanicis*, were the only sources of information in regard to the first voyage accessible to the world at large. The translation here given is that contained in Quaritch's *The Spanish Letter of Columbus* (London, 1893), with a few minor changes in the wording. An English translation of the Latin or Sanchez letter may be found in the first edition of Major's *Select Letters of Columbus* (London, 1847). This version is reprinted in P.L. Ford's *Writings of Christopher Columbus*, New York, 1892. By an error in the title of the first edition, Rome, 1493, Sanchez's Christian name is given as Raphael.

The text of the Santangel letter published by Navarrete in 1825 was derived from a manuscript preserved in the Spanish Archives at Simancas.
In 1858 the Brazilian scholar Varnhagen published an edition of the Sanchez letter from a manuscript discovered by him in Valencia. Neither of these manuscripts, however, has the authority of the first printed editions.

E.G.B.

Letter from Columbus to Luis de Santangel

SIR: As I know that you will have pleasure from the great victory which our Lord hath given me in my voyage, I write you this, by which you shall know that in thirty-three days I passed over to the Indies with the fleet which the most illustrious King and Queen, our Lords, gave me; where I found very many islands peopled with inhabitants beyond number. And, of them all, I have taken possession for their Highnesses, with proclamation and the royal standard displayed; and I was not gainsaid. To the first which I found, I gave the name Sant Salvador, in commemoration of His High Majesty, who marvellously hath given all this: the Indians call it Guanaham.[369] The second I named the Island of Santa Maria de Concepcion, the third Ferrandina, the fourth, Fair Island,[370] the fifth La Isla Juana; and so for each one a new name. When I reached Juana, I followed its coast westwardly, and found it so large that I thought it might be mainland, the province of Cathay. And as I did not thus find any towns and villages on the sea-coast, save small hamlets with the people whereof I could not get speech, because they all fled away forthwith, I went on further in the same direction, thinking I should not miss of great cities or towns. And at the end of many leagues, seeing that there

---

[369] Guanahani in the Journal; see entry covering October 11 and 12.
[370] The original text has Isla bella, which was a misprint for Isabella. *Cf.* Journal, October 20.

was no change, and that the coast was bearing me northwards, whereunto my desire was contrary, since the winter was already confronting us, I formed the purpose of making from thence to the South, and as the wind also blew against me, I determined not to wait for other weather and turned back as far as a port agreed upon; from which I sent two men into the country to learn if there were a king, or any great cities. They travelled for three days, and found innumerable small villages and a numberless population, but nought of ruling authority; wherefore they returned.[371] I understood sufficiently from other Indians whom I had already taken, that this land, in its continuousness, was an island;[372] and so I followed its coast eastwardly for a hundred and seven leagues as far as where it terminated; from which headland I saw another island to the east, eighteen leagues distant from this, to which I at once gave the name La Spañola.[373] And I proceeded thither, and followed the northern coast, as with La Juana, eastwardly for a hundred and eighty-eight great leagues in a direct easterly course, as with La Juana. The which, and all the others, are most fertile to an excessive degree, and this extremely so. In it, there are many havens on the sea-coast, incomparable with any others that I know in Christendom, and plenty of rivers so good and great that it is a marvel. The lands thereof are high, and in it are very many ranges of hills, and most lofty mountains incomparably beyond the island of Tenerife,[374] all most beautiful in a thousand shapes, and all accessible, and full of trees of a thousand kinds, so lofty that they seem to reach the sky. And I am assured that they never lose their foliage; as may be imagined,

---

[371] Cf. Journal, November 2 and 6.

[372] Cf. Journal, November 1, for Columbus's strong inclination to regard Cuba as mainland.

[373] Cf. Journal, December 9.

[374] Cf. Journal, December 20 and note.

since I saw them as green and as beautiful as they are in Spain during May. And some of them were in flower, some in fruit, some in another stage according to their kind. And the nightingale was singing, and other birds of a thousand sorts, in the month of November, there where I was going. There are palm-trees of six or eight species, wondrous to see for their beautiful variety; but so are the other trees, and fruits, and plants therein. There are wonderful pine-groves, and very large plains of verdure, and there is honey, and many kinds of birds, and many various fruits. In the earth there are many mines of metals; and there is a population of incalculable number.[375] Española is a marvel; the mountains and hills, and plains, and fields, and the soil, so beautiful and rich for planting and sowing, for breeding cattle of all sorts, for building of towns and villages. There could be no believing, without seeing, such harbors as are here, as well as the many and great rivers, and excellent waters, most of which contain gold. In the trees and fruits and plants, there are great diversities from those of Juana. In this, there are many spiceries, and great mines of gold and other metals. The people of this island, and of all the others that I have found and seen, or not seen, all go naked, men and women, just as their mothers bring them forth; although some women cover a single place with the leaf of a plant, or a cotton something which they make for that purpose. They have no iron or steel, nor any weapons; nor are they fit thereunto; not because they be not a well-formed people and of fair stature, but that they are most wondrously timorous. They have no other

---

[375] The prevalent Spanish, estimate of the population of Española at the time of the first colonization was 1,100,000. The modern ethnologist and critical historian, Oscar Peschel, placed it at less than 300,000 and more than 200,000. The estimates of Indian population by the early writers were almost invariably greatly exaggerated. *Cf.* Bourne, *Spain in America*, pp. 213-214. and notes.

weapons than the stems of reeds in their seeding state, on the end of which they fix little sharpened stakes. Even these, they dare not use; for many times has it happened that I sent two or three men ashore to some village to parley, and countless numbers of them sallied forth, but as soon as they saw those approach, they fled away in such wise that even a father would not wait for his son. And this was not because any hurt had ever been done to any of them:--on the contrary, at every headland where I have gone and been able to hold speech with them, I gave them of everything which I had, as well cloth as many other things, without accepting aught therefor;--but such they are, incurably timid. It is true that since they have become more assured, and are losing that terror, they are artless and generous with what they have, to such a degree as no one would believe but him who had seen it. Of anything they have, if it be asked for, they never say no, but do rather invite the person to accept it, and show as much lovingness as though they would give their hearts. And whether it be a thing of value, or one of little worth, they are straightways content with whatsoever trifle of whatsoever kind may be given them in return for it. I forbade that anything so worthless as fragments of broken platters, and pieces of broken glass, and strap buckles,[376] should be given them; although when they were able to get such things, they seemed to think they had the best jewel in the world, for it was the hap of a sailor to get, in exchange for a strap,[377] gold to the weight of two and a half castellanos,[378] and others much more for

---

[376] *Cabos de agugetas.* Rather the metallic tips of lacings or straps. *Agugeta* is a leather lacing or strap. The contemporary Latin translator used *bingulae*, shoe-straps, shoe-latchets.

[377] The *castellano* was one-sixth of an ounce of gold.

[378] The *castellano* was one-sixth of an ounce of gold.

other things of far less value; while for new blancas[379] they gave everything they had, even though it were the worth of two or three gold castellanos, or one or two arrobas[380] of spun cotton. They took even pieces of broken barrel-hoops, and gave whatever they had, like senseless brutes; insomuch that it seemed to me bad. I forbade it, and I gave gratuitously a thousand useful things that I carried, in order that they may conceive affection, and furthermore may become Christians; for they are inclined to the love and service of their Highnesses and of all the Castilian nation, and they strive to combine in giving us things which they have in abundance, and of which we are in need. And they knew no sect, nor idolatry; save that they all believe that power and goodness are in the sky, and they believed very firmly that I, with these ships and crews, came from the sky; and in such opinion, they received me at every place where I landed, after they had lost their terror. And this comes not because they are ignorant: on the contrary, they are men of very subtle wit, who navigate all those seas, and who give a marvellously good account of everything, but because they never saw men wearing clothes nor the like of our ships. And as soon as I arrived in the Indies, in the first island that I found, I took some of them by force, to the intent that they should learn [our speech] and give me information of what there was in those parts. And so it was, that very soon they understood [us] and we them, what by speech or what by signs; and those [Indians] have been of much service. To this day I carry them [with me] who are still of the opinion that I come from Heaven [as appears] from much conversation which they have had with me. And they were the first to proclaim it wherever I arrived; and the others went running from house to house and to the

---

[379] *Blancas* were little coins worth about one-third of a cent.
[380] The *arroba* was 25 pounds.

neighboring villages, with loud cries of "Come! come to see the people from Heaven!" Then, as soon as their minds were reassured about us, every one came, men as well as women, so that there remained none behind, big or little; and they all brought something to eat and drink, which they gave with wondrous lovingness. They have in all the islands very many *canoas*,[381] after the manner of rowing-galleys,[382] some larger, some smaller; and a good many are larger than a galley of eighteen benches. They are not so wide, because they are made of a single log of timber, but a galley could not keep up with them in rowing, for their motion is a thing beyond belief. And with these, they navigate through all those islands, which are numberless, and ply their traffic. I have seen some of those *canoas* with seventy and eighty men in them, each one with his oar. In all those islands, I saw not much diversity in the looks of the people, nor in their manners and language; but they all understand each other, which is a thing of singular advantage for what I hope their Highnesses will decide upon for converting them to our holy faith, unto which they are well disposed. I have already told how I had gone a hundred and seven leagues, in a straight line from West to East, along the sea-coast of the Island of Juana; according to which itinerary, I can declare that that island is larger than England and Scotland combined;[383] as, over and above those hundred and seven leagues, there remain for me, on the western side, two provinces whereto I did not go--one of which they call Avan, where the people are born with tails[384] --which provinces cannot be less in length than

---

[381] The first appearance of this West Indian word in Europe.

[382] *Fustas de remo.*

[383] Cf. Journal, December 23, and note. The reader will observe the tone of exaggeration in the letter as compared with the Journal.

[384] Marco Polo reported that in the kingdom of Lambri in Sumatra "there are men who have tails like dogs, larger than a palm, and who are covered with hair." Marco Polo, pt. III., ch. XIV. See Yule's note on the

fifty or sixty leagues, according to what may be
understood from the Indians with me, who know all the
islands. This other, Española, has a greater circumference
than the whole of Spain from Colibre in Catalunya, by
the sea-coast, as far as Fuente Ravia in Biscay; since,
along one of its four sides, I went for a hundred and
eighty-eight great leagues in a straight line from west to
east.[385] This is [a land] to be desired,--and once seen,
never to be relinquished--in which (although, indeed, I
have taken possession of them all for their Highnesses,
and all are more richly endowed than I have skill and
power to say, and I hold them all in the name of their
Highnesses who can dispose thereof as much and as
completely as of the kingdoms of Castile) in this
Española, in the place most suitable and best for its
proximity to the gold mines, and for traffic with the
mainland both on this side and with that over there
belonging to the Great Can,[386] where there will be great
commerce and profit, I took possession of a large town
which I named the city of Navidad.[387] And I have made
fortification there, and a fort (which by this time will have
been completely finished) and I have left therein men
enough for such a purpose, with arms and artillery, and

---

legend of men with tails, Yule's *Marco Polo*, II. 284. The name Avan
(Anan in the Latin letter) does not occur in the Journal. Bernaldez,
Historia de las Reyes Catolicos, [TN-5] II. 19, gives Albao as one of
the provinces of Española. As this name is not found in his chief
source, Dr. Chanca's letter, he may have got it from Columbus and
through a lapse of memory transferred it from Cuba to Española.
[385] The area of Spain is about 191,000 square miles; that of Española
or Hayti is 28,000. The extreme length of Hayti is 407 miles.
[386] That is, with the mainland of Europe on this side of the Atlantic and with
the mainland on that side of the ocean belonging to the Great Can, *i.e.*,
China.
[387] *I.e.*, Nativity, Christmas, because the wreck occurred on that day. *Cf.*
Journal, December 25 and January 4, and note to entry of December 28.

provisions for more than a year, and a boat, and a [man who is] master of all seacraft for making others; and great friendship with the king of that land, to such a degree that he prided himself on calling and holding me as his brother. And even though his mind might change towards attacking those men, neither he nor his people know what arms are, and go naked. As I have already said, they are the most timorous creatures there are in the world, so that the men who remain there are alone sufficient to destroy all that land, and the island is without personal danger for them if they know how to behave themselves. It seems to me that in all those islands, the men are all content with a single wife; and to their chief or king they give as many as twenty. The women, it appears to me, do more work than the men. Nor have I been able to learn whether they held personal property, for it seemed to me that whatever one had, they all took share of, especially of eatable things. Down to the present, I have not found in those islands any monstrous men, as many expected,[388] but on the contrary all the people are very comely; nor are they black like those in Guinea, but have flowing hair; and they are not begotten where there is an excessive violence of the rays of the sun. It is true that the sun is there very strong, although it is twenty-six degrees distant from the equinoctial line.[389] In those islands, where there are lofty mountains, the cold was very keen there, this winter; but they endure it by being accustomed thereto, and by the help of the meats which they eat with

---

[388] Columbus had read in the *Imago Mundi* of Pierre d'Ailly and noted in the margin the passage which says that in the ends of the earth there "were monsters of such a horrid aspect that it were hard to say whether they were men or beasts."*Raccolta Colombiana*, pt. I., vol. II., p. 468. *Cf.* also the stories in the *Book of Sir John Mandeville*, chs. XXVII. and XXVIII.
[389] Columbus apparently revised his estimate of the latitude on the return, without, however, correcting his Journal; *cf.* entries for October 30 and November 21.

many and inordinately hot spices. Thus I have not found, nor had any information of monsters, except of an island which is here the second in the approach to the Indies, which is inhabited by a people whom, in all the islands, they
regard as very ferocious, who eat human flesh. These have many canoes with which they run through all the islands of India, and plunder and take as much as they can. They are no more ill-shapen than the others, but have the custom of wearing their hair long, like women; and they use bows and arrows of the same reed stems, with a point of wood at the top, for lack of iron which they have not. Amongst those other tribes who are excessively cowardly, these are ferocious; but I hold them as nothing more than the others. These are they who have to do with the women of Matinino[390] --which is the first island that is encountered in the passage from Spain to the Indies--in which there are no men. Those women practise no female usages, but have bows and arrows of reed such as above mentioned; and they arm and cover themselves with plates of copper of which they have much. In another island, which they assure me is larger than Española, the people have no hair. In this there is incalculable gold; and concerning these and the rest I bring Indians with me as witnesses. And in conclusion, to speak only of what has been done in this voyage, which has been so hastily performed, their Highnesses may see that I shall give them as much gold as they may need, with very little aid which their Highnesses will give me; spices and cotton at once, as much as their Highnesses will order to be shipped, and as much as they shall order to be shipped of mastic,--which till now has never been found except in Greece, in the island of Xio,[391] and the Seignory sells it for

---

[390] See Journal, January 15, and note. The island is identified with Martinique.
[391] See Journal, November 12, and note. The Seignory was the

what it likes; and aloe-wood as much as they shall order
to be shipped; and slaves as many as they shall order to
be shipped,--and these shall be from idolaters. And I
believe that I have discovered rhubarb and cinnamon, and
I shall find that the men whom I am leaving there will
have discovered a thousand other things of value; as
I made no delay at any point, so long as the wind gave me
an opportunity of sailing, except only in the town of
Navidad till I had left things safely arranged and well
established. And in truth I should have done much more if
the ships had served me as well as might reasonably have
been expected. This is enough; and [thanks to] Eternal
God our Lord who gives to all those who walk His way,
victory over things which seem impossible; and this was
signally one such, for although men have talked or
written of those lands,[392] it was all by conjecture, without
confirmation from eyesight, amounting only to this much
that the hearers for the most part listened and judged
that there was more fable in it than anything actual,
however trifling. Since thus our Redeemer has given to
our most illustrious King and Queen, and to their famous
kingdoms, this victory in so high a matter, Christendom
should have rejoicing therein and make great festivals,
and give solemn thanks to the Holy Trinity for the great
exaltation they shall have by the conversion of so many
peoples to our holy faith; and next for the temporal
benefit which will bring hither refreshment and profit, not
only to Spain, but to all Christians. This briefly, in
accordance with the facts. Dated, on the caravel, off the
Canary Islands,[393] the 15 February of the year 1493.

---

government of Genoa to which Chios [Scio] belonged at this time.

[392] Such writers, for example, as Pierre d'Ailly, Marco Polo, and the author
of the *Book of Sir John Mandeville*, from whom Columbus had derived
most of his preconceptions which often biassed or misled him in
interpreting the signs of the natives.

[393] According to the Journal, Columbus thought he was off the Azores,
February 15.

At your command,

THE ADMIRAL.

POSTSCRIPT WHICH CAME WITHIN THE LETTER

After having written this letter, and being in the sea of
Castile, there rose upon me so much wind, South and
South-east,[394] that it has caused me to lighten the vessels;
however I ran hither to-day into this port of Lisbon, which
was the greatest wonder in the world; where I decided to
write to their Highnesses. I have always found the
seasons like May in all the Indies, whither I passed in
thirty-three days, and returned in twenty-eight, but that
these storms have delayed me twenty-three days running
about this sea.[395] All the seamen say here that there
never has been so bad a winter nor so many shipwrecks.

Dated the 14th of March.[396]

---

[394] The storm of March 3d; see Journal.

[395] The time of the return voyage, like that of the outgoing voyage, is
reckoned as that consumed in making the Atlantic passage from the last
island left on one side to the first one reached on the other. Just how the
twenty-three days is to be explained is not altogether clear. The editor of
Quaritch's *The Spanish Letter of Columbus* supposed Columbus to refer to
the time which elapsed from February 16, when he arrived at the Azores,
to March 13, when he left Lisbon.

[396] Columbus arrived at Lisbon March 4, and he is supposed by R.H. Major
to have written the postscript there, but not to have despatched the letter
until he reached Seville, March 15, when he redated it March 14.

Colom sent this letter to the Escrivano de Racion.[397] Of the islands found in the Indies. Received with another for their Highnesses.[398]

---

[397] The *Escrivano de Racion* in the kingdom of Aragon was the high steward or controller of the king's household expenditures. In Castile the corresponding official was the *contador mayor*, chief auditor or steward. Navarrete, I. 167.

[398] No longer extant. These lines are a memorandum appended to the text by Santangel or the printer, and might have been used as a title, as the similar memorandum was used in the publication of the Latin letter. The Admiral's name is spelled as in the Articles of Agreement "Colom."

Letter from Columbus to Ferdinand and Isabella concerning the Colonization and commerce of Española[399]

MOST HIGH AND POWERFUL LORDS: In obedience to what your Highnesses command me, I shall state what occurs to me for the peopling and management of the

---

[399] The original text of this letter will be most accessible in Thacher, *Christopher Columbus*, III. 100-113. It is there accompanied by a facsimile of the original manuscript and an English translation. The translation here given is a revision of that made by Dr. José Ignacio Rodriguez of Washington and printed in the *Report of the American Historical Association*, 1894, pp. 452-455, as part of a paper by W.E. Curtis on *Autographs of Christopher Columbus*. The text was first printed by Justo Zaragoza in his *Cartas de Indias*, etc. (Madrid, 1877). It was first translated by George Dexter in the *Proceedings of the Massachusetts Historical Society*, Vol. XVI. This translation, which contains some errors which seriously affect the meaning, is also to be found in P.L. Ford, *Writings of Christopher Columbus*, pp. 67-74. Zaragoza placed the date of this letter in 1497. It is the opinion of the present editor that it should be placed between the first and the second voyage. The arguments advanced by Lollis in favor of 1493 are conclusive. See *Raccolta Colombiana*, parte I., tomo I., pp. lxxv-lxxx.

The letter is of great importance as the first draft of a systematic colonial policy for the newly discovered islands. Several of its suggestions were incorporated in the letter of instructions which the Sovereigns gave Columbus May 29, 1493, for the second voyage. See Navarrete, *Viages*, II. 66-72. It was supplemented in 1494 by the memorandum which the Admiral sent back to the sovereigns by Antonio de Torres and the two together entitle Columbus to be considered the pioneer lawgiver as well as the discoverer of the New World. *Cf.* Bourne, *Spain in America*, pp. 204-206.

Spanish Island[400] and of all others, whether already discovered or hereafter to be discovered, submitting myself, however, to any better opinion. In the first place, in regard to the Spanish Island: that there should go there settlers up to the number of two thousand[401] who may want to go so as to render the possession of the country safer and cause it to be more profitable and helpful in the intercourse and traffic with the neighboring islands.

Likewise, that in the said island three or four towns be founded at convenient places, and the settlers be properly distributed among said places and towns.

Likewise, in order to secure the better and prompter settlement of the said island, that the privilege of getting gold be granted exclusively to those who actually settle and build dwelling-houses in the settlement where they may be, in order that all may live close to each other and more safely.

Likewise, that in each place and settlement there be a mayor[402] or mayors and a clerk[403] according to the use and custom of Castile.

Likewise, that a church be built, and that priests or friars be sent there for the administration of the sacraments, and for divine worship and the conversion of the Indians.

---

[400] *La ysla Española*. So translated, for so it would sound to the Sovereigns. There had not been time for Española to sound like a proper name.
[401] See Bourne, *Spain in America*, pp. 34-35, for the actual equipment of the second voyage.
[402] Alcalde.
[403] *Escribano del pueblo*.

Likewise, that no settler be allowed to go and gather gold unless with a permit from the governor or mayor of the town in which he lives, to be given only upon his promising under oath to return to the place of his residence and faithfully report all the gold which he may have gathered, this to be done once a month, or once a week, as the time may be assigned to him, the said report to be entered on the proper registry by the clerk of the town in the presence of the mayor, and if so deemed advisable, in the presence of a friar or priest selected for the purpose.

Likewise, that all the gold so gathered be melted forthwith, and stamped with such a stamp as the town may have devised and selected, and that it be weighed and that the share of that gold which belongs to your Highnesses be given and delivered to the mayor of the town, the proper record thereof being made by the clerk and by the priest or friar, so that it may not pass through only one hand and may so render the concealing of the truth impossible.

Likewise, that all the gold which may be found without the mark or seal aforesaid in the possession of any one who formerly had reported once as aforesaid, be forfeited and divided by halves, one for the informer and the other for your Highnesses.

Likewise, that one per cent. of all the gold gathered be set apart and appropriated for building churches, and providing for their proper furnishing and ornamentation, and to the support of the priests or friars having them in their charge, and, if so deemed advisable, for the payment of some compensation to the mayors and clerks of the respective towns, so as to cause them to fulfil their duties faithfully, and that the balance be delivered to the governor and treasurer sent there by your Highnesses.

Likewise, in regard to the division of the gold and of the share which belongs to your Highnesses, I am of the opinion that it should be entrusted to the said governor and treasurer, because the amount of the gold found may sometimes be large and sometimes small, and, if so deemed advisable, that the share of your Highnesses be established for one year to be one-half, the other half going to the gatherers, reserving for a future time to make some other and better provision, if necessary.

Likewise, that if the mayors and clerks commit any fraud or consent to it, the proper punishment be inflicted upon them, and that a penalty be likewise imposed upon those settlers who do not report in full the whole amount of the gold which is in their possession.

Likewise, that there be a treasurer[404] in the said island, who shall receive all the gold belonging to your Highnesses, and shall have a clerk to make and keep the proper record of the receipts, and that the mayors and clerks of the respective towns be given the proper vouchers for everything which they may deliver to the said treasurer.

Likewise, that whereas the extreme anxiety of the colonists to gather gold may induce them to neglect all other business and occupations, it seems to me that prohibition should be made to them to engage in the search of gold during some season of the year, so as to give all other business, profitable to the island, an opportunity to be established and carried on.

---

[404] As the King and Queen on May 7, 1493, appointed Gomez Tello to go with Columbus on the second voyage to act as receiver of the royal dues, Thacher argues strongly, on the ground that this recommendation presumably antedates the appointment of a treasurer, that this letter of Columbus's was written earlier than May 7, 1493.

Likewise, that as far as the business of discovering other lands is concerned,[405] it is my opinion that permission to do so should be given to everyone who desires to embark in it, and that some liberality should be shown in reducing the fifth to be given away, so as to encourage as many as possible for entering into such undertakings.

And now I shall set forth my opinion as to the manner of sending vessels to the said Spanish Island, and the regulation of this subject which must be made, which is as follows: That no vessels should be allowed to unload their cargoes except at one or two ports designated for that purpose, and that a record should be made of all that they carry and unload; and that no vessels should be allowed either to leave the island except from the same ports, after a record has been made also of all that they have taken on board, so that nothing can be concealed.

Likewise, in regard to the gold to be brought from the island to Castile, that the whole of it, whether belonging to your Highnesses or to some private individual, must be kept in a chest, with two keys, one to be kept by the master of the vessel and the other by some person chosen by the governor and the treasurer, and that an official record must be made of everything put in the said chest, in order that each one may have what is his, and that any other gold, much or little, found outside of the said chest in any manner be forfeited to the benefit of your Highnesses, so as to cause the transaction to be made faithfully.

---

[405] Such an authorization was given by the sovereigns, April 10, 1495, reserving Columbus's rights to one-eighth of the trade. Navarrete, II. 166-167. The Admiral protested that this authorization led to infringement of his rights and it was in so far revoked, June 2, 1497.

Likewise, that all vessels coming from the said island must come to unload to the port of Cadiz, and that no person shall be allowed to leave the vessels or get in them until such person or persons of the said city as may be appointed for this purpose by your Highnesses go on board the same vessels, to whom the masters must declare all that they have brought, and show the statement of everything they have in the cargoes, so that it may be seen and proved whether the said ships have brought anything hidden and not declared in the manifests at the time of shipment.

Likewise, that in the presence of the Justice of the said city of Cadiz and of whosoever may be deputed for the purpose by your Highnesses, the said chest shall be opened in which the gold is to be brought and that to each one be given what belongs to him.[406]

May your Highnesses keep me in their minds, while I, on my part, shall ever pray to God our Lord to preserve the lives of your Highnesses and enlarge their dominions.

S.
S.A.S.
X.M.Y.
XPO FERENS.[407]

Sent by the admiral.

---

[406] On the development of the fiscal and commercial regulations of the Spanish colonial administration, see Bourne, *Spain in America*, pp. 282-301 and 337; Moses, *Establishment of Spanish Rule in America*, pp. 27-67.

[407] The formal signature of Columbus which he enjoined upon his heir in his deed of entail, February 28, 1498. See P.L. Ford, *Writings of Christopher Columbus*, p. 90. If this letter was written, as is supposed, in 1493, this is the earliest use of this monogram. Its meaning has never been determined. The various conjectures are presented by Thacher, *Christopher Columbus*, III. 454-458.

Letter of Dr. Chanca on the second voyage of Columbus

INTRODUCTION

Dr. Chanca of Seville volunteered to go to the Indies, and on May 23, 1493, the King and Queen appointed him surgeon (Navarrete, *Viages*, II. 54). This letter was written to the cabildo or town council of Seville and is the first narrative of one of Columbus's voyages that we have exactly as it was written by a private observer. It is also the first description of the natives that we have from an observer of scientific training. The original text was first printed by Navarrete in his *Viages* in 1825. The original manuscript or a copy came into the possession of the historian Bernaldez, who embodied it with a few trifling changes and omissions in his *Historia de Los Reyes Catolicos*, chs. CXIX., CXX. (Seville ed., 1870), Vol. II., pp. 5-36.

Columbus kept a journal on this voyage which is no longer extant. Abridgments of it are preserved to us in the *Historie* of Ferdinand Columbus and in the *Historia de las Indias* of Las Casas. There are other contemporary narratives of the voyage from private hands, but they are either made up from conversations with those who went on the voyage, like the letters of Simone Verde, printed in Harrisse, *Christophe Colomb*, II. 68-78, or the account in Books II. and III. of the first decade of Peter Martyr's *De Rebus Oceanicis*, or a literary embellishment of some private letters like the translation into Latin by Nicolo Syllacio of some letters he received from Guillelmo Coma who went on the voyage. The Syllacio-Coma letter and Peter Martyr's account in its earliest published form, the Venetian *Libretto de tutta la Navigatione de Re de Spagna de le Isole et Terreni novamente Trovati*, are accessible in English in Thacher, *Christopher Columbus*, II. 243-262, 489-502. These two narratives gave the European public its first knowledge of the second voyage. The Syllacio-Coma letter was published late in 1494 or early in 1495, and the *Libretto* in Venice in 1504.

The translation of Dr. Chanca's letter given here is that of R.H. Major. It has been carefully revised to bring it into closer conformity to the original. Any noteworthy changes will be indicated. Attention may be called to a somewhat important correction of the text on p. 304.

Of Dr. Chanca personally little or nothing is known beyond what has been mentioned except that he devoted himself with zeal and self-sacrifice to his duties. In the report of the Second Voyage which Columbus prepared January 30, 1494, and sent off by Antonio de Torres February 2, he charged Torres as follows in regard to Dr. Chanca. "You will inform their Highnesses of the labor that Dr. Chanca is performing on account of the many that are ill and the lack of supplies and that with all this he is conducting himself with great diligence and kindness in everything that concerns his duties," etc. Major, *Select Letters of Columbus*, pp. 93, 94.

E.G.B.

Letter of Dr. Chanca on the second voyage of Columbus

A letter addressed to the Town Council of Seville by Dr. Chanca, a native of that city, and physician to the fleet of Columbus, on his second voyage to the Indies, describing the principal events which occurred during that voyage

Most noble Lord:--

Since the occurrences which I relate in private letters to other persons are not of such general interest as those which are contained in this epistle, I have resolved to give you a distinct narrative of the events of our voyage, as well as to treat of the other matters which form the subject of my petition to your Lordship. The news I have to communicate are as follows: The expedition which their Catholic Majesties sent, by Divine permission, from Spain to the Indies, under the command of Christopher Columbus, Admiral of the Ocean, left Cadiz on the twenty-fifth of September, of the year [1493, with seventeen ships well equipped and with 1200 fighting men or a little less,][408] with wind and weather favorable for the voyage. This weather lasted two days, during which time we managed to make nearly fifty leagues; the weather then changing, we made little or no progress for the next two days; it pleased God, however, after this, to restore us fine weather, so that in two days more we reached the Great Canary. Here we put into harbor, which we were obliged to do, to repair one of the ships which made a great deal of water; we remained all that

---

[408] There is a gap here in the text of the original which has been filled by taking the corresponding words in Bernaldez's text.

day, and on the following set sail again, but were several times becalmed, so that we were four or five days before we reached Gomera. We had to remain at Gomera some days[409] to lay in our stores of meat, wood, and as much water as we could stow, preparatory to the long voyage which we expected to make without seeing land: thus through the delay at these two ports, and being calmed one day after leaving Gomera, we were nineteen or twenty days before we arrived at the island of Ferro. After this we had, by the goodness of God, a return of fine weather, more continuous than any fleet ever enjoyed during so long a voyage, so that leaving Ferro on the thirteenth of October, within twenty days we came in sight of land; and we should have seen it in fourteen or fifteen days, if the ship *Capitana*[410] had been as good a sailer as the other vessels; for many times the others had to shorten sail, because they were leaving us much behind. During all this time we had great good fortune, for throughout the voyage we encountered no storm, with the exception of one on St. Simon's eve,[411] which for four hours put us in considerable jeopardy.

On the first Sunday after All Saints, namely the third of November, about dawn, a pilot of the flagship cried out, "The reward, I see the land!"

The joy of the people was so great, that it was wonderful to hear their cries and exclamations of pleasure; and they had good reason to be delighted; for they had become so wearied of bad living, and of working the water out of the

---

[409] Major here translated *algun dia* "one day." It should be "some days." Bernaldez has *algunos dias*, and Coma says the tarry at Gomera was nearly six days.

[410] *La nao Capitana* means the flagship. The name of the flagship on the second voyage was *Marigalante*. *Historie* of Ferdinand Columbus, cap. XLV. (London, ed. 1867), p. 137.

[411] October 27.

ships, that all sighed most anxiously for land. The pilots of the fleet reckoned on that day, that between leaving Ferro and first reaching land, we had made eight hundred leagues; others said seven hundred and eighty (so that the difference was not great), and three hundred more between Ferro and Cadiz, making in all eleven hundred leagues; I do not therefore feel as one who had not seen enough of the water. On the morning of the aforesaid Sunday, we saw lying before us an island, and soon on the right hand another appeared: the first was high and mountainous, on the side nearest to us; the other[412] flat, and very thickly wooded. As soon as it became lighter, other islands began to appear on both sides; so that on that day, there were six islands to be seen lying in different directions, and most of them of considerable size. We directed our course towards that which we had first seen, and reaching the coast, we proceeded more than a league in search of a port where we might anchor, but without finding one; all that part of the island which met our view, appeared mountainous, very beautiful, and green even up to the water, which was delightful to see, for at that season, there is scarcely any thing green in our own country. When we found that there was no harbor there, the Admiral decided that we should go to the other island, which appeared on the right, and which was at four or five leagues distance; one vessel however still remained on the first island all that day seeking for a harbor, in case it should be necessary to return thither. At length, having found a good one, where they saw both people and dwellings, they returned that night to the fleet, which had put into harbor at the other island,[285-3] and there the Admiral, accompanied by a great number of men, landed with the royal banner in his hands, and

---

[412] The island Marigalante, which was so called from the name of the ship in which Columbus sailed. *Historie, ibid.*

took formal possession on behalf of their Majesties. This island was filled with an astonishingly thick growth of wood; the variety of unknown trees, some bearing fruit and some flowers, was surprising, and indeed every spot was covered with verdure. We found there a tree whose leaf had the finest smell of cloves that I have ever met with; it was like a laurel leaf, but not so large: but I think it was a species of laurel. There were wild fruits of various kinds, some of which our men, not very prudently, tasted; and upon only touching them with their tongues, their countenances became inflamed[413] and such great heat and pain followed, that they seemed to be mad, and were obliged to resort to refrigerants to cure themselves. We found no signs of any people in this island, and concluded it was uninhabited; we remained only two hours, for it was very late when we landed, and on the following morning we left for another very large island,[414] situated below this at the distance of seven or eight leagues. We approached it under the side of a great mountain, that seemed almost to reach the skies, in the middle of which rose a peak, higher than all the rest of the mountain, whence many streams diverged into different channels, especially towards the part at which we arrived. At three leagues distance, we could see a fall of water as broad as an ox, which discharged itself from such a height that it appeared to fall from the sky; it was seen from so great a distance that it occasioned many wagers to be laid on board the ships, some maintaining that it was but a series of white rocks, and others that it was water. When we came nearer to it, it showed itself distinctly, and it was the most beautiful thing in the

---

[413] One would infer from this that it was the fruit of the *manzanillo*, which produces similar effects. (Navarrete.) On the Manzanillo (Manchineel), see Oviedo, lib. IX., cap. XII. He says the Caribs used it in making their arrow poisons.

[414] Guadeloupe.

444

world to see from how great a height and from what a small space so large a fall of water was discharged. As soon as we neared the island the Admiral ordered a light caravel to run along the coast to search for a harbor; the captain put into land in a boat, and seeing some houses, leapt on shore and went up to them, the inhabitants fleeing at sight of our men; he then went into the houses and there found various household articles that had been left unremoved, from which he took two parrots, very large and quite different from any we had before seen; he found a great quantity of cotton, both spun and prepared for spinning, and articles of food, of all of which he brought away a portion; besides these, he also brought away four or five bones of human arms and legs. On seeing these we suspected that we were amongst the Caribbee islands, whose inhabitants eat human flesh; for the Admiral, guided by the information respecting their situation which he had received from the Indians of the islands discovered in his former voyage, had directed his course with a view to their discovery, both because they were the nearest to Spain, and because this was the direct track for the island of Española, where he had left some of his people. Thither, by the goodness of God and the wise management of the Admiral, we came in as straight a track as if we had sailed by a well known and frequented route. This island is very large, and on the side where we arrived it seemed to us to be twenty-five leagues in length. We sailed more than two leagues along the shore in search of a harbor; on the part towards which we moved appeared very high mountains, and on that which we left extensive plains; on the sea-coast there were a few small villages, whose inhabitants fled as soon as they saw the sails: at length after proceeding two leagues we found a port late in the evening. That night the Admiral resolved that some of the men should land at break of day in order to confer with the natives, and learn what sort of people they were; although it was suspected, from the appearance of those who had fled at our approach, that they were naked, like those whom the Admiral had seen in his former voyage. That morning certain captains started out; one of them arrived at the dinner hour, and brought away a boy of about fourteen years of age, as it afterwards appeared, who said that he was one of the prisoners taken by these people. The others divided themselves, and one party took a little boy whom a man was leading by the hand, but who left him and fled; this boy they sent on board immediately with some of our men; others remained, and took certain women, natives of the island, together with other women from among the captives who came of their own accord One captain of this last company, not knowing that any intelligence of the people had been obtained, advanced farther into the island and lost himself, with the six men who accompanied him: they could not find their way back until after four days, when they lighted upon the sea-shore, and following the line of coast returned to the fleet.[415] We had already looked upon them as killed and eaten by the people that are called Caribbees; for we could not account for their long absence in any other way, since they had among them some pilots who by their knowledge of the stars could navigate either to or from Spain, so that we imagined that they could not lose themselves in so small a space. On this first day of our landing several men and women came on the beach up to the water's edge, and gazed at the ships in astonishment at so novel a sight;

---

[415] It was Diego Marquez, the inspector, who with eight other men went on shore into the interior of the island, without permission from the Admiral, who caused him to be sought for by parties of men with trumpets, but without success. One of those who were sent out with this object was Alonzo Ojeda, who took with him forty men, and on their return they reported that they had found many aromatic plants, a variety of birds, and some considerable rivers. The wanderers were not able to find their way to the ships until the 8th of November. [Navarrete, condensed from Las Casas, Historia de las Indias, II. 7-8.]

and when a boat pushed on shore in order to speak with them, they cried out, "tayno, tayno,"[416] which is as much as to say, "good, good," and waited for the landing of the sailors, standing by the boat in such a manner that they might escape when they pleased. The result was, that none of the men could be persuaded to join us, and only two were taken by force, who were secured and led away. More than twenty women of the captives were taken with their own consent, and other women, natives of the island, were surprised and carried off; several of the boys, who were captives, came to us fleeing from the natives of the island who had taken them prisoners. We remained eight days in this port in consequence of the loss of the aforesaid captain, and went many times on shore, passing amongst the dwellings and villages which were on the coast; we found a vast number of human bones and skulls hung up about the houses, like vessels intended for holding various things.[417] There were very few men to be seen here, and the women informed us that this was in consequence of ten canoes having gone to make an attack upon other islands. These islanders appeared to us to be more civilized than those that we had hitherto seen; for although all the Indians have houses of straw, yet the houses of these people are constructed in a much superior

---

[416] Tayno was also the tribal name of these people, who differentiated themselves from the Caribs. Peter Martyr reports the assertions of the followers of Guacamari that they were Taynos not Caribs: "Se Tainos, id est, nobiles esse, non Canibales, inclamitant." *De Rebus Oceanicis*, Dec. I., lib. II., p. 25. (Cologne ed. of 1574.)

[417] Las Casas, *Historia de las Indias*, II. 8, remarks of these bones, 'They must have belonged to lords or persons whom they loved since it is not probable that they belonged to those they ate, because if they ate as many as some say, the cabins would not hold all the bones and skulls, and it seems that after having eaten them there would be no object in keeping the skulls and bones for relics unless they belonged to some very notable enemies. The whole matter is a puzzle."

fashion, are better stocked with provisions, and exhibit more evidences of industry, both on the part of the men and the women. They had a considerable quantity of cotton, both spun and prepared for spinning, and many cotton sheets, so well woven as to be no way inferior to those of our country. We inquired of the women, who were prisoners in the island, what people these islanders were; they replied that they were Caribbees.

As soon as they learned that we abhorred such people,[418] on account of their evil practice of eating human flesh, they were much delighted; and, after that, if they brought forward any woman or man of the Caribbees, they informed us (but secretly) that they were such, still evincing by their dread of their conquerors, that they belonged to a vanquished nation, though they knew them all to be in our power.

We were enabled to distinguish which of the women were Caribbees, and which were not, by the Caribbees wearing on each leg two bands of woven cotton, the one fastened round the knee, and the other round the ankle; by this means they make the calves of their legs large, and the above-mentioned parts very small, which I imagine that they regard as a mark of elegance: by this peculiarity we distinguished them.[419] The habits of these Caribbees are brutal. There are three islands: this is called Turuqueira; the other, which was the first that we saw, is called Ceyre; the third is called Ayay:[420] all these are alike as if they were of one race, who do no injury to each other; but

---

[418] The name *Caribe* here obviously has begun to have the meaning "cannibal," which is in origin the same word.

[419] This practice still survives among the Caribs. Im Thurn describes it in almost the same words as Dr. Chanca. See *Among the Indians of Guiana*, p. 192.

[420] These are the native names for Dominica (Ceyre) and Guadeloupe (Turuqueira and Ayay), which consists of two islands separated by a narrow channel.

each and all of them wage war against the other
neighboring islands, and for the purpose of attacking
them, make voyages of a hundred and fifty leagues at sea,
with their numerous canoes, which are a small kind of
craft with one mast. Their arms are arrows, in the place of
iron weapons and as they have no iron, some of them
point their arrows with tortoise-shell, and others make
their arrow-heads of fish spines, which are naturally
barbed like coarse saws: these prove dangerous weapons
to a naked people like the Indians, and may cause death
or severe injury, but to men of our nation, are not very
formidable. In their attacks upon the neighboring
islands, these people capture as many of the women as
they can, especially those who are young and beautiful,
and keep them for servants and to have as concubines;
and so great a number do they carry off, that in fifty
houses no men were to be seen; and out of the number of
the captives, more than twenty were young girls. These
women also say that the Caribbees use them with such
cruelty as would scarcely be believed; and that they eat
the children which they bear to them, and only bring up
those which they have by their native wives. Such of their
male enemies as they can take alive, they bring to their
houses to slaughter them, and those who are killed they
devour at once. They say that man's flesh is so good, that
there is nothing like it in the world; and this is pretty
evident, for of the bones which we found in their houses,
they had gnawed everything that could be gnawed, so
that nothing remained of them, but what from its great
hardness, could not be eaten: in one of the houses we
found the neck of a man, cooking in a pot. When they take
any boys prisoners, they cut off their member and make
use of them as servants until they grow up to manhood,
and then when they wish to make a feast they kill and eat
them; for they say that the flesh of boys and women is

not good to eat. Three of these boys came fleeing to us thus mutilated.

At the end of four days arrived the captain who had lost himself with his companions, of whose return we had by this time given up all hope; for other parties had been twice sent out to seek him, one of which came back on the same day that he rejoined us, without having gained any information respecting the wanderers; we rejoiced at their arrival, regarding it as a new accession to our numbers. The captain and the men who accompanied him brought back some women and boys, ten in number. Neither this party, nor those who went out to seek them, had seen any of the men of the island, which must have arisen either from their having fled, or possibly from there being but very few men in that locality; for, as the women informed us, ten canoes had gone away to make an attack upon the neighboring islands. The wanderers had returned from the mountains in such an emaciated condition, that it was distressing to see them; when we asked them how it was that they lost themselves, they said that the trees were so thick and close that they could not see the sky; some of them who were mariners had climbed the trees to get a sight of the stars, but could never see them, and if they had not found their way to the sea-coast, it would have been impossible to have returned to the fleet. We left this island eight days after our arrival.[421] The next day at noon we saw another island, not very large,[422] at about twelve leagues distance from the one we were leaving; the greater part of the first day of our departure we were kept close in to the coast of this island by a calm, but as the Indian women whom we brought with us said that it was not inhabited, but had been dispeopled by the Caribbees, we made no stay in it. On that evening we saw

---

[421] They left on Sunday, the 10th of November. Las Casas, *Historia*, II. 9.

[422] The island Montserrat. Las Casas, *ibid.*

another island;[423] and in the night finding there were some sandbanks near, we dropped anchor, not venturing to proceed until the morning. On the morrow another island appeared, of considerable size, but we touched at none of these because we were anxious to convey consolation to our people who had been left in Española; but it did not please God to grant us our desire, as will hereafter appear. Another day at the dinner hour we arrived at an island which seemed to be worth the finding, for judging by the extent of cultivation in it, it appeared very populous. We went thither and put into harbor, when the Admiral immediately sent on shore a well manned barge to hold speech with the Indians, in order to ascertain what race they were, and also because we considered it necessary to gain some information respecting our course; although it afterwards plainly appeared that the Admiral, who had never made that passage before, had taken a very correct route. But as matters of doubt should always be brought to as great a certainty as possible by inquiry, he wished that communication should be held with the natives at once, and some of the men who went in the barge leapt on shore and went up to a village, whence the inhabitants had already withdrawn and hidden themselves. They took in this island five or six women and some boys, most of whom were captives, like those in the other island; we learned from the women whom we had brought with us, that the natives of this place also were Caribbees. As this barge was about to return to the ships with the capture which they had made, a canoe came along the coast containing four men, two women, and a boy; and when they saw the fleet they were so stupefied with amazement, that for a good hour they remained motionless at the distance of nearly two cannon shots

---

[423] The island of St. Martin. Las Casas, *ibid.*

from the ships. In this position they were seen by those who were in the barge and also by all the fleet. Meanwhile those in the barge moved towards the canoe, but so close in shore, that the Indians, in their perplexity and astonishment as to what all this could mean, never saw them, until they were so near that escape was impossible; for our men pressed on them so rapidly that they could not get away, although they made considerable effort to do so.

When the Caribbees saw that all attempt at flight was useless, they most courageously took to their bows, both women and men; I say most courageously, because they were only four men and two women, and our people were twenty-five in number. Two of our men were wounded by the Indians, one with two arrow-shots in his breast, and another with one in his side, and if it had not happened that they carried shields and wooden bucklers, and that they soon got near them with the barge and upset their canoe, most of them would have been killed with their arrows. After their canoe was upset, they remained in the water swimming and occasionally wading (for there were shallows in that part), still using their bows as much as they could, so that our men had enough to do to take them; and after all there was one of them whom they were unable to secure till he had received a mortal wound with a lance, and whom thus wounded they took to the ships. The difference between these Caribbees and the other Indians, with respect to dress, consists in their wearing their hair very long, while the latter have it clipt and paint their heads with crosses and a hundred thousand different devices, each according to his fancy; which they do with sharpened reeds. All of them, both the Caribbees and the others, are beardless, so that it is a rare thing to find a man with a beard: the Caribbees whom we took had their eyes and eyebrows stained, which I imagine they do from ostentation and to give them a more frightful appearance. One of these captives said, that in an island belonging to them called Cayre[424] (which is the first we saw, though we did not go to it), there is a great quantity of gold; and that if we were to take them nails and tools with which to make their canoes, we might bring away as much gold as we liked. On the same day we left that island, having been there no more than six or seven hours; and steering for another point of land[425] which appeared to lie in our intended course, we reached it by night. On the morning of the following day we coasted along it, and found it to be a large extent of country, but not continuous for it was divided into more than forty islets.[426] The land was very high and most of it barren, an appearance which we have never observed in any of the islands visited by us before or since: the surface of the ground seemed to suggest the probability of its containing metals. None of us went on shore here, but a small latteen caravel went up to one of the islets and found in it some fishermen's huts; the Indian women whom we brought with us said they were not inhabited. We proceeded along the coast the greater part of that day, and on the evening of the next we discovered another island called Burenquen,[427] which we judged to be thirty leagues in length, for we were coasting along it the whole of one day. This island is very beautiful and apparently fertile; hither the Caribbees come with the view of subduing the inhabitants, and often carry away many of the people. These islanders have no boats nor any knowledge of

---

[424] Dominica.

[425] Santa Cruz. November 14. Las Casas, *ibid*.

[426] The Admiral named the largest of these islands St. Ursula, and all the others The Eleven Thousand Virgins. Las Casas, *Historia*, II. 10.

[427] The island of Porto Rico, to which the Admiral "gave the name of St. John the Baptist, which we now call Sant Juan and which the Indians called Boriquen." Las Casas, II. 10.

navigation; but, as our captives inform us, they use bows as well as the Caribbees, and if by chance when they are attacked they succeed in taking any of their invaders, they will eat them in like manner as the Caribbees themselves in the contrary event would devour them. We remained two days in this island, and a great number of our men went on shore, but could never get speech of the natives, who had all fled, from fear of the Caribbees. All the above-mentioned islands were discovered in this voyage, the Admiral having seen nothing of them in his former voyage; they are all very beautiful and possess a most luxuriant soil, but this last island appeared to exceed all the others in beauty. Here terminated the islands, which on the side towards Spain had not been seen before by the Admiral, although we regard it as a matter of certainty that there is land more than forty leagues beyond the foremost of these newly discovered islands, on the side nearest to Spain. We believe this to be the case, because two days before we saw land we observed some birds called rabihorcados,[428] marine birds of prey which do not sit or sleep upon the water, making circumvolutions in the air at the close of evening previous to taking their flight towards land for the night. These birds could not be going to settle at more than twelve or fifteen leagues distance, because it was late in the evening, and this was on our right hand on the side towards Spain; from which we all judged that there was land there still undiscovered; but we did not go in search of it, because it would have taken us round out of our intended route. I hope that in a few voyages it will be discovered. It was at dawn that we left the before-mentioned island of Burenquen,[429] and on that day before nightfall we caught sight of land, which though not

---

[428] See note to Journal, September 29. Frigate-bird is the accepted English name; a species of pelican.
[429] Porto Rico.

recognized by any of those who had come hither in the former voyage, we believed to be Española, from the information given us by the Indian women whom we had with us; and in this island we remain at present.[430] Between this island and Burenquen another island appeared at a distance, but of no great size. When we reached Española the land, at the part where we approached it, was low and very flat,[431] on seeing which, a general doubt arose as to its identity; for neither the Admiral nor his companions, on the previous voyage, had seen it on this side.

The island being large, is divided into provinces; the part which we first touched at, is called Hayti; another province adjoining it, they call Xamaná;[432] and the next province is named Bohio,[433] where we now are. These provinces are again subdivided, for they are of great extent. Those who have seen the length of its coast, state that it is two hundred leagues long, and I myself should judge it not to be less than a hundred and fifty leagues: as to its breadth, nothing is hitherto known; it is now forty days since a caravel left us with the view of circumnavigating it,[434] and is not yet returned. The country is very remarkable, and contains a vast number of large rivers, and extensive chains of mountains, with broad open valleys, and the mountains are very high; it does not appear that the grass is ever cut throughout the

---

[430] On Friday, the 22d of November, the Admiral first caught sight of the island of Española. Las Casas, II. 10.

[431] Cape Engaño, in the island of Española. (Navarrete.)

[432] Preserved in the Bay of Samana.

[433] See Journal, October 21. and note.

[434] Of this voyage of exploration there seems to be no record. Our natural sources, the *Historie* and Las Casas, are silent. Columbus suspended his writing in his Journal from December 11, 1493, till March 12, 1494. Antonio de Torres sailed for Spain February 2, 1494, when Dr. Chanca sent off his letter. Probably this exploration was begun about December 20.

year. I do not think they have any winter in this part, for at Christmas were found many birds-nests, some containing the young birds, and others containing eggs. No four-footed animal has ever been seen in this or any of the other islands, except some dogs of various colors, as in our own country, but in shape like large house-dogs;[435] and also some little animals, in color and fur like a rabbit, and the size of a young rabbit, with long tails, and feet like those of a rat; these animals climb up the trees, and many who have tasted them, say they are very good to eat:[436] there are not any wild beasts.

There are great numbers of small snakes, and some lizards, but not many; for the Indians consider them as great a luxury as we do pheasants; they are of the same size as ours, but different in shape. In a small adjacent island[437] (close by a harbor called Monte Cristo, where we stayed several days), our men saw an enormous kind of lizard, which they said was as large round as a calf, with a tail as long as a lance, which they often went out to kill: but bulky as it was, it got into the sea, so that they could not catch it.[438] There are, both in this and the other islands, an infinite number of birds like those in our own country, and many others such as we had never seen. No

---

[435] *Unos gosques grandes.* The French translation has *gros carlins,* "large pug-dogs." Bernaldez calls these dogs, *gozcos pequeños,* "small curs." "Cur" is the common meaning for *gozque* or *gosque.* See Oviedo, lib. XII., cap. V., for a description of these native dogs which soon became extinct.

[436] Bernaldez, II. 34, supplies the native name, *Utia.* Oviedo, lib. XII., cap. I., describes the _hutia_. When he wrote it had become so scarce as to be seen only on rare occasions. It was extinct in Du Tertre's time, a century later. Of the four allied species described by Oviedo, the *hutia,* the *quemi,* the *mohuy,* and the *cori* (agouti), only the last has survived to the present day.

[437] Cabra, or Goat Island, between Puerto de Plata and Cas Rouge Point. (Major.)

[438] Apparently the cayman or South American alligator.

kind of domestic fowl has been seen here, with the exception of some ducks in the houses in Zuruquia; these ducks were larger than those of Spain, though smaller than geese,--very pretty, with flat crests on their heads, most of them as white as snow, but some black.

We ran along the coast of this island nearly a hundred leagues, concluding, that within this range we should find the spot where the Admiral had left some of his men, and which we supposed to be about the middle of the coast. As we passed by the province called Xamaná, we sent on shore one of the Indians, who had been taken in the previous voyage, clothed, and carrying some trifles, which the Admiral had ordered to be given him. On that day died one of our sailors, a Biscayan, who had been wounded in the affray with the Caribbees, when they were captured, as I have already described, through their want of caution. As we were proceeding along the coast, an opportunity was afforded for a boat to go on shore to bury him, the boat being accompanied by two caravels to protect it. When they reached the shore, a great number of Indians came out to the boat, some of them wearing necklaces and ear-rings of gold, and expressed a wish to accompany the Spaniards to the ships; but our men refused to take them, because they had not received permission from the Admiral. When the Indians found that they would not take them, two of them got into a small canoe, and went up to one of the caravels that had put in to shore; they were received on board with great kindness, and taken to the Admiral's ship, where, through the medium of an interpreter, they related that a certain king had sent them to ascertain who we were, and to invite us to land, adding that they had plenty of gold, and also of provisions, to which we should be welcome. The Admiral desired that shirts, and caps, and other trifles, should be given to each of them, and said that as he was going to the place where Guacamari dwelt, he would not stop then, but that another time there would be an opportunity of seeing him, and with that they departed. We continued our route till we came to an harbor called Monte Cristi, where we remained two days, in order to observe the character of the land; for the Admiral had an objection to the spot where his men had been left with the view of making a settlement. We went on shore therefore to see the character of the land: there was a large river of excellent water close by;[439] but the ground was inundated, and very ill-calculated for habitation. As we went on making our observations on the river and the land, some of our men found two dead bodies by the river's side, one with a rope round his neck, and the other with one round his foot; this was on the first day of our landing. On the following day they found two other corpses farther on, and one of these was observed to have a great quantity of beard; this was regarded as a very suspicious circumstance by many of our people, because, as I have already said, all the Indians are beardless. This harbor is twelve leagues[440] from the place where the Spaniards had been left under the protection of Guacamari,[441] the king of that province, whom I suppose to be one of the chief men of the island. After two days we set sail for that spot, but as it was late when we arrived there,[442] and there were some shoals, where the Admiral's ship had been lost, we did not venture to put in close to the shore, but remained that night at a little less than a league from the coast, waiting until the morning, when we might enter securely. On that evening, a canoe, containing five or six Indians,

---

[439] The river Yaque.

[440] The river Yaque.

[441] This chief's name is Guacanagari in Las Casas, *Historia de las Indias*, and in the *Histori* of Ferdinand Columbus, Goathanari in the Syllacio-Coma letter, Guacanari in Bernaldez and Guaccanarillus in Peter Martyr's *De Rebus Oceanicis*.

[442] The admiral anchored at the entrance of the harbor of Navidad, on Wednesday, the 27th of November, towards midnight. Las Casas, II. 11.

came out at a considerable distance from where we were, and approached us with great celerity. The Admiral believing that he insured our safety by keeping the sails set, would not wait for them; they, however, perseveringly rowed up to us within a cannon shot[443] and then stopped to look at us; but when they saw that we did not wait for them, they put back and went away. After we had anchored that night at the spot in question,[444] the Admiral ordered two cannons to be fired, to see if the Spaniards, who had remained with Guacamari, would fire in return, for they also had cannons with them; but when we received no reply, and could not perceive any fires, nor the slightest symptom of habitations on the spot, the spirits of our people became much depressed, and they began to entertain the suspicion which the circumstances were naturally calculated to excite. While all were in this desponding mood, and when four or five hours of the night had passed away, the same canoe which we had seen in the evening, came up, and the Indians with a loud voice addressed the captain of the caravel, which they first approached, inquiring for the Admiral;[445] they were conducted to the Admiral's vessel, but would not go on board till he had spoken to them, and they had asked for a light, in order to assure themselves that it was he who conversed with them. One of them was a cousin of Guacamari, who had been sent by him once before: it appeared, that after they had turned back the previous evening, they had been charged by Guacamari with two masks of gold as a present; one for the Admiral, the other for a captain who had accompanied him on the former voyage. They remained on board for three hours,

---

[443] See Journal of First Voyage, December 25.

[444] The Bay of Caracol, four leagues west of Fort Dauphin. (Major.)

[445] "Toward midnight a canoe came full of Indians and reached the ship of the Admiral, and they called for him saying 'Almirante, Almirante.'" Las Casas, II. 11.

talking with the Admiral in the presence of all of us, he showing much pleasure in their conversation, and inquiring respecting the welfare of the Spaniards whom he had left behind. Guacamari's cousin replied, that those who remained were all well, but that some of them had died of disease, and others had been killed in quarrels that had arisen amongst them; and that Guacamari was at some distance, lying ill of a wound in his leg, which was the occasion of his not appearing, but that he would come on the next day. He said also that two kings named Caonabó and Mayreni, had come to fight with him and that they had burned the village. The Indians then departed, saying they would return on the following day with the said Guacamari, and left us consoled for that night. On the morning of the next day, we were expecting that Guacamari would come; and, in the meantime, some of our men landed by command of the Admiral, and went to the spot where the Spaniards had formerly been: they found the building which they had inhabited, and which they had in some degree fortified with a palisade, burnt and levelled with the ground; they found also some cloaks and clothing which the Indians had brought to throw upon the house. They observed too that the Indians who were seen near the spot, looked very shy, and dared not approach, but, on the contrary, fled from them. This appeared strange to us, for the Admiral had told us that in the former voyage, when he arrived at this place, so many came in canoes to see us, that there was no keeping them off; and as we now saw that they were suspicious of us, it gave us a very unfavorable impression. We threw trifles, such as hawk bells[446] and beads, towards them, in order to conciliate them, but only four, a relation of Guacamari's and three others, took courage to enter the

---

[446] The hawk bell was a small open bell used in hawking. The discoverers used hawk bells as a small measure as of gold dust.

boat, and were rowed on board. When they were asked concerning the Spaniards, they replied that all of them were dead; we had been told this already by one of the Indians whom we had brought from Spain, and who had conversed with the two Indians that on the former occasion came on board with their canoe, but we had not believed it. Guacamari's kinsman was asked who had killed them; he replied that the king of Caonabó and king Mayreni had made an attack upon them, and burnt the buildings on the spot, that many were wounded in the affray, and among them Guacamari, who had received a wound in his thigh, and had retired to some distance. He also stated that he wished to go and fetch him; upon which some trifles were given to him, and he took his departure for the place of Guacamari's abode. All that day we remained in expectation of them, and when we saw that they did not come, many suspected that the Indians who had been on board the night before, had been drowned; for they had had wine given them two or three times, and they had come in a small canoe that might be easily upset. The next morning the Admiral went on shore, taking some of us with him; we went to the spot where the settlement had been, and found it utterly destroyed by fire, and the clothes of the Spaniards lying about upon the grass, but on that occasion we saw no dead body. There were many different opinions amongst us; some suspecting that Guacamari himself was concerned in the betrayal and death of the Christians; others thought not, because his own residence was burnt: so that it remained a very doubtful question. The Admiral ordered all the ground which had been occupied by the fortifications of the Spaniards to be searched, for he had left orders with them to bury all the gold that they might get. While this was being done, the Admiral wished to examine a spot at about a league's distance, which seemed to be suitable for building a town, for it was already time to do so;--and some of us went thither with him, making our observations of the land as we went along the coast, until we reached a village of seven or eight houses, which the Indians forsook when they saw us approach, carrying away what they could, and leaving the things which they could not remove, hidden amongst the grass, around the houses. These people are so like beasts that they have not even the sense to select a fitting place to live in; those who dwell on the shore, build for themselves the most miserable hovels that can be imagined, and all the houses are so covered with grass and dampness, that I am amazed at the way they live. In these houses we found many things belonging to the Spaniards, which it could not be supposed they would have bartered; such as a very handsome Moorish mantle which had not been unfolded since it was brought from Spain, stockings and pieces of cloth, also an anchor belonging to the ship which the Admiral had lost here on the previous voyage; with other articles, which the more confirmed our suspicions. On examining some things which had been put away to keep in a basket, closely woven and very secure, we found a man's head kept with great care; this we judged might be the head of a father, or mother, or of some person whom they much regarded: I have since heard that many were found in the same state, which makes me believe that our first impression was the true one. After this we returned. We went on the same day to the site of the settlement; and when we arrived, we found many Indians, who had regained their courage, bartering gold with our men: they had bartered to the extent of a mark;[447] we also learned that they had shown where the bodies of eleven of the dead Spaniards were laid, which were already covered with the grass that

---

[447] The mark was a weight of eight ounces, two-thirds of a Troy pound. The mark of gold in Spain was equivalent to 50 castellanos, or in bullion value to-day about $150.

had grown over them; and they all with one voice asserted that Caonabó and Mayreni had killed them; but notwithstanding all this, we began to hear complaints that one of the Spaniards had taken three women to himself, and another four; from whence we drew the inference that jealousy was the cause of the misfortune that had occurred. On the next morning, as no spot in that vicinity appeared suitable for our making a settlement, the Admiral ordered a caravel to go in one direction to look for a convenient locality, while some of us went with him another way. In the course of our explorations, we discovered a harbor, of great security, and a very favorable situation for a settlement; but as it was far from where we wanted to have the gold mine, the Admiral decided to settle only in some spot which would give us greater certainty of attaining that object, provided the position of the land should prove equally convenient. On our return, we found the other caravel arrived, in which Melchior[448] and four or five other trustworthy men had been exploring with a similar object. They reported that as they went along the coast, a canoe came out to them in which were two Indians, one of whom was the brother of Guacamari, and was recognized by a pilot who was in the caravel. When he asked them "who goes there," they replied that Guacamari sent to beg the Spaniards to come on shore, as he had his settlement near, with nearly fifty houses. The chief men of the party then went on shore in the boat, proceeded to the place where Guacamari was, and found him stretched on his bed, complaining of a severe wound. They conferred with him, and inquired respecting the Spaniards; his reply was, in accordance with the account already given by the

---

[448] Melchior Maldonado, apparently the Melchiorius from whom Peter Martyr derived some of his material for his account of the second voyage. See his *De Rebus Oceanicis*, ed. 1574, p. 26.

others, viz.--that they had been killed by Caonabó and Mayreni, who also had wounded him in the thigh; which he showed to them bandaged up: on seeing which, they concluded that his statement was correct. At their departure he gave to each of them a jewel of gold, according to his estimation of their respective merits. The Indians beat the gold into very thin plates, in order to make masks of it, and to be able to set it in bitumen; if it were not so prepared it could not be mounted; other ornaments they make of it, to wear on the head and to hang in the ears and nostrils, for these also they require it to be thin; since they set no store by it as wealth but only for adornment. Guacamari desired them by signs and as well as he was able, to tell the Admiral that as he was thus wounded, he prayed him to have the goodness to come to see him. The sailors told this to the Admiral when he arrived. The next morning he resolved to go thither, for the spot could be reached in three hours, being scarcely three leagues distance from the place where we were; but as it would be the dinner-hour when we arrived, we dined before we went on shore. After dinner, the Admiral gave orders that all the captains should come with their barges to proceed to the shore, for already on that morning, previous to our departure, the aforesaid brother of Guacamari had come to speak with the Admiral to urge him to come to the place where Guacamari was. Then the Admiral went on shore accompanied by all the principal officers, so richly dressed that they would have made a fine appearance even in any of our chief cities. He took with him some articles as presents, having already received from Guacamari a certain quantity of gold, and it was reasonable that he should make a commensurate response to his acts and expressions of good-will: Guacamari had also provided himself with a present. When we arrived, we found him stretched upon his bed, which was made of cotton network, and, according to their custom, suspended.[449] He did not arise, but made from his bed the best gesture of courtesy of which he was capable. He showed much feeling with tears in his eyes for the death of the Spaniards, and began speaking on the subject, with explaining to the best of his power, how some died of disease, others had gone to Caonabó in search of the mine of gold, and had there been killed, and that the rest had been attacked and slain in their own town. According to the appearance of the dead bodies, it was not two months since this had happened. Then he presented the Admiral with eight marks and a half of gold and five or six belts worked with stones[450] of various colors, and a cap of similar jewel-work, which I think they must value very highly, because in it was a jewel, which was presented to him with great reverence. It appears to me that these people put more value upon copper than gold. The surgeon of the fleet and myself being present,

---

[449] The familiar hammock.

[450] The original reads "cinco o seiscientos labrados de pedreria," which Major translated "five or six hundred pieces of jewellery," and Thacher "five or six hundred cut stones." The dictionaries recognize *labrado* as a noun only in the plural *labrados*, "tilled lands." Turning to Bernaldez, *Historia de los Reyes Catolicos*, in which Dr. Chanca's letter was copied almost bodily, we find, II. 27, "cinco ó seis labrados de pedreria," which presents the ame difficulty. The omission of *cientos* is notable, however. I think the original text of Dr. Chanca's letter read "cinco ó seis cintos labrados de pedreria," i.e., five or six belts worked with jewellery. *Cintos* being written blindly was copied *cientos* by Antonio de Aspa, from whom our text of Dr. Chanca's letter has come down (Navarrete, I. 224), and was omitted perhaps accidentally in Bernaldez's copy. This conjecture is rendered almost certain by the *Historie*, where it is recorded that "the Cacique gave the Admiral eight belts worked with small beads made of white, green, and red stones," p. 148, London ed. of 1867. This passage enables us to correct the text of Las Casas, II. 14, changing "ochocientas cuentas menudas de piedra," "eight hundred small beads of stone," to "ocho cintos de cuentas menudas," etc., "eight belts of small beads," and again, *ciento de oro* to *cinto de oro*. In the Syllacio-Coma letter the gift is *balteos duodecim*, "twelve belts." Thacher, *Columbus*, II. 235. Cf. Las Casas's description of the girdle or belt that this chief wore when Columbus first saw him, Dec. 22, above, p. 194.

the Admiral told Guacamari that we were skilled in the treatment of human disorders, and wished that he would shew us his wound; he replied that he was willing; upon which I said it would be necessary that he should, if possible, go out of the house, because we could not see well on account of the place being darkened by the crowd of people; to this he consented, I think more from timidity than inclination, and left the house leaning on the arm of the Admiral. After he was seated, the surgeon approached him and began to untie the bandage; then he told the Admiral that the wound was made with a *ciba*, by which he meant with a stone. When the wound was uncovered, we went up to examine it: it is certain that there was no more wound on that leg than on the other, although he cunningly pretended that it pained him much. Ignorant as we were of the facts, it was impossible to come to a definite conclusion. There were certainly many proofs of an invasion by a hostile people, so that the Admiral was at a loss what to do; he with many others thought, however, that for the present, and until they could ascertain the truth, they ought to conceal their distrust; for after ascertaining it, they would be able to claim whatever indemnity they thought proper. That evening Guacamari accompanied the Admiral to the ships, and when they showed him the horses and other objects of interest, their novelty struck him with the greatest amazement;[451] he took supper on board, and returned that evening to his house. The Admiral told him that he wished to settle there and to build houses; to which he assented but said that the place was not wholesome, because it was very damp: and so it most certainly was.

---

[451] These were not only the first horses seen in the New World since the extinction of the prehistoric varieties, but the first large quadrupeds the West Indians had seen.

All this passed through the interpretation of two of the Indians who had gone to Spain in the last voyage, and who were the sole survivors of seven who had embarked with us; five died on the voyage, and these but narrowly escaped. The next day we anchored in that port: Guacamari sent to know when the Admiral intended leaving, and was told that he would do so on the morrow. The same day Guacamari's brother, and others with him, came on board, bringing gold to barter: on the day of our departure also they bartered a great quantity of gold. There were ten women on board, of those who had been taken in the Caribbee islands, principally from Boriquen, and it was observed that the brother of Guacamari spoke with them; we think that he told them to make an effort to escape that night; for certainly during our first sleep they dropped themselves quietly into the water, and went on shore, so that by the time they were missed they had reached such a distance that only four could be taken by the boats which went in pursuit, and these were secured when just leaving the water: they had to swim considerably more than half a league. The next morning the Admiral sent to desire that Guacamari would cause search to be made for the women who had escaped in the night, and that he would send them back to the ships. When the messengers arrived they found the place forsaken and not a soul there; this made many openly declare their suspicions, but others said they might have removed to another village, as was their custom. That day we remained quiet, because the weather was unfavorable for our departure. On the next morning the Admiral resolved that as the wind was adverse, it would be well to go with the boats to inspect a harbor on the coast at two leagues distance further up,[452] to see if the formation of the land was favorable for a settlement;

---

[452] Port Dauphin. (Navarrete.)

and we went thither with all the ship's boats, leaving the ships in the harbor. As we moved along the coast the people manifested a sense of insecurity, and when we reached the spot to which we were bound all the natives had fled. While we were walking about this place we found an Indian stretched on the hill-side, close by the houses, with a gaping wound in his shoulder caused by a dart, so that he had been disabled from fleeing any further. The natives of this island fight with sharp darts, which they shoot with straps in the same manner as boys in Spain shoot their little darts, and with these they shoot with considerable skill to a great distance; and certainly upon an unarmed people these weapons are calculated to do serious injury. The man told us that Caonabó and his people had wounded him and burnt the houses of Guacamari. Thus we are still kept in uncertainty respecting the death of our people, on account of the paucity of information on which to form an opinion, and the conflicting and equivocal character of the evidence we have obtained. We did not find the position of the land in this port favorable for healthy habitation, and the Admiral resolved upon returning along the upper coast by which we had come from Spain, because we had had tidings of gold in that direction. But the weather was so adverse that it cost more labor to sail thirty leagues in a backward direction than the whole voyage from Spain; so that, what with the contrary wind and the length of the passage, three months had elapsed when we landed.[453] It pleased God, however, that through the check upon our progress caused by contrary winds, we succeeded in finding the best and most suitable spot that we could have selected for a settlement, where there was an excellent

---

[453] That is, three months from the time the fleet left Spain, September 25, 1493. Neither the *Historie* nor Las Casas mentions the date of landing. In the Syllacio-Coma letter the date is given as "eight days from Christmas." See Thacher, *Columbus*, II. 236, 257.

harbor[454] and abundance of fish, an article of which we stand in great need from the scarcity of meat. The fish caught here are very singular and more wholesome than those of Spain. The climate does not allow the fish to be kept from one day to another, for it is hot and moist, so that all animal food[455] spoils very quickly. The land is very rich for all purposes; near the harbor there are two rivers: one large,[456] and another of moderate breadth somewhat near it; the water is of a very remarkable quality. On the bank of it is being built a city called Marta,[457] one side of which is bounded by the water with a ravine of cleft rock so that at that part there is no need of fortification; the other half is girt with a plantation of trees so thick that a rabbit could scarcely pass through it; and so green that fire will never be able to burn it. A channel has been commenced for a branch of the river, which the managers say they will lead through the middle of the settlement, and will place on it grist-mills and saw-mills and mills of other kinds requiring to be worked by water. Great quantities of vegetables have been planted, which certainly attain a more luxuriant growth here in eight days than they would in Spain in twenty. We are frequently visited by numbers of Indians, among whom are some of their *caciques* or chiefs, and many women.

---

[454] Port Isabelique, or Isabella, ten leagues to the east of Monte Cristi. (Navarrete.)

[455] *Cosas introfatibles* in the Spanish. The translation follows the French version. The text perhaps is corrupt. The word *introfatibles* is not found in any of the Spanish dictionaries nor is it a learned compound whose meaning is apparent from its etymology. Professor H.R. Lang suggests that *cosas corruptibles* may be the proper reading. The sentence is omitted in the corresponding passage in Bernaldez, II. 30.

[456] The river Isabella.

[457] I can offer no explanation for this name, which is found only in Dr. Chanca's letter. Bernaldez, who copied Dr. Chanca, gives Isabela as the name of the city, II. 30, and the *Historie* and Las Casas, who preserve for us the gist of Columbus's own narrative, both say that "he named the city Isabela in memory of Queen Isabela." Las Casas, II. 21. *Historie*, p. 150.

They all come loaded with *ages*,[458] which are like turnips, very excellent for food, which we dressed in various ways. This food was so nutritious as to prove a great support to all of us after the privations we endured when at sea, which were more severe than ever were suffered by man; for as we could not tell what weather it would please God to send us on our voyage, we were obliged to limit ourselves most rigorously with regard to food, in order that, at all events, we might at least have the means of supporting life.

This *age* the Caribbees call *nabi*, and the Indians *hage*.[459] The Indians barter gold, provisions, and everything they bring with them, for tips of lacings, beads, and pins, and pieces of porringers and dishes. They all, as I have said, go naked as they were born, except the women of this island, who have their private parts covered, some with a covering of cotton, which they bind round their hips, while others use grass and leaves of trees.[460] When they wish to adorn themselves, both men and women paint themselves, some black, others white, and various colors, in so many devices that the effect is very laughable;[461] they shave some parts of their heads, and in others wear long tufts of matted hair, which have an indescribably ridiculous appearance: in short, whatever would be looked upon in our country as characteristic of a madman, is here regarded by the highest of the Indians as a mark of distinction.

---

[458] Yams, the *Dioscorea sativa*. Columbus had seen the yam in Guinea an applied the African negro name, *igname*, *ñame*, whence the English, yam. See note to Journal, November 4.

[459] By the Indians Dr. Chanca means the Tainos, the native inhabitants of Española.

[460] "Every woman wears a tiny apron called a *queyu*, suspended by tying its strings around her waist." Im Thurn, *Among the Indians of Guiana*, 194.

[461] On this body painting, see Im Thurn, *ibid*.

In our present position, we are in the neighborhood of many mines of gold, not one of which, we are told, is more than twenty or twenty-five leagues off: the Indians say that some of them are in Niti, in the possession of Caonabó, who killed the Christians; the others are in another place called Cibao, which, if it please God, we shall see with our eyes before many days are over; indeed we should go there at once, but that we have so many things to provide that we are not equal to it at present. One third of our people have fallen sick within the last four or five days, which I think has principally arisen from the toil and privations of the journey; another cause has been the variableness of the climate; but I hope in our Lord that all will be restored to health. My idea of this people is, that if we could converse with them, they would all become converted, for they do whatever they see us do, making genuflections before the altars at the *Ave Maria* and the other parts of the devotional service, and making the sign of the cross. They all say that they wish to be Christians, although in truth they are idolaters, for in their houses they have many kinds of figures; when asked what such a figure was, they would reply it is a thing of *Turey*, by which they meant "of Heaven." I made a pretence of throwing them on the fire, which grieved them so that they began to weep: they believe that everything we bring comes from Heaven, and therefore call it *Turey*, which, as I have already said, means heaven in their language. The first day that I went on shore to sleep, was the Lord's day. The little time that we have spent on land, has been so much occupied in seeking for a fitting spot for the settlement, and in providing necessaries, that we have had little opportunity of becoming acquainted with the products of the soil, yet although the time has been so short, many marvellous things have been seen. We have met with trees bearing wool, of a sufficiently fine quality (according to the opinion of those who are acquainted with the art) to be woven into good cloth; there are so many of these trees that we might load the caravels with wool, although it is troublesome to collect, for the trees are very thorny,[462] but some means may be easily found of overcoming this difficulty. There are also cotton trees, perennials, as large as peach trees, which produce cotton in the greatest abundance.[463] We found trees producing wax as good both in color and smell as bees-wax and equally useful for burning; indeed there is no great difference between them.[464] There are vast numbers of trees which yield surprisingly fine turpentine; and there is also a great abundance of tragacanth, also very good. We found other trees which I think bear nutmegs, because the bark tastes and smells like that spice, but at present there is no fruit on them; I saw one root of ginger, which an Indian wore hanging round his neck. There are also aloes; not like those which we have hitherto seen in Spain, but no doubt they are one of the species used by us doctors.[465] A sort of cinnamon also has been found; but, to tell the truth, it is not so fine as that with which we are already acquainted in Spain. I do not know whether this arises from ignorance of the proper season to gather it, or whether the soil does not produce better. We have also seen some lemon-colored myrobolans; at this season they are all lying under the trees, and have a bitter flavor, arising, I think, from the rottenness occasioned by the moisture of the ground; but the taste of such parts as

---

[462] A species of the N.O. *Bombaceae*; perhaps the *Eriodendron anfractuosum*. (Major.) The English name is silk-cotton tree. The fibre, however, cannot be woven. Von Martius suggests the *Bombax ceiba*.

[463] *Cf*. Hazard, *Santo Domingo*, p. 350, "the cotton plant which instead of being a simple bush planted from the seed each year, is here a tree, growing two or three years, which needs only to be trimmed and pruned to produce a large yield of the finest cotton."

[464] Probably the so-called Carnauba wax or perhaps palm-tree wax. *Cf*. the *Encyclopædia Britannica*, art. "Wax."

[465] The Spanish here is *linaloe*, but the reference seems to be to the medicinal aloes and not to lign aloes. On lign aloes, see Columbus's Journal, November 12, and note.

have remained sound, is that of the genuine myrobolan.[466] There is also very good mastic.[467] None of the natives of these islands, as far as we have yet seen, possess any iron; they have, however, many tools, such as axes and adzes, made of stone, which are so handsome and well finished, that it is wonderful how they contrive to make them without the use of iron. Their food consists of bread, made of the roots of a vegetable which is between a tree and a vegetable, and the *age*,[468] which I have already described as being like the turnip, and very good food; they use, to season it, a spice called *agi*,[469] which they also eat with fish, and such birds as they can catch of the many kinds which abound in the island. They have, besides, a kind of grain like hazel-nuts very good to eat. They eat all the snakes, and lizards, and spiders, and worms, that they find upon the ground;[470] so that, to my fancy, their bestiality is greater than that of any beast upon the face of the earth. The Admiral had at one time determined to leave the search for the mines until he had first despatched the ships which were to return to Spain, on account of the great sickness which

---

[466] The myrobolan is an East Indian fruit with a stone, of the prune genus. Crude or preserved myrobolans were a more important article of commerce in the Middle Ages than now. There were five varieties, one of which, the *Mirobalani citrini*, were so named because they were lemon-colored. Heyd, *Histoire du Commerce du Levant au Moyen-Age*, II. 641. A species of myrobolan grows in South America.

[467] The product of the *Bursera gummifera*.

[468] *Cf.* Columbus's Journal, November 4, and note.

[469] *Agi*, also written *Axi*, is the *Capsicum annuum* or Spanish pepper. Most of the cayenne or red pepper of commerce comes from the allied species, *Capsicum frutescens*. In Mexico the name of this indigenous pepper plant was Quauhchilli, *Chili* tree. *Chili* was taken over into Spanish as the common name for capsicum and has come down in English in the familiar Chili sauce. See Peschel, *Zeitalter der Entdeckungen*, p. 139; De Candolle, *Origin of Cultivated Plants*, pp. 289-290. *Encyclopædia Britannica*, art. "Cayenne Pepper."

[470] *Cf.* Im Thurn, *Among the Indians of Guiana*, 266.

had prevailed among the men,[471] but afterwards he resolved upon sending two bands under the command of two captains, the one to Cibao, and the other to Niti, where, as I have already said, Caonabó lived. These parties went, one of them returning on the twentieth, and the other on the twenty-first of January. The party that went to Cibao saw gold in so many places as to seem almost incredible, for in truth they found it in more than fifty streamlets and rivers, as well as upon their banks; so that, the captain said they had only to seek throughout that province, and they would find as much as they wished. He brought specimens from the different parts, namely, from the sand of the rivers and small springs. It is thought, that by digging, it will be found in greater pieces, for the Indians neither know how to dig nor have the means of digging more than a hand's depth. The other captain, who went to Niti, returned also with news of a great quantity of gold in three or four places; of which he likewise brought specimens.[472]

---

[471] The Admiral, "having described the country at length and the condition in which he was and where he had settled for the Catholic sovereigns and sending them the specimen of gold which Guacanagari had given him and that which Hojeda had brought, and informing them of all that he saw to be needed, despatched the twelve ships before mentioned, placing in command of them all Antonio de Torres, brother of the nurse of the prince Don Juan, to whom he intrusted the gold and all his despatches. They made sail the 2d of February, 1494." Las Casas, *Historia de las Indias*, II. 25-26. Columbus's letter to Ferdinand and Isabella mentioned here has not been preserved. That part of it which related to future needs was apparently duplicated in the "memorial" which he gave to Torres. This document is given in English in Thacher, *Christopher Columbus*, II. 297-308, and Major, *Select Letters of Christopher Columbus*, ed. 1870, pp. 72-107. See p. 73, *ibid.*, for a reference to letters of the Admiral no longer extant.

[472] Alonso de Hojeda was sent to explore the region of Cibao with fifteen men. He found Cibao to be fifteen or twenty leagues from Isabella. The other exploring party was headed by Gines de Gorbalan. Further details of these expeditions are given in the Syllacio-Coma letter. Thacher, *Columbus*, II. 258-260. According to Coma, or his translator Syllacio, Cibao was identified with the Sheba of the Bible. Columbus, on the other hand, identified Cibao and Cipango. *Cf., e.g.*,

Thus, surely, their Highnesses the King and Queen may henceforth regard themselves as the most prosperous and wealthy sovereigns in the world; never yet, since the creation, has such a thing been seen or read of; for on the return of the ships from their next voyage, they will be able to carry back such a quantity of gold as will fill with amazement all who hear of it. Here I think I shall do well to break off my narrative. I think those who do not know me, who hear these things, may consider me prolix, and a man who has exaggerated somewhat, but God is my witness, that I have not exceeded, by one tittle, the bounds of truth.[473]

Peter Martyr, *De Rebus Oceanicis*, ed. 1574, p. 31.

[473] "The preceding is the transcript of that part of Doctor Chanca's letter, which refers to intelligence respecting the Indies. The remainder of the letter does not bear upon the subject, but treats of private matters, in which Doctor Chanca requests the interference and support of the Town Council of Seville (of which city he was a native), in behalf of his family and property, which he had left in the said city. This letter reached Seville in the month of [March] in the year fourteen hundred and ninety-three [four]." This note is no doubt from the hand of Friar Antonio de Aspa, who formed the collection of papers in which Navarrete found the text of Dr. Chanca's letter. The collection was made about the middle of the sixteenth century. See Navarrete, II. 224. The returning fleet arrived at Cadiz in March, 1494. Bernaldez, *Historia de los Reyes Catolicos*, (ed. 1870), II. 37.

Narrative of the third voyage of Columbus as contained in las Casas's History

INTRODUCTION

The narrative given here of the third voyage of Columbus in which he discovered the mainland of South America is taken from the *Historia de las Indias* of Las Casas. In preparing his History Las Casas had the use of a larger body of Columbus's papers than has come down to us. Among these papers was a journal of this third voyage which was incorporated in a condensed form by Las Casas in his History, just as he did in the case of the journals of the first and second voyages. This narrative is found in the second volume of the *Historia de las Indias*, pp. 220-317. The translation is, as is mentioned in the preface to this volume, that given in John Boyd Thacher's *Christopher Columbus*.

In certain places the text differs slightly from that in the printed edition of Las Casas, as Mr. Thacher followed the critical text of Cesare de Lollis prepared for the *Raccolta Colombiana* by a collation of the manuscript in the Archives at Madrid with the recently discovered autograph manuscript of Las Casas. Mr. Thacher, following Lollis, omitted passages that were obviously comments on the text by Las Casas. These have been supplied either from Mr. Thacher's notes or translated by the editor from the printed text. The editor has gone over the whole translation and can testify to its exceptional accuracy. A few slight changes have been made in the wording for the sake of greater clearness or exactness.

Columbus described this voyage in a letter to Ferdinand and Isabella. This letter is included in Major's *Select Letters of Columbus* and in P.L. Ford's *Writings of Columbus*. This letter is of great importance in the study of Columbus's geographical ideas. Other contemporary accounts of this voyage are contained in Ferdinand Columbus's *Historie*, the life of his father, where the journal abridged by Las Casas is still further condensed, in Peter Martyr's *De Rebus Oceanicis*, Dec. I., lib. VI., and in the letter of Simone Verde and the three letters of Angelo Trivigiano which will be found in Harrisse, *Christophe Colomb*, II. 95-98 and 119-123.

E.G.B.

Narrative of the third voyage of Columbus as contained in las Casas's history

May 30- August 31, 1498

He started then (our First Admiral)[474] "in the name of the Most Holy Trinity" (as he says and as he was always accustomed to say) from the port of San Lucar de Barrameda, Wednesday, May 30, 1498, with the intention of discovering new land not yet discovered, with his six ships, "greatly fatigued," he says, "with my voyage, since as I was hoping for some quietude, when I left the Indies, I experienced double hardships;" they being the result of the labors, new obstacles and difficulties with which he obtained the funds for his starting upon the expedition and the annoyances in connection therewith received from the royal officials and the hindrance and the evil reports the people around about the Sovereigns gave concerning the affairs in the Indies, wherefore it appeared to him that what he already had done was not sufficient but that he must renew his labors to gain new credit. And because war had then broken out with France,[475] he had news of a French fleet which was waiting for the Admiral beyond the Cape of St. Vincent, to capture him. On this account he decided to steal away as they say and make a detour, directing his course straight to the island of Madeira.

---

[474] *I.e.*, the first Admiral of the Ocean and the Indies where Las Casas was when he was writing.

[475] This clause is probably an explanatory remark by Las Casas. It is misleading. The war in Naples growing out of the invasion of Italy by Charles VIII. of France, in which Ferdinand had taken an active part against the French, had been brought to a close so far as concerned France and Spain by a truce in March, 1497. The treaty of peace was signed August 5, 1498

He arrived at the island of Puerto Sancto, Thursday, June 7, where he stopped to take wood, water and supplies and to hear mass, and he found all the island disturbed and all the farms, goods and flocks guarded, fearing that the new-comers might be French; and then that night he left for the island of Madeira and arrived there the following Sunday, June 10. He was very well received in the town[476] and with much rejoicing, because he was well known there, having been a citizen thereof during some time.[477] He remained there six days, providing himself fully with water and wood and the other necessities for his journey.

Saturday, June 16, he left the island of Madeira with his six ships and arrived at the island of Gomera[478] the following Tuesday. At this island he found a French corsair with a French vessel and two large ships which the corsair had taken from the Castilians, and when the Frenchman saw the six vessels of the Admiral he left his anchors and one vessel and fled with the other vessel. The Admiral sent a ship after him and when the six Spaniards who were being carried away on the captured ship saw this ship coming to their aid, they attacked six Frenchmen who were guarding them and by force they placed them below decks and thus brought them back.

---

[476] Funchal.

[477] This positive assertion that Columbus had lived in Funchal, Madeira, has been overlooked by Vignaud and Harrisse. Vignaud, *Etudes Critiques sur la Vie de Colomb avant ses Découvertes* (Paris, 1905), p. 443, note 9, rejects as unauthenticated the tradition that Columbus lived in Madeira, without adequate grounds it seems to me. Diego Columbus told Las Casas in 1519 that he was born in the neighboring island of Puerto Santo and that his father had lived there. Las Casas, *Historia de las Indias*, I. 54. This passage is not noted by Vignaud.

[478] One of the Canary Islands.

Here in the island of Gomera the Admiral determined to send three ships directly to the island of Española, so that, if he should be detained here, they might give news of him and cheer and console the Christians with the supplies: and principally that they might give joy to his brothers, the Adelantado[479] and Don Diego, who were very desirous of hearing from him. He named Pedro de Arana, a native of Cordova, as captain of one ship,--a very honorable and prudent man, whom I knew very well, brother of the mother of Don Ferdinand Columbus,[480] the second son of the Admiral, and cousin of that Arana who remained in the fortress with the 38 men whom the Admiral on his return found dead. The other captain of the second ship was called Alonso Sanchez de Carvajal, governor of the city of Baçea, an honorable gentleman. The third captain for the remaining ship was Juan Antonio Columbo,[481] a Genoese, a relation of the Admiral, a very capable and prudent man and one of authority, with whom I had frequent conversation.

He gave them suitable instructions, in which instructions he ordered that, one week one captain, and another week another, each by turns should be captain-general of all the ships, as regarded the navigation and the placing of the night lantern, which is a lighted lantern placed in the stern of the ship in order that the other ships may know and follow where the captain guides. He ordered them to

---

[479] The Adelantado was Bartholomew Columbus. The title Adelantado was given in Spain to the military and political governors of border provinces. In this use it was transplanted to America in the earlier days. Cf. Moses, *The Establishment of Spanish Rule in America*, pp. 68-69.

[480] Beatrix Enriquez.

[481] This Juan Antonio Columbo seems to have been a first cousin of the admiral. Cf. Markham, *Christopher Columbus*, pp. 2 and 187. It is to be noted that he retained in Spain his family name and did not follow the discoverer in changing his name to Colon. On this change of name, see above, p. 77, note 2.

go to the west, quarter south-west,[482] for 850 leagues and told them that then they would arrive at the island of Dominica. From Dominica they should go west-north-west and they would then reach the island of Sant Juan,[483] and it would be the southern part of it, because that was the direct way to go to the New Isabella,[484] which now is Santo Domingo. Having passed the island of Sant Juan, they should leave the island of Mona to the north and from there they should make for the point of this Española,[485] which he called Sant Raphael, which now is the Cabo del Engaño, from there to Saona, which he says makes a good harbor between it and this Española. Seven leagues farther there is another island, which is called Santa Catherina, and from there to the New Isabella, which is the port of Santo Domingo, the distance is 25 leagues. And he told the captains that wherever they should arrive and land they should purchase all that they needed by barter and that for the little they might give the Indians, although they might be the canibales,[486] who are said to eat human flesh, they would obtain what they wished and the Indians would give them all that they had; and if they should undertake to procure things by force, the Indians would conceal themselves and remain hostile. He says further in the instructions that he was going by the Cape Verde Islands (which he says were called in ancient times Gorgodes[487] or according to others

---

[482] *I.e.*, west by south.

[483] Porto Rico.

[484] Founded in the summer of 1496 by Bartholomew Columbus in accordance with the directions of the Admiral to establish a new settlement on the south side of the island. Las Casas, II. 136.

[485] "This Española," so frequently repeated, is one of the indications that Las Casas was writing in Española.

[486] *Canibales*, here used still as a tribal name equivalent to Caribbees.

[487] The correct form of this name is Gargades. Columbus's knowledge of them was derived indirectly from Pliny's *Natural History*, book VI., XXXVII., through Cardinal d'Ailly's *Imago Mundi*. Cf. Columbus's marginal note to ch. XXXXI. of that work: "*De situ Gorgodum insule nunc de Capite Viride*

Hesperides) and that he was going in the name of the
Holy Trinity with the intention of navigating to the south
of these islands so as to arrive below the equinoctial line
and to follow the course to the west until this island of
Española should lie to the northwest, to see if there are
islands or lands. "Our Lord," he says, "guides me and
gives me things which may serve Him and the King and
Queen, our Lords, and which may be for the honor of the
Christians, for I believe that no one has ever gone this
way and that this sea is entirely unknown."[488] And here
the Admiral finished his instructions.

Having then taken water and wood and other provisions,
especially cheese, of which there are many and good ones
there, the Admiral made sail with his six ships on
Thursday, June 21, towards the island of Hierro,[489]
which is distant from Gomera about fifteen leagues, and
of the seven Canaries is the one farthest to the west.
Passing it, the Admiral took his course with one ship and
two caravels for the islands of Cape Verde, and dismissed
the other three ships in the name of the Holy Trinity; and
he says that he entreated the Holy Trinity to care for him
and for all of them; and at the setting of the sun they
separated and the three ships took their course for this
island. Here the Admiral makes mention to the
Sovereigns of the agreement they had made with the King
of Portugal that the Portuguese should not go to the
westward of the Azores and Cape Verde Islands, and also
mentions how the Sovereigns sent for him that he should

---

vel Antonii dicitur." Raccolta Colombiana, parte I., vol. II., p. 395.
According to Pliny's location of them they were probably the Canaries.
Pliny's knowledge of the location of the Hesperides is naturally vague, but
his text would support their identification with the Cape Verde Islands.
[488] In this Columbus was mistaken, although he had no means of
knowing it in 1498. Vasco da Gama had sailed in that sea the preceding
summer. Cf. Bourne, Spain in America, p. 72.
[489] Ferro.

be present at the meetings in regard to the partition,[490] and that he could not go on account of the grave illness which he had incurred in the discovery of the mainland of the Indies, that is to say of Cuba, which he always regarded as the mainland even until the present time as he could not circumnavigate it. He adds further that then occurred the death of Don Juan, before he could carry out the matter.[491]

Then the Admiral continuing on his way arrived at the Cape Verde Islands, which according to what he says, have a false name, because he never saw anything green but all things dry and sterile. The first thing he saw was the island of La Sal, Wednesday, June 27: and it is a small island. From there he went to another which is called Buenavista and is very sterile, where he anchored in a bay, and near it is a very small island. To this island come all the lepers of Portugal to be cured and there are not more than six or seven houses on it. The Admiral ordered the boats to go to land to provide themselves with salt and flesh, because there are a great number of goats on the island. There came to the ships a steward[492]

---

[490] August 16, 1494, the sovereigns included in the letter despatched to Columbus by Torres the essential articles of the Treaty of Tordesillas, signed June 7, 1494, and asked him if he could not co-operate in locating the Demarcation Line. Navarrete, *Coleccion de Viages*, II. 155; Harrisse, *Diplomatic History of America*, pp. 80-81.

[491] Columbus's illness began in September, 1494, and it was five months before he was fully recovered. Ferdinand Columbus, *Historie*, ed. 1867, p. 177. The death of Prince John took place October 4, 1497. No actual scientific conference to locate the line took place till that at Badajoz in 1524. See Bourne, *Essays in Historical Criticism*, pp. 205-211.

[492] *Escribano de la hacienda*. In 1497 Rodrigo Affonso, a member of the king's council, was granted the northern of the two captaincies into which São Thiago was divided and also the wild cattle on the island of Boavista (Buenavista in Spanish). D'Avezac, *Ils de l'Afrique* (Paris, 1848), p. 218. The word *mayordomo*, translated "steward," here stands for the high Portuguese title of honor *Mordomo môr da Casa Real*, a title in its origin

to whom that island belonged, named Roderigo Alonso, notary public of the exchequer[493] of the King of Portugal, who offered to the Admiral what there was on the island of which he might be in need. The Admiral thanked him and ordered that he should be given some supplies from Castile, which he enjoyed very much.

Here he relates how the lepers came there to be cured because of the great abundance of turtles on that island, which commonly are as large as shields. By eating the flesh and constantly bathing in the blood of these turtles, the lepers become cured.[494] The turtles in infinite number come there three months in the year, June, July, and August, from the mainland, which is Ethiopia,[495] to lay eggs in the sand and with the claws and legs they scratch places in the sand and spawn more than five hundred eggs, as large as those of a hen except that they have not a hard shell but a tender membrane which covers the yolk, like the membrane which covers the yolk of the hen's egg after taking off the hard shell. They cover the eggs in the sand as a person would do, and there the sun hatches them, and the little live turtles come out and then run in search of the sea as if they had come out of it alive. They take the turtles there in this manner: At night with lights which are torches of dry wood, they go searching for the track of the turtle which is easily traced, and find the turtle tired and sleeping. They come up quickly and turn it over with the belly up and leave it, sure that it cannot

---

similar to the *majores domus* or mayors of the palace of the early French kings. *Escribano de la hacienda del Rey* means rather the king's treasurer.
[493] *Mayordomo.*
[494] This account of Boavista and its lepers is not noticed in the histories of the Cape Verde Islands so far as I know.
[495] From Pliny's time through the Middle Ages the name Ethiopia embraced all tropical Africa. He calls the Atlantic in the tropics the "Ethiopian Sea." Pliny's *Natural History*, book VI., chs. XXXV. And XXXVI.

turn itself back, and go in search of another. And the Indians do the same in the sea; if they come upon one asleep and turn it over it remains safe for them to take it whenever they wish. The Indians, however, have another greater device for taking them on the sea, which will be explained God willing when we give a description of Cuba.[496]

The healthy persons on that island of Buenavista who lead a laborious life were six or seven residents who have no water except brackish water from wells and whose employment is to kill the big goats and salt the skins and send them to Portugal in the caravels which come there for them, of which in one year they kill so many and send so many skins that they are worth 2000 ducats to the notary public, to whom the island belonged. Such a great multitude of goats, male and female, have been grown there, from only eight original head. Those who live there neither eat bread nor drink wine during four or five months, nor anything else except goat flesh or fish or turtles. All this they told to the Admiral.

He left there Saturday, June 30, at night for the island of Santiago, where he arrived on Sunday at the hour of vespers, because it is distant 28 leagues: and this is the principal one of the Cape Verde Islands. He wished to take from this island a herd of black cattle in order to carry them to Española as the Sovereigns had ordered, and he was there eight days and could not get them; and because the island is very unhealthy since men are burned with heat there and his people commenced to fall ill, he decided to leave it. The Admiral says again that he wishes to go to the south, because he intends with the aid

---

[496] A remark by Las Casas, of which many are interspersed with the material from Columbus's Journal of this voyage.

of the Most Holy Trinity, to find islands and lands, that
God may be served and their Highnesses and Christianity
may have pleasure, and that he wishes to see what was
the idea of King Don Juan of Portugal, who said that
there was mainland to the south: and because of this, he
says that he had a contention with the Sovereigns of
Castile, and finally the Admiral says that it was
concluded that the King of Portugal should have 370
leagues to the west from the islands of the Azores[497] and
Cape Verde, from north to south, from pole to pole. And
the Admiral says further that the said King Don Juan
was certain that within those limits famous lands and
things must be found.[498] Certain principal inhabitants of
the island of Santiago came to see them and they said
that to the south-west of the island of Huego, which is one
of the Cape Verde Islands distant 12 leagues from this,
may be seen an island, and that the King Don Juan was
greatly inclined to send to make discoveries to the southwest, and that canoes had been found which start from
the coast of Guinea and navigate to the west with
merchandise. Here the Admiral says again as if he was
speaking with the Sovereigns,--"He that is Three and One
guides me by His pity and mercy that I may serve Him
and give great pleasure to your Highnesses and to all
Christianity, as was done in the discovery of the Indies
which resounded throughout all the world."

---

[497] The Tordesillas line was 370 leagues west of the Cape Verde Islands
alone.

[498] This reason for the desire of King John of Portugal to have the
Demarcation Line moved further west has escaped all the writers on the
subject. If Columbus reported the king's ideas correctly, we may have
here a clew to one of the reasons why Cabral went so far to the
southwest in 1500 that he discovered Brazil when on his voyage to India,
and perhaps also one of the reasons why Vasco da Gama struck off so
boldly into the South Atlantic. Cf. Bourne, *Spain in America*, pp. 72, 74.

Wednesday, July 4, he ordered sail made from that island in which he says that since he arrived there he never saw the sun or the stars, but that the heavens were covered with such a thick mist that it seemed they could cut it with a knife and the heat was so very intense that they were tormented, and he ordered the course laid to the way of the south-west, which is the route leading from these islands to the south, in the name, he says, of the Holy and Indivisible Trinity, because then he would be on a parallel with the land of the sierra of Loa[499] and cape of Sancta Ana in Guinea, which is below the equinoctial line, where he says that below that line of the world are found more gold and things of value; and that after, he would navigate, the Lord pleasing, to the west, and from there would go to this Española, in which route he would prove the theory of the King John aforesaid; and that he thought to investigate the report of the Indians of this Española who said that there had come to Española from the south and south-east, a black people who have the tops of their spears made of a metal which they call *guanin*, of which he had sent samples to the Sovereigns to have them assayed, when it was found that of 32 parts, 18 were of gold, 6 of silver and 8 of copper.

Following this course to the south-west he commenced to find grasses like those encountered in the direct way to these Indies; and the Admiral says here that after having gone 480 miles which make 120 leagues, that at nightfall he took the latitude and found that the North Star was in five degrees. Yet it seems to me that he must have gone more than 200 leagues, and that the text is in error because it is necessary to traverse more than 200 leagues on that course from the Cape Verde Islands and Santiago whence he started to put a ship within five degrees of the equator, as any sailor will observe who will

---

[499] Sierra Leone.

judge it by the map and by the latitude. And he says that there, Friday, July 13, the wind deserted him and he entered into heat so great and so ardent that he feared the ships would take fire and the people perish. The ceasing of the wind and coming of the excessive and consuming heat was so unexpected and sudden that there was no person who dared to descend below to care for the butts of wine and water, which swelled, breaking the hoops of the casks; the wheat burned like fire; the pork and salted meat roasted and putrefied. This ardent heat lasted eight days. The first day was clear with a sun which burned them. God sent them less suffering because the seven following days it rained and was clouded; however with all this, they could not find any hope of saving themselves from perishing and from being burned, and if the other seven days had been like the first, clear and with the sun, the Admiral says here that it would have been impossible for a man of them to have escaped alive. And thus they were divinely succored by the coming of some showers and by the days being cloudy. He determined from this, if God should give him wind in order to escape from this suffering, to run to the west some days, and then if he found himself in any moderation of temperature to return to the south, which was the way he desired to follow. "May our Lord," says he, "guide me and give me grace that I may serve Him, and bring pleasing news to your Highnesses." He says he remembered, being in this burning latitude, that when he came to the Indies in the past voyages, always when he reached 100 leagues toward the west from the Azores Islands he found a change in the temperature from north to south, and for this he wished to go to the west to reach the said place.

The Admiral must have been on that same parallel or rather meridian, on which Hanno the Carthaginian was

with his fleet, who departing from Cadiz and going out
into the Ocean to the left[500] of Lybia or Ethiopia
after thirty days' voyaging toward the south, among other
distresses that he suffered the heat and fire were so
intense that it seemed as if they were roasting; they heard
such thundering and lightning that their ears pained
them and their eyes were blinded and it appeared no
otherwise than as if flames of fire fell from heaven.
Amianus narrates this--a Greek historian, a follower of
the truth, and very famous--in the *History of India* near
the end, and Ludovico Celio quotes it in Book I., ch. XXII.,
of the *Lectiones Antiguas.*[501] Returning to these days of
toil:--

Saturday, which they counted July 14, the Guards[502]
being on the left hand, he says the *North* was in seven
degrees: he saw black and white jays,[503] which are birds
that do not go far from land, and from this he considered
it a sign of land. He was sick at this point of the journey,
from gout and from not sleeping; but because of this he
did not cease to watch and work with great care and
diligence.

---

[500] As one faces north.

[501] On Hanno's voyage see _Encyclopœdia Britannica_ under his name.
There was no Greek historian Amianus; the name should be Arrianus, who
wrote the history of Alexander the Great's expedition to India and a history
of India. The reference is to the latter work, ch. XLIII., sects. 11, 12.
Ludovico Celio: Ludovico Ricchieri, born about 1450. He was for a time a
professor in the Academy at Milan. He took the Latin name Rhodiginus
from his birthplace Rovigo, and sometimes his name appears in full as
Ludovicus Coelius Richerius Rhodiginus. His *Antiquarum Lectionum Libri
XVI.* was published at Venice in 1516, at Paris in 1517, and in an extended
form at Basel, 1542. It is a collection of passages from the classical authors
relating to all branches of knowledge, with a critical commentary.

[502] The Guards, "the two brightest stars in Ursa Minor." (Tolhausen.)

[503] *Grajos* The meaning given in the dictionaries for *grajo* is
"daw."

Sunday and Monday, they saw the same birds and more swallows, and some fish appeared which they called *botos*,[504] which are little smaller than great calves, and which have the head very blunt. The Admiral says here incidentally that the Azores Islands which in ancient times were called Casetérides,[505] were situated at the end of the fifth clime.[506]

Thursday, July 19, there was such intense and ardent heat that they thought the men and ships would burn, but as our Lord at sight of the afflictions which He gives is accustomed by interfering to the contrary to alleviate them, He succored him by His mercy at the end of seven or eight days, giving him very good weather to get away from that fire; with which good weather he navigated towards the west 17 days, always intending to return to the south, and place himself, as above said, in such a region, that this Española should be to the north or *septentrion*, where he thought he must find land before or beyond the said place: and thus he intended to repair the ships which were already opening from the past heat, and the supplies, of which he had a large quantity, because of the necessity of taking them to this island and them great difficulty in getting them from Castile, and which were becoming worthless and damaged.

Sunday, July 22, in the afternoon, as they were going with good weather, they saw innumerable birds pass from the west-south-west to the north-east: he says that they

---

[504] This word, as a name of a fish, is Portuguese. It means "blunted."

[505] See Pliny, *Natural History*, book IV., ch. XXXVI. The Cassiterides are commonly identified with the Scilly Islands.

[506] The fifth clime or climate is a term in Ptolemy's geographical system. The fifth climate was a strip 255 Roman miles in width lying between 41° and 45° north latitude. *Cf. Raccolta Columbiana*, Parte I., Tomo 2, p. 293. The latitude of the Azores is about 37°-40°.

were a great sign of land. They saw the same the Monday following and the days after, on one of which days a pelican came to the ship of the Admiral, and many others appeared another day, and there were other birds which are called "frigate pelicans."[507]

On the seventeenth day of the good weather which they were experiencing, the Admiral was hoping to see land, because of the said signs of the birds, and as he did not see it Monday, or the next day, Tuesday, July 31, as they lacked water, he decided to change his route, and this was to the west, and to go to the right, and make for the island of Dominica, or some of the islands of the Canibales, which to-day are called the Caribes, and thus he ordered the course to the north, quarter north-east, and went that way until midday. "But as His Divine Majesty," he says, "has always used mercy with me, a sailor from Guelva,[508] my servant, who was called Alonso Pérez, by chance and conjecture ascended to the round top and saw land to the west, and he was 15 leagues from it, and that part which appeared were three rocks or mountains." These are his words. He named this land "The Island of the Trinity,"[509] because he had determined that the first land he discovered should be named thus. "And it pleased our Lord," he says, "by His Exalted Majesty, that the first lands seen were three rocks all united at the base, I say three mountains, all at one time and in one glance." "His High Power by His pity guides me," he says, "in such a manner, that He may have much service, and your Highnesses much pleasure: as it is certain that the discovery of this land in this place was as great a miracle as the discovery of the first voyage." These are his words.

---

[507] The names are *alcatraz* and *rabihorcado*. See above, note to Journal of First Voyage, p. 98.
[508] Huelva, near Palos.

He gave infinite thanks to God as was his custom, and all praised the divine goodness, and with great rejoicings and merriment the *Salve Regina*[510] was sung with other devout songs which contain praises of God and our Lady, according to the custom of sailors, at least our sailors of Spain, who in tribulations and rejoicings are accustomed to say them.

Here he makes a digression and recapitulation of the services he has rendered the Sovereigns, and of the will he always had keen to serve them, "not as false tongues," says he, "and as false witnesses from envy said."[511] And surely, I believe that such as these God took for instruments to chasten him because he loved him since many without cause and without object maligned him and disturbed these efforts, and brought it about that the Sovereigns grew lukewarm and wearied of expense and of keeping up their attachment and expectation that these Indies were likely to be of profit, at least that it should be more than the expenses with increase that came to them. He repeats a mention of the heat he suffered, and how they were nevertheless now going by the same parallel, except they had drawn near to the land when he ordered the course directed to the west, because the land emits coolness from its fountains and rivers, and by its waters causes moderation and softness; and because of this he says the Portuguese who go to Guinea which is below the equinoctial line are able to navigate because they go along the coast. He says further, that now he was in the same parallel from which the King of Portugal brought gold, from which he believed that whoever would search those

---

[510] Salve Regina, one of the great hymns to the Virgin in the Catholic service. "The antiphon said after Lauds and Compline from Trinity Sunday to Advent." Addis and Arnold, *Catholic Dictionary*.

[511] *I.e.*, that his will was not to serve the sovereigns but to advance himself.

seas would find things of value. He confesses here that there is no man in the world for whom God has shown so much grace, and entreats Him that He will furnish something from which their Highnesses and Christianity may receive great pleasure; and he says that, although he should not find any other thing of benefit except these beautiful lands, which are so green and full of groves and palms, that they are superior to the gardens of Valencia in May, they would deserve to be highly valued. And in this he speaks the truth and later on he will place a still higher value on it with much reason. He says that it is a miraculous thing that the Sovereigns of Castile should have lands so near the equinoctial as 6 degrees, Ysabela being distant from the said line 24 degrees.

Having seen the land then to the great consolation of all, he left the course which he desired to follow in search of some of the islands of the Canibales in order to provide himself with water, of which he was greatly in need, and made a short excursion towards the land which he had seen, towards a cape which appeared to be to the west, which he called "Cabo de la Galera,"[512] from a great rock which it had, which from a distance appeared like a galley sailing. They arrived there at the hour of compline.[513] They saw a good harbor but it was not deep, and the Admiral regretted that they could not enter it. He pursued his course to the point he had seen, which was seven leagues toward the south. He did not find a harbor. On all the coast he found that the groves reached to the sea, the most beautiful coast that eyes ever saw. He says that this island must be large; a canoe appeared at a distance filled with people who must have been fishing, and made towards the land to some houses which

---

[512] Cape of the Galley. To-day, Cape Galeota.
[513] The last of the canonical hours of prayer, after sunset or early evening.

appeared there. The land was very cultivated and high and beautiful.

Wednesday, August 1, he ran down the coast toward the west, five leagues, and arrived at a point, where he anchored with all three ships, and took water from fountains and streams. They found signs of people, instruments for fishing, signs of goats, but they were only of deer of which there are many in those lands. He says that they found aloes and great groves of palms, and very beautiful lands: "for which infinite thanks may be given to the Holy Trinity." These are his words. He saw much tilled land along the coast and many settlements. He saw from there towards the south, another island, which is distant more than 20 leagues. (And he might well say five hundred since this is the mainland which, as he saw a part of it, seemed to him to be an island); to this he gave the name of "Ysla Sancta." He says here that he would not take any Indians in order not to disturb the land. From the Cape of Galera to the point where he took the water, which I believed he named "Punta de la Playa," he says that having been a great way, and running east-west (he should say that he went from east to west) there was no port in all that way, but the land was well populated and tilled, and with many trees and thick groves, the most beautiful thing in the world, the trees reaching to the sea. Here it may be remarked that when the trees of the country grow down to the water's edge it indicates that such a coast is not exposed to high seas, because when the coast is so exposed trees do not grow down to the water, but there is an open sandy shore. The current, *surgente*, which is that which comes down, and the *montante*, which is that which ascends from below, he says appear to be great. The island which lies to the south he says is very large, because he was already going along with the mainland in sight although he did not think so, but that it was an island.

He says that he came to search for a harbor along the island of Trinidad, Thursday, August 2, and arrived at the cape of the island of Trinidad, which is a point, to which he gave the name "Punta del Arenal,"[514] which is to the west: so that he had in a sense already entered in the gulf which he called "de la Ballena,"[515] where he underwent great danger of losing his ships, and he as yet did not know that he was becoming encircled by land as will be seen. This gulf is a wonderful thing and dangerous on account of the very great river that flows into it which is called the Yuyapari,[516] the last syllable long. It comes from more than 300 and I believe more than 400 leagues, and it has been traversed for 300 leagues up stream partly with a ship, partly with brigantines and partly with large canoes. And since the force of the water is very great at all times and particularly so in this season of July and August in which the Admiral was there, which is the season of high water as in Castile in October and November, and since it wants naturally to get to the sea, and the sea with its great mass under the same natural impulse wants to break upon the land, and since this gulf is enclosed by the mainland on one side and on the other by the island of Trinidad, and since it is very narrow for such a violent force of contrary waters, it must needs be that when they meet a terrific struggle takes place and a conflict most perilous for those that find themselves in that place.

He says here that the island of Trinidad is large, because from the Cape of Galera to the Point of Arenal, where he

---

[514] Sandy Point.

[515] Of the whale.

[516] One of the native names of the Orinoco, here referring to one of the northern branch mouths. A detailed map of the region is given Winsor's *Columbus*, p. 353.

was at the present time, he says it is 35 leagues. I say that it is more than 45, as he that desires may see by the charts, although now those names are not written on the charts as they have been forgotten, and to understand the matter they must consider the course the Admiral pursued until he arrived there, and at what point he first saw land, and from there where he went till he stopped, and in that way, one will find out what he called the Cape of Galera and what the Point of Arenal. It is not a matter of surprise that the Admiral did not make an accurate estimate of the leagues of the island because he went along it piece by piece.

He ordered that his people should land on this Point of Arenal, the end of the island toward the west, to enjoy themselves and obtain recreation, because they had become wearied and fatigued; who found the land very much trampled by deer, although they believed they were goats. This Thursday, August 2, a large canoe came from towards the east, in which came twenty-five men, and having arrived at the distance of a Lombard shot, they ceased to row, and cried out many words. The Admiral believed, and I also believe, that they were asking what people they were, as the others of the Indies were accustomed to do, to which they did not respond in words, but by showing them certain small boxes of brass and other shining things, in order that they should come to the ship, coaxing them with motions of the body and signs. They approached somewhat, and afterwards became terrified by the ship; and as they would not approach, the Admiral ordered a tambourine player to come up to the poop deck of the ship and that the young boys of the ship should dance, thinking to please them. But they did not understand it thus, but rather, as they saw dancing and playing, taking it for a signal of war, they distrusted them. They left all their oars and laid hold of their bows and arrows; and each one embracing his wooden shield, they commenced to shoot a great cloud of arrows. Having seen this, the Admiral ordered the playing and dancing to cease, and that some cross-bows should be drawn on deck and two of them shot off at them, nothing more than to frighten them. The Indians then, having shot the arrows, went to one of the two caravels, and suddenly, without fear, placed themselves below the poop, and the pilot of the caravel, also without any fear, glided down from the poop and entered with them in the canoe with some things which he gave them; and when he was with them he gave a smock frock and a bonnet to one of them who appeared to be the principal man. They took them and as if in gratitude for what had been given them, by signs said to him that he should go to land with them, and there they would give him what they had. He accepted and they went away to land. The pilot entered the boat and went to beg permission of the Admiral on the ship, and when they saw that he did not go directly with him, they did not expect him longer, and so they went away and neither the Admiral nor any other ever saw them more. From the sudden change in their bearing because of the playing on the tambourine and the dancing, it appears that this must be considered among them a sign of hostility.

A servant of the Admiral, called Bernaldo de Ibarro, who was on this voyage with him, told me and gave it to me in writing and I have this writing in my possession to-day, that a cacique came to the ship of the Admiral and was wearing upon his head a diadem of gold; and he went to the Admiral who was wearing a scarlet cap and greeted him and kissed his own diadem, and with the other hand he removed the cap of the Admiral and placed upon-him the diadem, and he himself put upon his own head the scarlet cap, appearing very content and pleased.

The Admiral says here that these were all youths and very well shaped and adorned, although I do not believe they wore much silk or brocade, with which, also, I believe the Spaniards and the Admiral might be more pleased; but they came armed with bows and arrows and wooden shields. They were not as short as others he had seen in the Indies and they were whiter, and of very good movements and handsome bodies, the hair long and smooth and cut in the manner of Castile. They had the head tied with a large handkerchief of cotton, symmetrically woven in colors, which the Admiral believed to be the *almaiçar*;[517] he says that others had this cloth around them, and they covered themselves with it in place of trousers. He says that they are not black although they are near the equinoctial,[518] but of an Indian color like all the others he has found. They are of very fine stature, go naked, are warlike, wear the hair very long like the women in Castile, carry bows and arrows with plumes, and at the end of the arrows a sharp bone with a point like a fish-hook, and they carry wooden shields, which he had not seen before; and according to the signs and gestures which they made, he says he could understand from them that they believed the Admiral came from the south, from which he judged that there must be great lands toward the south, and he said well since the mainland is so large that it occupies a large part of the south.

---

[517] "A sort of veil, or head attire used by the Moorish women, made of thin silk, striped of several colors, and shagged at the ends, which hangs down on the back." John Stevens, *A New Dictionary, Spanish and English*, etc. (London. 1726.)

[518] The exploration of the west coast of Africa, the only equatorial regions then known to Europeans, had led to the conclusion that black was the natural color of the inhabitants of the tropics.

The temperature of this land, he says, is very high, and according to him this causes the color of the people, and the hair which is all flowing, and the very thick groves which abound everywhere. He says it must be believed that when once the boundary is passed, 100 leagues to the west of the Azores, that many times he has said that there is a change in the sky and the sea and the temperature, "and this," he says, "is manifest," because here where he was, so near to the equinoctial line, each morning, he says, it was cool and the sun was in Leo. What he says is very true, since I who write this have been there and required a robe nights and mornings especially at Navidad.[519]

The waters were running toward the west with a current stronger than the river of Seville; the water of the sea rose and fell 65 paces and more, as in Barrameda so that they are able to beach carracks;[520] he says that the current flows very strongly going between these two islands, Trinidad and that one which he called Sancta, and the land which afterwards and farther on he called Isla de Gracia. And he calls the mainland an island, since he was

---

[519] The Navidad referred to by Las Casas was near the Gulf of Paria. (Thacher.)

[520] *Poner á monte carracas. Poner á monte_* is not given in the Spanish dictionaries, and is apparently a sea phrase identical with the Portuguese "pôr um navio a monte," to beach or ground a vessel. The translator went entirely astray in this passage. See Thacher's *Columbus*, II. 388. The figure here given and the use of word *pasos*, normally, a land measure of length, instead of *braza*, "fathom," would seem to indicate that the 65 paces refers to the extent of shore laid bare, and not to the height of the tide. The corresponding passage in the *Historie* reads: "so that it seemed a rapid river both day and night and at all hours, notwithstanding the fact that the water rose and fell along the shore (*per la spiaggia*) more than sixty paces between the waves (*alle marette*) as it is wont to do in San Lucar di Barrameda where the waters [of the river] are high since although the water rises and falls it never ceases to run toward the sea," *Historie* (London ed.), p. 229. In this passage *maree*, "tides," should be read instead of *marette*.

already between the two which are two leagues apart which [*i.e.*, the channel] is like a river as it appears on the map. They found fruits[521] like those of this Española, and the trees and the soil, and the temperature of the sky. In this Española they found few fruits native to the soil. The temperature of that country is much higher than it is in this Española, except in the mines of Cibao and in some other districts, as has been said above.

They found *hostias* or oysters, very large, infinite fish, parrots as large as hens, he says. In this land and in all the mainland the parrots are larger than any of those in these islands and are green, the color being very light, but those of the islands are of a green somewhat darker. Those of the mainland have the yellow with spots and the upper part of the wings with reddish spots, and some are of yellow plumage; those of the islands have no yellow, the neck being red with spots. The parrots of Española have a little white over the back; those of Cuba have that part red and they are very pretty. Those of the island of San Juan I believe are similar to those of this island [Española] and I have not observed this feature in those of Jamaica. Finally it appears that those of each island are somewhat different. In this mainland where the Admiral is now, there is a species of parrots which I believe are found nowhere else, very large, not much smaller than hens, reddish with blue and black feathers in the wings. These never speak nor are attractive except in appearance. They are called by the Indians *guacamayas*. It is marvellous how all the other kinds can speak except the smallest, which are called *xaxaues*.

---

[521] Accepting the emendation of de Lollis which substitutes *fructas* for *fuentes*, "springs."

Being at this Point of Arenal, which is the end of the island of Trinidad, they saw toward the north, quarter north-east,[522] a distance of 15 leagues, a cape or point of the same mainland, and this is that which is called Paria. The Admiral believing that it was another distinct island named it "Isla de Gracia": which island he says goes to the west [Oeste] which is the west [*poniente*], and that it is a very high land. And he says truly, for through all that land run great chains of very high mountains.

Saturday, August 4, he determined to go to the said island of Gracia and raised the anchors and made sail from the said Point of Arenal, where he was anchored; and because that strait by which he entered into the Gulf of Ballena was not more than two leagues wide between Trinidad on one side and the mainland on the other, the fresh water came out very swiftly. There came from the direction of the Arenal, on the island of Trinidad, such a great current from the south, like a mighty flood (and it was because of the great force of the river Yuyaparí which is toward the south and which he had not yet seen), with such great thundering and noise, that all were frightened and did not think to escape from it, and when the water of the sea withstood it, coming in opposition, the sea was raised making a great and very high swell[523] of water which raised the ship and placed it on top of the swell, a thing which was never heard of nor seen, and raised the anchors of the other ship which must have been already cast and forced it toward the sea, and the Admiral made sail to get away from the said slope. "It pleased God not to injure us," says the Admiral here, and when he wrote this thing to the Sovereigns he said, "even to-day I feel the

---

[522] *I.e., north by east.*
[523] *Loma.*

fear in my body which I felt lest it should upset the ship when it came under her."[524] For this great danger, he named the mouth "Boca de la Sierpe."[525]

Having reached that land which he saw in that direction and believed was an island, he saw near that cape two small islands in the middle of another channel which is made by that cape which he called Cabo de Lapa and another cape of the Trinidad which he called Cabo Boto, because of being thick and blunt,--the one island he named El Caracol, the other El Delfin.[526] It is only five leagues in this strait between the Point of Paria and Cape Boto of Trinidad, and the said islands are in the middle of the strait. The impetus of the great river Yuyaparí and the tempestuous waves of the sea make the entrance and exit by this strait greatly dangerous, and because the Admiral experienced this difficulty and also danger, he called that difficult entrance Boca del Drago[527] and thus it is called to this day. He went along the coast of the mainland of Paria,[528] which he believed to be an island, and named it Isla de Gracia, towards the west in search of a harbor. From the point of the Arenal, which is one cape of Trinidad as has been said, and is towards the south, as far as the other Cape Boto, which is of the same island and is towards the sea, the Admiral says it is 26 large leagues, and this part appears to be the width of the island, and these two said capes are north and south. There were great currents, the one against the other; there came many showers as it was the rainy season, as aforesaid. The Isla de Gracia is, as has been said,

---

[524] Las Casas here quotes Columbus's letter to Ferdinand and Isabella on this voyage. See Major, *Select Letters of Columbus*, p. 123.

[525] Serpent's mouth. The name is still retained.

[526] *Lapa* means barnacle; *caracol*, periwinkle; and *delfin*, dolphin.

[527] Dragon's mouth. The name is still retained.

[528] *I.e.*, along the south shore of the peninsula of Paria in the Gulf of Paria.

mainland. The Admiral says that it is a very high land and all full of trees which reach to the sea; this is because the gulf being surrounded by land, there is no surf and no waves which break on the land as where the shores are uncovered. He says that, being at the point or end of it, he saw an island of very high land to the north-east, which might be 26 leagues from there. He named it "Belaforma," because it must have looked very well from a distance, yet all this is the mainland, which, as the ships changed their position from one side to the other within the gulf enclosed by land, some inlets appeared as if they separated lands which might be detached, and these the Admiral called islands; for such was his opinion.[529]

He navigated Sunday, August 5, five leagues from the point of the Cape of Lapa, which is the eastern end of the island of Gracia. He saw very good harbors adjacent to each other, and almost all this sea he says is a harbor, because it is surrounded by islands and there are no waves. He called the parts of the mainland which disclosed themselves to him "islands," but there are only the island of Trinidad and the mainland, which inclose the gulf which he now calls the sea. He sent the boats to land and found fish and fire, and traces of people, and a great house visible to the view. From there he went eight leagues where he found good harbors. This part of this island of Gracia he says is very high land, and there are many valleys, and "all must be populated," says he, because he saw it all cultivated. There are many rivers because each valley has its own from league to league; they found many fruits, and grapes like [our] grapes and of good taste, and myrobolans very good, and others like apples, and others, he says, like oranges, and the inside is

---

[529] The grammatical form of this sentence follows the original, which is irregular.

like figs. They found numberless monkeys.[530] The waters, he says, are the best that they saw. "This island," he says, "is all full of harbors, this sea is fresh, although not wholly so, but brackish like that of Carthagena"; farther down he says that it is fresh like the river of Seville, and this was caused when it encountered some current of water from the sea, which made that of the river salty.

He sailed to a small port Monday, August 6, five leagues from whence he went out and saw people, and then a canoe with four men came to the caravel which was nearest the land and the pilot called the Indians as if he wished to go to land with them, and in drawing near and entering he submerged the canoe, and they commenced swimming; he caught them and brought them to the Admiral. He says that they are of the color of all the others of the Indies. They wear the hair (some of them) very long, others as with us; none of them have the hair cut as in Española and in the other lands. They are of very fine stature and all well grown; they have the genital member tied and covered, and the women all go naked as their mothers gave them birth. This is what the Admiral says, but I have been, as I said above, within 30 leagues of this land yet I never saw women that did not have their private parts, at least, covered.[531] The Admiral must have meant that they went as their mothers bore them as to the rest of the body.

"To these Indians," says the Admiral, "as soon as they were here, I gave hawks' bells and beads and sugar, and sent them to land, where there was a great battle among

---

[530] *Galos paules* (Cat-Pauls). A species of African monkey was so called in Spain. The name occurs in Marco Polo. On its history and meaning, see Yule's *Marco Polo*, II. 372.

[531] Im Thurn, *Among the Indians of Guiana*, p. 193, says, "Indians after babyhood are never seen perfectly naked."

them, and after they knew the good treatment, all wished to come to the ships. Those who had canoes came and they were many, and to all we gave a good welcome and held friendly conversation with them, giving them the things which pleased them." The Admiral asked them questions and they replied, but they did not understand each other. They brought them bread and water and some beverage like new wine; they are very much adorned with bows and arrows and wooden shields, and they almost all carry arrows poisoned.

Tuesday, August 7, there came an infinite number of Indians by land and by sea and all brought with them bread and maize and things to eat and pitchers of beverages, some white, like milk, tasting like wine, some green, and some of different colors; he believes that all are made from fruits. Most or all of it is made from maize but as the maize itself is white or violet and reddish, it causes the wine to be of different colors. I do not know of what the green wine is made. They all brought their bows and poisoned arrows, very pointed;[532] they gave nothing for beads, but would give as much as they had for hawks' bells, and asked nothing else. They gave a great deal for brass. It is certain that they hold this in high estimation and they gave in this Española for a little brass as much gold as any one would ask, and I believe that in the beginning it was always thus in all these Indies. They called it *turey* as if it came from Heaven because they called Heaven *hureyo*.[533] They find in it I do not know

---

[532] *Flechas con hierba muy á punto*, literally, arrows with grass very sharp. Gaffarel, *Histoire de la Découverte de l'Amérique*, II. 196, interprets this to mean arrows feathered with grass; but *hierba* used in connection with arrows usually means poison. Cf. Oviedo, lib. IX., title of cap. XII., "*Del árbol ó mançanillo con cuya fructa los indios caribes flecheros haçen la hierba con que tiran é pélean.*"

[533] *Hureyos* is *Tureyos* in the printed edition of Las Casas, an obvious correction of the manuscript reading. On *turey*, see above, p. 310.

what odor, but one which is agreeable to them. Here the Admiral says whatever they gave them from Castile they smelled it as soon as it was given them. They brought parrots of two or three kinds, especially the very large ones like those in the island of Guadeloupe, he says, with the large tail. They brought handkerchiefs of cotton very symmetrically woven and worked in colors like those brought from Guinea, from the rivers of the Sierra Leona and of no difference, and he says that they cannot communicate with the latter, because from where he now is to Guinea the distance is more than 800 leagues; below he says that these handkerchiefs resemble *almayzars*. He desired, he says, to take a half-dozen Indians, in order to carry them with him, and says that he could not take them because they all went away from the ships before nightfall.

But Wednesday, August 8, a canoe came with 12 men to the caravel and they took them all, and brought them to the ship of the Admiral, and from them he chose six and sent the others to land. From this it appears that the Admiral did it without scruple as he did many other times in the first navigation, it not appearing to him that it was an injustice and an offence against God and his neighbor to take free men against their will, separating fathers from their sons and wives from their husbands and [not reflecting] that according to natural law they were married, and that other men could not take these women, or those men other women, without sin and perhaps a mortal sin of which the Admiral was the efficient cause-- and there was the further circumstance that these people came to the ships under tacit security and promised confidence which should have been observed toward them; and beyond this, the scandal and the hatred of the

Christians not only there, but in all the earth and among the peoples that should hear of this.

He made sail then towards a point which he calls "de l'Aguja,"[534] he does not say when he gave it this name, and from there he says that he discovered the most beautiful lands that have been seen and the most populated, and arriving at one place which for its beauty he called Jardines,[535] where there were an infinite number of houses and people, and those whom he had taken told him there were people who were clothed, for which reason he decided to anchor, and infinite canoes came to the ships. These are his words. Each one, he says, wore his cloth so woven in colors, that it appeared an *almayzar*, with one tied on the head and the other covering the rest, as has been already explained. Of these people who now came to the ships, some he says wore gold leaf[536] on the breast, and one of the Indians he had taken told him there was much gold there, and that they made large mirrors of it, and they showed how they gathered it. He says mirrors, wherefore the Admiral must have given some mirrors and the Indian must have said by signs that of the gold they made those things, for they did not understand the language. He says that, as he was going hastily along there, because he was losing the supplies which it had cost him so much labor to obtain, and this island Española is more than 300 leagues from there, he did not tarry, which he would have wished very much in order to discover much more land, and says that it is all full of very beautiful islands, much populated, and very high lands and valleys and plains, and all are very

---

[534] Needle. Alcatrazes, to-day. (Navarrete.)

[535] Gardens.

[536] *Ojas de oro*. The translator took *ojas* (*hojas*) for *ojos* and rendered it eyes of gold." See Thacher, *Columbus*, II. 393.

large. The people are much more politic than those of Española and warlike, and there are handsome houses. If the Admiral had seen the kingdom of Xaraguá as did his brother the Adelantado and the court of the King Behechio[537] he would not have made so absolute a statement.

Arriving at the point of Aguja, he says that he saw another island to the south 15 leagues which ran south-east and north-west, very large, and very high land, and he called it Sabeta, and in the afternoon he saw another to the west, very high land. All these islands I understand to be pieces of the mainland which by reason of the inlets and valleys that separate them seem to be distinct islands notwithstanding that he went clear inside the gulf which he called Ballena enclosed as is said by land; and this seems clear since when one is, as he was, within the said gulf no land bears off to the south, except the mainland; next, the islands which he mentioned were not islands but pieces of the mainland which he judged to be islands.

He anchored at the place he had named the Jardines, and then there came an infinite number of canoes, large and small, full of people, according to what he says. Afterwards in the afternoon there came more from all the territory, many of whom wore at the neck pieces of gold of the size of horseshoes. It appeared that they had a great deal of it: but they gave it all for hawks' bells and he did not take it. And this is strange that a man as provident as the Admiral and desiring to make discoveries should not have seized this opportunity for trading, as he did on his first voyage. Yet he had some specimens from them and it was of very poor quality so that it appeared plated. They said, as well as he could understand by signs, that

---

[537] I.e., in Española.

there were some islands there where there was much of that gold, but that the people were canibales, and the Admiral says here that this word "Canibales" every one there held as a cause for enmity, or perhaps they said so because they did not wish the Christians to go yonder, but that they should remain there all their life. The Christians saw one Indian with a grain of gold as large as an apple.

Another time there came an infinite number of canoes loaded with people, and all wore gold and necklaces, and beads of infinite kinds, and had handkerchiefs tied on their heads as they had hair well cut, and they appeared very well. It rained a great deal, and for this reason the people ceased to go and come. Some women came who wore on the arms strings of beads, and mingled with them were pearls or *aljofars*,[538] very fine, not like the colored ones which were found on the islands of Babueca; they traded for some of them, and he says that he would send them to their Highnesses.

I never knew of these pearls that were found in the islands of Babueca, which are near Puerto de Plata, in this Española; and these besides are low under the water and not islands, and they are very dangerous to ships that pass that way if they are not aware of them; and so they have the name Abre el Ojo.[539]

The Admiral asked the Indians where they found them or fished them, and they showed him some mother-of-pearl where they are formed; and they replied to him by very clear signs, that they grow and are gathered towards the west, behind that island, which was the Cape of Lapa, the

---

[538] Irregularly shaped pearls, seed pearls.
[539] "Keep your eyes open."

Point of Paria and mainland, which he believed to be an island, but it was the mainland. He sent the boats to land to know if there was any new thing which he had not seen, and they found the people so tractable, says the Admiral, that, "although the sailors did not go intending to land, there came two principal persons with all the village, who induced them to descend and who took them to a large house, built near two streams and not round, like a camp-tent, in the manner of the houses of the islands, where they received them very well and made them a feast and gave them a collation, bread and fruit of many kinds; and the drink was a white beverage which had a great value, which every one brought there, at this time, and some of it is tinted and better than the other, as the wine with us. The men were all together at one end of the house and the women at the other. Having taken the collation at the house of the older man, the younger conducted them to the other house, where they went through the same function. It appeared that one must be the cacique and lord, and the other must be his son. Afterwards the sailors returned to the boats and with them went back to the ships, very pleased with this people." These are all the words of the Admiral. He says further: "They are of very handsome stature, and all uniformly large," and whiter than any other he had seen in these Indies, and that yesterday he saw many as white as we are, and with better hair and well cut, and of very good speech. "No lands in the world can be more green and beautiful or more populated; moreover the temperature since I have been in this island," says he, "is, I say, cool enough each morning for a lined gown, although it is so near the equinoctial line; the sea is however fresh. They called the island Paria." All are the words of the Admiral. He called the mainland an island, however, because so he believed it to be.

Friday, August 10, he ordered sail to be made and went to the west of that which he thought to be an island, and travelled five leagues and anchored. For fear of not finding bottom, he went to search for an opening [mouth] by which to get out of that gulf, within which he was going, encircled by mainland and islands, although he did not believe it to be mainland, and he says it is certain that that was an island, because the Indians said thus, and thus it appears he did not understand them. From there he saw another island facing the south, which he called Ysabeta,[540] which extends from the south-east to north-west, afterwards another which he called La Tramontana,[541] a high land and very beautiful, and it seemed that it ran from north to south. It appeared very large. This was the mainland. The Indians whom he had taken said--according to what he understood--that the people there were *Canibales* and that yonder was where the gold was found and that the pearls which they had given the Admiral they had sought and found on the northern part of Paria toward the west. The water of that sea he says was as fresh as that of the river of Seville and in the same manner muddy. He would have wished to go to those islands except for turning backward because of the haste he felt in order not to lose the supplies that he was taking for the Christians of Española, which with so much labor, difficulty and fatigue he had gathered for them; and as being a thing for the sake of which he had suffered much, he repeats this about the provisions or supplies many times. He says he believes that in those islands he had seen, there must be things of value because they are all large and high lands with valleys and plains and with many waters and very well cultivated and

---

[540] Isabela in the printed text.
[541] The north wind.

populated and the people of very good speech, as their gestures showed. These are the words of the Admiral.

He says also that if the pearls are born as Pliny[542] says from the dew which falls in the oysters while they are open, there is good reason for having them there because much dew falls in that place and there are an infinite number of oysters and very large ones and because there are no tempests there, but the sea is always calm, a sign of which is that the trees enter into the sea, which shows there is never a storm there, and every branch of the trees which were in the water (and there are also roots of certain trees in the sea, which according to the language of this Española are called *mangles*[543]) was full of an infinite number of oysters so that breaking a branch, it comes out full of oysters attached to it. They are white within, and their flesh also, and very savory, not salt but fresh and they require some salt, and he says that they do not know or spring from mother-of-pearl. Wherever the pearls are generated, he says, they are extremely fine and they pierce them as in Venice. As for this that the Admiral says that the branches were full of oysters there, we say that those oysters that he saw and that are on the branches above the water and a little under the water are not those that produce pearls, but another species; because those that bear pearls are more careful from their natural instinct to hide themselves as much further under water as they can than those he saw on the branches....[544]

---

[542] Pliny, *Natural History*, book IX., ch. LIV.

[543] The name is still used. It is the *Rhicopharia mangle*. See the description of it in Thompson's Alcedo's *Geographical and Historical Dictionary of America and the West Indies*, Appendix.

[544] Las Casas here inserts a long disquisition on pearls which is omitted. It covers pp. 246-252 of the printed edition, Vol. II.

Returning to where I dropped the thread of the history, at this place the Admiral mentions many points of land and islands and the names he had given them, but it does not appear when. In this and elsewhere the Admiral shows himself to be a native of another country and of another tongue, because he does not apprehend all the signification of the Castilian words nor the manner of using them. He gave names to the Punta Seca, the Ysla Ysabeta, the Ysla Tramontana, the Punta Llana, Punta Sara, assuming them to be known, although he has said nothing of them or of any of them. He says that all that sea is fresh, and he does not know from whence it proceeds, because it did not appear to have the flow from great rivers, and that, if it had them, he says it would not cease to be a marvel. But he was mistaken in thinking there were no rivers, since the river Yuyaparí furnished so great a flow of fresh water, as well as others which come from near there.

Desiring to get out of this Gulf of Ballena, where he was encircled by mainland and La Trinidad, as already said, in going to the west by that coast of the mainland, which he called "de Gracia" towards the point Seca, although he does not say where it was, he found two fathoms of water, no more. He sent the small caravel to see if there was an outlet to the north, because, in front of the mainland and of the other which he called Ysabeta, to the west, there appeared a very high and beautiful island. The caravel returned, and said that they found a great gulf, and in it four great openings which appeared small gulfs, and at the end of each one a river. This gulf he named Golpho de las Perlas, although I believe there are no pearls there. It appears that this was the inside corner of all this great gulf,[545] in which the Admiral was going enclosed by the mainland and the island of Trinidad; those four bays or

---

[545] *I.e., the western end of the Gulf of Paria.*

openings, the Admiral believed were four islands, and
that there did not appear to be a sign of a river, which
would make all that gulf, of 40 leagues, of sea, all fresh;
but the sailors affirmed that those openings were mouths
of rivers. And they say true, at least in regard to two of
these openings, because by one comes the great river
Yuyaparí and by the other comes another great river
which to-day is called the river of Camarí.[546]

The Admiral would have liked very much to find out the
truth of this secret, which was the cause of this great gulf
being 40 leagues in length by 26 in width, containing
fresh water, which was a thing, he says, for wonder, (and
he was certainly right), and also to penetrate the secrets
of those lands, where he did not believe it to be possible
that there were not things of value, or that they were not
in the Indies, especially from having found there traces of
gold and pearls and the news of them, and discovered
such lands, so many and such people in them; from which
the things there and their riches might easily be known;
but because the supplies he was carrying for the people
who were in this Española, and which he carried that
they who were in the mines gathering gold might have
food, were being lost, which food and supplies he had
gathered with great difficulty and fatigue, he did not
allow himself to be detained, and he says that, if he had
the hope of having more as quickly, he would postpone
delivering them, in order to discover more lands and see
the secrets of them; and finally he resolves to follow that
which is most sure, and come to this island, and send
from it moneys to Castile to bring supplies and people

---

[546] These mouths of the Orinoco supplied the fresh water, but they
can hardly be the streams referred to by the sailors who explored the
western end of the Gulf of Paria. Las Casas had no good map of this
region.

under hire, and at the earliest opportunity to send also his brother, the Adelantado, to prosecute his discovery and find great things, as he hoped they would be found, to serve our Lord and the Sovereigns.

Yet, just at the best time, the thread was cut, as will appear, of these his good desires, and he says thus: "Our Lord guides me by His pity and presents me things with which He may be served, and your Highnesses may have great pleasure, and certainly they ought to have pleasure, because here they have such a noble thing and so royal for great princes. And it is a great error to believe any one who speaks evil to them of this undertaking, but to abhor them, because there is not to be found a prince who has had so much grace from our Lord, and so much victory from a thing so signal and of so much honor to their high estate and realms, and by which God may receive endlessly more services and the people of Spain more refreshment and gains. Because it has been seen that there are infinite things of value, and although now this that I say may not be known, the time will come when it will be accounted of great excellence, and to the great reproach of those persons who oppose this project to your Highnesses; and although they may have expended something in this matter, it has been in a cause more noble and of greater account than any undertaking of any other prince until now, nor was it proper to withdraw from it hastily, but to proceed and give me aid and favor; because the Sovereigns of Portugal spent and had courage to spend in Guinea, for four or five years, money and people, before they received any benefit, and afterward God gave them advantages and gold. For certainly, if the people of the kingdom of Portugal be counted, and those of them who died in this undertaking of Guinea be enumerated, it would be found that they are more than half of the kingdom;[547] and certainly, it would be the greatest thing to have in Spain a revenue which would come from this undertaking. Your Highnesses would leave nothing of greater memory; and they may examine, and discover that no prince of Castile may be found, and I have not found such by history or by tradition,--who has ever gained land outside of Spain. And your Highnesses will gain these lands, so very great, which are another world,[548] and where Christianity will have so great pleasure, and our faith in time so great an increase.[549] All this I say with very honest intention, and because I desire that Your Highnesses may be the greatest Lords in the world,[550] I say Lords of it all; and that it may all be with great service and contentment of the Holy Trinity, for which at the end of their days they may have the glory

---

[547] Columbus elaborated this point in his letter to Ferdinand and Isabella. Major, *Select Letters of Columbus*, p. 113. Columbus's estimate of the sacrifice of lives in the exploration of the west coast of Africa must be considered a most gross exaggeration. The contemporary narratives of those explorations give no such impression.

[548] *Cf.* Columbus's letter to the sovereigns, "Your Highnesses have here another world." Major, *Select Letters of Columbus*, p. 148, and the letter to the nurse of Prince John, p. 381, *post.* "I have placed under the dominion of the King and Queen our sovereigns another world." These passages clearly show that Columbus during and after this voyage realized that he accomplished something quite different from merely reaching Asia by a western route. He had found a hitherto unknown portion of the world, unknown to the ancients or to Marco Polo, but not for that reason necessarily physically detached from the known Asia. For a fuller discussion of the meaning of the phrase "*another world*," "*New World*," and of Columbus's ideas of what he had done, see Bourne, *Spain in America*, pp. 94-98.

[549] A noteworthy prediction. In fact the discovery of the New World has effected a most momentous change in the relative strength and range of Christianity among the world-religions. During the Middle Ages Christianity lost more ground territorially than it gained. Since the discovery of America its gain has been steady.

[550] Such in fact their Highnesses' grandson, Charles I. (V. as Emperor), was during his long reign, and such during a part of his reign if not the whole, was their great-grandson Philip II. See Oviedo's reflections upon Columbus's career. Bourne, *Spain in America*, p. 82.

of Paradise, and not for that which concerns me myself, whose hope is in His High Majesty, that Your Highnesses will soon see the truth of it, and this is my ardent desire." All these are the actual words of the Admiral....[551]

So, in order to get out of this gulf, within which he was surrounded by land on all parts, with the intention already told of saving the supplies which he carried, which were being lost, in coming to this island of Española, --Saturday, August 11, at the appearance of the moon, he raised the anchors, spread the sails, and navigated toward the east (*el leste*), that is towards the place where the sun rises,[552] because he was in the corner of the gulf where was the river Yuyaparí as was said above, in order to go out between the Point of Paria and the mainland, which he called the Punta or Cabo de Lapa, and the land he named Ysla de Gracia, and between the cape which he called Cabo Boto of the island of Trinidad. He arrived at a very good harbor, which he called Puerto de Gatos,[553] which is connected with the mouth where are the two little islands of the Caracol and Delfin, between the capes of Lapa and Cape Boto. And this occurred Sunday, August 12.

He anchored near the said harbor, in order to go out by the said mouth in the morning. He found another port near there, to examine which he sent a boat. It was very good. They found certain houses of fishermen, and much

[551] Las Casas here comments at some length on these remarks of Columbus and the great significance of his discoveries. The passage omitted takes further down.
[552] Las Casas explains *leste*, which would seem to have been either peculiar to sailors or at least not in common usage then for "east."
[553] Probably *gatos* in the sense of *gatos paules*, monkeys, noted above, p. 341, as very plentiful.

water and very fresh. He named it Puerto de las abañas.[554] They found, he says, myrobolans on the land: near the sea, infinite oysters attached to the branches of the trees which enter into the sea, the mouths open to receive the dew which drops from the leaves and which engenders the pearls, as Pliny says and as is alleged in the vocabulary which is called *Catholicon*.[555]

Monday, August 13, at the rising of the moon, he weighed anchor from where he was, and came towards the Cape of Lapa, which is Paria, in order to go to the north by the mouth called Del Drago, for the following cause and danger in which he saw himself there; the Mouth of the Dragon, he says, is a strait which is between the Point of Lapa, the end of the island of Gracia, which is at the east end of the land of Paria and between Cape Boto which is the western end of the island of Trinidad. He says it is about a league and a half between the two capes. This must be after having passed four little islands which he says lie in the centre of the channel, although now we do not really see more than two, by which he could not go out, and there remained of the strait only a league and a half in the passage. From the Punta de la Lapa to the Cabo de Boto it is five leagues. Arriving at the said mouth at the hour of tierce,[556] he found a great struggle between the fresh water striving to go out to the sea and the salt water of the sea striving to enter into the gulf, and it was so strong and fearful, that it raised a great swell, like a very high hill, and with this, both waters made a noise

---

[554] Port of the Cabins.

[555] The *Catholicon* was one of the earliest Latin lexicons of modern times and the first to be printed. It was compiled by Johannes de Janua (Giovanni Balbi of Genoa) toward the end of the thirteenth century and first printed at Mainz in 1460, and very frequently later.

[556] The third of the canonical hours of prayer, about nine o'clock in the morning.

and thundering, from east to west, very great and fearful, with currents of water, and after one came four great waves one after the other, which made contending currents; here they thought to perish, no less than in the other mouth of the Sierpe by the Cape of Arenal when they entered into the gulf. This danger was doubly more than the other, because the wind with which they hoped to get out died away, and they wished to anchor, because there was no remedy other than that, although it was not without danger from the fierceness of the waters, but they did not find bottom, because the sea was very deep there. They feared that the wind having calmed, the fresh or salt water might throw them on the rocks with their currents, when there would be no help. It is related that the Admiral here said, although I did not find it written with his own hand as I found the above, that if they escaped from that place they could report that they escaped from the mouth of the dragon, and for this reason that name was given to it and with reason.

It pleased the goodness of God that from the same danger safety and deliverance came to them and the current of the fresh water overcame the current of the salt water and carried the ships safely out, and thus they were placed in security; because when God wills that one or many shall be kept alive, water is a remedy for them.[557] Thus they went out, Monday, August 13, from the said dangerous Gulf and Mouth of the Dragon. He says that there are 48 leagues from the first land of La Trinidad to the gulf which the sailors discovered whom he sent in the caravel, where they saw the rivers and he did not believe them, which gulf he called "de las Perlas," and this is the interior angle of all the large gulf, which he called "de la Ballena," where he travelled so many days encircled by

---

[557] *El agua les es medicina, i.e., a means of curing the ill.*

land. I add that it is a good 50 leagues, as appears from the chart.

Having gone out of the gulf and the Boca del Drago and having passed his danger, he decides to go to the west by the coast below[558] of the mainland, believing yet that it was the island of Gracia, in order to get abreast, on the right, of the said Gulf of the Pearls, north and south, and to go around it,[559] and see whence comes so great abundance of water, and to see if it proceeded from rivers, as the sailors affirmed and which he says he did not believe because he had not heard that either the Ganges, the Nile or the Euphrates[560] carried so much fresh water. The reason which moved him was because he did not see lands large enough to give birth to such great rivers, "unless indeed," he says, "that this is mainland." These are his words. So that he was already beginning to suspect that the land of Gracia which he believed to be an island is mainland, which it certainly was and is, and the sailors had been right, from which land there came such a quantity of water from the rivers, Yuyaparí and the other which flows out near it, which we now call Camarí, and others which must empty there, so that, going in search of

---

[558] *Abajo*. Las Casas views the mainland as extending up from the sea. Columbus was going west along the north shore of the peninsula of Paria.

[559] *I.e.*, to go west along the north shore of this supposed island until looking south he was to the right of it and abreast of the Gulf of Pearls.

[560] Three of the greatest known rivers, each of which drained a vast range of territory. This narrative reveals the gradual dawning upon Columbus of the fact that he had discovered a hitherto unknown continental mass. In his letter to the sovereigns his conviction is settled and his efforts to adjust it with previous knowledge and the geographical traditions of the ages are most interesting. See Major, *Select Letters of Columbus*, pp. 134 *et seqq*. "Ptolemy," he says, on p. 136, "and the others who have written upon the globe had no information respecting this part of the world, for it was most unknown."

that Gulf of the Pearls, where the said rivers empty, thinking to find it surrounded by land, considering it an island and to see if there was an entrance there, or an outlet to the south, and if he did not find it, he says he would affirm then that it was a river, and that both were a great wonder,--he went down the coast that Monday until the setting of the sun.

He saw that the coast was filled with good harbors and a very high land; by that lower coast he saw many islands toward the north and many capes on the mainland, to all of which he gave names: to one, Cabo de Conchas; to another, Cabo Luengo; to another, Cabo de Sabor; to another, Cabo Rico. A high and very beautiful land. He says that on that way there are many harbors and very large gulfs which must be populated, and the farther he went to the west he saw the land more level and more beautiful. On going out of the mouth, he saw an island to the north, which might be 26 leagues from the north, and named it La Isla de la Asuncion; he saw another island and named it La Concepcion, and three other small islands together he called Los Testigos.[561] They are called this to-day. Another near them he called El Romero, and three other little small islands he called Las Guardias. Afterwards he arrived near the Isla Margarita, and called it Margarita, and another near it he named El Martinet.

This Margarita is an island 15 leagues long, and 5 or 6 wide, and is very green and beautiful on the coast and is very good within, for which reason it is inhabited; it has near it extending lengthwise east and west, three small islands, and two behind them extending north and south.

---

[561] The Witnesses.

The Admiral did not see more than the three, as he was going along the southern part of Margarita. It is six or seven leagues from the mainland, and this makes a small gulf between it and the mainland, and in the middle of the gulf are two small islands, east and west, beside each other: the one is called Coche, which means deer, and the other Cubagua, which is the one we have described in chapter 136, and said that there are an infinite quantity of pearls gathered there. So that the Admiral, although he did not know that the pearls were formed in this gulf, appears to have divined that fact in naming it Margarita; he was very near it, although he does not express it, because he says he was nine leagues from the island of Martinet, which he says was near Margarita, on the northern part, and he says near it, because as he was going along the southern part of Margarita, it appeared to be near, although it was eight or nine leagues away; and this is the small island to the north, near Margarita, which is now called Blanca, and is distant eight or nine leagues from Margarita as I said. For here it seems that the Admiral must have been close to or near Margarita and I believe that he anchored because the wind failed him. Finally of all the names that he gave to the islands and capes of the mainland which he took for the island of Gracia none have lasted or are used to-day except Trinidad, Boca del Drago, Los Testigos, and Margarita.

There the eyes of the Admiral became very bad from not sleeping. Because always, as he was in so many dangers sailing among islands, it was his custom himself to watch on deck, and whoever takes ships with cargo should for the most part do that very thing, like the pilots, and he says that he found himself more fatigued here than when he discovered the other mainland, which is the island of Cuba, (which he regarded as mainland even until now), because his eyes were bloodshot; and thus his labors on the sea were incomparable. For this reason he was in bed this night, and therefore he found himself farther out in the sea than he would have been if he had himself watched, from which he did not trust himself to the sailors, nor should any one who is a diligent and perfect pilot trust to anybody, because dependent on him and on his head are all those who go in the ship, and that which is most necessary and proper to his office is to watch and not sleep all the time while he navigates.

The Admiral appears to have gone down the coast after he came out of the Mouth of the Dragon, yesterday Monday and to-day Tuesday, 30 or 40 leagues at least, although he does not say so, as he complains that he did not write all that he had to write, as he could not on account of his being so ill here. And as he saw that the land was becoming very extended below to the west, and appeared more level and more beautiful, and the Gulf of the Pearls which was in the back part of the gulf, or fresh-water sea, whence the river of Yuyaparí flowed, in the search of which he was going, had no outlet, which he hoped to see, believing that this mainland was an island, he now became conscious that a land so great was not an island, but mainland, and as if speaking with the Sovereigns, he says here: "I believe that this is mainland, very great, which until to-day has not been known. And reason aids me greatly because of this being such a great river and because of this sea which is fresh, and next the saying of Esdras aids me, in the 4th book, chapter 6th, which says that the six parts of the world are of dry land and the one of water.[562] Which book St. Ambrose approves in his

---

[562] The reference is to *II. Esdras*, VI. 42, in the Apocrypha of the English Bible. The Apocryphal books of I. and II. Esdras were known as III. and IV. Esdras in the Middle Ages, and the canonical books in the Vulgate called I. and II. Esdras are called Ezra and Nehemiah in the English Bible. II. Esdras is an apocalyptic work and dates from the close of the first century A.D. The passage to which Columbus referred reads as follows: "Upon the third

Examenon[563] and St. Augustine on the passage, 'Morietur filius meus Christus,' as Francisco de Mayrones alleges.[564] And further, I am supported by the sayings of many Canibales Indians, whom I took at other times, who said that to the south of them was mainland, and at that time I was on the island of Guadeloupe, and also I heard it from others of the island of Sancta Cruz and of Sant Juan, and they said that in it there was much gold, and, as your Highnesses know, a very short time ago, there was no other land known than that which Ptolemy wrote of, and there was not in my time any one who would believe that one could navigate from Spain to the Indies; about which matter I was seven years in your Court, and there were few who understood it; and finally the very great courage of your Highnesses caused it to be tried, against the opinion of those who contradicted it. And now the truth appears, and it will appear before long, much greater; and if this is mainland, it is a thing of wonder, and it will be so among all the learned, since so great a river flows out that it makes a fresh-water sea of 48 leagues." These are his words....[565]

---

day thou didst command that the waters should be gathered in the seventh part of the earth; six parts hast thou dried up, and kept them, to the intent that of these some being planted of God and tilled might serve thee."

[563] The reference is wrong, as Las Casas points out two or three pages further on (II. 266); it should be to the treatise *De Bono Mortis*, cap. 10

[564] Francis de Mayrones was an eminent Scotist philosopher. He died in 1327. Columbus here quotes from his Theologicae Veritates (Venice, 1493). See *Raccolta Colombiana*, Parte I., tomo II., p. 377. Las Casas (II. 266) was unable to verify the citation from St. Augustine.

[565] The passage omitted, Las Casas, II. 265-307, consists first, pp. 265-267, of his comments on these words of Columbus, and second, pp. 268-274, of a criticism of Vespucci's claim to have made a voyage in 1497 to this region of Paria, and of his narratives and the naming of America from him. This criticism is translated with Las Casas's other trenchant criticisms of Vespucci's work and claims by Sir Clements R. Markham in his *Letters of Amerigo Vespucci* (London, 1894), pp. 68 *et seq.* These passages are very interesting as perhaps the earliest piece of detailed critical work relating to the discoveries, and they still constitute the cornerstone of the case

Having finished this digression let us return then to our history and to what the Admiral resolved to do in the place where he was, and that is, going as fast as possible, he wished to come to this Española, for some reasons which impelled him greatly: one, because he was going with great anxiety and affliction, as he had not had news of the condition of this island for so many days; and it would seem that he had some, premonition of the disorder and the losses and the travail which with the rising of Francisco Roldan[566] all this land and his brothers were suffering; the other in order to despatch immediately the Adelantado, his brother, with three ships, to continue his discovery of the mainland which he had already begun to explore; and it is certain that if Francisco Roldan with his rebellion and shamelessness had not prevented him, the Admiral or his brother for him would have discovered the mainland as far as New Spain; but, according to the decree of Divine Providence, the hour of its discovery had not come, nor was the permission recalled[567] by which many were being enabled to distinguish themselves in unjust works under color of making discoveries.

The third cause which hastened him in coming to this island, was from seeing that the supplies were spoiling

---

against Vespucci. The third portion of the omitted passage, pp. 275-306, is a long essay on the location of the earthly paradise which Columbus placed in this new mainland he had just discovered. *Cf.* Columbus's letter on the Third Voyage. Major, *Select Letters of Columbus*, pp. 140-146.

[566] On the Roldan revolt, see Irving, *Christopher Columbus*, II. 199 *et seqq.*

[567] April 10, 1495, the sovereigns authorized independent exploring expeditions. Columbus protested that such expeditions infringed upon his rights, and so, June 2, 1497, the sovereigns modified their ordinance and prohibited any infringements. Apparently Las Casas is in error in saying the permission had not been recalled in 1498, but the independent voyages of Hojeda and Pinzon, who first explored the northern coast of South America (Paria) in 1499-1500, may have led him to conclude that the authorization had not been recalled.

and being lost, of which he had such great need for the relief of those who were here, which made him weep again, considering that he had obtained them with great difficulties and fatigues, and he says that, if they are lost, he has no hope of getting others, from the great opposition he always encountered from those who counselled the Sovereigns, "who," he says here, "are not friends nor desire the honor of the high condition of their Highnesses, the persons who have spoken evil to them of such a noble undertaking. Nor was the cost so great that it should not be expended, although benefits might not be had quickly to recompense it, since the service was very great which was rendered our Lord in spreading His Holy Name through unknown lands. And besides this, it would be a much greater memorial than any Prince had left, spiritual and temporal." And the Admiral says further, "And for this the revenue of a good bishopric or archbishopric would be well secured, and I say," says he, "as good as the best in Spain, since there are here so many resources and as yet no priesthood. They may have heard that here there are infinite peoples, which may have determined the sending here of learned and intelligent persons and friends of Christ to try and make them Christians and commence the work; the establishment of which bishopric I am very sure will be made, please our Lord, and the revenues will soon come from here and be carried there." These are his words. How much truth he spoke and how clear a case there was of inattention and remissness and lukewarmness of charity in the men of that day, spiritual or ecclesiastical and temporal, who held the power and resources, not to make provision for the healing and conversion of these peoples, so disposed and ready to receive the faith, the day of universal judgment will reveal.

The fourth cause for coming to this island and not stopping to discover more, which he would have very much wished, as he says, was because the seamen did not come prepared to make discoveries, since he says that he did not dare to say in Castile that he came with intention to make discoveries, because they would have placed some impediments in his way, or would have demanded more money of him than he had, and he says that the people were becoming very tired. The fifth cause, was because the ships he had were large for making discoveries, as the one was of more than 100 tons and the other more than 70, and only smaller ones are needed to make discoveries; and because of the ship which he took on his first voyage being large, he lost it in the harbor of Navidad, kingdom of the King Guacanagarí.[568] Also the sixth reason which very much constrained him to leave the discoveries and come to this island, was because of having his eyes almost lost from not sleeping, from the long and continued watches or vigils he had had; and in this place he says thus: "May it please our Lord to free me from this malady," he says. "He well knows that I did not suffer these fatigues in order to find treasures for myself, since surely I recognize that all is vanity which is done in this age, save that which is for the honor and service of God, which is not to amass pomps or riches, nor the many other things we use in this world, in which we are more inclined than to the things which can save us." These are his words.

Truly this man had a good Christian purpose and was very contented with his own estate and desired in a moderate degree to maintain himself in it, and to rest from such sore travail, which he fully merited; yet the result of his sweat and toil was to impose a greater burden on the Sovereigns, and I do not know what greater was necessary than had already fallen to them, and even

---

[568] See Journal of First Voyage, December 25.

he had imposed obligations on them, except that he kept seeing that little importance was made of his distinguished services that he had performed, and that all at once the estimation of these Indies which was held at first was declining and coming to naught, through those that had the ears of the Sovereigns, so that he feared each day greater disfavors and that the Sovereigns might give up the whole business and thus his sweat and travail be entirely lost.

Having determined, then, to come as quickly as he could to this island, Wednesday, August 15, which was the day of the Assumption of Our Lady, after the rising of the sun, he ordered the anchors weighed from where he was anchored, which must have been within the small gulf which Margarita and the other islands make with the mainland (and he must have been near Margarita as we said above), and sailed on the way to this island; and, pursuing his way, he saw very clearly Margarita and the little islands which were there, and also, the farther away he went, he discovered more high land of the continent. And he went that day from sunrise to sunset 63 leagues, because of the great currents which supplemented the wind....[569]

Let us return to the voyage of the Admiral, whom we left started from the neighborhood of the island of Margarita, and he went that day, Wednesday, 63 leagues from sun to sun, as they say. The next day, Thursday, August 16, he navigated to the north-west, quarter of the north,[570] 26 leagues, with the sea calm, "thanks be to God," as he always said. He tells here a wonderful thing, that when

---

[569] The passage omitted, II. 309-313, of the printed edition, gives an account of the voyage and arrival of the vessels which came to Española directly from the Canaries.
[570] Northwest by north.

he left the Canaries for this Española, having gone 300 leagues to the west, then the needles declined to the north-west[571] one quarter, and the North Star did not rise but 5 degrees, and now in this voyage it has not declined to the north-west until last night, when it declined more than a quarter and a half, and some needles declined a half wind which are two quarters;[572] and this happened suddenly last night. And he says each night he was marvelling at such a change in the heavens, and of the temperature there, so near the equinoctial line, which he experienced in all this voyage, after having found land; especially the sun being in Leo, where, as has been told, in the mornings a loose gown was worn, and where the people of that place--Gracia--were actually whiter than the people who have been seen in the Indies. He also found in the place where he now came, that the North Star was in 14 degrees when the Guardians had passed from the head after two hours and a half. Here he again exhorted the Sovereigns to esteem this affair highly, since he had shown them that there was in this land gold, and he had seen in it minerals without number, which will have to be extracted with intelligence, industry and labor, since even the iron, as much as there is, cannot be taken out without these sacrifices; and he has taken them a nugget of 20 ounces and many others, and where this is, it must be believed there is plenty, and he took their Highnesses a lump of copper originally of six *arrobas*,[573] lapis-lazuli, gum-lac, amber, cotton, pepper, cinnamon, a great quantity of Brazil-wood, aromatic gum,[574] white and

---

[571] Northeast in the printed text.

[572] The circle of the horizon, represented by the compass card, was conceived of as divided into eight winds and each wind into halves and quarters, the quarters corresponding to the modern points of the compass, which are thirty-two in number. The declination observed was two points of the compass, or 22° 30'.

[573] An arroba was twenty-five pounds.

[574] *Estoraque*, officinal storax, a gum used for incense.

yellow sandalwood, flax, aloes, ginger, incense, myrobolans of all kinds, very fine pearls and pearls of a reddish color, which Marco Polo says are worth more than the white ones,[575] and that may well be so in some parts just as it is the case with the shells that are gathered in Canaria and are sold for so great a price in the Mine of Portugal. "There are infinite kinds of spices which have been seen of which I do not care to speak for fear of prolixity." All these are his words.

As to what he says of cinnamon, and aloes and ginger, incense, myrobolans, sandal woods, I never saw them in this island, at least I did not recognize them; what he says of flax must mean *cabuya*[576] which are leaves like the *cavila* from which thread is made and cloth or linen can be made from it, but it is more like hemp cloth than linen. There are two sorts of it, *cabuya* and *nequen*; *cabuya* is coarse and rough and *nequen* is soft and delicate. Both are words of this island Española. Storax gum I never smelled except in the island of Cuba, but I did not see it, and this is certain that in Cuba there must be trees of it, or of a gum that smells like it, because we never smelled it except in the fires that the Indians make of wood that they burn in their houses. It is a most perfect perfume, certainly. I never knew of incense being found in these islands.

Returning to the journey, Friday, August 17, he went 37 leagues, the sea being smooth, "to God our Lord," he says, "may infinite thanks be given." He says that not finding islands now, assures him that that land from whence he came is a vast mainland, or where the Earthly Paradise

[575] Cf. Marco Polo, bk. III., ch. II.
[576] Pita, the fibre of the American agave.

is, "because all say that it is at the end of the east, and this is the Earthly Paradise,"[577] says he.

Saturday, between day and night, he went 39 leagues.

Sunday, August 19, he went in the day and the night 33 leagues, and reached land; and this was a very small island which he called Madama Beata, and which is now commonly so called. This is a small island of a matter of a league and a half close by this island of Española, and distant from this port of Sancto Domingo about 50 leagues and distant 15 leagues from the port of Yaquino, which is more to the west. There is next to it another smaller one which has a small but somewhat high mountain, which from a distance looks like a sail, and he named it Alto Velo.[578] He believed that the Beata was a small island which he called Sancta Catherina when he came by this southern coast, from the discovery of the island of Cuba, and distant from this port of Sancto Domingo 25 leagues, and is next to this island. It weighed upon him to have fallen off in his course so much, and he says it should not be counted strange, since during the nights he was from caution beating about to windward, for fear of running against some islands or shoals; there was therefore reason for this error, and thus in not following a straight course, the currents, which are very strong here, and which flow down towards the mainland and the west, must have carried the ships, without realizing it, so low. They run so violently there toward La Beata that it has happened that a ship has been eight months in those waters without

---

[577] *Cf.* the letter on the Third Voyage, Major, *Select Letters of Columbus*, p. 140, for Columbus's reasoning and beliefs about the Earthly Paradise or Garden of Eden; for Las Casas's discussion of the question, see *Historia de las Indias*, II. 275-306.
[578] High sail.

being able to reach this port and that much of delay in coming from there here, has happened many times.

Therefore he anchored now between the Beata and this island, between which there are two leagues of sea, Monday, August 20. He then sent the boats to land to call Indians, as there were villages there, in order to write of his arrival to the Adelantado; having come at midday, he despatched them. Twice there came to the ship six Indians, and one of them carried a crossbow with its cord, and nut and rack,[579] which caused him no small surprise, and he said, "May it please God that no one is dead." And because from Sancto Domingo the three ships must have been seen to pass downward, and concluding that it certainly was the Admiral as he was expecting him each day, the Adelantado started then in a caravel and overtook the Admiral here. They both were very much pleased to see each other. The Admiral having asked him about the condition of the country, the Adelantado recounted to him how Francisco Roldan had arisen with 80 men, with all the rest of the occurrences which had passed in this island, since he left it. What he felt on hearing such news, there is small need to recite.

He left there, Wednesday, August 22, and finally with some difficulty because of the many currents and the north-east breezes which are continuous and contrary there he arrived at this port of Sancto Domingo, Friday, the last day of August of the said year 1498, having set out from Isabela for Castile, Thursday the tenth day of March, 1496, so that he delayed in returning to this island two years and a half less nine days.

---

[579] The rack was used to bend the crossbow.

Letter of Columbus to the Nurse of Prince John

INTRODUCTION

This letter was addressed by Columbus to Doña Juana de Torres, who had been a nurse of the lately deceased royal prince John, the son of Ferdinand and Isabella, and who was the sister of Antonio de Torres, who had accompanied Columbus on his second voyage and was subsequently a commander in other voyages to the New World. It was probably written on shipboard when Columbus was sent back to Spain in irons in the autumn of the year 1500. It is at once a cry of distress and an impassioned self-defence, and is one of the most important of the Admiral's writings for the student of his career and character.

In the letter to Santangel the discoverer announces his success in his long projected undertaking; in the letter to the nurse he is at the lowest point in the startling reverse of fortune that befell him because of the troubles in Santo Domingo, and in the letter on the fourth voyage he appears as one struggling against the most adverse circumstances to vindicate his career, and to demonstrate the value of what he had previously accomplished, and to crown those achievements by actually attaining the coast of Asia. Columbus regarded his defence as set forth in this letter as of such importance that he included it in the four codices or collections of documents and papers prepared in duplicate before his last voyage to authenticate his titles and honors and to secure their inheritance by his son. The text of the letter from which the present translation was made is that of the Paris Codex of the *Book of Privileges*, as it is called. This is regarded by Harrisse as the best. The translation is by George F. Barwick of the British Museum, and was originally published in *Christopher Columbus, Facsimile of his Own Book of Privileges*, 1502, edited by B.F. Stevens (London, 1903). The letter remained unpublished until it was printed in Spotorno's *Codice Diplomatico* in 1822. In 1825 it appeared again in Navarrete's *Viages*, in a slightly varying text. It was first published in English in the translation of the *Codice Diplomatico* issued in London in 1823 under the title of *Memorials of Columbus*, etc.

E.G.B.

TRANSCRIPT OF A LETTER WHICH THE ADMIRAL OF THE INDIES SENT TO THE NURSE OF PRINCE DON JOHN OF CASTILE

IN THE YEAR 1500 WHEN HE WAS RETURNING FROM THE INDIES AS A PRISONER

Most virtuous Lady:--

Though my complaint of the world is new, its habit of ill-using is very ancient. I have had a thousand struggles with it, and have thus far withstood them all, but now neither arms nor counsels avail me, and it cruelly keeps me under water. Hope in the Creator of all men sustains me; His help was always very ready; on another occasion, and not long ago, when I was still more overwhelmed, he raised me with his right arm, saying, O man of little faith, arise, it is I; be not afraid.[580]

I came with so much cordial affection to serve these Princes, and have served them with such service, as has never been heard of or seen.

Of the new heaven and earth which our Lord made, when Saint John was writing the Apocalypse,[581] after what was spoken by the mouth of Isaiah,[582] he made me the

---

[580] An echo of the words of Jesus to Peter when he began to sink, "O thou of little faith, wherefore didst thou doubt?" *Matthew*, XIV. 31.

[581] *Revelation*, XXI. 1. "And I saw a new heaven and a new earth; for the first heaven and the first earth were passed away."

[582] "For, behold, I create new heavens and a new earth." Isaiah, LXV. 17.

messenger, and showed me where it lay. In all men there was disbelief, but to the Queen my Lady He gave the spirit of understanding, and great courage, and made her heiress of all, as a dear and much loved daughter. I went to take possession of all this in her royal name. They sought to make amends to her for the ignorance they had all shown by passing over their little knowledge, and talking of obstacles and expenses. Her Highness, on the other hand, approved of it, and supported it as far as she was able.

Seven years passed in discussion, and nine in execution.[583] During this time very remarkable and noteworthy things occurred whereof no idea at all had been formed. I have arrived at, and am in such a condition that there is no person so vile but thinks he may insult me; he shall be reckoned in the world as valor itself who is courageous enough not to consent to it.

If I were to steal the Indies or the land which lies towards them,[584] of which I am now speaking, from the altar of Saint Peter, and give them to the Moors, they could not show greater enmity towards me in Spain. Who would believe such a thing where there was always so much magnanimity?

I should have much desired to free myself from this affair had it been honorable towards my Queen to do so. The support of Our Lord and of Her Highness made me persevere; and to alleviate in some measure the sorrows

---

[583] 1485-1491 inc. and 1492-1500 inc.

[584] *Sy yo robara las Yndias o tierra que jaz fase ellas*, etc. In the translation *jaz fase* is taken to stand for *yace hacia*. This supposition makes sense and is probably correct. The reading of the other text is "*que san face ellas.*" Navarrete says that neither one is intelligible.

which death had caused her,[585] I undertook a fresh voyage to the new heaven and earth which up to that time had remained hidden; and if it is not held there in esteem like the other voyages to the Indies, that is no wonder because it came to be looked upon as my work.

The Holy Spirit inflamed Saint Peter and twelve others with him, and they all fought here below, and their toils and hardships were many, but last of all they gained the victory.

This voyage to Paria[586] I thought would somewhat appease them on account of the pearls, and of the discovery of gold in Española. I ordered the pearls to be collected and fished for by people with whom an arrangement was made that I should return for them, and, as I understood, they were to be measured by the bushel.[587] If I did not write about this to their Highnesses, it was because I wished to have first of all done the same thing with the gold. The result to me in this has been the same as in many other things; I should not have lost them nor my honor, if I had sought my own advantage, and had allowed Española to be ruined, or if my privileges and contracts had been observed. And I say just the same about the gold which I had then collected, and [for] which with such great afflictions and toils I have, by divine power, almost perfected [the arrangements].

When I went from Paria I found almost half the people of Española in revolt,[588] and they have waged war against

---

[585] The death of Prince John, October 4, 1497.

[586] The name given to that part of the mainland of South America which Columbus discovered on his third voyage.

[587] I.e. so great was their abundance.

[588] On this revolt, see Bourne, *Spain in America*, p. 49 *et seqq.*, and in greater detail, Irving, *Columbus*, ed. 1868, II. 109 *et seqq.*

me until now, as against a Moor; and the Indians on the other side grievously [harassed me]. At this time Hojeda arrived[589] and tried to put the finishing stroke: he said that their Highnesses had sent him with promises of gifts, franchises and pay; he gathered together a great band, for in the whole of Española there are very few save vagabonds, and not one with wife and children. This Hojeda gave me great trouble; he was obliged to depart, and left word that he would soon return with more ships and people, and that he had left the royal person of the Queen our Lady at the point of death. Then Vincent Yañez[590] arrived with four caravels; there was disturbance and mistrust, but no mischief; the Indians talked of many others at the Canibales [Caribbee Islands] and in Paria; and afterwards spread the news of six other caravels, which were brought by a brother of the Alcalde,[591] but it was with malicious intent. This occurred at the very last, when the hope that their Highnesses would ever send any ships to the Indies was almost abandoned, nor did we expect them; and it was commonly reported that her Highness was dead.

A certain Adrian about this time endeavored to rise in rebellion again, as he had done previously, but Our Lord did not permit his evil purpose to succeed. I had purposed in myself never to touch a hair of anybody's head, but I lament to say that with this man, owing to his

---

[589] Hojeda sailed in May 1499. Las Casa's account of his voyage is translated by Markham in his *Letters of Amerigo Vespucci*, Hakluyt Society (London, 1894), p. 78 *et seqq.* See also Irving, *Columbus*, III. 23-42, He was accompanied on this voyage by Amerigo Vespucci.

[590] Vicente Yañez Pinzon set sail from Palos, November 18, 1499. For his voyage, see Irving, *Columbus*, III. 49-58.

[591] The Alcalde was Roldan, the leader of the revolt. He was alcalde mayor of the city of Isabela and of the whole island, *i.e.*, the chief justice. Las Casas, *Historia de las Indias*, II. 124.

ingratitude, it was not possible to keep that resolve as I had intended; I should not have done less to my brother, if he had sought to kill me, and steal the dominion which my King and Queen had given me in trust.[592] This Adrian, as it appears, had sent Don Ferdinand[593] to Xaragua to collect some of his followers, and there a dispute arose with the Alcalde from which a deadly contest ensued, but he [Adrian] did not effect his purpose. The Alcalde seized him and a part of his band, and the fact was that he would have executed them if I had not prevented it; they were kept prisoners awaiting a caravel in which they might depart. The news of Hojeda which I told them, made them lose the hope that he would now come again.

For six months I had been prepared to return to their Highnesses with the good news of the gold, and to escape from governing a dissolute people, who fear neither God, nor their King and Queen, being full of vices and wickedness. I could have paid the people in full with six hundred thousand,[594] and for this purpose I had four millions of tenths and somewhat more, besides the third of the gold. Before my departure I many times begged their Highnesses to send there, at my expense, some one to take charge of the administration of justice; and after finding the Alcalde in arms I renewed my supplications to have either some troops or at least some servant of theirs with letters patent; for my reputation is such that even if I build churches and hospitals, they will always be called dens of thieves. They did indeed make provision at last, but it was the very contrary of what the matter demanded: may it be successful,

---

[592] On the career in Española of Adrian de Muxica and his execution, see Irving, *Columbus*, II. 283 *et seqq*.

[593] Ferdinand de Guevara. See Irving, *Columbus*, II. 283 *et seqq*.

[594] *I.e.*, maravedis, equivalent to about $4000.

since it was according to their good pleasure.

I was there for two years without being able to gain a decree of favor for myself or for those who went there, yet this man[595] brought a coffer full; whether they will all redound to their [Highnesses'] service, God knows. Indeed, to begin with, there are exemptions for twenty years, which is a man's lifetime; and gold is collected to such an extent that there was one person who became worth five marks[596] in four hours; whereof I will speak more fully later on.

If it would please their Highnesses to remove the grounds of a common saying of those who know my labors, that the calumny of the people has done me more harm than much service and the maintenance of their [Highnesses'] property and dominion has done me good, it would be a charity, and I should be re-established in my honor, and it would be talked about all over the world; for the undertaking is of such a nature that it must daily become more famous and in higher esteem.

When the commander Bobadilla came to Santo Domingo,[597] I was at La Vega, and the Adelantado[598] at Xaragua, where that Adrian had made a stand, but then all was quiet, and the land rich and all men at peace. On the second day after his arrival he created himself Governor, and appointed officers and made executions,

---

[595] Bobadilla, the successor of Columbus as governor, who sent him back in chains.
[596] A mark was eight ounces or two-thirds of a Troy pound. Here it is probably the silver mark as a measure of value, which was about $3.25. If the word is used as a measure of weight of gold, it would be about $150.
[597] Bobadilla arrived at Santo Domingo August 23, 1500.
[598] Bartholomew Columbus.

and proclaimed immunities of gold and tenths and in general of everything else for twenty years, which is a man's lifetime, and that he came to pay everybody in full up to that day, even though they had not rendered service; and he publicly notified that, as for me, he had charge to send me in irons, and my brothers likewise, as he has done, and that I should nevermore return thither, nor any other of my family; alleging a thousand disgraceful and discourteous things about me. All this took place on the second day after his arrival, as I have said, and while I was absent at a distance, without my knowing either of him or of his arrival.

Some letters of their Highnesses signed in blank, of which he brought a number, he filled up and sent to the Alcalde and to his company, with favors and commendations; to me he never sent either letter or messenger, nor has he done so to this day. Imagine what any one holding my office would think when one who endeavored to rob their Highnesses, and who has done so much evil and mischief, is honored and favored, while he who maintained it at such risks is degraded.

When I heard this, I thought that this affair would be like that of Hojeda or one of the others, but I restrained myself when I learnt for certain from the friars that their Highnesses had sent him. I wrote to him that his arrival was welcome, and that I was prepared to go to the Court and had sold all I possessed by auction; and that with respect to the immunities he should not be hasty, for both that matter and the government I would hand over to him immediately as smooth as my palm. And I wrote to the same effect to the friars, but neither he nor they gave me any answer. On the contrary, he put himself in a warlike attitude, and compelled all who went there to take an oath to him as Governor; and they told me that it was for twenty years.

Directly I knew of those immunities, I thought that I would repair such a great error and that he would be pleased, for he gave them without the need or occasion necessary in so vast a matter; and he gave to vagabond people what would have been excessive for a man who had brought wife and children. So I announced by word and letters that he could not use his patents because mine were those in force; and I showed them the immunities which Juan Aguado[599] brought. All this was done by me in order to gain time, so that their Highnesses might be informed of the condition of the country, and that they might have an opportunity of issuing fresh commands as to what would best promote their service in that respect.

It is useless to publish such immunities in the Indies; to the settlers who have taken up residence it is a pure gain, for the best lands are given to them, and at a low valuation they will be worth two hundred thousand at the end of the four years when the period of residence is ended, without their digging a spadeful in them. I would not speak thus if the settlers were married, but there are not six among them all who are not on the lookout to gather what they can and depart speedily. It would be a good thing if people should go from Castile, and also if it were known who and what they are, and if the country could be settled with honest people.

I had agreed with those settlers that they should pay the third of the gold, and the tenths, and this at their own request; and they received it as a great favor from their Highnesses. I reproved them when I heard that they

---

[599] Juan Aguado arrived from Spain in October, 1495. Las Casas, *Historia de las Indias*, II. 109 *et seqq.*, gives a full account of his mission. See also Irving, *Columbus*, ed. 1868, II. 77 *et seqq.*

ceased to do this, and hoped that the Commander would do likewise, but he did the contrary. He incensed them against me by saying that I wanted to deprive them of what their Highnesses had given them; and he endeavored to set them at variance with me, and did so; and he induced them to write to their Highnesses that they should never again send me back to the government, and I likewise make the same supplication to them for myself and for my whole family, as long as there are not different inhabitants. And he together with them ordered inquisitions concerning me for wickednesses the like whereof were never known in hell. Our Lord, who rescued Daniel and the three children,[600] is present with the same wisdom and power as he had then, and with the same means, if it should please him and be in accordance with his will.

I should know how to remedy all this, and the rest of what has been said and has taken place since I have been in the Indies, if my disposition would allow me to seek my own advantage, and if it seemed honorable to me to do so, but the maintenance of justice and the extension of the dominion of Her Highness has hitherto kept me down. Now that so much gold is found, a dispute arises as to which brings more profit, whether to go about robbing or to go to the mines. A hundred castellanos[601] are as easily obtained for a woman as for a farm, and it is very general, and there are plenty of dealers who go about looking for girls; those from nine to ten are now in demand, and for all ages a good price must be paid.

I assert that the violence of the calumny of turbulent persons has injured me more than my services have

---

[600] Cf. *Daniel*, chs. III. and VI.

[601] The castellano was one-sixth of an ounce, or in value about $3.

profited me; which is a bad example for the present and for the future. I take my oath that a number of men have gone to the Indies who did not deserve water in the sight of God and of the world; and now they are returning thither, and leave is granted them.[602]

I assert that when I declared that the Commander[603] could not grant immunities, I did what he desired, although I told him that it was to cause delay until their Highnesses should receive information from the country, and should command anew what might be for their service. He excited their enmity against me, and he seems, from what took place and from his behavior, to have come as my enemy and as a very vehement one; or else the report is true that he has spent much to obtain this employment. I do not know more about it than what I hear. I never heard of an inquisitor gathering rebels together and accepting them, and others devoid of credit and unworthy of it, as witnesses against their governor.

If their Highnesses were to make a general inquisition there, I assure you that they would look upon it as a great wonder that the island does not founder.

I think your Ladyship will remember that when, after losing my sails, I was driven into Lisbon by a tempest, I was falsely accused of having gone there to the King in order to give him the Indies. Their Highnesses afterwards learned the contrary, and that it was entirely malicious.

---

[602] See Bourne, *Spain in America*, p. 50, for Columbus's bitter characterization of the Spaniards in Española in 1498, and p. 46 for the royal authorization in June, 1497, to transport criminals to the island. The terrible consequences of this policy led the Spanish government later to adopt the strictest regulations controlling emigration to the New World. *Cf. Spain in America*, ch. XVI.

[603] Bobadilla was a knight commander of the military order of Calatrava.

Although I may know but little, I do not think anyone considers me so stupid as not to know that even if the Indies were mine I could not uphold myself without the help of some prince. If this be so, where could I find better support and security than in the King and Queen our Lords, who have raised me from nothing to such great honor, and are the most exalted princes of the world on sea and on land, and who consider that I have rendered them service, and preserve to me my privileges and rewards; and if anyone infringes them, their Highnesses increase them still more, as was seen in the case of Juan Aguado; and they order great honor to be conferred upon me, and, as I have already said, their Highnesses have received service from me, and keep my sons in their household;[604] all which could by no means happen with another prince, for where there is no affection, everything else fails.

I have now spoken thus in reply to a malicious slander, but against my will, as it is a thing which should not recur to memory even in dreams; for the Commander Bobadilla maliciously seeks in this way to set his own conduct and actions in a brighter light; but I shall easily show him that his small knowledge and great cowardice, together with his inordinate cupidity, have caused him to fail therein.

I have already said that I wrote to him and to the friars, and immediately set out, as I told him, almost alone, because all the people were with the Adelantado, and likewise in order to prevent suspicion on his part. When he heard this, he seized Don Diego[605] and sent him on

---

[604] Diego Columbus had been appointed a page to Prince John in 1492. Navarrete, iages, II. 17. At this time, 1500, both Diego and Ferdinand were pages in the Queen's household. *Historie*, ed. 1867, p. 276.
[605] The younger brother of the Admiral.

board a caravel loaded with irons, and did the same to me upon my arrival, and afterwards to the Adelantado when he came; nor did I speak to him any more, nor to this day has he allowed anyone to speak to me; and I take my oath that I cannot understand why I am made a prisoner. He made it his first business to seize the gold, which he did without measuring or weighing it, and in my absence; he said that he wanted it to pay the people, and according to what I hear he assigned the chief part to himself and sent fresh exchangers for the exchanges. Of this gold I had put aside certain specimens, very big lumps, like the eggs of geese, hens, and pullets, and of many other shapes, which some persons had collected in a short space of time, in order that their Highnesses might be gladdened, and might comprehend the business upon seeing a quantity of large stones full of gold. This collection was the first to be given away, with malicious intent, so that their Highnesses should not hold the matter in any account until he has feathered his nest, which he is in great haste to do. Gold which is for melting diminishes at the fire; some chains which would weigh about twenty marks have never been seen again. I have been more distressed about this matter of the gold than even about the pearls, because I have not brought it to Her Highness.

The Commander at once set to work upon anything which he thought would injure me. I have already said that with six hundred thousand I could pay everyone without defrauding anybody, and that I had more than four millions of tenths and constabulary [dues], without touching the gold. He made some free gifts which are ridiculous, though I believe that he began by assigning the chief part to himself. Their Highnesses will find it out when they order an account to be obtained from him, especially if I should be present thereat. He does nothing but reiterate that a large sum is owing, and it is what I have said, and even less. I have been much distressed that there should be sent concerning me an inquisitor who is aware that if the inquisition which he returns is very grave he will remain in possession of the government.

Would that it had pleased our Lord that their Highnesses had sent him or some one else two years ago, for I know that I should now be free from scandal and infamy, and that my honor would not be taken from me, nor should I lose it. God is just, and will make known the why and the wherefore.

They judge me over there as they would a governor who had gone to Sicily, or to a city or town placed under regular government, and where the laws can be observed in their entirety without fear of ruining everything; and I am greatly injured thereby. I ought to be judged as a captain who went from Spain to the Indies to conquer a numerous and warlike people, whose customs and religion are very contrary to ours; who live in rocks and mountains, without fixed settlements, and not like ourselves; and where, by the divine will, I have placed under the dominion of the King and Queen, our sovereigns, another world,[606] through which Spain, which was reckoned a poor country, has become the richest. I ought to be judged as a captain who for such a long time up to this day has borne arms without laying them aside for an hour, and by gentlemen adventurers and by customs and not by letters,[607] unless they were Greeks or Romans, or others of modern times of whom there are so

---

[606] *Un otro mundo.* See note, p. 352 above.

[607] *Caballeros de conquistas y del uso, y no de letras.* This should be: "Knights of Conquests and by profession and not of letters." I.e., by nobles that have actually been conquerors and had conquered territory awarded to them and who are knights by practice or profession and not gentlemen of letters.

many and such noble examples in Spain;[608] or otherwise I receive great injury, because in the Indies there is neither town nor settlement.

The gate to the gold and pearls is now open, and plenty of everything--precious stones, spices, and a thousand other things--may be surely expected, and never could a worse misfortune befall me; for by the name of our Lord the first voyage would yield them just as much as would the traffic of Arabia Felix as far as Mecca, as I wrote to their Highnesses by Antonio de Torres in my reply respecting the repartition of the sea and land with the Portuguese; and afterwards it would equal that of Calicut, as I told them and put in writing at the monastery of Mejorada.

The news of the gold that I said I would give is, that on the day of the Nativity, while I was much tormented, being harassed by wicked Christians and by Indians, and when I was on the point of giving up everything and, if possible, escaping from life, our Lord miraculously comforted me and said, "Fear not violence, I will provide for all things; the seven years of the term of the gold have not elapsed, and in that and in everything else I will afford thee a remedy." On that day I learned that there were eighty leagues of land with mines at every point thereof. The opinion now is that it is all one. Some have collected a hundred and twenty castellanos in one day, and others ninety, and even the number of two hundred and fifty has been reached. From fifty to seventy, and in many more cases from fifteen to fifty, is considered a good day's work, and many carry it on. The usual quantity is from six to twelve, and any one obtaining less than this is

---

[608] What this means is not altogether clear. Apparently Columbus means that men of letters or lawyers in Greece and Rome, great conquering nations, would know what standards to apply in his case, and that there were some such men of breadth in Spain.

not satisfied. It seems too that these mines are like others, and do not yield equally every day. The mines are new, and so are the workers: it is the opinion of everybody that even if all Castile were to go there, every individual, however inexpert he might be, would not obtain less than one or two castellanos daily, and now it is only commencing. It is true that they keep Indians, but the business is in the hands of the Christians. Behold what discernment Bobadilla had, when he gave up everything for nothing, and four millions of tenths, without any reason or even being requested, and without first notifying it to their Highnesses. And this is not the only loss.

I know that my errors have not been committed with the intention of doing evil, and I believe that their Highnesses regard the matter just as I state it; and I know and see that they deal mercifully even with those who maliciously act to their disservice. I believe and consider it very certain that their clemency will be both greater and more abundant towards me, for I fell therein through ignorance and the force of circumstances, as they will know fully hereafter; and I indeed am their creature, and they will look upon my services, and will acknowledge day by day that they are much profited. They will place everything in the balance, even as Holy Scripture tells us good and evil will be at the day of judgment. If, however, they command that another person do judge me, which I cannot believe, and that it be by inquisition in the Indies, I very humbly beseech them to send thither two conscientious and honorable persons at my expense, who I believe will easily, now that gold is discovered, find five marks in four hours. In either case it is needful for them to provide for this matter.

The Commander on his arrival at Santo Domingo took up his abode in my house, and just as he found it so he appropriated everything to himself. Well and good; perhaps he was in want of it. A pirate never acted thus towards a merchant. About my papers I have a greater grievance, for he has so completely deprived me of them that I have never been able to obtain a single one from him; and those that would have been most useful in my exculpation are precisely those which he has kept most concealed. Behold the just and honest inquisitor! Whatever he may have done, they tell me that there has been an end to justice, except in an arbitrary form. God our Lord is present with his strength and wisdom, as of old, and always punishes in the end, especially ingratitude and injuries.

Letter of Columbus on the fourth voyage

INTRODUCTION

The letter on Columbus's last voyage when he explored
the coast of Central America and of the Isthmus of
Panama was written when he was shipwrecked on the
island of Jamaica, 1503. It is his last important writing
and one of great significance in understanding his
geographical conceptions.

The Spanish text of this letter is not older than the
sixteenth century and perhaps not older than the
seventeenth. The Spanish text was first published by
Navarrete in his *Coleccion de los Viages y
Descubrimientos*, 1825. An Italian translation, however,
was published in 1505 and is commonly known as the
Lettera Rarissima. Mr. John Boyd Thacher has
reproduced this early Italian translation in facsimile in
his *Christopher Columbus*, accompanied by a translation
into English. Cesare de Lollis prepared a critical edition of
the Spanish text for the *Raccolta Colombiana*, which was
carefully collated with and in some instances corrected by
this contemporary translation. Most of his changes in
punctuation and textual emendations have been adopted
in the present edition, and attention is called to them in
the notes.

The translation is that of R.H. Major as published in the revised edition of his *Select Letters of Columbus*. It has been carefully revised by the present editor, and some important changes have been made. As hitherto published in English a good many passages in this letter have been so confused and obscure and some so absolutely unintelligible, that the late Justin Winsor characterized this last of the important writings of Columbus as "a sorrowful index of his wandering reason."[609] Almost every one of these passages has yielded up the secret of its meaning either through a more exact translation or in the light of the textual emendations suggested by de Lollis or proposed by the present editor. Among such revisions and textual emendations attention may be called to those discussed on pp. 392, 396, 397. As here published this letter of Columbus is as coherent and intelligible as his other writings.

The editor wishes here to acknowledge his obligations to Professor Henry R. Lang of Yale University, whom he has consulted in regard to perplexing passages or possible emendations, and from whom he has received valuable assistance.

The other important accounts of this voyage, or of the part of it covered by this letter, are the brief report by Diego de Porras, of which a translation is given in Thacher's *Columbus*, and those by Ferdinand Columbus in the *Historie* and Peter Martyr in his *De Rebus Oceanicis*. On this voyage Las Casas's source was the account of Ferdinand Columbus. Lollis presents some striking evidence to show that the accounts of Ferdinand Columbus and Peter Martyr were based upon the same

---

[609] *Christopher Columbus*, p 459; cf. also the passages quoted on p. 460.

original, a lost narrative of the Admiral. It will be remembered, however, that Ferdinand accompanied his father on this voyage, and although only a boy of thirteen his narrative contains several passages of vivid personal recollection. The editor has carefully compared Ferdinand's narrative with the account in this letter and noted the important differences.

E.G.B.

THE FOURTH VOYAGE OF COLUMBUS

A Letter written by Don Christóbal Colon, Viceroy and Admiral of the Indies, to the most Christian and mighty King and Queen of Spain, our Sovereigns, in which are described the events of his voyage, and the countries, provinces, cities, rivers and other marvellous matters therein discovered, as well as the places where gold and other substances of great richness and value are to be found

Most Serene, and very high and mighty Princes, the King and Queen our Sovereigns:--

My passage from Cadiz to the Canary occupied four days, and thence to the Indies sixteen days. From which I wrote, that my intention was to expedite my voyage as much as possible while I had good vessels, good crews and stores, and that Jamaica was the place to which I was bound. I wrote this in Dominica:[610]--

Up to the period of my reaching these shores I experienced most excellent weather, but the night of my arrival came on with a dreadful tempest, and the same bad weather has continued ever since. On reaching the island of Española[611] I despatched a packet of letters, by which I begged as a favor that a ship should be supplied

---

[610] The punctuation of this first paragraph has been changed in the light of the contemporary Italian translation known as the *Lettera Rarissima,* which is given in facsimile and English translation in Thacher's *Christopher Columbus,* II. 671 *et seqq.*

[611] June 29. Las Casas, III. 29.

me at my own cost in lieu of one of those that I had brought with me, which had become unseaworthy, and could no longer carry sail. The letters were taken, and your Highnesses will know if a reply has been given to them. For my part I was forbidden to go on shore;[612] the hearts of my people failed them lest I should take them further, and they said that if any danger were to befall them, they should receive no succor, but, on the contrary, in all probability have some great affront offered them. Moreover every man had it in his power to tell me that the new Governor would have the superintendence of the countries that I might acquire.[613]

The tempest was terrible throughout the night, all the ships were separated, and each one driven to the last extremity, without hope of anything but death; each of them also looked upon the loss of the rest as a matter of certainty. What man was ever born, not even excepting Job, who would not have been ready to die of despair at finding himself as I then was, in anxious fear for my own safety, and that of my son, my brother[614] and my friends, and yet refused permission either to land or to put into harbor on the shores which by God's mercy I had gained for Spain sweating blood?

But to return to the ships: although the tempest had so completely separated them from me as to leave me single, yet the Lord restored them to me in His own good time.

---

[612] By the letter of the King and Queen, March 14, 1502, Columbus had been forbidden to call at Española on the outward voyage. Las Casas, *Historia de las Indias*, III. 26.

[613] The new governor, Ovando, who had been sent out to supersede Bobadilla, had reached Santo Domingo in April of this year, 1502.

[614] Columbus was accompanied by his younger son Ferdinand and his elder brother Bartholomew. Las Casas, III. 25.

The ship which we had the greatest fear for, had put out to sea to escape [being blown] toward the island. The *Gallega*[615] lost her boat and a great part of her provisions, which latter loss indeed all the ships suffered. The vessel in which I was, though dreadfully buffeted, was saved by our Lord's mercy from any injury whatever; my brother went in the ship that was unsound, and he under God was the cause of its being saved. With this tempest I struggled on till I reached Jamaica, and there the sea became calm, but there was a strong current which carried me as far as the Queen's Garden[616] without seeing land. Hence as opportunity afforded I pushed on for the mainland, in spite of the wind and a fearful contrary current, against which I contended for sixty days, and after all only made seventy leagues. All this time I was unable to get into harbor, nor was there any cessation of the tempest, which was one continuation of rain, thunder and lightning; indeed it seemed as if it were the end of the world. I at length reached the Cape of Gracias á Dios, and after that the Lord granted me fair

---

[615] The translation here follows Lollis's emendation of the text which changed the printed text, "*habia, echado á la mar, por escapar, fasta la isola la Gallega; perdio la barca,*" etc., to "*habia echado á la mar, por escapar fasta la isla; la Gallega perdio la barca.*" One of the ships was named *La Gallega*, and there is no island of that name in that region.

[616] Columbus set forth from the harbor of Santo Domingo in the storm, Friday, July 1. The ships found refuge in the harbor of Azua on the following Sunday, July 3. (Ferdinand Columbus in the *Historie*, ed. 1867, pp. 286-287.) Azua is about 50 miles west of Santo Domingo in a straight line, but much farther by water. After a rest and repairs the Admiral sailed to Yaquimo, the present Jacmel in the territory of Hayti, into which port he went to escape another storm. He left Yaquimo, July 14. (Las Casas, III. 108; Ferdinand Columbus, *Historie*, p. 289.) He then passed south of Jamaica, and was carried by the currents northwest till he reached the Queen's Garden, a group of many small islands south of Cuba and east of the Isle of Pines, so named by him in 1494 on his exploration of the coast of Cuba.

wind and tide; this was on the twelfth of September.[617]
Eighty-eight days did this fearful tempest continue,
during which I was at sea, and saw neither sun nor stars;
my ships lay exposed, with sails torn, and anchors,
rigging, cables, boats and a great quantity of provisions
lost; my people were very weak and humbled in spirit,
many of them promising to lead a religious life, and all

---

[617] From the Queen's Garden he sailed south July 27 (the Porras narrative
of this voyage, Navarrete, II. 283; in English in Thacher, *Columbus*, II. 640 *et
seqq.*), and after a passage of ninety leagues sighted an island Saturday,
July 30. (Porras in Thacher, II. 643.) This was the island of Guanaja about
twelve leagues north of Trujillo, Honduras. (Las Casas, III. 109.) Here a
landing was made and a canoe was encountered which was covered
with an awning and contained Indians well clothed and a load of
merchandise. Notwithstanding these indications of a more advanced
culture than had hitherto been found, the Admiral decided not to explore
the country of these Indians, which would have led him into Yucatan and
possibly Mexico, but to search for the strait which he supposed separated
Asia from the continental mass he had discovered on his third voyage
(Paria, South America). He struck the mainland near Trujillo, naming the
point Caxinas. At or near this place they landed Sunday, August 14, to say
mass. (Las Casas, III. 112; Ferdinand Columbus, *Historie*, p. 295.) From this
point he coasted very slowly, sailing in sight of land by day and anchoring
at night, distressed by storms and headwinds, some days losing as much
ground as could be gained in two, till September 12, when he reached
Cape Gracias á Dios. (Las Casas, III. 113; *Historie*, p. 297; Porras narrative in
Thacher, *Columbus*, II. 644.) It will be seen from this collation of the sources
that the statements in our text are far from exact, that they are in fact a
very general and greatly exaggerated recollection of a most trying
experience.
It will be remembered that Ferdinand was on this voyage, but his narrative
says nothing of any storm between July 14 when he left the Queen's
Gardens and the arrival at Guanaja, a passage which Porras says took
three days. This passage, however, Las Casas describes apparently on
the basis of this letter as having taken sixty days (*Historia*, III. 108). Next the
text of the *Historie* presents a difficulty, for it places the tedious stormy
voyage of *sixty* leagues and *seventy* days between Caxinas (Trujillo) and
Cape Gracias á Dios (*Historie*, p. 296), although in another place it gives
the beginning of this coasting as after August 14 and the date of arrival at
the Cape as September 12. This last chronological difficulty may perhaps
be accounted for in this way: The original manuscript of the *Historie* may
have had "XXX dias," which a copyist or the Italian translator may have
taken for "LXX dias."

making vows and promising to perform pilgrimages, while some of them would frequently go to their messmates to make confession.[618] Other tempests have been experienced, but never of so long a duration or so fearful as this: many whom we looked upon as brave men, on several occasions showed considerable trepidation; but the distress of my son who was with me grieved me to the soul, and the more when I considered his tender age, for he was but thirteen years old, and he enduring so much toil for so long a time. Our Lord, however, gave him strength even to enable him to encourage the rest, and he worked as if he had been eighty years at sea, and all this was a consolation to me. I myself had fallen sick, and was many times at the point of death, but from a little cabin that I had caused to be constructed on deck, I directed our course. My brother was in the ship that was in the worst condition and the most exposed to danger; and my grief on this account was the greater that I brought him with me against his will.

Such is my fate, that the twenty years of service[619] through which I have passed with so much toil and danger, have profited me nothing, and at this very day I do not possess a roof in Spain that I can call my own; if I wish to eat or sleep, I have nowhere to go but to the inn or tavern, and most times lack wherewith to pay the

[618] A review of the chronology of the voyage in the preceding note will show that no such storm of eighty-eight days' duration could have occurred in the first part of this voyage. Columbus was only seventy-four days in going from Santo Domingo to Cabo Gracias á Dios. Either the text is wrong or his memory was at fault. The most probable conclusion is that in copying either LXXXVIII got substituted for XXVIII or *Ochenta y ocho* for *Veinte y ocho*. In that case we should have almost exactly the time spent in going from Trujillo to Cape Gracias á Dios, August 14 to September 12, and exact agreement between our text, the *Historie*, and the Porras narrative.

[619] Twenty years, speaking approximately. This letter was written in 1503, and Columbus entered the service of Spain in 1485.

bill. Another anxiety wrung my very heartstrings, which was the thought of my son Diego, whom I had left an orphan in Spain, and dispossessed of my honor and property, although I had looked upon it as a certainty, that your Majesties, as just and grateful Princes, would restore it to him in all respects with increase.[620]

I reached the land of Cariay,[621] where I stopped to repair my vessels and take in provisions, as well as to afford relaxation to the men, who had become very weak. I myself (who, as I said before, had been several times at the point of death) gained information respecting the gold mines of which I was in search, in the province of Ciamba;[622] and two Indians conducted me to Carambaru,[623] where the people (who go naked) wear golden mirrors round their necks, which they will neither sell, give, nor part with for any consideration. They named to me many places on the sea-coast where there were both gold and mines. The last that they mentioned was Veragua,[624] which was five-and-twenty leagues

---

[620] Diego was the heir of his father's titles. He was appointed governor of the Indies in 1508, but a prolonged lawsuit was necessary to establish his claims to inherit his father's rights.

[621] Their course was down the Mosquito coast. Cariay was near the mouth of the San Juan River of Nicaragua. Las Casas gives the date of the arrival at Cariarí, as he gives the name, as September 17 (III. 114). The *Historie* gives the date as September 5 and the name as Cariai (p. 297).

[622] Peter Martyr, *De Rebus Oceanicis* (ed. 1574), p. 239, says that Columbus called Ciamba the region which the inhabitants called Quiriquetana, a name which it would seem still survives in Chiriqui Lagoon just east of Almirante Bay. The name "Ciamba" appears on Martin Behaim's globe, 1492, as a province corresponding to Cochin-China. It is described in Marco Polo under the name "Chamba"; see Yule's *Marco Polo*, II. 248-252 (bk. III., ch. V.).

[623] Carambaru is the present Almirante Bay, about on the border between Costa Rica and Panama. Las Casas describes the bay as six leagues long and over three broad with many islands and coves. He gives the name as Caravaró (III. 118). Ferdinand Columbus's account is practically identical.

[624] Veragua in this letter includes practically all of the present republic of Panama. The western quarter of it was granted to Luis Colon, the Admiral's

distant from the place where we then were. I started with the intention of visiting all of them, but when I had reached the middle of my journey I learned that there were other mines at so short a distance that they might be reached in two days. I determined on sending to see them. It was on the eve of St. Simon and St. Jude,[625] which was the day fixed for our departure; but that night there arose so violent a storm, that we were forced to go wherever it drove us, and the Indian who was to conduct us to the mines was with us all the time. As I had found every thing true that had been told me in the different places which I had visited, I felt satisfied it would be the same with respect to Ciguare,[626] which according to their account, is nine days journey across the country westward: they tell me there is a great quantity of gold there, and that the inhabitants wear coral ornaments on their heads, and very large coral bracelets and anklets,

---

grandson, in 1537, as a dukedom in partial compensation for his enouncing his hereditary rights. Hence the title Dukes of Veragua borne by the Admiral's descendants. The name still survives in geography in that of the little island Escudo de Veragua, which lies off the northern coast.

[625] The eve or vigil of St. Simon and St. Jude is October 27. According to the narrative in the *Historie*, on October 7, they went ashore at the channel of Cerabora (Carambaru). A few days later they went on to Aburema. October 17 they left Aburema and went twelve leagues to Guaigo, where they landed. Thence they went to Cateva (Catiba, Las Casas) and cast anchor in a large river (the Chagres). Thence easterly to Cobrava; thence to five towns, among which was Beragua (Veragua); the next day to Cubiga. The distance from Cerabora to Cubiga was fifty leagues. Without landing, the Admiral went on to Belporto (Puerto Bello), which he so named. ("Puerto Bello, which was a matter of six leagues from what we now call El Nombre de Dios." Las Casas, III. 121.) He arrived at Puerto Bello November 2, and remained there seven days on account of the rains and bad weather. (*Historie*, pp. 302-306.) Apparently Columbus put this period of bad weather a few days too early in his recollection of it.

[626] Ciguare. An outlying province of the Mayas lying on the Pacific side of southern Costa Rica. Peter Martyr, *De Rebus Oceanicis*, p. 240, says, "In this great tract (*i.e.*, where the Admiral was) are two districts, the near one called Taia, and the further one Maia."

with which article also they adorn and inlay their seats, boxes, and tables. They also said that the women there wore necklaces hanging down to their shoulders. All the people agree in the report I now repeat, and their account is so favorable that I should be content with the tithe of the advantages that their description holds out. They are all likewise acquainted with the pepper-plant; according to the account of these people, the inhabitants of Ciguare are accustomed to hold fairs and markets for carrying on their commerce, and they showed me also the mode and form in which they transact their various exchanges; others assert that their ships carry cannon, and that the men go clothed and use bows and arrows, swords and cuirasses, and that on shore they have horses which they use in battle, and that they wear rich clothes and have good things.[627] They also say that the sea surrounds Ciguare, and that at ten days' journey from thence is the river Ganges; these lands appear to hold the same relation to Veragua, as Tortosa to Fontarabia, or Pisa to Venice.[628] When I left Carambaru and reached the places in its neighborhood, which I have mentioned above as being spoken of by the Indians, I found the customs of the people correspond with the accounts that had been given of them, except as regarded the golden mirrors: any man who had one of them would willingly part with it for three hawks'-bells, although they were equivalent in weight to ten or fifteen ducats. These people resemble the natives of

---

[627] Probably *casas*, houses, should be the reading here. In the corresponding passage of the contemporary Italian version the word is "houses." This information, mixed as it is with Columbus's misinterpretations of the Indian signs and distorted by his preconceptions, was first made public in the Italian translation of this letter in 1505 and then gave Europe its first intimations of the culture of the Mayas.

[628] I.e., in being on either side of a peninsula, Tortosa and Fontarabia being on opposite sides of the narrowest part of the Spanish peninsula.

Española in all their habits. They have various modes of collecting the gold, none of which will bear comparison with the plans adopted by the Christians.

All that I have here stated is from hearsay. This, however, I know, that in the year ninety-four I sailed twenty-four degrees to the westward in nine hours,[629] and there can be no mistake upon the subject, because there was an eclipse; the sun was in Libra and the moon in Aries.[630] What I had learned by the mouth of these people I already knew in detail from books. Ptolemy thought that he had satisfactorily corrected[631] Marinus, and yet this latter appears to have come very near to the truth. Ptolemy placed Catigara[632] at a distance of twelve lines to the west

---

[629] The Spanish reads, "Lo que yo sé es que el año de noventa y cuatro en veinte y cuatros grados al Poniente en termino de nueve horas." The translation in the text and that in Thacher (II. 687) of the Italian makes nonsense. The translation should be "what I know is that in the year '94 (1494) I sailed westward on the 24th parallel (lit. on 24 degrees) a total of nine hours (lit. to a limit of nine hours)." That is, he reckoned that he had gone 9/24 round the world on the 24th parallel, and he knew it because there was an eclipse by which he found out the difference in time between Europe and where he was. The "termino" of nine hours refers to the western limit of his exploration of the southern coast of Cuba when he concluded it was a projection of the mainland of Asia. After reaching the conclusion that this is the correct interpretation of this passage, I discovered that it had been given by Humboldt in his *Kritische Untersuchungen über die historische Entwickelung der geographischen Kenntnisse von der Neuen Welt*, I. 553, and by Peschel in his *Zeitalter der Entdeckungen*, p. 97, note 2. It may be objected to this explanation that in reality Columbus had only gone about 75 degrees west of Cape St. Vincent in Portugal. The accurate calculation of longitude at that time, however, was impossible, and as will be seen in the following note Columbus's calculation was biassed by powerful preconceptions.

[630] In his *Libro de Profecias* Columbus recorded the data of this eclipse which took place February 29, 1494, from which he drew the conclusion, "The difference between the middle of the island Jamaica in the Indies and the island of Cadiz in Spain is seven hours and fifteen minutes." Navarrete, *Viages*, II. 272.

[631] Reading *remendiado* or *remendado* instead of *remedado*.

[632] Catigara was in China on the east side of the Gulf of Tonquin.

of his meridian, which he fixes at two degrees and a third beyond Cape St. Vincent, in Portugal. Marinus comprised the earth and its limits in fifteen lines.[633] Marinus on Ethiopia gives a description covering more than twenty-four degrees beyond the equinoctial line, and now that the Portuguese have sailed there they find it correct.[634]

---

[633] Marinus of Tyre divided the earth into 24 meridians, 15 degrees or one hour apart. His first meridian passed the Fortunate Isles, which he supposed to be 2-1/2 degrees west of Cape St. Vincent, and his fifteenth through Catigara, southeastern China. The inhabited world embraced fifteen of these lines, 225 degrees, and the unknown portion east of India and west of Spain, nine lines, or hours, or 135 degrees. *Cf.* Vignaud, *Toscanelli and Columbus*, p. 74; Bunbury, *History of Ancient Geography*, II. 519 *et seqq*. Columbus, therefore, according to his calculations, had in 1494 completely covered this unknown section and reached India (or China), and so had demonstrated the correctness of Marinus's views. In reality his strong preconceptions as to where he was distorted his calculations of the longitude. Ptolemy corrected Marinus's estimate of 225 degrees from Cape St. Vincent to Sera in China, and, as noted in Columbus's letter, placed Catigara in China (on the east side of the Gulf of Tonquin) at twelve lines or 180 degrees west of his meridian (2-1/2 degrees west of Cape St. Vincent). If Ptolemy was right, Columbus had not reached India (or more exactly China) or come, on his own calculation, within 45 degrees or 2700 geographical miles of it measured on the equator. The outline reproduction of the map of Bartholomew Columbus made after his return from this voyage given in Channing's *Student's History of the United States*, p. 27 (photographic reproduction in Bourne, *Spain in America*, p. 96) illustrates the Admiral's ideas and conclusions. This region (*i.e.*, Costa Rica and Panama) is a southern extension of Cochin-China and Cambodia and is connected with *Mondo Novo*, *i.e.*, South America.

[634] The translation here adopts the emended text of Lollis, substituting "ali[e]nde" for "al Indo" in the sentence "Marino en Ethiopía escribe al Indo la línea equinoçial." *Raccolta Colombiana*, parte I., tomo II., p. 184. The translation of the unamended text as printed by Major was "the same author describes the Indus in Ethiopia as being more than four and twenty degrees from the equinoctial line." Apparently the 24 should be 44. With these changes the statements in the text agree with Columbus's marginalia to the *Imago Mundi*, where he notes that the Cape of Good Hope is Agesinba and that Bartholomew Diaz found it to be 45 degrees south of the equator. "This," he goes on, "agrees with the dictum of Marinus, whom Ptolemy corrects, in regard to the expedition to the Garamantes, who said it traversed 27,500 stadia beyond the equinoctial." *Raccolta Colombiana*, parte II., tomo II., p. 377. On Marinus's

Ptolemy says also that the most southern land is the first boundary, and that it does not go lower down than fifteen degrees and a third.[635] The world is but small; out of seven divisions of it the dry part occupies six, and the seventh is entirely covered by water.[636] Experience has shown it, and I have written it with quotations from the Holy Scripture, in other letters, where I have treated of the situation of the terrestrial paradise, as approved by the Holy Church;[637] and I say that the world is not so large as vulgar opinion makes it, and that one degree of the equinoctial line measures fifty-six miles and two-thirds; and this may be proved to a nicety.[638]

---

exaggerated estimate of the distance covered by the Romans in tropical Africa, see Bunbury, *History of Ancient Geography*, II. 524.

[635] This is unintelligible. The Spanish is, "Tolomeo diz que la tierra mas austral es el plazo primero." The meaning of *plazo* is not "boundary" but "term" (allotted time). The reading should be: "la tierra mas austral es el praso promontorio," and the translation should be, "Ptolemy says that the most southern land is the promontory of Prasum," etc. Prasum promontorium was Ptolemy's southern limit of the world. He placed it at about 16 degrees south latitude. See Bunbury, *History of Ancient Geography*, II. 572, and Smith's *Dictionary of Greek and Roman Geography*, art. "Prasum Promontorium"; also Ptolemy's *Geography*, bk. IV., ch. IX., the descriptive matter relating to Map 4 on Africa.

[636] *II. Esdras*, VI. 42, see p. 358, note 1.

[637] See the Letter of Columbus on his Third Voyage. Major, *Select Letters of Columbus*, p. 141.

[638] Ptolemy reckoned the length of the degree on the equator at 62-1/2 miles. The shorter measurement of 56-2/3 was the estimate adopted by the Arab astronomer Alfragan in the ninth century and known to Columbus through Cardinal d'Ailly's *Imago Mundi*, the source of much if not most of his information on the geographical knowledge and opinions of former times. Cardinal d'Ailly's source of information about Alfragan was Roger Bacon's *Opus Majus*. Columbus was deeply impressed with Alfragan's estimate of the length of the degree and annotated the passages in the *Imago Mundi*. Cf. *Raccolta Colombiana*, Parte I., tomo II., pp. 378, 407, and frequently. See this whole question in Vignaud, *Toscanelli and Columbus*, p. 79 *et seqq.*

But I leave this subject, which it is not my intention now to treat upon, but simply to give a narrative of my laborious and painful voyage, although of all my voyages it is the most honorable and advantageous. I have said that on the eve of St. Simon and St. Jude I ran before the wind wherever it took me, without power to resist it; at length I found shelter for ten days from the roughness of the sea and the tempest overhead, and resolved not to attempt to go back to the mines, which I regarded as already in our possession.[639] When I started in pursuance of my voyage it was under a heavy rain, and reaching the harbor of Bastimentos I put in, though much against my will.[640] The storm and a rapid current kept me in for fourteen days, when I again set sail, but not with favorable weather. After I had made fifteen leagues with great exertions, the wind and the current drove me back[641] again with great fury, but in again making for the port which I had quitted, I found on the way another port, which I named Retrete, where I put in for shelter with as much risk as regret, the ships being in sad condition, and my crews and myself exceedingly fatigued.[642] I remained there fifteen days, kept in by stress of weather, and when I fancied my troubles were at an end, I found them only

---

[639] In Puerto Bello. See p. 394, note 2. Porto Bello, to use the Anglicized form, became the great shipping port on the north side of the isthmus for the trade with Peru. Cf. Bourne, *Spain in America*, p. 292.

[640] Columbus left Porto Bello November 9 and went eight leagues, but the next day he turned back four and took refuge at what is now Nombre de Dios. From the abundance of maize fields he named it Port of Provisions (Puerto de Bastimentos). *Historie*, p. 306.

[641] *Me reposó atrás il viento*, etc. For *reposó* the text apparently should be either *repuso*, "put back," or *rempujó*, "drove back," and the translation is based on this supposition.

[642] They remained at Bastimentos till November 23, when they went on to Guiga, but did not tarry but pushed on to a little harbor (November 26), which the Admiral called Retrete (Closet) because it was so small that it could hold only five or six vessels and the entrance was only fifteen or twenty paces wide. *Historie*, p. 306.

begun. It was then that I changed my resolution with respect to proceeding to the mines, and proposed doing something in the interim, until the weather should prove more favorable for my voyage.[643] I had already made four leagues when the storm recommenced, and wearied me to such a degree that I absolutely knew not what to do; my wound reopened, and for nine days my life was despaired of; never was the sea seen so high, so terrific, and so covered with foam; not only did the wind oppose our proceeding onward, but it also rendered it highly dangerous to run in for any headland, and kept me in that sea which seemed to me as a sea of blood, seething like a cauldron on a mighty fire. Never did the sky look more fearful; during one day and one night it burned like a furnace, and every instant I looked to see if my masts and my sails were not destroyed; these flashes came with such alarming fury that we all thought the ships must have been consumed. All this time the waters from heaven never ceased, not to say that it rained, for it was like a repetition of the deluge. The men were at this time so crushed in spirit that they longed for death as a deliverance from so many martyrdoms. Twice already had the ships suffered loss in boats, anchors, and rigging, and were now lying bare without sails.

When it pleased our Lord, I returned to Puerto Gordo,[644] where I recruited my condition as well as I could. I then once more turned towards Veragua; for my voyage,

---

[643] That is, Columbus turns back to explore the mines on account of the violence of the east and northeast winds. This was December 5. *Historie*, p. 309.

[644] Not mentioned in the *Historie* by name. It was the place where they stayed from December 26 to January 3 to repair the ship *Gallega* as appears in the *Probanzas del Almirante*. Navarrete, *Viages*, III. 600. It was between Rio de los Lagartos and Puerto Bello. Lollis, *Raccolta Colombiana*, Parte I., tomo II., p. 187.

although I was [ready] for it, the wind and current were still contrary.[645] I arrived at nearly the same spot as before, and there again the wind and currents still opposed my progress; and once again I was compelled to put into port, not daring to await the opposition of Saturn[646] with Mars so tossed on an exposed coast; for it almost always brings on a tempest or severe weather. This was on Christmas-day, about the hour of mass.

Thus, after all these fatigues, I had once more to return to the spot from whence I started; and when the new year had set in, I returned again to my task: but although I had fine weather for my voyage, the ships were no longer in a sailing condition, and my people were either dying or very sick. On the day of the Epiphany,[647] I reached Veragua in a state of exhaustion; there, by our Lord's goodness, I found a river and a safe harbor, although at the entrance there were only ten spans of water. I succeeded in making an entry, but with great difficulty; and on the following day the storm recommenced, and had I been still on the outside at that time, I should have been unable to enter on account of the reef. It rained without

---

[645] Adopting de Lollis's text and punctuation.

[646] *La oposicion de Saturno con Marte tan desvaratado en costa brava,* adopting de Lollis's text following the suggestion of the contemporary Italian translation. According to the doctrines of astrology the influence of Saturn was malign. "When Saturn is in the first degree of Aries, and any other Planet in the first degree of Libra, they being now an hundred and eighty degrees each from other, are said to be in Opposition: A bad Aspect." William Lilly, *Christian Astrology* (London, 1647), p. 27.

[647] Epiphany, January 6. It will be remembered that Columbus had passed Veragua the previous October when working eastward. See p. 394, note 2. He now found he could enter the river of Veragua, but found another near by called by the Indians Yebra, but which Columbus named Belem in memory of the coming of the three kings (the wise men of the East) to Bethlehem. (Las Casas, III. 128; Porras in Thacher, II. 645.) The name is still preserved attached to the river.

ceasing until the fourteenth of February, so that I could find no opportunity of penetrating into the interior, nor of recruiting my condition in any respect whatever; and on the twenty-fourth of January, when I considered myself in perfect safety, the river suddenly rose with great violence to a considerable height, breaking my cables and the breastfasts,[648] and nearly carrying away my ships altogether, which certainly appeared to me to be in greater danger than ever. Our Lord, however, brought a remedy as He has always done. I do not know if any one else ever suffered greater trials.

On the sixth of February, while it was still raining, I sent seventy men on shore to go into the interior, and at five leagues' distance they found several mines. The Indians who went with them conducted them to a very lofty mountain, and thence showing them the country all around, as far as the eye could reach, told them there was gold in every part, and that, towards the west, the mines extended twenty days' journey; they also recounted the names of the towns and villages where there was more or less of it. I afterwards learned that the Quibian,[649] who had lent these Indians, had ordered them to show the distant mines, and which belonged to an enemy of his; but

---

[648] *Proeses.* In nautical Spanish *prois* or *proiza* is a breastfast or headfast, that is a large cable for fastening a ship to a wharf or another ship. In Portuguese *proiz* is a stone or tree on shore to which the hawsers are fastened. Major interpreted it in this sense, translating the words *las amarras y proeses,* "the cables and the supports to which they were fastened." The interpretation given first seems to me the correct one, especially as Ferdinand says that the flood came so suddenly that they could not get the cables on land. *Historie,* p. 315.

[649] *Quibian* is a title, as indicated a few lines further on, and not a proper name as Major, Irving, Markham, and others following Las Casas have taken it to be. The Spanish is uniformly "El Quibian." Peter Martyr says: "They call a kinglet (*regulus*) Cacicus, as we have said elsewhere, in other places Quebi, in some places also Tiba. A chief, in some places Sacchus, in others Jurá." *De Rebus Oceanicis,* p. 241.

that in his own territory one man might, if he would, collect in ten days as much as a child could carry.[650] I bring with me some Indians, his servants, who are witnesses of this fact.

The boats went up to the spot where the dwellings of these people are situated; and, after four hours, my brother returned with the guides, all of them bringing back gold which they had collected at that place. The gold must be abundant, and of good quality, for none of these men had ever seen mines before; very many of them had never seen pure gold, and most of them were seamen and lads. Having building materials in abundance, I established a settlement, and made many presents to the Quibian, which is the name they gave to the lord of the country. I plainly saw that harmony would not last long, for the natives are of a very rough disposition, and the Spaniards very encroaching; and, moreover, I had taken possession of land belonging to the Quibian. When he saw what we did, and found the traffic increasing, he resolved upon burning the houses, and putting us all to death; but his project did not succeed, for we took him prisoner, together with his wives, his children, and his servants. His captivity, it is true, lasted but a short time, for he eluded the custody of a trustworthy man, into whose charge he had been given, with a guard of men; and his sons escaped from a ship, in which they had been placed under the special charge of the master.

---

[650] "*Una mozada de oro*." *Mozada* is not given in any of the Spanish dictionaries I have consulted. The Academy dictionary gives *mojoda* as a square measure, deriving it from the low Latin *modiata* from *modius*. Perhaps one should read *mojada* instead of *mozada* and give it a meaning similar to that of *modius* or about a peck. Major's translation follows the explanation of De Verneuil, who says: "*Mozada signifie la mesure que peut porter un jeune garçon.*"

In the month of January the mouth of the river was
entirely closed up,[651] and in April the vessels were so
eaten by the shipworm,[652] that they could scarcely be kept
above water. At this time the river forced a channel for
itself, by which I managed, with great difficulty, to
extricate three of them after I had unloaded them. The
boats were then sent back into the river for water and
salt, but the sea became so high and furious, that it
afforded them no chance of exit; upon which the Indians
collected themselves together in great numbers, and made
an attack upon the boats, and at length massacred the
men.[653] My brother, and all the rest of our people, were in
a ship which remained inside; I was alone, outside, upon
that dangerous coast, suffering from a
severe fever and worn with fatigue. All hope of escape was
gone. I toiled up to the highest part of the ship, and, with
a voice of fear crying, and very urgently, I called upon
your Highnesses' war-captains in every direction for help,
but there was no reply. At length, groaning with
exhaustion, I fell asleep, and heard a compassionate voice
address me thus: "O fool, and slow to believe and to serve
thy God, the God of all! what did He do more for Moses, or
for David his servant, than He has done for thee? From
thine infancy He has kept thee under His constant and

---

[651] The mouth of the river was closed by sand thrown up by the violent
storms outside. *Historie*, p. 321.

[652] The teredo.

[653] During the weeks that he was shut in the River Belem Columbus had
his brother explore the country. The prospects for a successful colony
led him to build a small settlement and to plan to return to Spain for
re-enforcements and supplies. The story is told in detail in the *Historie* and
by Irving, *Columbus*, II. 425-450, and more briefly by Markham, *Columbus*,
pp. 259-207. This was the first settlement projected on the American
Continent. The hostility of the Indians culminating in this attack rendered
the execution of the project impracticable. In the manuscript copy of Las
Casas's *Historia de las Indias* Las Casas noted on the margin of the
passage containing the account of this incident, "This was the first
settlement that the Spaniards made on the mainland, although in a short
time it came to naught." See Thacher, *Columbus*, II. 608.

watchful care. When He saw thee arrived at an age which suited His designs respecting thee, He brought wonderful renown to thy name throughout all the land. He gave thee for thine own the Indies, which form so rich a portion of the world, and thou hast divided them as it pleased thee, for He gave thee power to do so. He gave thee also the keys of those barriers of the ocean sea which were closed with such mighty chains;[654] and thou wast obeyed through many lands, and gained an honorable fame throughout Christendom. What did he more for the people of Israel, when he brought them out of Egypt? or for David, whom from a shepherd He made to be king in Judea? Turn to Him, and acknowledge thine error--His mercy is infinite. Thine old age shall not prevent thee from accomplishing any great undertaking. He holds under His sway many very great possessions. Abraham had exceeded a hundred years of age when he begat Isaac; nor was Sarah young. Thou criest out for uncertain help: answer, who has afflicted thee so much and so often, God or the world? The privileges promised by God, He never fails in bestowing; nor does He ever declare, after a service has been rendered Him, that such was not agreeable with His intention, or that He had regarded the matter in another light; nor does he inflict suffering, in order to give effect to the manifestation of His power. His word goes according to the letter; and He performs all his promises with interest. This is [his] custom. Thus I have told thee what thy Creator has done for thee, and what He does for all men. Just now He gave me a specimen of

---

[654] De Lollis points out that these striking words are a paraphrase of the famous lines in Seneca's *Medea*, Chorus, Act II.:-- *Venient annis saecula seris Quibus Oceanus vincula rerum Laxet, et ingens pateat tellus, Tethysque novos detegat orbes Nec sit terris ultima Thule.* Columbus copied these verses into his *Libro de las Profecias* and translated them. Navarrete, *Viages*, II. 272.

the reward of so many toils and dangers incurred by thee in the service of others."[655]

I heard all this, as it were, in a trance; but I had no answer to give in definite words, and could but weep for my errors. He who spoke to me, whoever it was, concluded by saying,--"Fear not, but trust; all these tribulations are recorded on marble, and not without cause." I arose as soon as I could; and at the end of nine days there came fine weather, but not sufficiently so to allow of drawing the vessels out of the river. I collected the men who were on land, and, in fact, all of them that I could, because there were not enough to admit of one party remaining on shore while another stayed on board to work the vessels. I myself should have remained with my men to defend the settlement, had your Highnesses known of it; but the fear that ships might never reach the spot where we were, as well as the thought, that when provision is to be made for bringing help, everything will be provided,[656] made me decide upon leaving. I departed, in the name of the Holy Trinity, on Easter night,[657] with the ships rotten, worm-eaten and full of holes. One of them I left at Belen, with a supply of necessaries; I did the same at Belpuerto. I then had only two left, and they in the same state as the others. I was without boats or provisions, and in this condition I had to cross seven thousand miles of sea; or, as an alternative, to die on the passage with my son, my brother, and so many of my people. Let those who are accustomed to finding fault and censuring ask, while they sit in security at home, "Why did you not do so and so under such circumstances?" I wish they now had this voyage to make. I verily believe that another journey of another kind awaits them, or our faith is nothing.

---

[655] Accepting de Lollis's emended text.
[656] "Quando se aia de proveer de socorro, se proveera de todo."
[657] April 16, 1503.

On the thirteenth of May I reached the province of Mago [Mango],[658] which borders on Cathay, and thence I started for the island of Española. I sailed two days with a good wind, after which it became contrary. The route that I followed called forth all my care to avoid the numerous islands, that I might not be stranded on the shoals that lie in their neighborhood. The sea was very tempestuous, and I was driven backward under bare poles. I anchored at an island, where I lost, at one stroke, three anchors; and, at midnight, when the weather was such that the world appeared to be coming to an end, the cables of the other ship broke, and it came down upon my vessel with such force that it was a wonder we were not dashed to pieces; the single anchor that remained to me was, next to the Lord, our only preservation. After six days, when the weather became calm, I resumed my journey, having already lost all my tackle; my ships were pierced by borers more than a honey-comb and the crew entirely paralyzed with fear and in despair. I reached the island a little beyond the point at which I first arrived at it, and

---

[658] Cuba. According to Ferdinand Columbus the course was as follows: The Admiral followed the coast of the isthmus eastward beyond El Retrete to a place he named Marmoro (near Punto de Mosquitos) somewhat west of the entrance to the Gulf of Darien; then May 1 in response to the urgency of the pilots he turned north. May 10 they sighted two little islands, Caymanos Chicos, and the 12th they reached the Queen's Garden just south of Cuba (see p. 301, note 1). The next day they landed in Cuba and secured supplies. It is significant of the tenacity of Columbus's conviction that Cuba was a part of the mainland of Asia that he here calls it Mago (*i.e.*, Mango). June 12, 1494, when he had explored the southern coast of Cuba, he reached this conviction and compelled his officers and crew to take oath that "it (*i.e.*, Cuba) is mainland and in particular the province of Mango." Navarrete, *Viages*, II. 144. (The affidavits are translated in Thacher, *Columbus*, II. 327.) Mangi (southern China) is described by Marco Polo at great length. In the second Toscanelli letter Quinsay is said to be "in the province of Mangi, *i.e.*, near the province of Cathay." It is noted several times in Columbus's marginalia to Marco Polo.

there I turned in to recover myself after the storm;[659] but I afterwards put into a much safer port in the same island. After eight days I put to sea again, and reached Jamaica by the end of June;[660] but always beating against contrary winds, and with the ships in the worst possible condition. With three pumps, and the use of pots and kettles, we could scarcely clear the water that came into the ship, there being no remedy but this for the mischief done by the ship-worm. I steered in such a manner as to come as near as possible to Española, from which we were twenty-eight leagues distant, but I afterwards wished I had not done so, for the other ship which was half under water was obliged to run in for a port. I determined on keeping the sea in spite of the weather, and my vessel was on the very point of sinking when our Lord miraculously brought us upon land. Who will believe what I now write? I assert that in this letter I have not related one hundredth part of the wonderful events that occurred in this voyage; those who were with the Admiral can bear witness to it. If your Highnesses would be graciously pleased to send to my help a ship of above sixty-four tons, with two hundred quintals of biscuits and other provisions, there would then be sufficient to carry me and my crew from Española to Spain. I have already said that there are not twenty-eight leagues between Jamaica and Española; and I should not have gone there, even if the ships had been in a fit condition for so doing, because your Highnesses ordered me not to land there. God knows if this command has proved of any service. I send this letter by means of

---

[659] *Allí me torné á reposar atrás la fortuna.* De Lollis, following the Italian translation, reads: *Allí me torné á reposar atrás la fortuna*, etc. "There the storm returned to drive me back; I stopped in the same island in a safer port." As this gives an unknown meaning to *reposar*, he suggests that Columbus may have written *repujar*, "to drive."
[660] June 23. *Historie*, p. 334.

and by the hands of Indians; it will be a miracle if it reaches its destination.

This is the account I have to give of my voyage. The men who accompanied me were a hundred and fifty in number, among whom were many calculated for pilots and good sailors, but none of them can explain whither I went nor whence I came;[661] the reason is very simple: I started from a point above the port of Brazil[662] in Española. The storm prevented me from following my intended route, for I was obliged to go wherever the wind drove me; at the same time I fell very sick, and there was no one who had navigated in these parts before. However, after some days, the wind and sea became tranquil, and the storm was succeeded by a calm, but accompanied with rapid currents. I put into harbor at an island called Isla de las Pozas, and then steered for mainland;[663] but it is impossible to give a correct account of all our movements, because I was carried away by the current so many days without seeing land. I ascertained, however, by the compass and by observation, that I moved parallel with the coast of the mainland. No one could tell under what part of the heavens we were, and when I set out from there to come to the island of Española, the pilots thought we had come to the island of St. John, whereas it was the land of Mango, four hundred leagues to the westward of where they said.[664] Let them answer and say if they know

---

[661] On the contrary the narrative of Diego de Porras, which he prepared after his return to Spain in November, 1504, is a much clearer account of the voyage in most respects than this letter of Columbus's. For it, see Thacher, *Columbus*, II. 640-646. Porras relates that during this voyage the Admiral took all the charts away that the seamen had had. Thacher, *Columbus*, II. 646.

[662] "*El puerto de Jaquimo* [Jacmel], which he called the port of Brasil." Las Casas, *Historia*, III. 108.

[663] Cuba.

[664] The pilots thought that they were east of Española when Columbus

where Veragua is situated. I assert that they can give no
other account than that they went to lands, where there
was an abundance of gold, and this they can certify surely
enough; but they do not know the way to return thither
for such a purpose; they would be obliged to go on a
voyage of discovery as much as if they had never been
there before.

There is a mode of reckoning derived from astronomy
which is sure and safe, and a sufficient guide to any one
who understands it. This resembles a prophetic vision.[665]
The Indies ships[666] do not sail except with the wind abaft,
but this is not because they are badly built or clumsy, but
because the strong currents in those parts, together with
the wind, render it impossible to sail with the bowline,[667]
for in one day they would lose as much way as they might
have made in seven; for the same reason I could make no
use of caravels, even though they were Portuguese
lateens.[668] This is the cause that they do not sail unless
with a regular breeze, and they will sometimes stay in
harbor waiting for this seven or eight months at a time;
nor is this anything wonderful, for the same very often
occurs in Spain.

The nation of which Pope Pius II. describes the situation
and characteristics has now been found,[669] excepting the

---

turned north, and consequently thought that Cuba (Mango) was Porto
Rico (San Juan). *Cf. Historie*, p. 333.

[665] *I.e.* in that it is clear to one who understands it, and blind to one who
does not.

[666] *Las naos de las Indias, i.e.*, the large ships for the Indies, i.e., Española.

[667] Bow-lines are ropes employed to keep the windward edges of the
principal sails steady, and are only used when the wind is so unfavorable
that the sails must be all braced sideways, or close hauled to the wind.
(Major.)

[668] *I.e.*, rigged with lateen sails in the Portuguese fashion.

[669] Columbus, in his marginal notes to his copy of the *Historia Rerum
ubique Gestarum* of Pope Pius II. (Aeneas Sylvius Piccolomini; Venice,

horses with the saddles and poitrels and bridles of gold; but this is not to be wondered at, for the lands on the sea-coast are only inhabited by fishermen, and moreover I made no stay there, because I was in haste to proceed on my voyage. In Cariay and the neighboring country there are great enchanters of a very fearful character. They would have given the world to prevent my remaining there an hour. When I arrived they sent me immediately two girls very showily dressed; the eldest could not be more than eleven years of age and the other seven, and both exhibited so much immodesty, that more could not be expected from public women; they carried concealed about them a magic powder; when they came I gave them some articles to dress themselves out with, and directly sent them back to the shore.[670] I saw here, built on a mountain, a sepulchre as large as a house, and elaborately sculptured; the body lay uncovered and embalmed in it. They also spoke to me of other very excellent works of art.[671] There are many species of

---

1477), summarized the description of the Massagetae in ch. XII. in part as follows: they "use golden girths and golden bridles and silver breast-pieces and have no iron but plenty of copper and gold." *Raccolta Colombiana*, parte I., tomo II., p. 300. This description of the Massagetae goes back to Herodotus. While some habits ascribed to the Massagetae were like what Columbus observed in Veragua, their home was nowhere near eastern China.

[670] The account in the *Historie* is radically at variance with this. The girls were brought on board and "showed themselves very brave since although the Christians in looks, acts, and race were very strange, they gave no signs of distress or sadness, but maintained a cheerful and modest (*honesto*) bearing, wherefore they were very well treated by the Admiral who gave them clothes and something to eat and then sent them back." *Historie*, p. 299. Ferdinand gives the ages as eight and fourteen and says nothing of witchcraft except that the Indians were frightened and thought they were being bewitched when Bartholomew the next day ordered the ships' clerks to write down the replies he got to his questions; *ibid.*

[671] A specimen of the Maya sculptures, of which such imposing remains are found in Yucatan. The translation follows Lollis's emendation, which substitutes *mirrado* for *mirando*.

animals both small and large, and very different from those of our country. I had a present of two pigs, and an Irish dog was afraid to face them. A cross-bowman had wounded an animal like a monkey,[672] except that it was larger, and had a face like a man's; the arrow had pierced it from the neck to the tail, and since it was fierce he was obliged to cut off an arm and a leg; the pig bristled up on seeing it and tried to get away. I, when I saw this, ordered the *begare*[673] as it is called to be thrown to the pig where he was, and though the animal was nearly dead, and the arrow had passed quite through his body, yet he threw his tail round the snout of the boar, and then holding him firmly, seized him by the nape of the neck with his remaining hand, as if he were engaged with an enemy. This action was so novel and so extraordinary, that I have thought it worth while to describe it here. There is a great variety of animals here, but they all die of *barra*.[674] I saw some very large fowls (the feathers of which resemble wool),[675] lions, stags, fallow-deer and birds.

When we were so harassed with our troubles at sea, some of our men imagined that we were under the influence of sorcery, and even to this day entertain the same notion.

---

[672] *Gato paulo*. On this name, see p. 341, note 3. Ferdinand, in the *Historie*, relates this incident in more detail, from which it is clear that the pigs were peccaries which had been captured by the men. On the other hand, Ulloa, the Italian translator of the *Historie*, mistranslated *gato paulo* by "gatto," "cat."

[673] *Begare*. Columbus in recollecting this incident transferred to the monkey the Indian name of the wild pigs. The *begare* is the "peccary," a native of America. Oviedo, lib. XII., cap. XX, gives *baquira* as the name of wild pigs in Nicaragua, and *baquira* and *begare* are obviously identical.

[674] For the word *barra* no explanation can be offered except what is derived from the context. As the Italian has *diverse malattie*, "divers diseases," de Lollis suggests that *barra* should be *varias* and that *maladias* was somehow dropped from the text.

[675] *Leones*. The American lion or puma.

Some of the people whom I discovered eat men, as was evidenced by the brutality of their countenances. They say that there are great mines of copper in the country, of which they make hatchets[676] and other elaborate articles both cast and soldered; they also make of it forges, with all the apparatus of the goldsmith, and crucibles. The inhabitants go clothed; and in that province I saw some large sheets of cotton very elaborately and cleverly worked, and others very delicately painted in colors.[677] They tell me that more inland towards Cathay they have them interwoven with gold. For want of an interpreter we were able to learn but very little respecting these countries, or what they contain. Although the country is very thickly peopled, yet each nation has a very different language; indeed so much so, that they can no more understand each other than we understand the Arabs. I think, however, that this applies to the barbarians on the sea-coast, and not to the people who live more inland. When I discovered the Indies, I said that they composed the richest lordship in the world; I spoke of gold and pearls and precious stones, of spices and the traffic that might be carried on in them; and because all these things were not forthcoming at once I was abused. This punishment causes me to refrain from relating anything but what the natives tell me. One thing I can venture upon stating, because there are so many witnesses of it, viz., that in this land of Veragua I saw more signs of gold in the first two days than I saw in Española during fours years, and that there is not a more fertile or better cultivated country in all the world, nor one whose inhabitants are more timid; added to which there is a

---

[676] A misunderstanding. The Mayas made no metal tools. Brinton, *The American Race*, p. 156.

[677] Possibly Columbus may have seen some Maya codices, of which such remarkable specimens have been preserved.

good harbor, a beautiful river, and the whole place is capable of being easily put into a state of defence. All this tends to the security of the Christians and the permanency of their sovereignty, while it affords the hope of great increase and honor to the Christian religion; moreover the road hither will be as short as that to Española, because there is a certainty of a fair wind for the passage. Your Highnesses are as much lords of this country as of Xerez or Toledo; your ships if they should go there, go to your own house. From there they will take gold; in other lands to have what there is in them, they will have to take it by force or retire empty-handed, and on the land they will have to trust their persons in the hands of a savage.[678]

Of the other [matter] that I refrain from saying, I have already said why I kept silent. I do not speak so, neither [do I say] that I make a threefold affirmation in all that I have ever said or written nor that I am at the source.[679] The Genoese, Venetians and all other nations that possess pearls, precious stones, and other articles of value, take them to the ends of the world to exchange them for gold. Gold is most excellent; gold is treasure, and he who possesses it does all he wishes to in this world, and succeeds in helping souls into paradise. They say that when one of the lords of the country of Veragua dies, they bury all the gold he possessed with his body. There were brought to Solomon at one journey[680] six hundred and sixty-six quintals of gold, besides what the merchants and sailors brought, and that which was paid in Arabia.

---

[678] Considering Columbus's experience at Veragua this account exhibits boundless optimism. Still it is not to be forgotten that through the conquest of Mexico to the north this prediction was rather strikingly fulfilled.

[679] It is not clear to what Columbus refers in this sentence.

[680] *De un camino.* The texts to which Columbus refers just below show that this should read *de un año*, in one year.

Of this gold he made two hundred lances[681] and three hundred shields, and the flooring[682] which was to be above them was also of gold, and ornamented with precious stones; many other things he made likewise of gold, and a great number of vessels of great size, which he enriched with precious stones. This is related by Josephus in his Chronicle *De Antiquitatibus*; mention is also made of it in the Chronicles and in the Book of Kings.[683] Josephus thinks that this gold was found in the Aurea;[684] if it were so, I contend that these mines of the Aurea are identical with those of Veragua, which, as I have said before, extends westward twenty days' journey, and they are at an equal distance from the Pole and the Line.[685] Solomon bought all of it, --gold, precious stones, and silver, --but your Majesties need only send to seek them to have them at your pleasure. David, in his will, left three thousand quintals of Indian gold to Solomon, to assist in

---

[681] In the Latin version of Josephus used by Columbus the Greek θυρεός, a target, was rendered *lancea*. See *Raccolta Colombiana*, parte I., tomo II., p. 367.

[682] *Tablado*. In the Italian translation *tavolato*, a "partition wall," wainscoting," also "floor." *Tablado* also means "scaffold" and "stage" or "staging." We have here a curious series of mistakes. The Greek text of Josephus has ἐκπώματα, "cups." The old Latin translator, perhaps having a defective text, took ἐκπώματα apparently to be equivalent to πώματα, which has as its secondary meaning, "lids," and translated it by the uncommon word *coopercula*, "lids" (cf. Georges, *Lateinischdeutsches Handwörterbuch, sub voce cooperculum*). The meaning of this word Columbus guessed at, not having the text before him to see the connection, and from its derivation from *cooperio*, "to cover," took it to be a "covering" in the sense of flooring, or perhaps ceiling, above where the shields were hung "in the house of the forest of Lebanon," and rendered it *tablado*. The whole passage from the old Latin version (published in 1470 and frequently later), Columbus copied into a fly-leaf of his copy of the *Historia Rerum ubique Gestarum* of Pope Pius II. See *Raccolta olombiana*, parte I., tomo II., pp. 366-367.

[683] Josephus, *Antiquities of the Jews*, bk. VIII., ch. VII., sect. 4; *I. Kings*, X. 14, 15; *II. Chronicles*, IX. 13, 14.

[684] The Chersonesus Aurea of Ptolemy, or the Malay Peninsula.

[685] That is, Veragua and the Golden Chersonese are in the same latitude.

building the Temple; and, according to Josephus, it came from these lands.[686] Jerusalem and Mount Sion are to be rebuilt by the hands of Christians, who it is to be God told by the mouth of His prophet in the fourteenth Psalm.[687] The Abbot Joaquim said that he who should do this was to come from Spain;[688] Saint Jerome showed the holy woman the way to accomplish it;[689] and the emperor of Cathay, a long time ago, sent for wise men to instruct him in the faith of Christ.[690] Who will offer himself for this work?[691] Should any one do so, I pledge myself, in the name of God, to convey him safely thither, provided the Lord permits me to return to Spain.

---

[686] Josephus wrote that the gold came from the "Land of Gold," "*a terra que vocatur aurea*," as the passage in the Latin version reads. The Greek is, ἀπὸ τῆς χρυσῆς καλουμένης γῆς. Josephus gives no further identification of the location.

[687] I have not been able to verify this reference. There is nothing in the fourteenth Psalm relating to this matter, nor is the fourteenth Psalm mentioned among the many citations from the Psalms in the *Libro de las Profecias*.

[688] In his *Libro de las Profecias* Columbus wrote, "El abad Johachín, calabrés, diso que habia de salir de España quien havía de redificar la Casa del Monte Sion." "The abbot Joachim, the Calabrian, said that he who was destined to rebuild the House of Mount Sion was to come from Spain." Lollis remarks that Columbus interpreted in his own way the "Oraculum Turcicum," which concludes the thirty prophecies of Joachim of Flora in regard to the popes. In the edition (Venice, 1589) which Lollis had seen, this prophecy was interpreted to mean Charles VIII. Of France. *Raccolta Colombiana*, parte II., tomo II., p. 83.

[689] The reference to St. Jerome I have not found in Columbus's marginalia.

[690] The father and uncle of Marco Polo had been given this mission by Cublay Kaan. See Marco Polo, bk. I., ch. VII. Opposite the passage in his copy of the Latin Marco Polo which he had, Columbus wrote, "magnus kam misit legatos ad pontificem." *Raccolta Colombiana*, parte II., tomo II., p. 446.

[691] The recovery of the Holy Sepulchre had been long a cherished object with Columbus. See the Journal of the First Voyage, December 26; the letter to Pope Alexander VI., February, 1502 (Navarrete, *Viages*, II. 280), and his *Libra de Profecias*, a collection of Scripture texts compiled under his supervision relating to the restoration of Zion, etc. *Raccolta Colombiana*, parte I., tomo II., pp. 77-160.

The people who have sailed with me have passed through incredible toil and danger, and I beseech your Highnesses, since they are poor, to pay them promptly, and to be gracious to each of them according to their respective merits; for I can safely assert, that to my belief they are the bearers of the best news that ever was carried to Spain. With respect to the gold which belongs to the Quibian of Veragua, and other chiefs in the neighboring country, although it appears by the accounts we have received of it to be very abundant, I do not think it would be well or desirable, on the part of your Highnesses, to take possession of it in the way of plunder; by fair dealing, scandal and disrepute will be avoided, and all the gold will thus reach your Highnesses' treasury without the loss of a grain.

With one month of fair weather I shall complete my voyage. As I was deficient in ships, I did not persist in delaying my course; but in everything that concerns your Highnesses' service, I trust in Him who made me, and I hope also that my health will be re-established. I think your Highnesses will remember that I had intended to build some ships in a new manner, but the shortness of the time did not permit it. I had certainly foreseen how things would be. I think more of this opening for commerce, and of the lordship over such extensive mines, than of all that has been done in the Indies[692]. This is not a child to be left to the care of a stepmother.

I never think of Española, and Paria, and the other countries, without shedding tears. I thought that what had occurred there would have been an example for others; on the contrary, these settlements are now in a

---

[692] An opinion abundantly justified through the conquest of Mexico and the establishment of the kingdom of New Spain.

languid state, although not dead, and the malady is incurable, or at least very extensive. Let him who brought the evil come now and cure it, if he knows the remedy, or how to apply it; but when a disturbance is on foot, every one is ready to take the lead. It used to be the custom to give thanks and promotion to him who placed his person in jeopardy; but there is no justice in allowing the man who opposed this undertaking, to enjoy the fruits of it with his children. Those who left the Indies, avoiding the toils consequent upon the enterprise, and speaking evil of it and me, have since returned with official appointments, --such is the case now in Veragua: it is an evil example, and profitless both as regards the business in which we are embarked, and as respects the general maintenance of justice. The fear of this, with other sufficient considerations, which I clearly foresaw, caused me to beg your Highnesses, previously to my coming to discover these islands and mainland, to grant me permission to govern in your royal name. Your Highnesses granted my request; and it was a privilege and treaty granted under the royal seal and oath, by which I was nominated viceroy, and admiral, and governor-general of all: and your Highnesses limited the extent of my government to a hundred leagues beyond the Azores and Cape Verde islands, by a line passing from one pole to the other, and gave me ample power over all that I might discover beyond this line; all which is more fully described in the official document.[693]

But the most important affair of all, and that which cries most loudly for redress, remains inexplicable to this moment. For seven years was I at your royal court, where every one to whom the enterprise was mentioned treated

[693] See the Capitulation, above. The limit mentioned was fixed by the Papal Demarcation line; the limit agreed upon by Spain and Portugal was 370 leagues west of the Cape Verde Islands.

it as ridiculous; but now there is not a man, down to the very tailors, who does not beg to be allowed to become a discoverer. There is reason to believe, that they make the voyage only for plunder, and that they are permitted to do so, to the great disparagement of my honor, and the detriment of the undertaking itself.[694] It is right to give God His own,--and to Caesar[695] that which belongs to him.[696] This is a just sentiment, and proceeds from just feelings. The lands in this part of the world, which are now under your Highnesses' sway, are richer and more extensive than those of any other Christian power, and yet, after that I had, by the Divine will, placed them under your high and royal sovereignty, and was on the point of bringing your majesties into the receipt of a very great and unexpected revenue; and while I was waiting for ships, to convey me in safety, and with a heart full of joy, to your royal presence, victoriously to announce the news of the gold that I had discovered, I was arrested and thrown, with my two brothers, loaded with irons, into a ship, stripped, and very ill-treated, without being allowed any appeal to justice.[697]

Who could believe, that a poor foreigner would have risen against your Highnesses, in such a place, without any motive or argument on his side; without even the assistance of any other prince upon which to rely; but

---

[694] A reference to such voyages as those of Vicente Yañez Pinzon, Hojeda, Diego de Lepe, and Rodrigo de Bastidas which occurred in 1499-1502. Cf. Bourne, *Spain in America*, pp. 67-71, and for details Irving, *Columbus*, III. 15-62.

[695] Accepting de Lollis's emendation *á César* instead of the MS. reading *açetar* which Navarrete printed *aceptar*. The Italian has *a Cesaro*.

[696] "Render therefore unto Caesar the things which are Caesar's; and unto God, the things which are God's." *Matthew*, XXII. 21.

[697] At Española in 1500 by Bobadilla. Cf. the letter to the nurse above.

on the contrary, amongst your own vassals and natural subjects, and with my sons staying at your royal court? I was twenty-eight years old when I came into your Highnesses' service,[698] and now I have not a hair upon me that is not gray; my body is infirm, and all that was left to me, as well as to my brothers, has been taken away and sold, even to the frock that I wore, to my great dishonor. I cannot but believe that this was done without your royal permission. The restitution of my honor, the reparation of my losses, and the punishment of those who have inflicted them, will redound to the honor of your royal character; a similar punishment also is due to those who plundered me of my pearls, and who have brought a disparagement upon the privileges of my admiralty. Great and unexampled will be the glory and fame of your Highnesses, if you do this; and the memory of your Highnesses, as just and grateful sovereigns, will survive as a bright example to Spain in future ages. The honest devotedness I have always shown to your Majesties' service, and the so unmerited outrage with which it has been repaid, will not allow my soul to keep silence, however much I may wish it: I implore your Highnesses to forgive my complaints. I am indeed in as ruined a condition as I have related; hitherto I have wept over others; --may Heaven now have mercy upon me, and may the earth weep for me. With regard to temporal things, I

---

[698] This is one of the most important passages bearing upon the age of Columbus. As he came to Spain at the end of 1484 according to Ferdinand Columbus, *Historie*, ch. XII., Peschel fixed his birth in 1456, *Zeitalter der Entdeckungen*, p. 76. The majority of modern critics, however, have agreed upon the basis of notarial documents in Genoa that 1446 was the date of his birth and propose therefore to emend the text here by substituting "treinta y ocho" for "veinte y ocho." On the various dates set for his birth see Vignaud, *The Real Birth-date of Christopher Columbus*. Vignaud fixes upon 1451.

have not even a blanca,[699] for an offering; and in spiritual
things, I have ceased here in the Indies from observing
the prescribed forms of religion. Solitary in my trouble,
sick, and in daily expectation of death, surrounded by a
million of hostile savages full of cruelty, and thus
separated from the blessed sacraments of our holy
Church, how will my soul be forgotten if it be separated
from the body in this foreign land? Weep for me, whoever
has charity, truth, and justice! I did not come out on this
voyage to gain to myself honor or wealth; this is a certain
fact, for at that time all hope of such a thing was dead. I
do not lie when I say, that I went to your Highnesses with
honest purpose of heart, and sincere zeal in your cause. I
humbly beseech your Highnesses, that if it please God to
rescue me from this place, you will graciously sanction my
pilgrimage to Rome and other holy places. May the Holy
Trinity protect your Highnesses' lives, and add to the
prosperity of your exalted position.

Done in the Indies, in the island of Jamaica, on the
seventh of July, in the year one thousand five hundred
and three.

---

[699] *Blanca*, a copper coin worth about one-third of a cent.

Bibliography

The life of Christopher Columbus. From authentic Spanish and Italian documents by Roselly de Lourges, 1870. ISBN: 978-1503104532

History of the Indies by Bartolome de las Casas (European perspectives) Paperback; 1971. ISBN: 978-0061315404

Notes on Columbus, by Henry Herrisse, 1866; out of print.

De Orbe Novo, The Eight Decades of Peter Martyr D'Anghera, 1530; ISBN: 978-0526406531

Book of Prophecies by Christopher Columbus; ISBN 978-1592446483

"Colección de los viages y descubrimientos que hicieron por mar los españoles desde fines del siglo XV" - Collection of the voyages and discoveries made by the Spaniards since the late 15th century (1825-1837) by Martín Fernández de Navarrete

If you enjoyed this authentic reproduction of the account of Columbus' discoveries, read the other books in the Knowledge Keepers Bookstore series!

Available on Amazon as well as KnowledgeKeepersBookstore.com.

Made in the USA
Coppell, TX
03 October 2023

22350744R00331